PICTORIAL
ATLAS
OF THE
WORLD

CLB 2502
© 1992 Colour Library Books Ltd., Godalming, Surrey
Printed and bound in Spain by Graficromo, S.A.
ISBN 0 86283 933 5

PICTORIAL
ATLAS
OF THE
WORLD

COLOUR LIBRARY BOOKS

FOREWORD

In 1636 a bound collection of maps was published by Gerard Mercator and John Hondt with a frontispiece illustrating the titan Atlas bearing the world on his shoulders. As a result, the word 'atlas' entered the vocabulary as a synonym for a book of maps. In the seventeenth century only the very rich could afford the luxury of an atlas. Cartographic masterpieces by Dutch map engravers offered their patrons the first view of a world the horizons of which were being swiftly broadened by maritime discovery.

Today, most households can afford an atlas even if they do not own one. Certainly, the need for and the attraction of the atlas have never been greater. Never have so many people been on the move around the world. Never have so many been concerned with the impact of world events. 'Atlas-eaters', Dylan Thomas called those who were hungry for world news. The atlas, through its co-ordinates of latitude and longitude, can answer the question 'Where?'. Or, perhaps, more precisely, the index to the atlas provides the answer – hence the importance of the extended index to the *Pictorial Atlas of the World*.

In an atlas, the science of map-making is married to the art of map presentation. Techniques of production are increasingly refined; sources of information are increasingly precise. Satellite imagery, photogrammetry and computerisation have transformed map production. Most of the *Pictorial Atlas of the World* consists of topographical maps, with our own respective home areas receiving generous treatment. Additionally, the pictorial section provides useful and fascinating information on the world's nations and peoples.

An atlas is no substitute for a globe. The two are complementary, for not even the larger globes can include a fraction of the information that is packed into an atlas. The task of projecting the globe onto a flat surface has taxed the ingenuity of mathematicians since the Greeks first attempted to measure the circumference of the Earth. The variety of formidably-named projections employed in the *Pictorial Atlas of the World* illustrates the extended range of options available to present-day cartographers.

Atlases have a romantic appeal as well as a utilitarian value. The novelist Alan Sillitoe, in a memorable essay on maps, recalls the flights of fancy set in motion by his 'first cheap layer-tinted atlas'. To turn the pages of the *Pictorial Atlas of the World* – to contemplate the controlling features of land and sea, to reflect upon the boundaries that define the outlines and shape the destinies of countries and to respond to the magic of the infinity of place-names – is to experience a stimulus to the imagination as well as to the intellect.

William R. Mead
PROFESSOR EMERITUS OF GEOGRAPHY, UNIVERSITY COLLEGE LONDON.

MAP LEGEND

SETTLEMENT

For scales larger than 1:2,000,000

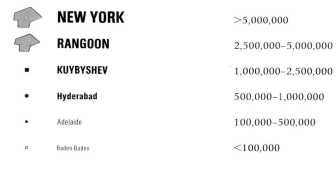

		Population
➤	**BIRMINGHAM**	>1,000,000
➤	**GLASGOW**	500,000–1,000,000
➤	**CARDIFF**	250,000–500,000
➤	**LIMERICK**	50,000–250,000
•	**Dover**	10,000–50,000
•	Lossiemouth	5,000–10,000
○	Church Stretton	<5,000
➤	*CROYDON*	London Borough

For scales between 1:2,000,000 and 1:12,000,000

➤	**NEW YORK**	>5,000,000
➤	**RANGOON**	2,500,000–5,000,000
▪	**KUYBYSHEV**	1,000,000–2,500,000
•	**Hyderabad**	500,000–1,000,000
•	Adelaide	100,000–500,000
○	Baden-Baden	<100,000

For scales smaller than 1:12,000,000

▪	**DAR ES SALAAM**	>1,000,000
•	**Maracaibo**	500,000–1,000,000
•	Tiranë	<500,000

<u>**Lisboa**</u>	National capital	<u>**Winnipeg**</u>	State, provincial capital

COMMUNICATIONS

―――――	Motorway
=========	Motorway under construction
―――――	Principal road
- - - - - -	Principal road under construction
―――――	Other main road
– – – –	Track, seasonal road
⊢――⊣	Road tunnel
―――――	Principal railway
– – – –	Principal railway under construction
⊢――⊣	Railway tunnel
✈	International, main airport

BOUNDARIES

▭▭▭▭	International
▬ ▬ ▬ ▬	Undefined, disputed
―――――	Internal, state, provincial
– – – –	Armistice, cease-fire line

The representation of a boundary in this atlas does not denote its international recognition and therefore the *defacto* situation has been depicted.

HYDROGRAPHIC FEATURES

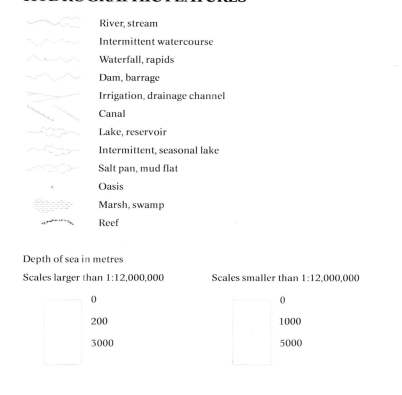

	River, stream
	Intermittent watercourse
	Waterfall, rapids
	Dam, barrage
	Irrigation, drainage channel
	Canal
	Lake, reservoir
	Intermittent, seasonal lake
	Salt pan, mud flat
	Oasis
	Marsh, swamp
	Reef

Depth of sea in metres

Scales larger than 1:12,000,000	Scales smaller than 1:12,000,000
0	0
200	1000
3000	5000

OTHER FEATURES

▲ 3798	Elevation above sea level (metres)
▼ −133	Depression, below sea level (metres)
≂	Pass
•―⌃―▪	Oil, gas pipeline with field

ENVIRONMENTAL TYPES

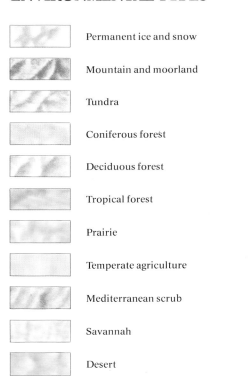

	Permanent ice and snow
	Mountain and moorland
	Tundra
	Coniferous forest
	Deciduous forest
	Tropical forest
	Prairie
	Temperate agriculture
	Mediterranean scrub
	Savannah
	Desert

This representation of the environment and its associated vegetation gives an overview of the landscape. It is not intended to be definitive.

CONVERSION SCALES

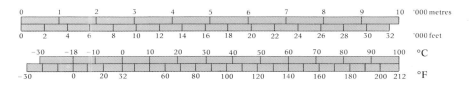

CONTENTS

◀ *Chicago, Illinois, one of the largest cities in the U.S.A.*

First page: Victoria Falls span the Middle Zambezi River at one of its widest points. Title Page: the well-known resort of Bled, in the Slovenian Highlands.

EUROPE

*A*s the cradle of Western civilisation and the industrial revolution which now dominates the world economies, Europe may justly claim to be the historical heart of the modern world. It was in Europe that technological advances made mass-production industry possible for the first time. This led to an economic dominance over the rest of the world, which continued until the same processes were taken up by the booming population of North America and the industrial lead crossed the Atlantic.

Geographically Europe is a highly diverse and fragmented continent without any of the vast plains, mountain ranges or deserts which characterise other land masses. In Europe everything is on a much smaller scale than elsewhere. The greatest mountain chain is the Alps, which stretch across northern Italy and on into eastern Europe, but these peaks are dwarfed by the Asian Himalayas or the American Andes. The largest plain is that of the Ukraine, now devoted to the production of grain crops, but again this is far smaller than the North American prairies or the Mongolian grasslands.

Europe is, however, immensely diverse, with a wide variety of landscape forms being found in relatively small areas. Fertile plains jostle with mountain ranges and dense forests with productive meadows. It is the sheer diversity of the geological make up of Europe which gives the continent its characteristic appearance. Nowhere is it possible to travel far without coming across a change in scenery.

Hidden beneath this fragmented landscape is a wide variety of mineral wealth. Pockets of every conceivable metal ore are to be found scattered across Europe. Though none occurs in the kind of mass deposit encountered on other continents, these ores have provided the raw materials for European industry for some centuries, and only now are being surpassed by bulk ores from elsewhere.

Until the immigration of racial groups from other continents in large numbers during the later 20th century, the population of Europe was remarkably homogeneous. Almost the entire population was descended from Indo-Europeans, who spread across the continent in antiquity. Earlier peoples were swamped by these new cultures, only surviving in isolated pockets, such as that of the Basques of northern Spain.

However, the populations of Europe have strong historic cultures and concepts of nationhood which transcend the rather academic classification of Indo-European. These nationalist identities are a powerful cultural impetus within Europe and sources of much pride. They may also lead to factional violence, and attempts at supra-national states have rarely survived. Most recent to fall before nationalist feelings is Yugoslavia, the federation of southern Slav peoples. As 1991 dawned the provinces of Slovenia and Croatia were attempting to become independent. The colossal USSR, too, was feeling separatist pressures as the unifying Communist ideology collapsed and nationalist pride in Estonia, Latvia, Lithuania and elsewhere reasserted itself.

The keynote of Europe is diversity. There is diversity in landscape, in geology and in human culture. Packed into the smallest of the continents are over thirty countries based around identifiable national groupings. Even within countries nationalist divisions are to be found. The nation state of Italy was united only a century ago and strong regional differences of culture, language and lifestyle are still apparent. Europe is nothing if not a continent of contrasts.

◄ Iceland – 'Land of fire and Ice'.　　▲ Traditional costume, Bulgaria.　　▲ Dubrovnik, Yugoslavia.　　▼ Pünderich, overlooking the Mosel, Germany.

ALBANIA

Population: 3.2 million
Area: 29,000 square kilometres
Capital: Tirana
Language: Albanian and Greek
Currency: Lek

The rugged mountain nation of Albania has been virtually cut off from the rest of Europe for decades. A province of first the Byzantine and later the Ottoman Empires, Albania gained independence as a kingdom in 1912 and as a Communist republic in 1946. The old-style Stalinist regime has retained a tight grip on running the country, and in 1991 President Ramiz Alia took full power to himself. Under Communism the nation has tried to revolutionise its economy by abandoning the traditional farming techniques which formerly employed the population. Today, less than half the workforce is in farming, the rest having moved to the towns to join the growing number of industrial workers. Copper, steel and electronics are among the growth industries.

ANDORRA

Population: 52,000
Area: 468 square kilometres
Capital: Andorra La Vella
Language: Catalan and French
Currency: French Franc and Spanish Peseta

The independent mountain state of Andorra has retained its freedom unchanged since 1278, when the rival powers of the region agreed on a compromise. Under the 700-year-old arrangement the state is ruled jointly by the Bishop of Urgel and the Count of Foix. As the estates of Foix have since passed to the French state, the present joint rulers are the Bishop of Urgel and the President of France. In practice the native Andorrans, who number around 10,000, govern themselves through a democratic system, though the agreement of the joint rulers is needed for all actions. Sheep are the mainstay of the agricultural economy, but tourism and duty-free shopping bolster the modern prosperity.

AUSTRIA

Population: 7.6 million
Area: 84,000 square kilometres
Capital: Vienna
Language: German
Currency: Schilling

Until 1918 the heart of the vast Hapsburg Empire, which encompassed the Danube Basin and much of the Balkans, Austria is now a democratic republic based upon the German-speaking parts of that Empire. The capital, Vienna, has a long tradition of sophisticated culture and excellence in the arts, music being particularly strongly represented. The economy of Austria is broadly based, though agriculture is limited by the terrain. The mountains, however, do attract large numbers of tourists who come to enjoy winter skiing and summer walking. The industrial sector was heavily nationalised after the Second World War, but has recently been returned to the private sector.

BELGIUM

Population: 10 million
Area: 31,000 square kilometres
Capital: Brussels
Language: Flemish, French and German
Currency: Belgian Franc

The present constitutional monarchy dates back to 1830, when the Belgian people rebelled against Dutch rule and invited a German prince to become their king. The constitution has been amended several times since, but consists of a two-chamber Parliament acting under the monarch. The Flemish- and French-speaking areas each enjoy a degree of regional self-government. The nation is predominantly urban, with industry and services leading the economy. The coal, steel and other metal industries dominate the scene, and these are in turn in the hands of a small number of conglomerates. Agriculture contributes only a small proportion to the economy, but Belgium is now almost self-sufficient in temperate-climate foods, only tropical fruits being imported in bulk.

▲ *An open-air restaurant, Brussels, Belgium.*

BULGARIA

Population: 9 million
Area: 111,000 square kilometres
Capital: Sofia
Language: Bulgarian
Currency: Lev

Bulgaria became independent of the Moslem Ottoman Empire in 1908 as a kingdom, and became a Communist republic following the Russian occupation in 1946. In 1989

▲ *Tranquil countryside, Finland.*

Above right: *The Schonbrunn Palace, Vienna, Austria.*

▼ *Old-world charm, Czechoslovakia.*

▼ *Nyhavn, in Copenhagen, Denmark.*

▲ *Corn harvest, Albania.*

▼ *An Orthodox priest, Cyprus.*

▲ *The Orthodox Cathedral, Tallinn, Estonia.*

▲ Vineyards, Santenay, France.

▲ The mountain state of Andorra.

street protests and demands for reform led the National Assembly to approve a multi-party democracy and free elections. In 1990 the Communist government stepped down to make way for a democratic election. The river valleys have fertile soils and a climate conducive to heavy grain crops and livestock rearing. In recent years the traditional dominance of agriculture has been overtaken by a growing industrial sector producing large quantities of iron, steel, textiles and agricultural equipment.

CYPRUS

Population: 700,000
Area: 9,000 square kilometres
Capital: Nicosia
Language: Greek and Turkish
Currency: Cypriot Pound

For centuries part of the Ottoman Empire, Cyprus passed to Britain as security for a loan which was never repaid. Britain, however, granted independence in 1960 under a constitution designed to calm ethnic rivalries between the Greek and Turkish populations. In 1974 a coup by the Greeks threatened to join Cyprus to Greece, and Turkey invaded to block the move. Today, the island is divided between the Turkish northern third and the southern section inhabited by Greeks. The traditional agricultural products of olives, grapes and fruits remain important. Tourists, attracted by the beautiful scenery and beaches, provide much foreign currency, though this business has been disrupted by the partition. There is no communication across the demarcation line and northern Cyprus has declared itself an independent state.

CZECHOSLOVAKIA

Population: 16 million
Area: 127,000 square kilometres
Capital: Prague
Language: Czech and Slovak
Currency: Koruna

As its name suggests, this is a nation formed from two distinct ethnic groups. The Czechs inhabit the western regions and have a predominantly urban culture with strong German influences. The Slovaks of the eastern regions are more agricultural in outlook and their culture shows strong Hungarian influence. Formerly part of the Hapsburg Empire, Czechoslovakia became independent in 1918. Communists took power with Soviet aid in 1948, and an attempt at liberalisation in 1968, known as the Prague Spring, was crushed by Russian tanks. In November 1989 mass public demonstrations led to the resignation of the Communist

government and the legalisation of opposition parties. In December the dissident playwright Vaclav Havel became President. Czechoslovakia is a heavily industrialised nation with iron and steel, chemicals and food processing being prominent.

DENMARK

Population: 5 million
Area: 43,000 square kilometres
Capital: Copenhagen
Language: Danish
Currency: Krone

The rich soil and temperate climate of Denmark have aided the traditionally-strong agricultural sector. Grains, potatoes and vegetables are grown in quantities, but it is livestock which dominates. There are estimated to be over nine million pigs and sixteen million chickens in Denmark, and bacon is a major export earner. Recently the industrial sector has grown significantly, using imported raw materials which are then processed for export as finished goods. Manufacturing now outstrips agriculture in terms of economic value by about four times. The constitution is based on the monarch, who cannot act without the consent of the democratically-elected parliament. Parliament includes members from Greenland and the Faroes, which are dependencies of the Danish Crown.

ESTONIA

Population: 1.5 million
Area: 45,000 square kilometres
Capital: Tallinn
Language: Estonian and Russian
Currency: Rouble

In September 1991 Estonia was accepted as an independent nation for the first time since it annexation by the Soviet Union in 1939. The republic has been dominated by economic central planning from Moscow for over five decades and relies heavily on agriculture for employment and prosperity. Gas-rich shale and phosphates represent the only mineral wealth and industrial base for this small nation. Co-operation with the other Baltic states is already established and other foreign economic links are being vigorously pursued.

FINLAND

Population: 5 million
Area: 338,000 square kilometres
Capital: Helsinki
Language: Finnish
Currency: Markka

Ruled in turn by Denmark, Sweden and Russia, Finland gained independence in 1917, when the people took advantage of the chaos

following the Russian Revolution to seize power for themselves. In 1940 war with Russia resulted in Finland losing much territory around Lake Ladoga to the Soviets. Modern foreign policy emphasises the need for friendly relations with Russia and with Scandinavian nations. The economy of the nation is mixed and broadly based. The vast forests provide raw material for a lumber trade. The small area of land suitable for agriculture is heavily used for the raising of livestock, particularly cattle in the south and reindeer in the north. Industry is concentrated on the extraction and processing of iron deposits, though many other businesses flourish.

FRANCE

Population: 56 million
Area: 543,000 square kilometres
Capital: Paris
Language: French
Currency: French Franc

The modern state of France is generally traced back to the accession of the Capetian dynasty to the throne of the Western Franks in 987, though Frankish power was established in the region as early as 500 a.d. The monarchy was overthrown in the Revolution of 1789, after which France was ruled by republics, emperors and kings. The Fifth Republic was established in 1958. The present constitution allows for a democratically-elected parliament, which operates under the guidance of an elected President. The economy of the nation is highly developed, with industry and services being dominant employers. Agriculture remains largely in the hands of small-scale farmers and produces quantities of grain and fruits, most notably grapes, from which the famous French wines are produced.

GERMANY

Population: 80 million
Area: 357,000 square kilometres
Capital: Berlin
Language: German
Currency: Mark

Unity and division have been the hallmarks of German history. The disparate German tribes were united under the Frankish Empire in the 9th century, but this fell apart, to be replaced by the Holy Roman Empire of the Middle Ages. Initially strong, the Empire broke up into dozens of petty feudal states and city republics. The Napoleonic Wars swept this pattern away and in 1871 the German states were united under Prussian rule as the German Empire. This nation remained together until 1945, when Germany lost much territory and was divided

as Communist East and Democratic West Germany. In 1990 the overthrow of the Communist regime in East Germany led to reunification. The strong West German economy is concentrating on raising the prosperity of East Germany. Agriculture is well developed throughout the country.

GREECE

Population: 10 million
Area: 132,000 square kilometres
Capital: Athens
Language: Greek
Currency: Drachma

Home of the ancient civilisation which has had such a profound influence on all Western culture, Greece is today working to join the front runners in European economies. The magnificent history, fine climate and attractive beaches have made Greece a favourite tourist resort for generations, and recent developments have boosted this business to the point where it welcomes over seven million visitors each year. Tourism is now the largest single industry in terms of foreign earnings. The mountainous terrain limits agriculture, but there are extensive olive groves and citrus orchards producing over a million tonnes of each product annually. Industry is less dominant than in other European nations and is concentrated on food processing, textiles and leatherwork. After a period of military rule in the 1970s, Greece has reverted to a democratic system.

HUNGARY

Population: 11 million
Area: 93,000 square kilometres
Capital: Budapest
Language: Magyar
Currency: Forint

Formerly a dominant state within the Hapsburg Empire, which ruled the Danube Basin from the Alps to the Black Sea, Hungary became independent in 1918. In 1949 a Communist government was imposed and the 1956 nationalist rising was put down by Russian tanks and troops. After popular protests and demands for reform, the Communist Party was disbanded in 1989 and opened the way for democratic elections, which took place in 1990. The great flat plain of Hungary has dominated the economy for generations. Its fertile soils and temperate climate make abundant crops possible. Wheat, maize and potatoes are the main crops, and large numbers of cattle and pigs are raised. In recent years industry has rapidly gained over agriculture and now dominates the economy, with metallurgy,

chemicals and electronics predominating.

ICELAND

Population: 253,000
Area: 103,000 square kilometres
Capital: Reykjavik
Language: Icelandic
Currency: Icelandic Krona

Viking settlers began arriving in Iceland in the 9th century, ousting the few Irish monks who had already established themselves. An independent society existed based on Viking social rules until 1264, when factional violence led to Norwegian control. In 1381 Iceland passed to the Danish crown, recovering full self-government in 1918 and severance from Denmark in 1946. The present republic operates with two chambers working under an elected President. Only two percent of land is farmed, producing potatoes, turnips and hay. Livestock is kept in small numbers. Fishing provides the basis of the economy, with Icelandic trawlers harvesting the rich reserves of white fish in the chill northern waters. Industry is very limited.

IRELAND

Population: 3.5 million
Area: 70,000 square kilometres
Capital: Dublin
Language: Gaelic and English
Currency: Irish Pound

After centuries of growing British influence, Ireland joined with Britain in 1801. In 1921 the Catholic southern counties of Ireland gained independence after an armed uprising and became the Republic of Eire in 1948, the Protestant counties of Ulster remaining part of Britain. Ongoing civil violence and terrorist activities have disrupted life in border counties and dominate Irish relations with Britain. The economy is traditionally agricultural. Large numbers of cattle produce dairy products, and sheep and pigs provide meat. The former reliance on potato crops has been reduced and larger areas are now under grains than under potatoes. Industrial activity has grown rapidly in recent years, and this is now more important to the economy than agriculture. Food processing, textiles and electrical engineering are the dominant industries.

ITALY

Population: 57 million
Area: 301,000 square kilometres
Capital: Rome
Language: Italian
Currency: Italian Lira

The various city states, kingdoms

and duchies of Italy were not united until 1861, and the republic was established in 1946. The present constitution allows for two chambers, the lower elected directly and the upper elected by the historic regions. The President is elected by the two houses of parliament. There are numerous political parties representing many shades of opinion, though fascism is banned. Southern parts of the country are generally less well developed than the north. Agriculture based on olives, wheat and sheep dominates in Sicily and the land south of Naples. More northerly farms tend to be large commercial concerns producing cash crops of sugar beet, tomatoes and fruits. Grapes are widely grown for wine production. Industry is concentrated in northern cities where textiles, food processing and the manufacture of machinery lead the sector.

LATVIA

Population: 2.6 million
Area: 64,000 square kilometres
Capital: Riga
Language: Latvian and Russian
Currency: Rouble

The troubled history of Latvia as an independent nation began with a democratic government being installed with British military support in 1919 after a brief Soviet regime and came to an end in 1940 when Soviet power was reimposed. Together with Lithuania and Estonia, Latvia became independent once again after the failed coup in Moscow of August 1991. Five decades of economic central planning has given Latvia a heritage of heavy industry, with steel, railway equipment and textiles dominating. The previous agricultural economic base has been reduced to a substantial minority of wealth-creating activity.

LIECHTENSTEIN

Population: 28,000
Area: 160 square kilometres
Capital: Vaduz
Language: German
Currency: Swiss Franc

The tiny principality of Liechtenstein dates back to 1434, when the Count of Vaduz gained control of Schellenberg. In 1712 the principality passed to the Liechtenstein family, which held it directly from the Holy Roman Emperor. When that empire collapsed in 1806 the family retained their domains, and in 1923 joined Switzerland in a customs and currency union. The present constitution places power in the hands of the Prince, though legislation needs approval of the democratically-elected parliament.

▲ *Dusk in Mykonos, Greece.*

▲ *A Round Tower, Co. Wicklow, Ireland.*

▼ *Luxembourg, one of Europe's smallest nations.*

▲ *The Principality of Monaco.*

▼ *The Principality of Liechtenstein.*

▲ *The River Danube, Budapest, Hungary.*

◄ *Heavy industry, Lithuania*

▲ *A characteristic view of Malta.*

▼ *The Old City, Riga, Latvia.*

◄ *The Colosseum, Rome, Italy.*

▲ *Kinderdijk, east of Rotterdam, Netherlands.*

The economy is based on a mixture of agriculture, light industry and commerce. Many companies have their nominal headquarters in Liechtenstein and their taxation contributes to the state income.

LITHUANIA

Population: 3.7 million
Area: 65,000 square kilometres
Capital: Vilnius
Language: Lithuanian and Russian
Currency: Rouble

With a population over 80 percent ethnic Lithuanians, the republic has long desired independence. In March 1991 an overwhelming majority voted for separation from the Soviet Union, but not until the failed coup of August 1991 did this freedom become a reality. Traditionally an agricultural nation, Lithuania is now dominated by industry. Heavy engineering and textiles dominate the economic scene, although forestry and agriculture are significant employers.

LUXEMBOURG

Population: 379,000
Area: 2,500 square kilometres
Capital: Luxembourg
Language: German and French
Currency: Luxembourg Franc

The tiny state of Luxembourg enjoyed varying degrees of self government until being conquered by France in 1795. In 1815 the current Grand Duchy came into being under the Dutch monarchy, and in 1890 full independence came when a junior branch of the Dutch royal family inherited Luxembourg. The Grand Duke is closely involved in administration with the democratically-elected parliament. The nation is part of a customs union with Belgium and Belgian currency can be used within Luxembourg. Industry is based on a thriving iron and steel business, though attempts are being made to diversify the economy. Agriculture plays a minor role in national life with the production of grain, market crops and meat as well as a small quantity of wine.

MALTA

Population: 354,000
Area: 316 square kilometres
Capital: Valletta
Language: Maltese and English
Currency: Maltese Pound

During World War II Malta was a vital British naval base and came under massive attack by German and Italian forces. In 1942 King George VI awarded the George Cross to the people of Malta. This medal is featured on the Maltese flag, together with the colours of the religious Knights of Malta, who ruled between 1530 and 1798. Malta gained independence from Britain in 1964, though economic ties remain close. Malta's strategic position in the Mediterranean makes commerce, trade and ship-building lucrative industries. Tourism has long been important and about 800,000 visitors arrive each year. Tourism is the biggest single earner of foreign currency for Malta. The constitution is a multi-party democracy in which two major parties dominate.

MONACO

Population: 30,000
Area: 1.5 square kilometres
Capital: Monaco
Language: Monegasque and French
Currency: French Franc

The small Principality of Monaco has been the domain of the Grimaldi family since 1297, placing itself under French protection in 1861. The traditional Grimaldi colours make up the flag, which is almost identical to that of Indonesia except that it is slightly shorter. The constitution allows for democratic government though the Prince retains much influence. The main economic base of Monaco is tourism, with nearly ten times as many visitors as residents in the course of a year. The scenic coastline and fine beach delight many tourists, but it is the famous casino which is the major attraction. The nightlife is hectic and provides entertainment for those tourists who have tired of gambling. Agriculture is virtually non-existent but the industrial sector is growing in importance.

NETHERLANDS

Population: 15 million
Area: 34,0000 square kilometres
Capital: Amsterdam and The Hague
Language: Dutch
Currency: Dutch Guilder

The present nation came into being in the late 16th century, when the prosperous Protestant cities rebelled against oppressive Catholic rule from Spain. Much of the Netherlands has been reclaimed from the sea by massive reclamation projects, culminating in over 1,000-square-kilometres being reclaimed from the Zuider Zee this century. Much of this land is devoted to agriculture, with potatoes, sugar beet and grain being major crops. Cut flowers and flower bulbs are produced in large quantities for export, while dairy cattle graze on meadows to produce milk from which famous Dutch cheeses are made. The nation's position at the mouth of the Rhine has long ensured

lucrative trade and commerce connections. The Netherlands still enjoy much trans-shipment trade and processes many raw materials for re-export.

NORWAY

Population: 4.2 million
Area: 324,000 square kilometres
Capital: Oslo
Language: Norwegian
Currency: Norwegian Krone

In 1905 Norway succeeded in gaining independence from Sweden and took Prince Carl of Denmark as its first monarch. The constitution places power in the hands of a democratically-elected parliament called the *Storting*, though the monarch retains control of the armed forces and has the power to veto any legislation. The mountainous terrain makes agriculture difficult and much food needs to be imported. Hydroelectric power is produced in quantity and supplies ninety-nine percent of domestic needs. Offshore oil and gas has added to the energy self-reliance of Norway. The metallurgy industries are based on aluminium, copper and iron. Industry is prosperous and is based on the processing of domestic metals, agricultural products and timber from the vast upland forests.

▲ *The Tatra Mountains, Poland.*

POLAND

Population: 38 million
Area: 312,000 square kilometres
Capital: Warsaw
Language: Polish
Currency: Zloty

The powerful kingdom of Poland collapsed in the late 18th century and was divided between the growing Prussian, Hapsburg and Russian empires. Reconstitution and independence did not occur until 1918. The German invasion of Poland in 1939 sparked the Second World War, and following liberation in 1945 Poland was ruled by a Communist regime imposed by Russia. Communist rule ended in 1989 after several years of

opposition from the Solidarity trade union. Free elections were called for 1991, with opposition parties campaigning for the first time in decades. The Polish economy is industrially based, with iron and steel, textiles and machine manufacture being the most important. The formerly dominant agricultural sector is still important, producing wheat, rye and potatoes, together with large quantities of dairy produce and meats.

PORTUGAL

Population: 10 million
Area: 92,000 square kilometres
Capital: Lisbon
Language: Portuguese
Currency: Escudo

The coup of 1974 overthrew the dictatorship which had governed Portugal since 1933, and in 1976 introduced a democratic constitution for only the second time in Portugal's 800-year history. The present constitution, adopted in 1982, allows for an elected President who chooses the Prime Minister from the Assembly, which is elected by universal suffrage. The economy is presently dominated by the dismantling of government control and privatisation of industry. Manufacturing is based on textiles and leather goods together with ceramics. Agriculture is based on grains and potatoes. Wine, cork and olives are important cash crops for export. Fishing is a major activity, especially for sardines, which are canned or dried for export.

ROMANIA

Population: 23 million
Area: 238,000 square kilometres
Capital: Bucharest
Language: Romanian and Hungarian
Currency: Leu

The overthrow of the Communist regime of President Ceausescu was attended by street fighting and great confusion. A temporary government was elected in 1990 to draw up a new constitution based on democratic principles. Until the Communist takeover in 1947 Romania was a traditionally agricultural kingdom with little industry. The past decades have seen massive government encouragement of industry, which today has overtaken agriculture as an employer and is concentrated on iron and steel, chemicals and textiles. The farms continue to produce large quantities of wheat and maize, while shepherding is as important as it was before the advent of the Communist regime. The collectivised farms are gradually being broken up and returned to former owners where possible.

Above left: *Interior of St Peter's, the Vatican, Italy.*

▲ *The Lofoten Islands, Norway.*

◄ *Carvoeiro, Portugal.*

▼ *Haymaking, Romania.*

▲ *The flower harvest, Spain.*

◄ *The golden domes of the Kremlin, Moscow, USSR.*

▼ *The Matterhorn and Stelli See, Switzerland.*

▼ *Gold Hill, Shaftesbury, Dorset, UK.*

▲ *Historic San Marino.*

SAN MARINO

Population: 23,000
Area: 61 square kilometres
Capital: San Marino
Language: Italian
Currency: Italian Lira

Legend has it that the 4th-century Saint Marinus founded the republic as a self-governing Christian community to escape Imperial persecution. The republic won full independence from the Pope in 1631, and in 1862 concluded a treaty of friendship with the newly-created Italian nation, which secured continued independence. San Marino is now part of a customs unions with Italy, so no duties are charged on imports or exports. The republic is governed by a Great Council elected by universal suffrage. Two members of the Great Council act as regents, fulfilling the roles of Heads of State. Agriculture is an important source of employment and wine is exported. Small-scale industrial activity includes chemicals, ceramics and paints. Much economic wealth comes from tourism and the sale of the unique coins and stamps of the republic.

SPAIN

Population: 40 million
Area: 492,000 square kilometres
Capital: Madrid
Language: Spanish and regional
Currency: Peseta

Spain regained its monarchy in 1975 after an interruption of forty-four years. King Juan Carlos is carefully leading his nation to democracy and stability. The constitution vests power in a parliament named the *Cortes*, with a main body elected by proportional representation and a senate elected by province. The traditional agricultural economic base has now been overtaken by industry, but remains important. Wheat and barley are the major crops, though wine is produced in vast quantities, both for local consumption and for lucrative export. Industry is dominated by motor vehicles, textiles, paper, and iron and steel, which together account for the majority of exports. The fishing fleet is large and catches of both fish and molluscs are high.

SWEDEN

Population: 8.5 million
Area: 450,000 square kilometres
Capital: Stockholm
Language: Swedish
Currency: Swedish Krona

Sweden acquired approximately its present boundaries a thousand years ago, but has since been united with other Scandinavian nations, and in the 17th century enjoyed Baltic hegemony. The present dynasty dates from 1809, when the highly-successful French general Jean Bernadotte was chosen to become king on the extinction of the native line. The constitution introduced in 1975 reduced the role of monarch to ceremonial and gave power to the democratic parliament. The highly-prosperous economy is based on iron ore deposits, the forests and immense hydro-electric power. Over half of all manufacturing is made up of metal smelting, metal machinery and other metal products. A further quarter of the sector is composed of timber, plywood and other wood products. Agriculture is well developed, but on a small scale, and much food needs to be imported.

▲ *A traditional church, Sweden.*

SWITZERLAND

Population: 6.7 million
Area: 41,000 square kilometres
Capital: Bern
Language: German, French, Italian and Romansch
Currency: Swiss Franc

The confederation of twenty-three cantons which makes up Switzerland is famous for its neutrality. But the state had its origins in a defensive alliance between Uri Schwyz and Unterwalden in 1291, and saw many wars in its early centuries of existence. The constitution vests supreme power in the electorate which can demand laws and changes to the constitution without regard to the wishes of the two-chamber parliament. Each canton is self-governing, with its own parliament; the federal government being responsible for war, peace and treaties. Isolated Alpine valleys continue to practise agriculture on traditional lines, but most crops are grown on the fertile central plain. Manufacturing is a major activity and is based on textiles, chemicals and the processing of agricultural produce into cheeses, sugar, beer and chilled meat. Banking and finance is a well-established sector of the economy which attracts much foreign money.

UNION OF SOVIET SOCIALIST REPUBLICS

Population: 290 million
Area: 22,400,000 square kilometres
Capital: Moscow
Language: Russian and numerous other languages
Currency: Rouble

The USSR came into being in 1922 with the establishment of Communist power throughout the territories of the former Tsarist Russian Empire. The abortive coup of August 1991 and the subsequent upheavals swept away the monolithic Communist state of the USSR. In its place have emerged a number of independent nations and a large but loose federation of states joined in voluntary association. This new form of constitution can be expected to evolve and develop for some years to come. The USSR is an economic giant, with output of iron and steel, machinery and other industrial goods being particularly high. Chronic problems of underproduction and shortages have dogged the economy recently. Agriculture uses one fifth of the workforce, producing grain, potatoes, meats and dairy products in large quantities. The economy of the area is rich and varied, but suffers from endemic inefficiency and years of neglect. Aid and advice from abroad is helping to improve the situation. The former states of the Soviet Union have retained their borders into the post Soviet era.

UNITED KINGDOM

Population: 57 million
Area: 243,000 square kilometres
Capital: London
Language: English, Welsh and Gaelic
Currency: Pound Sterling

The United Kingdom is a constitutional monarchy governing Britain, the northern counties of Ireland and neighbouring islands. The kingdoms of England and Scotland were united in 1603 when King James VI of Scotland inherited the English throne. The Parliaments merged a century later, but administration and justice remain distinct to some extent. The constitution allows for a single elected chamber together with a part-appointed, part-inherited House of Lords. The monarch has far-reaching powers, but in practice follows the wishes of Parliament. Agriculture is well developed, with highly-mechanised farms producing about half the nation's requirements. Industry and commerce are the basis of the economic wealth of this prosperous nation.

VATICAN

Population: 700
Area: 0.3 square kilometres
Capital: Vatican City
Language: Italian and Latin
Currency: Italian Lira

The Vatican is the smallest independent state in the world and exists solely as the residence of the Pope, the head of the Roman Catholic Church. Until 1860 the Pope ruled extensive areas of central Italy, but these were incorporated in the newly-created Kingdom of Italy, which in 1870 invaded Rome itself and confined the Pope to the complex of religious and administrative buildings known as the Vatican. In 1929 the Vatican was recognised as an independent state in return for the Pope relinquishing claims over Rome and surrounding territory. The Vatican has no industry, no agriculture and no commerce, though some income is gained from tourism. It is the administrative headquarters of the Catholic Church, which pays for its upkeep. The population is composed of religious and administrative personnel.

YUGOSLAVIA

Population: 24 million
Area: 255,000 square kilometres
Capital: Belgrade
Language: Serbian, Croat, Slovene, Macedonian and others
Currency: Yugoslavian Dinar

Yugoslavia came into being in 1918 as a confederation of southern Slavonic peoples newly independent of the Hapsburg Empire. A new constitution of 1946 made the nation a grouping of six republics, in which Communism was the only legal political party. Agriculture was formerly dominant and still employs about a quarter of the workforce. Maize, wheat and potatoes are the chief crops, with cattle, sheep and pigs the most important livestock. Industry has increased rapidly, particularly in the north. Iron and steel, chemicals and textiles are the primary industries, though numerous other areas are being exploited. Attempts in 1989-90 by the central government to curb the internal government of the republics led to widespread protest. The prosperous northern industrial republics of Slovenia and Croatia declared themselves independent, leading to invasion by the Federal army, fierce street fighting and a fragile ceasefire followed by negotiations between the republics and the federal government.

▲ *A village in Mozambique.*

▶ *A waterfall in Cameroon.*

▼ *Salisbury, Zimbabwe.*

ALGERIA

Population: 23 million
Area: 2,400,000 square kilometres
Capital: Algiers
Language: Arabic
Currency: Dinar

Algeria gained its independence from France in 1962 after nearly a decade of guerilla warfare. The bulk of the population lives along the Mediterranean coast and in the Atlas Mountains, where the climate is milder and the land more fertile than in the arid Sahara which makes up most of the country. The discovery of large natural gas fields has made Algeria relatively wealthy, and some of these resources are spent on free health treatment and high quality education. Many people continue to lead a traditional Islamic lifestyle, though European influences are strong in coastal towns. The single-party dictatorship which has held power since 1965 has recently announced its intention to allow rival political parties and to hold elections.

ANGOLA

Population: 10 million
Area: 1,200,000 square kilometres
Capital: Luanda
Language: Portuguese and various tribal languages
Currency: Kwanza

For most of its independent existence Angola has been racked by civil war between the communist MPLA party, which forms the central government, and the rebel UNITA organisation, which controls much of southern Angola. The long years of warfare have caused much hardship and have seriously disrupted the economy, making this one of the poorer African nations. However, oil production in the north and diamond mining provide a source of foreign capital which may lead to economic revival. The coastal region is the centre for industrialisation and urban lifestyles. The high plateau of the interior is heavily forested and inhabited by tribes which live in a traditional way with their own languages and religions.

BENIN

Population: 4 million
Area: 112,000 square kilometres
Capital: Porto Novo
Language: French and tribal languages
Currency: Franc CFA

The ideal of a revolutionary socialist state was recently abandoned in Benin, with the holding of free elections and the founding of several political parties. For the vast majority of the population the change probably meant little. Traditional agricultural lifestyles dominate in the interior, where tribal culture and animist cults are common. It is thought that about ninety percent of the population practice subsistence farming. In the mountainous far north Islamic culture has filtered down from the desert regions. Only on the coast is industry to be found, and even this is heavily based on the agricultural produce of the interior, particularly sugar and palm oil. A recently-exploited oilfield off the coast is expected to help boost the economy.

BOTSWANA

Population: 1.2 million
Area: 582,000 square kilometres
Capital: Gaborone
Language: English, Setswana
Currency: Pula

Botswana is rare among African nations in having maintained its democratic constitution throughout its period of independence. The constitution granted in 1966 allowed for an Elected Assembly of thirty-eight members and a House of Chiefs comprising the twelve tribal chiefs, and this arrangement is still in place. The vast majority of the population live in traditional villages, where cattle farming is the main activity, though some crops are also sown. Industry is limited to diamond and copper mining and many young men work in South Africa for some years in order to earn money for their families at home. The vast Kalahari Desert in the southwest of the nation is inhabited by nomadic bushmen tribes and they have little to do with national life.

BURKINA FASO

Population: 7.9 million
Area: 274,000 square kilometres
Capital: Ouagadougou
Language: French and tribal languages
Currency: Franc CFA

As one of the poorest and most unstable countries in Africa, Burkina Faso has experienced much hardship. Numerous coups and government changes have occurred, most recently in 1989. The nation is a largely artificial creation, being a former French administrative district covering the territory of several indigenous tribes. The vast majority of the population are engaged in subsistence farming in traditional tribal society. The country is periodically struck by drought and famine, being on the southern fringe of the Sahara. The recent discovery of gold and manganese deposits are unlikely to be exploited due to a poor transport system and lack of capital. The nation depends largely on foreign aid and remains chronically depressed.

BURUNDI

Population: 4.7 million
Area: 27,000 square kilometres
Capital: Bujumbura
Language: French, Kirundi and Swahili
Currency: Burundi Franc

Sometime in the 16th century Tutsi tribes invaded the area and conquered the Hutu peoples. Even today the nation is divided into the two ethnic groups, with the Tutsi wielding power. After a period of German and Belgian rule Burundi became independent in 1962 under a Tutsi monarch. In 1966 the king was overthrown by the Tutsi-dominated army, which has since suppressed Hutu unrest and dismissed Presidents at will. Tea and coffee plantations are the mainstays of both industry and the export economy. The majority of the population, however, remains dependent on subsistence agriculture based on bananas, maize and cattle. Less than one percent of the population is composed of pygmies, who inhabit dense forest and take little active part in national life.

CAMEROON

Population: 11.5 million
Area: 475,000 square kilometres
Capital: Yaounde
Language: English, French and tribal languages
Currency: Franc CFA

Much of the interior of Cameroon is virtually inaccessible during the rainy season, when torrential downpours wash away roads and flood large areas. This isolation is emphasised by ethnic diversity, with twenty-four languages and as many as 200 tribes. The fragmentation has slowed economic development, though the nation is relatively wealthy by African standards. The economy is based largely on agriculture, with coffee, cocoa and palm oil forming the bulk of export crops. The majority of farmland is, however, devoted to producing foods such as cassava, maize and groundnuts for local consumption. Industry is concentrated on aluminium smelting and the processing of agricultural products. Oil revenue has helped the government to invest in new projects.

CAPE VERDE

Population: 369,000
Area: 4,000 square kilometres
Capital: Praia
Language: French and Sangho
Currency: Cape Verde Escudo

The Cape Verde Islands have been independent only since 1975, when Portugal relinquished control. The

▲ Farm workers in Angola.

▲ A scene on the Chobe River, Botswana.

▲ Celebrations on the anniversary of the Algerian Revolution.

▲ *A village in Chad.*

▼ *A domestic scene in Burkina Faso.*

▲ *Barren, drought-ridden scenery, Cape Verde.*

▲ *Riverboat seller, Benin.*

▼ *The Central African Republic.*

▲ *Bathers in the Comoros.*

islands have strong historical links with Guinea Bisseau, also formerly Portuguese controlled, and have similar flags. The government is a single-party state, though the ruling elite joined several other African nations in 1990 by announcing an intention to allow democracy. The islands are small, rugged and arid, with little opportunity for farming. Coconuts, coffee and sugar are produced in small quantities on irrigated land. Fishing is far more productive for the local population with large numbers of tuna being landed each year. The climate and scenic coastline hold out the promise of an increase in tourism for the islands, though as yet this is underdeveloped.

CENTRAL AFRICAN REPUBLIC

Population: 2.9 million
Area: 622,000 square kilometres
Capital: Bangui
Language: French and tribal languages
Currency: Franc CFA

For thirteen years until 1979 this nation was ruled by Jean-Bedel Bokassa, who proclaimed himself Emperor and staged a lavish coronation ceremony. Bokassa was overthrown by the army and today the nation is a one-party state ostensibly committed to introducing democratic government. Though potentially rich in minerals and agriculture, the economy has been held back by political instability, poor communications, and particularly by the lack of a coastline. Diamond, gold and uranium mining lead the small industrial sector, while the majority of the population remain employed in subsistence agriculture. The southern rain-forests are beginning to be exploited, though ecological damage may result unless sustainable replanting is undertaken.

CHAD

Population: 5.5 million
Area: 1,284,000 square kilometres
Capital: N'djamena
Language: French, Arabic and tribal languages
Currency: Franc CFA

Endemic civil war has marked the history of Chad since independence from France in 1960. The fighting between various ethnic factions is based upon a struggle between the nomadic, Moslem north and the agricultural and animist south. The situation has been confused by shifting alliances and foreign intervention. Chad remains a dangerous and unstable country and the British ambassador to Chad is resident in London. The warfare has prevented exploitation of recently-discovered oilfields and deposits of gold and uranium.

The population remains desperately poor and is dependent on subsistence agriculture varied by fishing on the shores of Lake Chad. A new government was installed in March 1991, and it is to be hoped that this leads to some stability.

COMOROS

Population: 500,000
Area: 1,800 square kilometres
Capital: Moroni
Language: Arabic, French and Swahili
Currency: Franc CFA

When the three Comoros islands of Mwali, Njazidja and Nzwani declared themselves to be independent of France in 1975, the fourth island, Mayotte, refused to join them. The newly-independent nation has suffered three successful coups and has chronic problems of disease and poverty. The islands have, over the centuries, received influxes of Africans, Indonesian, Arabic and European peoples and today have a mixed population. The majority of the population engage in subsistence farming, producing such crops as cassava, bananas, coconuts and maize. In recent years commercial production of vanilla, cloves and coffee has been undertaken and these now account for much of the nation's exports. Though independent, the Comoros remain economically dependent on France.

▲ *The Congo's Sangha River.*

CONGO

Population: 2.2 million
Area: 341,000 square kilometres
Capital: Brazzaville
Language: French and tribal languages
Currency: Franc CFA

Formerly a French colony, the Congo is now a single-party, Marxist-Leninist state in which the army has a dominant influence. The army has engineered a total of four coups since independence. The nation is relatively wealthy by African standards, with oil reserves offshore and productive gold mines. Industry is well established around the capital and produces cement and textiles among other products. However, more than three-quarters of the population

remains engaged in farming, much of it at subsistence level. The vast bulk of the population is found in the southern parts of the country, for the northern regions are covered by dense forests and unfertile land.

DJIBOUTI

Population: 480,000
Area: 23,000 square kilometres
Capital: Djibouti City
Language: Somali, Afar, French
Currency: Djibouti Franc

Sandwiched between Ethiopia and Somalia, the tiny state of Djibouti is dominated by disputes between its ethnic Somalis and Afars. The hinterland is composed of arid grazing lands, although the bulk of the population lives in or around Djibouti City. The city has a long history as a trading centre and the economy is largely dependent on the port. Djibouti is a one-party state under President Hassan Aptidon.

EGYPT

Population: 50 million
Area: 1,000,000 square kilometres
Capital: Cairo
Language: Arabic
Currency: Egyptian Pound

Famous for its ancient history of pyramids and pharaohs, Egypt was conquered by the Arabs in 7th century, and today the nation is firmly Moslem in culture and outlook. People and prosperity are concentrated in the Nile Valley, as they have been since recorded history began here in around 3,000 BC. The waters of the Nile allow irrigation of the farmland which produces the bulk of the nation's food as well as export crops of cotton and citrus fruits. Industry is well advanced in the major towns and cities. Tourism plays a major role in the economy, with well over a million visitors to the country each year. The main attractions are the ancient temples and tombs, which are maintained by the government. Despite the assassination of President Sadat in 1981, Egypt has a relatively stable political system.

EQUATORIAL GUINEA

Population: 417,000
Area: 28,000 square kilometres
Capital: Malabo
Language: Spanish and tribal languages
Currency: Franc CFA

The single-party state of Equatorial Guinea is divided between the mainland territory on the Mbini River and the island of Bioko. Commercial farming has declined since independence in 1968, but cocoa and coffee remain important export crops. The majority of farmland is used for subsistence agriculture, with cassava and sweet potatoes being the chief products. The wet, hot tropical climate produces vast forests in the interior and these are beginning to be exploited for their timber, which accounts for one quarter of all exports. Although over half the population lives in towns, there is virtually no industry in the nation and foreign capital is difficult to attract due to the unstable nature of politics in the country.

ETHIOPIA

Population: 50 million
Area: 1,221,000 square kilometres
Capital: Addis Ababa
Language: Arabic and tribal languages
Currency: Birr

Drought, famine and civil war have placed Ethiopia in the world's headlines for several years. Much of the country is in the hands of rebel factions, one of which recently overthrew the central government. The violence is largely due to the many ethnic groups included within the nation, many of whom desire independence from strong central rule. The great famine of 1981-83 claimed hundreds of thousands of lives, and the country lives under the perpetual threat of another drought. Despite this, farming is generally in good condition and in productive years can account for valuable exports of coffee and sugar. Much potentially fertile ground remains untilled due to political instability. Peace would undoubtedly help ease the desperate plight of the Ethiopian peoples.

GABON

Population: 1.2 million
Area: 267,000 square kilometres
Capital: Libreville
Language: French and tribal languages
Currency: Franc CFA

Made up largely of the drainage basin of the Ogooue River, Gabon has numerous natural resources but lacks the finance and population to take best advantage of them. Offshore oil is being exploited, as are deposits of uranium and manganese, but the economy remains based chiefly on agriculture. The Equator runs through the centre of Gabon, and this dictates the climate and range of crops which can be produced. Most of the population supports itself on subsistence agriculture, though sugar cane is grown in large quantities near the coast for export. Government under a single-party state has been stable since 1967, but this was recently dismantled and free elections held, though allegations of ballot-rigging were made.

▲ *Thatched huts in Equatorial Guinea.*

Above right: *Children in Guinea -Bissau.*

▼ *Filling water pots, Ghana.*

▲ *Women cleaning groundnuts, Gambia.*

▲ *The mountain village of Ha Thuhlo, Lesotho.*

▶ *Landscape of Gabon.*

▼ *Kenyatta Centre, Nairobi, Kenya.*

▶ *Abidjan, Ivory Coast.*

GAMBIA

Population: 875,000
Area: 11,000 square kilometres
Capital: Banjul
Language: English and tribal languages
Currency: Dalasi

The Gambia exists because of the river from which it takes its name. The nation is made up of a narrow strip of land rarely more than twenty kilometres wide which follows the twists and turns of the river from Koina to the ocean. Several tribes have their territories along the river and their chiefs have an established position within the constitution. The nation is basically agricultural and has only one export of any importance. This is the groundnut, thousands of tons of which are shipped out each year. More recently the government has tried to break this hazardous dependence on a single crop and production of cotton is on the increase. In 1982 Gambia joined with Senegal, which virtually surrounds it, to form the Confederation of Senegambia.

GHANA

Population: 15 million
Area: 239,000 square kilometres
Capital: Accra
Language: English and tribal languages
Currency: Cedi

As the first Black African state to become independent of a European colonial power, in 1957, Ghana has set several trends in African history. The colours of the Ghanaian flag – red, green and yellow – have been adopted by several other colonies on achieving independence, while the black star of African freedom has also become a popular motif. Ghana has experienced several coups and is currently ruled by a Provisional Council led by Flight Lieutenant Jerry Rawlings. The economy is relatively healthy and is based on cash crop agriculture, with cocoa being by far the most important, though tobacco, coffee and tropical fruits are catching up. The small-scale industrial activities are based around the mining of gold, diamonds and, more recently, oil.

GUINEA

Population: 6.7 million
Area: 245,000 square kilometres
Capital: Conakry
Language: French and tribal languages
Currency: Syli

Guinea followed Ghana to independence one year later and adopted the same colours for its flag, though they are arranged in vertical rather than horizontal stripes. Several tribal groupings are included within Guinea, with the Fulani being the largest at around forty percent of the population. The nation is under the control of a military junta which seized power in 1984 following the death of the former president. The nation has a tropical climate, with a summer monsoon which brings heavy rain and high temperatures. Combined with fertile soils this climate creates ideal conditions for a variety of crops including rice, sugar cane and tropical fruits. Vast reserves of bauxite are now being mined as are iron ore deposits and high-grade diamonds.

GUINEA-BISSAU

Population: 0.9 million
Area: 36,000 square kilometres
Capital: Bissau
Language: Portuguese and tribal languages
Currency: Peso

The single party which has ruled Guinea-Bissau since the coup of 1980 has recently announced that it will be working towards multi-party democracy, though little progress has so far been made. The fertile soil and tropical climate allow the production of large quantities of rice, rubber and groundnuts, much of which is exported. Most of the population remains dependent on subsistence agriculture and industry is virtually non-existent. Guinea-Bissau has a crushing foreign debt more than one hundred times the size of the government's annual budget. Ethnically the population is divided between the coastal Balanta and the Muslim Fulani of the inland regions, though there are several smaller tribes.

IVORY COAST

Population: 12.1 million
Area: 322,000 square kilometres
Capital: Abidjan
Language: French and tribal languages
Currency: Franc FA

This nation takes its name from the early trade in ivory which dominated the region when it was first discovered by Europeans in the 15th century. Since then slavery, and more recently coffee, have been the mainstays of the economy. Today the rich soil of the coastal regions has been turned to support a wide variety of crops including yams, cassava and a number of tropical fruits for export. Despite this fertility the economy of the Ivory Coast is held back by massive foreign debts and limited mineral resources. The single party state which has existed for many years recently announced that it would begin a process of demo-cratisation and free elections have been held. The former sole party still retains power, having won over ninety percent of seats in Parliament.

KENYA

Population: 24 million
Area: 582,000 square kilometres
Capital: Nairobi
Language: English, Swahili and tribal languages
Currency: Kenya Shilling

Committed to the concept of "democracy with one party", the state of Kenya has enjoyed rather more stability than many other African nations since it achieved independence in 1963. This has combined with rich natural resources and a long history of international trade to make it economically viable, though not particularly wealthy. Most of the population inhabits the interior highlands, where coffee, tea and sugar are grown in large quantities for export, or the lower hills, where maize, cassava and sweet potatoes are produced for local consumption. The vast semi-arid plains are the home of gazelles, zebra and lions, which attract over half-a-million tourists each year, boosting the economy. The coastal towns have been trading with foreigners since the Arabs first arrived about the time of Christ and are thriving commercial centres.

LESOTHO

Population: 1.7 million
Area: 30,000 square kilometres
Capital: Maseru
Language: English, Sesotho
Currency: Loti

Lesotho is one of the few African tribal kingdoms to survive into modern times. Since a coup in 1986 the king acts on the advice of the army. In the early 19th century refugees from vicious warfare in the north fled to the mountains of Lesotho and became welded into a kingdom under Moshoeshoe I, who placed himself under British protection. This wise move ensured the Sotho clans retained some form of self-government throughout the colonial era, and in 1966 became independent outside the Union of South Africa. The country has few natural resources and little agricultural land. The young men work in South Africa for long periods of time, earning enough money to support their families and keep the fragile economy of the kingdom in balance.

LIBERIA

Population: 2.4 million
Area: 111,000 square kilometres
Capital: Monrovia
Language: English and tribal languages
Currency: Liberian Dollar

The flag of Liberia is similar to that of the United States of America, indicating the origins of the nation. In 1822 an American society landed a party of freed slaves on the coast in Monrovia in an attempt to establish a haven for such people. In 1847 the nation declared itself independent and adopted a constitution similar to that of the United States. Recent years have witnessed violent upheavals, with coups and civil war raging fiercely. The situation is not yet stable. Liberia has rich mineral resources, in particular massive iron ore deposits, which make up seventy percent of exports, together with gold and diamonds. The vast bulk of the population is engaged in farming, with numerous commercial farms growing coffee, rice and sugar cane.

▲ *A lake in the Fezzan desert, Libya.*

LIBYA

Population: 4 million
Area: 1,760,000 square kilometres
Capital: Tripoli
Language: Arabic
Currency: Libyan Dinar

Until recently one of the poorest Mediterranean nations, Libya is now one of the richest, following the discovery of massive oil fields in 1959. In 1969 King Idris was overthrown by an army faction led by Colonel Muammar Gadaffi, who established Libya as an Arab republic. The country has since vociferously supported Arab unity and nationalism, lending aid to various organisations such as the PLO and so earning Western enmity. The economy is based on natural oil and gas, which account for nearly all exports. Internally, however, agriculture dominates, with the most fertile lands of North Africa producing rich harvests of dates, citrus fruits and cereals. Ambitious irrigation projects are under way which aim at adding hundreds of square kilometres to the farmland.

29

MADAGASCAR

Population: 11.4 million
Area: 590,000 square kilometres
Capital: Antananarivo
Language: Malagasy and French
Currency: Malagasy Franc

The original kingdom, comprising a mixed population of Malaysians and Africans, was overrun by the French in 1897. In 1960 the island became independent as a republic, and since then has undergone several coups. It is now ruled by the Supreme Revolutionary Council and the President, who leads the sole political party. The economy of the nation is based on tropical agriculture and the exploitation of forests, both natural and planted. The fertile soils produce heavy crops of coffee, tobacco and tropical fruits, the processing of which forms the basis of the island's small-scale industries. Cattle breeding is a major activity in the highlands and there are nearly as many cattle on the island as people.

MALAWI

Population: 7 million
Area: 118,000 square kilometres
Capital: Lilongwe
Language: Chichewa and English
Currency: Kwacha

Ruled as a one-party state by Dr Kamuzu Banda, Malawi is a landlocked nation with few resources. Agriculture is the basic activity, with most of the population relying on subsistence farming for a livelihood. Tobacco and tea are grown for export, but occupy only a small part of the total agricultural land. Marble is the only major quarrying material and industry is restricted to local consumer goods. As a mountainous nation, however, Malawi has massive potential for hydro-electricity and this is now being exploited on a large scale. The economy remains reliant on its migrant workers, who leave Malawi for South Africa or Zambia to work in mines and factories to earn much needed income.

MALI

Population: 9 million
Area: 1,240,000 square kilometres
Capital: Bamako
Language: French, Bambara and tribal languages
Currency: Franc CFA

Mali is one of the world's poorest nations, being dependent on an agriculture at the mercy of drought and semi-desert conditions. The majority of the diverse population is concentrated in the southwest, where the Senegal and Niger rivers give a semblance of reliability to the water supply for irrigation. Millet, cassava and sweet potatoes are the chief crops for local consumption, while cotton is produced on a modest scale for export. The northern and eastern regions are covered by desert and are virtually uninhabited. Mineral wealth remains untapped due to poor transport and a lack of capital. The military coup of 1968 produced a stable government which is still headed by the coup leader, General Traore, who heads the only legal political party.

MAURITANIA

Population: 2 million
Area: 1,031,000 square kilometres
Capital: Nouakchott
Language: Arabic and French
Currency: Ouguiya

The crescent and star on Mauritania's green flag indicates the Islamic heritage of this desert nation. The vast desert region of the north and east is the home of nomadic herdsmen, but the majority of the population inhabits the Senegal Valley in the southwest. In this region millet, rice and dates are produced in large quantities for local consumption. Coastal villages land large catches of Atlantic fish, which are dried or salted locally to form the bulk of exports by value. Industry is virtually non-existent, what there is being restricted to iron-ore mining or food processing. A long-running war with Morocco over the Western Sahara territory, which ended in 1979, drained the Mauritanian economy, which is still attempting to recover. The country is ruled by a Military Committee which seized power in the coup of 1978.

MOROCCO

Population: 24.5 million
Area: 446,000 square kilometres
Capital: Rabat
Language: Arabic, Berber, French
Currency: Dirham

The Islamic kingdom of Morocco became independent of France in 1956, though the Sultan had always enjoyed some degree of control. The Sultanate became a Kingdom in 1957. The king holds supreme authority over both secular and religious life, though the government is actually carried out by a democratically-elected Parliament. The bulk of the nation's wealth is based on its rich mineral deposits, particularly phosphates and lead ore, which are extensively mined and provide much employment. Most of the population remains dependent on agriculture, however, and traditional crops of cereals, fruits and tomatoes dominate. Morocco has been involved in a lengthy war in the Western Sahara, where it claims large areas of territory.

MOZAMBIQUE

Population: 15 million
Area: 783,000 square kilometres
Capital: Maputo
Language: Portuguese and tribal languages
Currency: Metical

The national flag of Mozambique features a book, a hoe and a gun; symbols which are apt for this poverty-ridden nation in southern Africa. Since 1977 the Marxist Frelimo Party has been the only legal political party in Mozambique, though it recently announced its intention of allowing opposition. Opposition of a more violent kind has been maintained by the Renamo movement, which has been carrying on an armed struggle for many years. To counter this threat Mozambique maintains one of the largest armies in Africa, numbering 60,000 men. The hoe symbolises the agricultural base of the national economy, which relies on cereals, bananas and various types of nut. The long coastline on the Indian Ocean offers fine fishing opportunities and the prawn catch is substantial.

NAMIBIA

Population: 1.3 million
Area: 825,000 square kilometres
Capital: Windhoek
Language: English, Afrikaans and tribal languages
Currency: South African Rand

The vast desert nation of Namibia gained independence from South Africa in 1990, after many years of confused political instability. Cuban mercenaries from Communist Angola backed the SWAPO guerilla movement, while South Africa attempted to maintain its influence by enforcing a constitution. The independence elections resulted in victory for SWAPO, but not by the margin needed for them to fulfil their goal of one-party dictatorship. The political struggle was made more bitter by the vast mineral wealth of Namibia, which provides one the highest average incomes on the continent. Diamonds and uranium form the basis of the mineral industry. Most of the people are engaged in stock ranching of either cattle or sheep, which together outnumber humans in Namibia by six to one.

NIGER

Population: 7.5 million
Area: 1,268,000 square kilometres
Capital: Niamey
Language: French, Hausa and tribal languages
Currency: Franc CFA

▲ *A typical Senegalese, Senegal.*

▲ *Fertile river banks, Morocco.*

▼ *Terraced hillsides, Rwanda.*

▲ *Nevis Peak, St Christopher Nevis WI.*

▼ *Loading a schooner, St Vincent, WI.*

▲ *Washing clothes, Nicaragua.*

▼ *Punta del Este, Uruguay.*

▲ *Machu Picchu, Peru.*

▼ *Parmaribo, Surinam.*

▲ *Englishman's Bay, Trinidad and Tobago.*

▼ *The Panama Canal, Panama.*

▲ *Petit Piton and Soufrière, St Lucia, WI.*

▶ *Asuncion, Paraguay.*

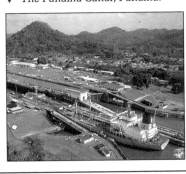

highly developed and extremely productive. Throughout the large area occupied by the nation are to be found deposits of a wide range of minerals, including oil, various metals and gemstones. The fertile soils are extensively farmed to produce huge crops; over two billion bushels of wheat alone. Industry is highly developed with high-tech industries leading the world in developing new processes. In other fields, too, the USA leads the industries of the world with a highly diversified range of businesses producing almost every type of goods imaginable. The nation is a democratic federal union of fifty states in which individual states have some rights of self-government, but the most important powers are held by the central administration.

URUGUAY

Population: 3.1 million
Area: 176,000 square kilometres
Capital: Montevideo
Language: Spanish
Currency: Uruguayan Nuevo Peso

A province of Brazil until it won its independence in 1828 after a brief war, in which Uruguay enjoyed Argentinian support. Uruguay then adopted a flag sharing the same colours and the Sun of May symbol as that of Argentina. In 1989 democratic elections were held after more than a decade of military intervention in government. The chief wealth of Uruguay is its land, which supports a flourishing pastoral economy. There are about eleven million cattle and twenty-five million sheep grazing on the rich grasslands of Uruguay, together with large numbers of farm animals. The processing of meat and leather are major industries in Uruguay, as is the spinning and weaving of wool. The nation has virtually no mineral resources and only a limited industrial base.

VENEZUELA

Population: 9.3 million
Area: 912,000 square kilometres
Capital: Caracas
Language: Spanish
Currency: Bolivar

The Republic of Venezuela came into being in 1830, when the area broke away from Colombia just nine years after jointly winning independence from Spain. Venezuela is more heavily dependent on industry than most other South American nations and has large and densely populated cities. Nearly ninety per cent of the population live in towns, far more than in neighbouring states. Vast oil reserves have recently been discovered and are slowly being exploited. More established is the mining of bauxite, which supports an aluminium smelting business. Iron ore similarly forms the basis of a metal working industry. Agriculture has steadily declined in importance, with more than half of those now employed in agriculture living at subsistence level.

AUSTRALASIA

*T*he nations of Australasia do not occupy a single continental entity, as do those of Asia, Africa or Europe. Instead they are united by cultural and ethnic traits more closely linked to the human populations than to the geographical limits of that region commonly called Australasia.

Strictly speaking, Australasia consists of the island continent of Australia, New Guinea, the Solomon Islands and possibly New Caledonia and New Zealand, though these latter are separate geological entities. The remaining islands strung across the vast spaces of the Pacific are isolated outcrops of volcanic rock or coral reefs with no geological or geographical connection at all.

These far flung islands and islets are, however, united by their human inhabitants. Several centuries ago, the ancestors of Polynesian and Melanesian islanders sailed across the vast, open stretches of the Pacific Ocean from Southeast Asia to colonise the remote islands of the tropical and sub-tropical regions. With them they brought taro, yams and other tropical crops with which to support themselves. Common ties of culture and religion bound these peoples together. Long voyages in open canoes were often undertaken between the various islands, preserving ties of technology and belief.

When European seamen arrived, from the 16th century onwards, they found the islands densely inhabited by peoples so similar that the entire region of Oceania came to be viewed as a cultural entity. European settlers and missionaries radically altered the society and cultures of the islands, though many features of Polynesian society remain even today.

The modern nations of Australasia are clearly divided into cultural and physical regions. The divides between the regions has as much to do with the economies and lifestyles of the peoples as with the physical location of the islands.

Dominating all is the great landmass of Australia. The Australian nation has a mixed culture based on the various immigrant groups, chiefly from Europe. To a much lesser extent Australian culture rests on the indigenous Aboriginal peoples who are now largely restricted to the Outback. The bulk of Australia is covered by arid deserts, where settlements are few and far between. The only populous centres are mining towns thriving on the exploitation of the rich mineral content of the nation's rocks.

Kinder climatic regions around the coasts are more densely populated, with farming communities producing crops according to the prevailing climate. All the major cities are on the coast, centred on the sites of historic ports. Here the population is engaged in industrial and service occupations more akin to developed western economies than to the prevailing culture of Australasia.

Sharing much of the flavour of Australia is New Zealand, with its largely European population and small indigenous element. The economy and lifestyle here is more rural than in Australia, while the temperate climate dictates the crops and livestock which can be produced.

Away from these economic giants of the region, the nations are far smaller and less developed, though the original cultures are more apparent. Nations may be as small as a single island with a population of just 7,000. The largest consist of archipelagoes spread across thousands of square kilometres of ocean, but even these never top one million in population. The cultures of the smaller nations are closely allied to the indigenous peoples. Christianity has generally replaced the violent ceremonies and beliefs of the former religions, and settlers from Europe and elsewhere often form sizeable minorities among the population.

The disparate nations of Australasia form a complex pattern of human adaptation to harsh environments. From the Australian deserts to the open ocean, Australasia is a place of extremes and superlatives. The differing cultures of European settlers and native populations are sometimes blended together and elsewhere stand in stark contrast to each other. But everywhere there is the great Pacific Ocean, dividing the nations and yet uniting them.

▲ Mount Tasman, New Zealand.

▶ A native girl on the beach, Kiribati.

◀ The world-famed Opera House, Sydney, Australia.

AUSTRALIA

Population: 17 million
Area: 7,682,000 square kilometres
Capital: Canberra
Language: English
Currency: Australian Dollar

The vast nation continent of Australia was the last major landmass to be discovered by Europeans, remaining largely unknown until the 18th century. Immigration,initially from the UK but later from the rest of Europe, and most recently from Asia, produced the dominant social profile of modern Australia. The extensive grazing lands support large numbers of sheep and cattle, while the smaller areas of arable land produce wheat, rice and market crops. The large desert regions are rich in mineral deposits. Industry is well developed, with a wide range of consumer goods and engineering equipment being produced. The nation is a federation of six states, with the central government being responsible for the Northern Territory. It came into being on the first day of the 20th century, when former British colonies joined to form the Commonwealth of Australia.

FIJI

Population: 730,000
Area: 18,000 square kilometres
Capital: Suva
Language: English, Fijian and Hindustani
Currency: Fijian Dollar

Britain annexed the 330 islands of Fiji in 1874 and stamped out the endemic tribal warfare. Independence was granted in 1970 and a troubled history has resulted. The population is almost equally divided between native Fijians of Melanesian and Polynesian ancestry and immigrants from India, who arrived during British rule. In 1987 an Indian coalition won power in Parliament. Within months a coup organised by the native Fijians placed the army in power. A new constitution has been imposed, which places political power in the hands of the native Fijians. The economy is based on agriculture, with sugar cane, coconuts and ginger being the primary crops. Industry is concentrated on processing the crops, while mineral wealth is restricted to two small gold mines.

KIRIBATI

Population: 66,000
Area: 717 square kilometres
Capital: Tarawa
Language: English, Gilbertese
Currency: Australian Dollar

Although Kiribati is independent it has no currency of its own, and its citizens use the Australian dollar. The islands are generally small but are spread over an immense area of the Pacific Ocean, being grouped into three coral archipelagos and one volcanic island. The islands voluntarily became British protectorates in 1892 and regained independence in 1979. The democratically-elected government consists of one chamber and a President. The agricultural economy of the islands relies almost exclusively on coconuts and copra, which make up over ninety percent of exports by value. The coconut tree grows well in the thin soil and tropical climate of Kiribati. Pigs, chickens and breadfruit trees are produced for local consumption, as is a local vegetable named *babai*.

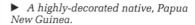

NAURU

Population: 8,100
Area: 21 square kilometres
Capital: Yaren
Language: Nauruan and English
Currency: Australian Dollar

With a population among the lowest in the world, Nauru does not support its own currency, using instead the Australian dollar. The population is a mix of Polynesian and Melanesians who arrived generations ago and have merged to produce a single racial group. The island fell under German control in 1881, passed to Australia in 1914, and became independent in 1968. The constitution allows an assembly elected every three years under a President. Nauru remains within the Commonwealth. The traditional crop of coconuts is widely grown and exported, while vegetables and livestock are kept for local consumption. Tourism is a growing business. The island nation's wealth, however, depends on phosphates mined on the island. This gives Nauru the highest per capita income in the Pacific islands and the wealth is being invested against the time when deposits run out.

NEW ZEALAND

Population: 3.4 million
Area: 268,000 square kilometres
Capital: Wellington
Language: English and Maori
Currency: New Zealand Dollar

Descendants of European immigrants form the bulk of New Zealand's population, though the native Maori form the largest minority. The exports of New Zealand have traditionally been agricultural and the pattern continues, with chilled meat, live animals, dairy products and wool far outstripping manufactured goods in value. However, industry

▲ *An isolated beach, Nauru.*

▶ *A highly-decorated native, Papua New Guinea.*

▼ *Niutao Island church, Tuvalu.*

▲ *Lefaga Beach, Upolu, Western Samoa.*

◀ *Yasur volcano, Vanuatu.*

▼ *Mananuca Islands, Fiji.*

is of growing importance internally, with iron and steel works and aluminium smelting being the largest heavy industrial works. The attractive scenery and relaxed lifestyle of the islands makes New Zealand an increasingly popular holiday attraction, with nearly a million tourists visiting each year. The government is based on universal suffrage, though some seats in the Assembly are reserved for Maoris and have an exclusively Maori electorate.

PAPUA NEW GUINEA

Population: 3.8 million
Area: 463,000 square kilometres
Capital: Port Moresby
Language: English, Motu and tribal languages
Currency: Kina

The rugged highlands of New Guinea are divided into isolated valleys covered by dense forests in which travel is difficult and communications are poor. The numerous tribes speak as many as 700 different languages, though the Motu form of pidgin English is a common *lingua franca*. Many of these tribes were untouched by the outside world, having no knowledge of Whites until the 1940s, and they still lead traditional lifestyles and pursue traditional tribal wars. Agriculture for export is concentrated around the coasts and produces coffee, copra and cocoa. Gold is mined on a commercial scale and there are large copper reserves on the island of Bougainville, though an active secessionist movement has disrupted mining. The constitution is based on that of the UK.

▲ *Native dance, Honiara, Solomon Islands.*

SOLOMON ISLANDS

Population: 309,000
Area: 28,000 square kilometres
Capital: Honiara
Language: English and tribal languages
Currency: Solomon Island Dollar

The Melanesian tribes of the Solomons retained their freedom until Britain declared a protectorate in 1893. The Japanese invaded during World War II, and Britain granted full independence in 1978. The country is governed by a Parliament elected by universal

suffrage. The Governor General, who represents the Queen, is appointed on the advice of the Parliament. The islands are predominantly agricultural, with property ownership held collectively by tribes and clans. Cocoa and coconuts are grown for export while yams, taro and sweet potatoes are consumed locally. The large fishing fleet exploits the tuna shoals of the region and the catch is canned before export. Industry is limited to processing crops for export.

▲ *The Tongatapu Island coastline, Tonga.*

TONGA

Population: 100,000
Area: 700 square kilometres
Capital: Nuku'alofa
Language: Tongan and English
Currency: Pa'anga

The kingdom of Tonga dates back to the early 19th century, when the warlike King Tupou of the Ha'apai conquered all the island tribes. Tupou overthrew the rule of petty chiefs and established a rudimentary democracy before Britain declared a protectorate in 1899. Internal government continued under the royal family and full independence came in 1970. The present constitution is based on that of King Topou. The Assembly consists of nine chiefs elected by the chiefs, nine people elected by the people and eleven privy councillors appointed by the king. The main exports are coconuts, fish and vanilla, while tourism brings in substantial quantities of foreign capital. Industry is virtually non-existent.

TUVALU

Population: 8,000
Area: 24 square kilometres
Capital: Fongafale
Language: Tuvaluan and English
Currency: Australian Dollar

As with other tiny Pacific states, Tuvalu uses the Australian dollar. However, it mints its own coins with unique and attractive designs. A British protectorate from 1892 to 1968, Tuvalu has a Parliament elected by universal suffrage and consisting of just twelve members,

four of whom are ministers. There are no political parties and candidates stand as individuals. The nine islands of the group are coral atolls with thin soils capable of supporting little other than coconut trees. Coconuts and copra comprise the main exports, with vegetables being grown for local consumption. The flag is highly symbolic, with the blue field representing the Pacific Ocean, the nine stars the nine islands, and the Union Jack standing for membership of the Commonwealth.

VANUATU

Population: 142,000
Area: 12,000 square kilometres
Capital: Vila
Language: Bislama and English
Currency: Vatu

On independence in 1980 the islands changed their name from New Hebrides to Vanuatu. The former name was given by Captain Cook because the rugged mountainous interiors reminded him of the Scottish islands, though the tropical climate is very different from that of the Scottish Hebrides. Power resides in an elected Parliament together with the tribal chiefs who sit in a separate Council. The Council advises primarily on matters of custom and tradition. The basis of the economy is the coconut tree, cocoa and coffee, which flourish in the hot, moist climate. A livestock industry based on cattle is becoming established. Tropical crops such as yams and taro are grown for local markets. Industry is limited to processing export crops and freezing the plentiful fish catch brought in by the numerous fishing boats.

WESTERN SAMOA

Population: 163,000
Area: 2,800 square kilometres
Capital: Apia
Language: English and Samoan
Currency: Tala

Formerly a German colony governed since 1920 by New Zealand, Western Samoa became independent in 1962. His Highness Malietoa Manumalfili became head of state for life, but after his death future heads of state are due to be elected. Though now independent, Western Samoa maintains direct diplomatic links only within the Pacific. Elsewhere New Zealand acts on its behalf. The economy of the islands is basically agricultural, with coconuts, bananas and cocoa being among the most important crops. Despite the tropical climate and a marked dry season, tourism is only poorly developed. Industry is limited to the processing of agricultural products.

45

POLAR REGIONS

*T*he polar regions have an image of being blizzard-swept wastes inhabited only by penguins and polar bears. In fact the polar regions are far more than that. It is true that both the North and South Poles are ice-bound throughout the year, but the wildlife of the regions is incredibly varied. In the north polar bears, seals and whales make up the mammal population and the oceans are teeming with fish. The south, which has the advantage of a solid rock continent, is home to a variety of fauna, including penguins.

Both poles have been divided between various nations which maintain scientific bases and conduct research. As the Arctic is open ocean beneath the ice, it is technically not subject to any state. However, those nations which have Arctic coasts maintain various bases, often military, in the area and patrol it regularly.

The political situation of Antarctica is more fraught. Officially, the vast continent is divided between Australia, New Zealand, France, Norway and Britain. Other nations, however, including Chile and Argentina, claim sections of the continent. All these nations, and others, maintain scientific research stations on Antarctica. The population of these outposts varies greatly with the season and from year to year, but there are rarely more than a thousand people on the continent. English is now the recognised scientific language, but each nationality speaks its own language on the continent.

In 1959 the Antarctic Treaty was signed by nations involved on the continent, and has since expanded to include thirty-eight nations. The Treaty bans military activity and tightly regulates commercial and scientific activity in Antarctica. It is unlikely that either polar region will ever maintain a sizeable human population but both remain rich in wildlife and environmental interest. It is to be hoped that international co-operation will ensure the continued existence of these great wilderness areas.

▲ An Eskimo in a hunting kayak, north-west Greenland.

► As temperatures drop, the sea near Signy Island starts to freeze.

▼ *Macaroni penguins on Bird Island, South Georgia.*

▲ *Heavy-bodied walruses resting on the beaches at Round Island, Alaska.*

▼ *Probing newly-formed ice in Antarctica.*

Miller Oblated Stereographic Projection

Designed and produced by E.S.R.

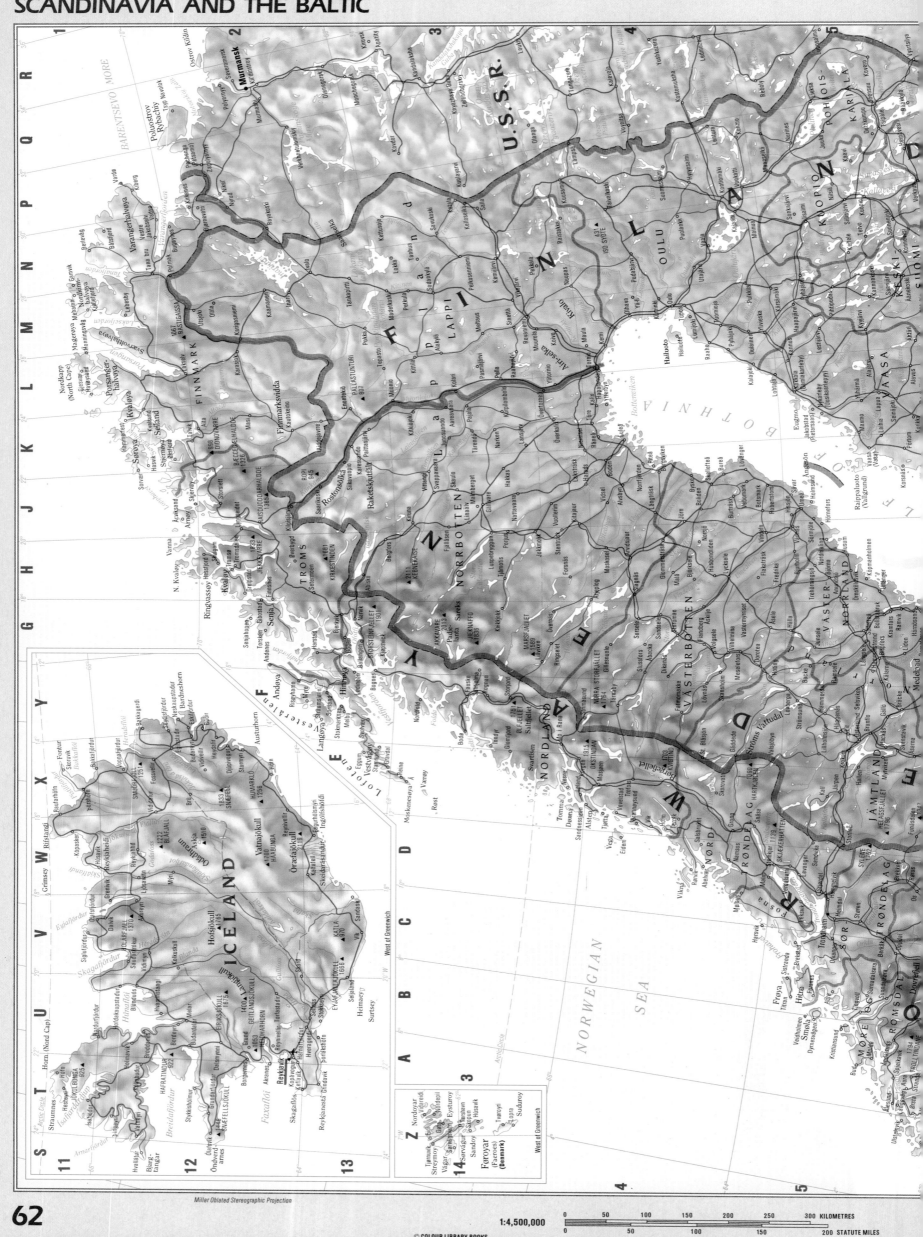

Miller Oblated Stereographic Projection

1:4,500,000

| 0 | 50 | 100 | 150 | 200 | 250 | 300 KILOMETRES |

| 0 | 50 | 100 | 150 | 200 STATUTE MILES |

© COLOUR LIBRARY BOOKS

East of Greenwich

Designed and produced by E.S.R.

BENELUX AND FRANCE

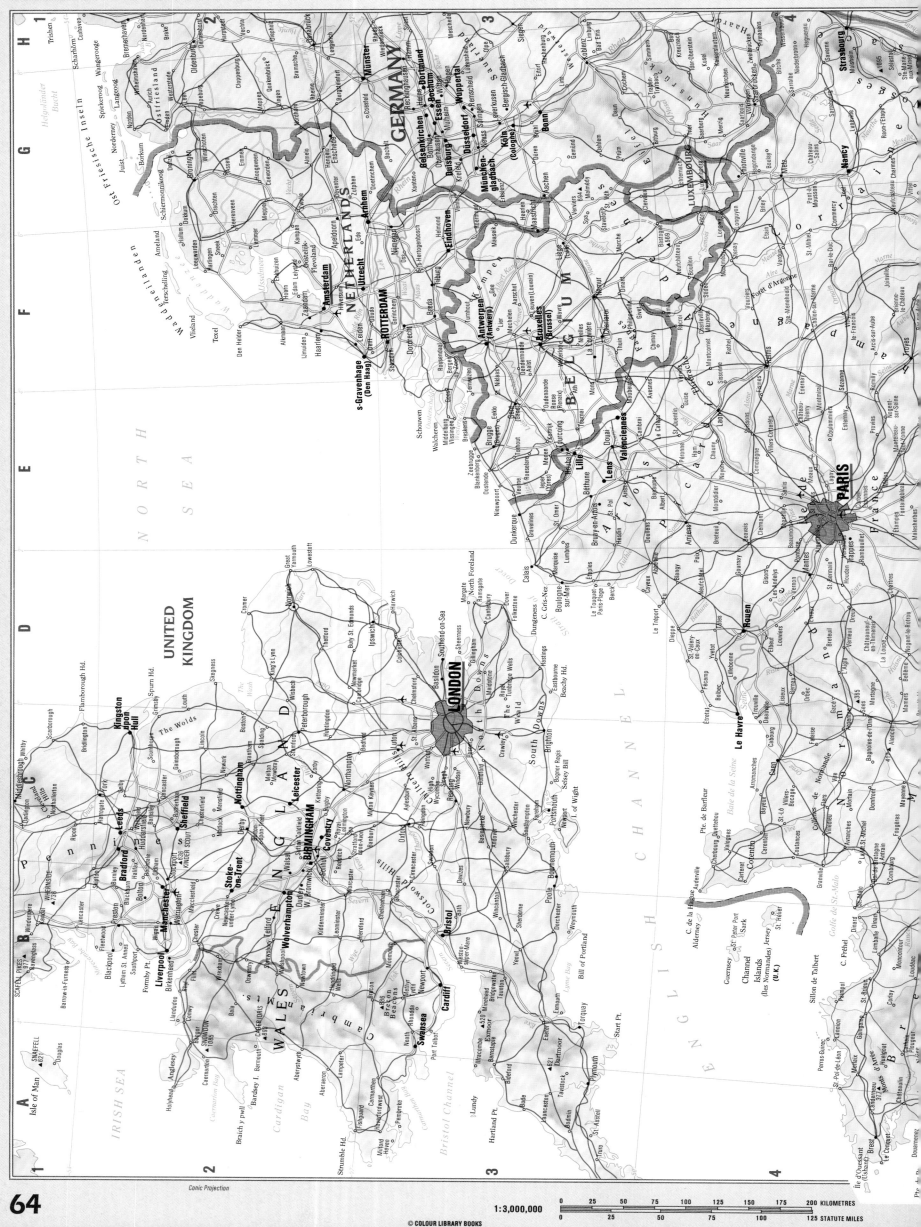

Conic Projection

1:3,000,000

© COLOUR LIBRARY BOOKS

| 0 | 25 | 50 | 75 | 100 | 125 | 150 | 175 | 200 KILOMETRES |

| 0 | 25 | 50 | 75 | 100 | 125 STATUTE MILES |

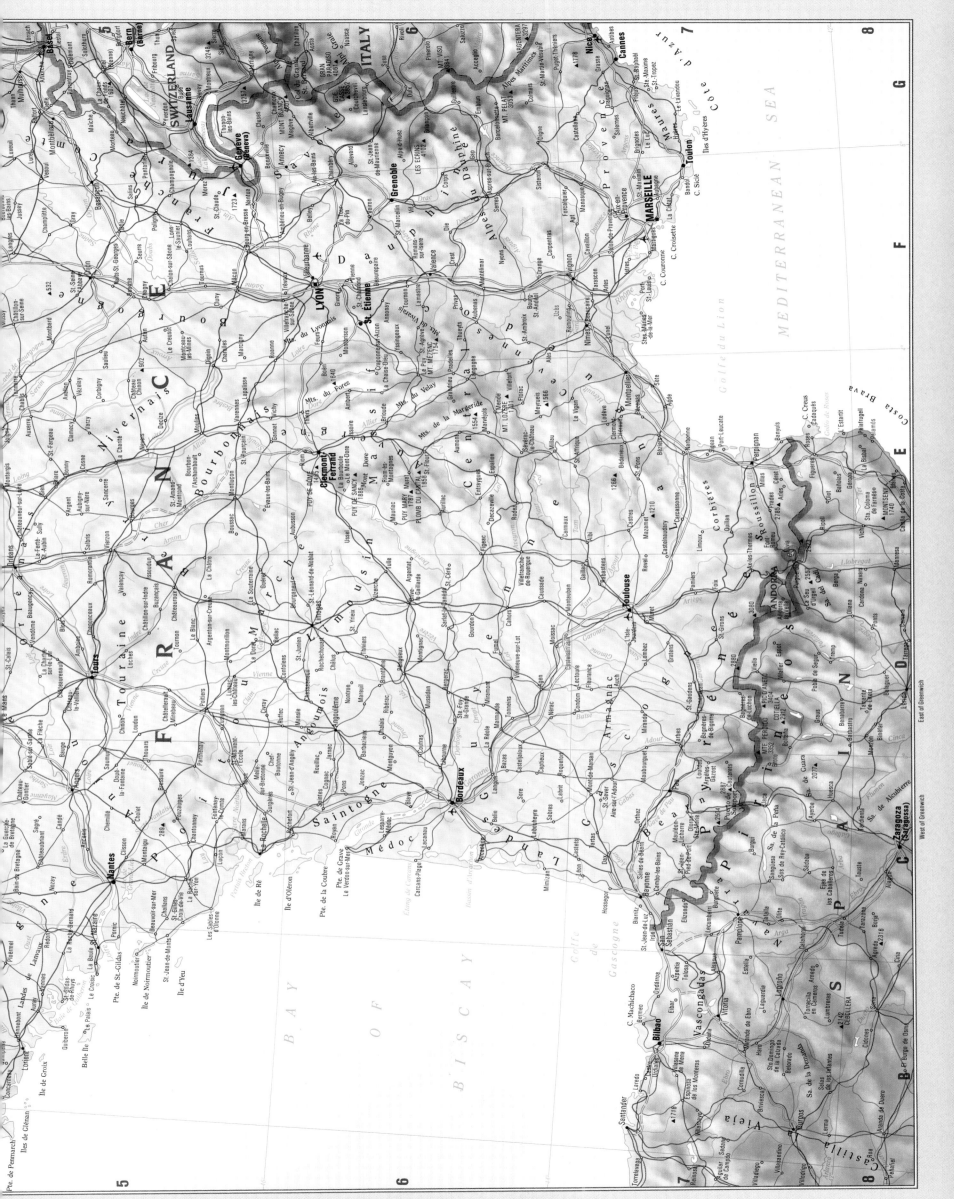

Designed and produced by E.S.R.

THE IBERIAN PENINSULA

1:3,000,000

© COLOUR LIBRARY BOOKS

Conic Projection

0   25   50   75   100   125   150   175   200 KILOMETRES

0   25   50   75   100   125 STATUTE MILES

Golfo de Gascuña

FRANCE

Armagnac

Gascogne

Béarn

Navarra

Pirineos Pyrénées

Andorra

Languedoc

Roussillon

Golfe du Lion

Provence

Maures

MARSEILLE

Toulon

Iles d'Hyères

Toulouse

San Sebastián

Bayonne

Pamplona

Zaragoza (Saragossa)

Cataluña

BARCELONA
Hospitalet

Costa Brava

Costa Dorada

Golfo de San Jorge

N

Valencia

Golfo de Valencia

Islas Columbretes

C. Caballeria

Ciudadela

Menorca (Minorca)

Mahón

C. de Formentor

Puerto de Pollensa

P. MAYOR
▲1445

Palma

Mallorca (Majorca)

Bahía de Palma

C. de Salinas

Cabrera

Ibiza (Iviza)

San Antonio Abad

Ibiza

San Francisco Javier

Formentera
Pta. Rotja

**Islas Baleares
(Balearic Islands)

(Spain)**

M E D I T E R R A N E A N   S E A

Murcia

Alicante

Costa Blanca

Murcia

Cartagena

C. de Palos

M E D I T E R R A N E A N

EL DJAZAÏR
(ALGIERS)

Golfe de Bejaïa

Kabylie

Petite Kabylie

Oran

ALGERIA

Massif de l'Ouarsenis

Mts. du Hodna

Chott El Hodna

F   G   H   J   K

1

2

3

4

5

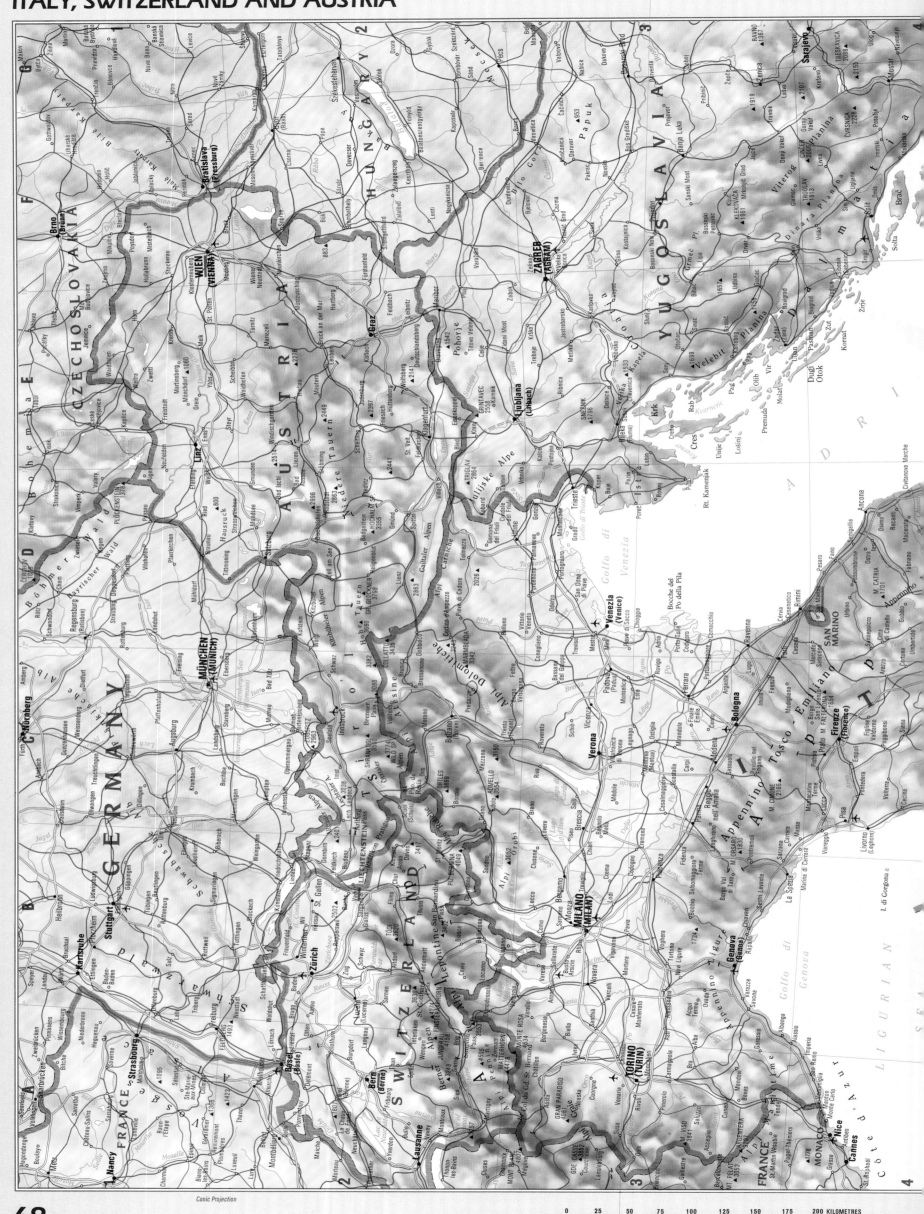

Conic Projection

1:3,000,000

© COLOUR LIBRARY BOOKS

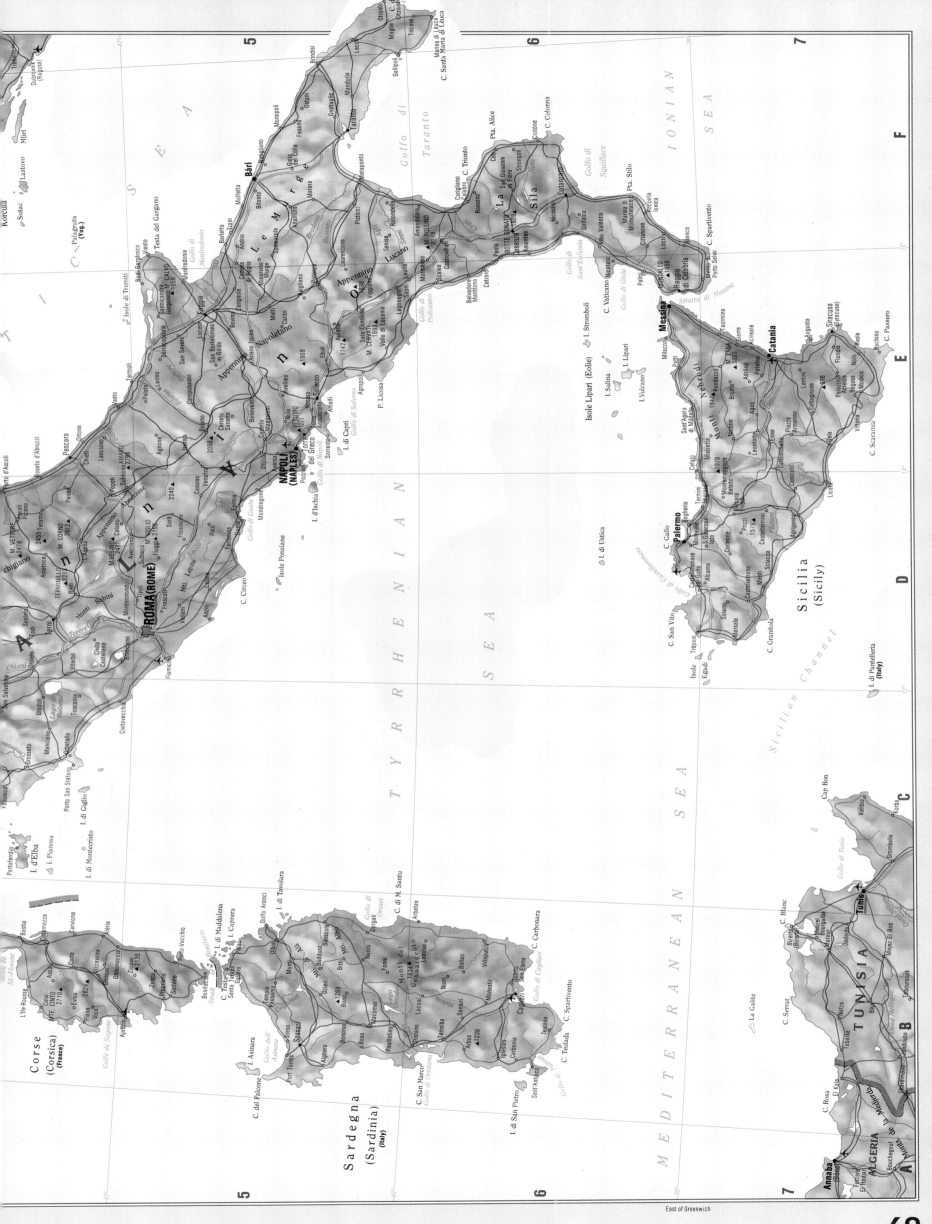

East of Greenwich

1:3,000,000

© COLOUR LIBRARY BOOKS

Conic Projection

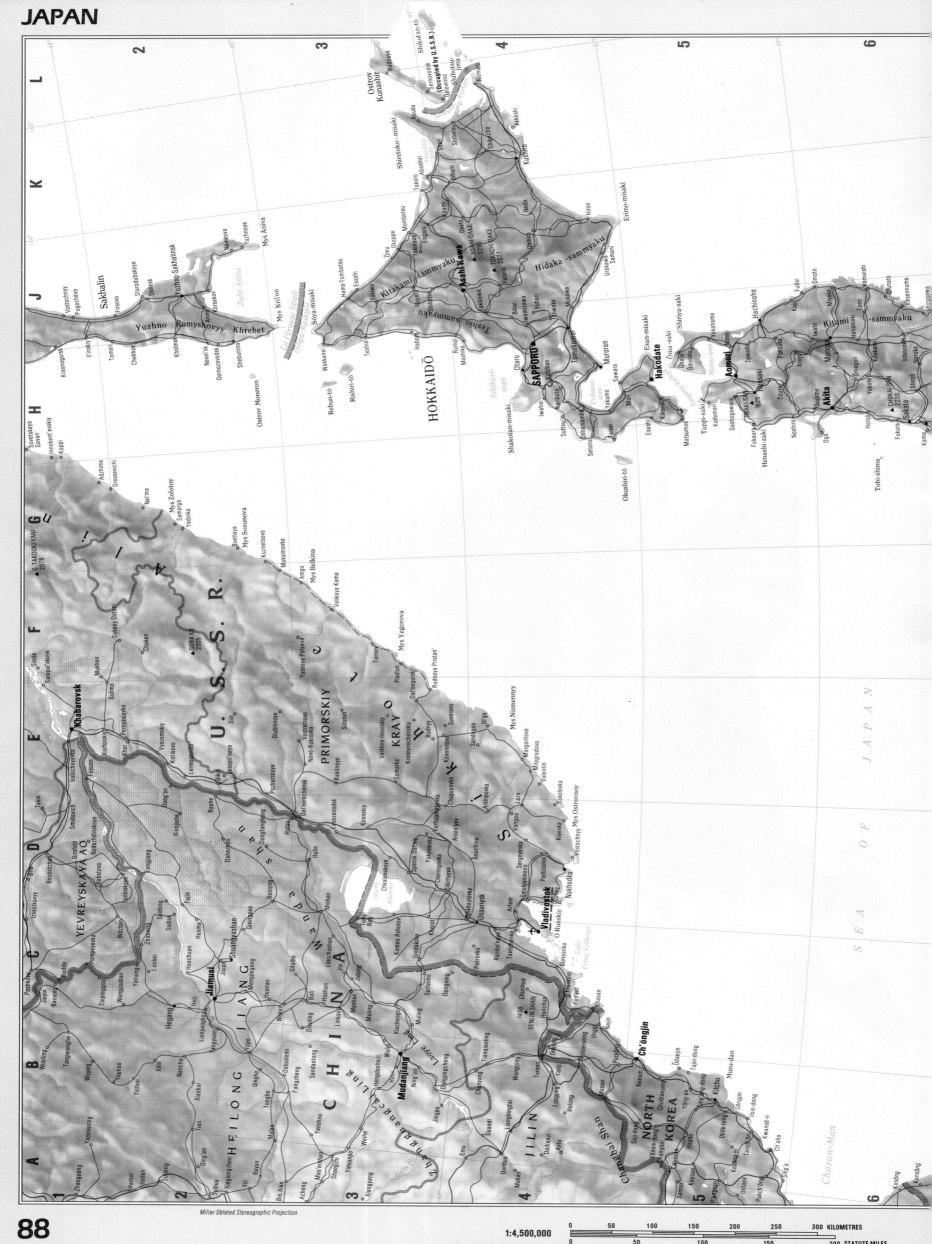

JAPAN

L
K
J
H
G
F
E
D
C
B
A

1 · 2 · 3 · 4 · 5 · 6

Shikotan-tō
Semovodsk
(Occupied by U.S.S.R.)
Ostrov
Kunashir
Kumame
Kunashir
Shibotsu
Shikotsu-jima
Nemuro

Shiretoko - misaki
Abashiri
Nemuro

Sakhalin
Yuzhno-Sakhalinsk
Korsakov
Mys Aniva
Zaliv Aniva

Novikovo
Yuzhno
Starodubskoye
Dolinsk

Vostochny
Pugachevo

Kitakami-sammyaku
Asahikawa
ASAHI-DAKE
2290
TOKACHI-DAKE
2017

HOKKAIDŌ

Hidaka -sammyaku

Erimo-misaki

Teshio -sammyaku

Ishikari-wan

SAPPORO

Otaru

Muroran

Uchiura-wan

Hakodate
Esan-misaki

Tsugaru-kaikyō

Tappi-saki

Kitakami -sammyaku
Aomori

Akita
CHŌKAI-SAN
2230

Shakotan-misaki

Rishiri-tō
Rebun-tō

Wakkanai

Sōya-misaki
La Pérouse Strait
(Soya-Kaikyō)

Yuzhno Kamyshovyy Khrebet

Mys Krilon

Ostrov Moneron

Okushiri-tō

Tobi-shima

Hachinohe

SEA OF JAPAN

Sovetskaya Gavan'
Innokent'evskiy
Koppi

G. TARDOKI-YANI
2078

Mys Zolotoy

Svetlaya

Mys Sosunova

Mys Belkina

PRIMORSKIY

KRAY

Khabarovsk

U.S.S.R.

YEVREYSKAYA AO

HEILONGJIANG

CHINA

Jiamusi

Mudanjiang

Zhangguangcai Ling

Laoye Ling

JILIN

Vladivostok
Nakhodka

Ch'ŏngjin

NORTH KOREA

Changbai Shan

Chosŏn-Man

Miller Oblated Stereographic Projection

88

1:4,500,000

0   50   100   150   200   250   300 KILOMETRES
0   50   100   150   200 STATUTE MILES

© COLOUR LIBRARY BOOKS

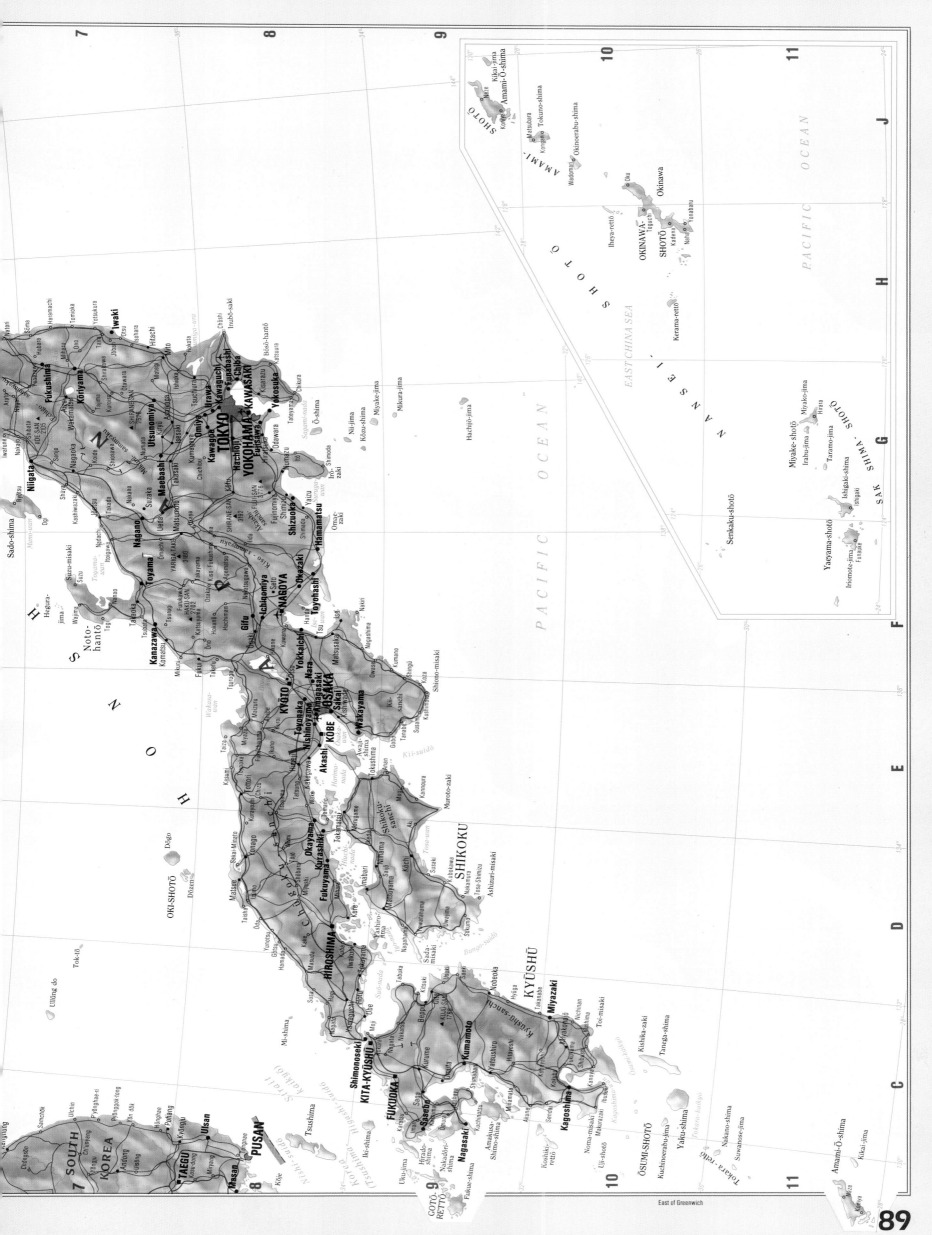

East of Greenwich

Designed and produced by E.S.R.

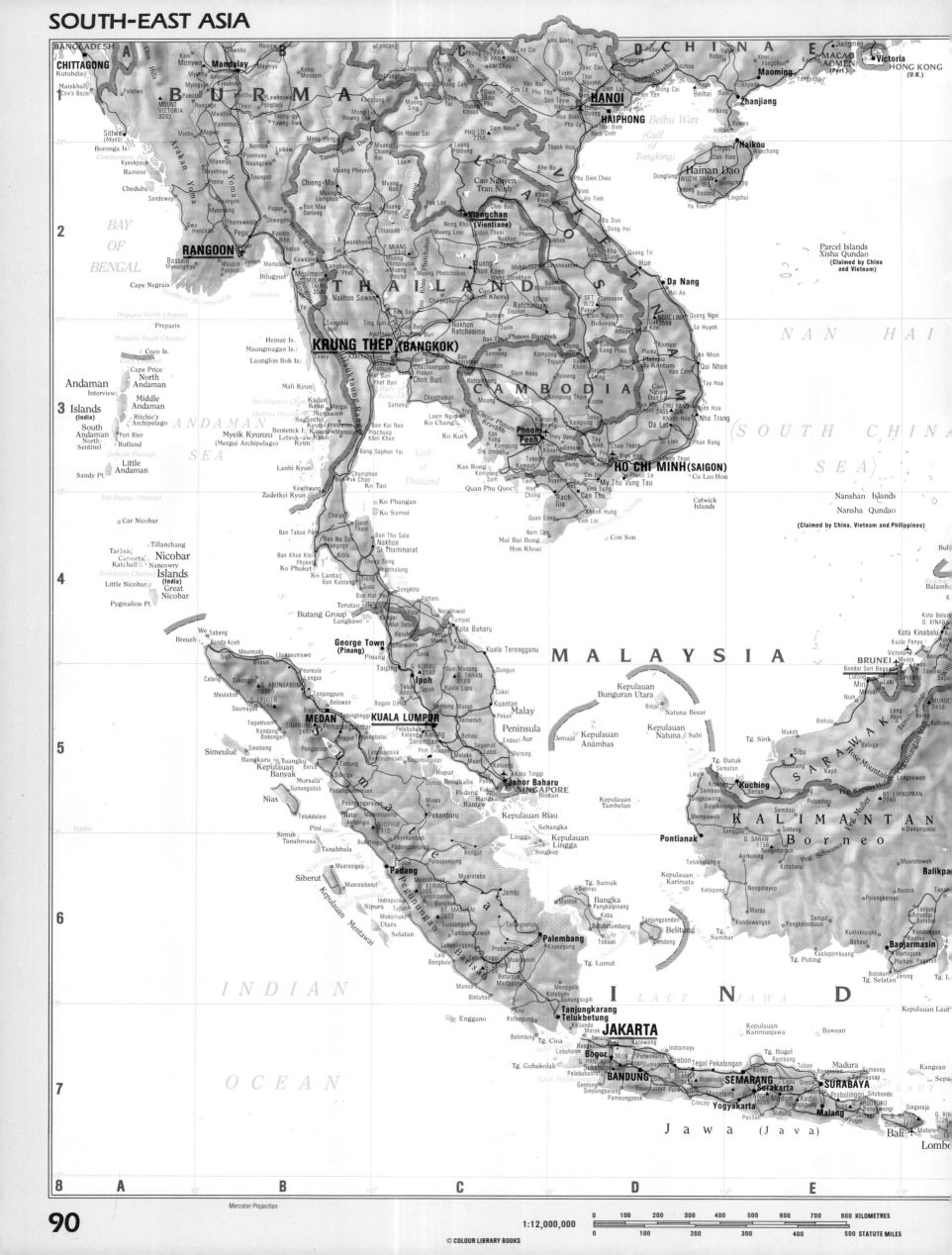

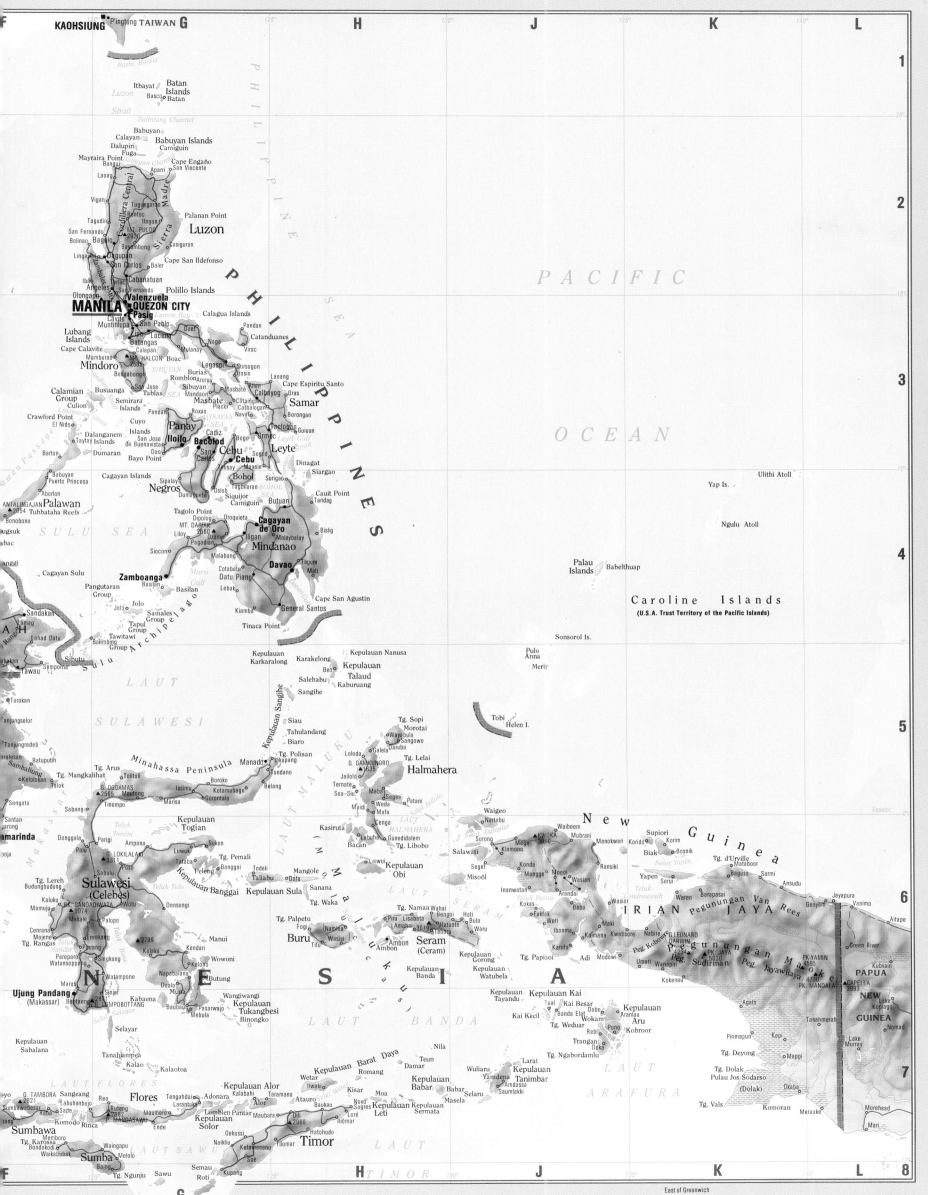

Miller Oblated Stereographic Projection

© COLOUR LIBRARY BOOKS

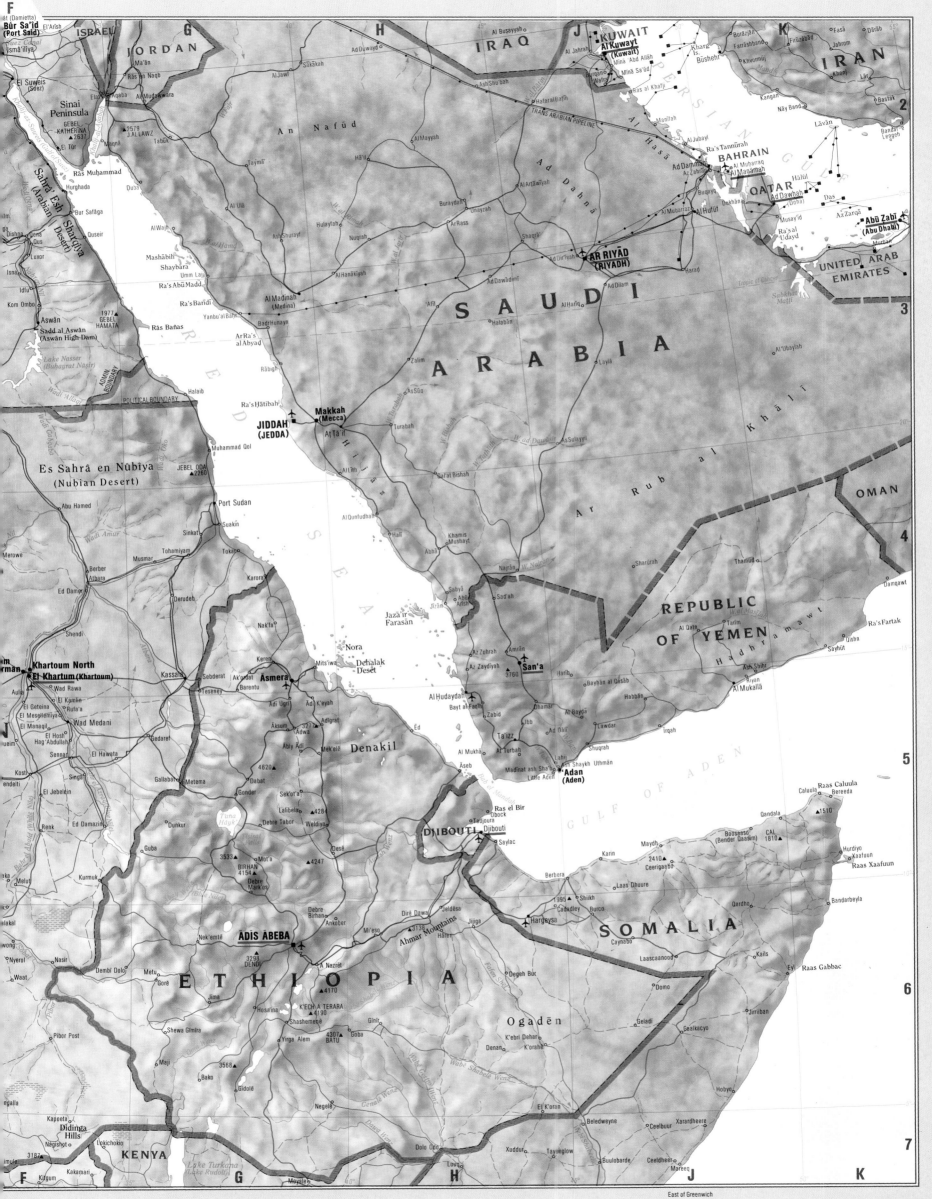

MAP CONTENTS:

WESTERN SAHARA — C. Barbas, Fadrik, Zouerate, Maktei, Tropic of Cancer, Erg Chech, Tanezrouft

MAURITANIA — Nouadhibou (Pt. Etienne), Ras Nouadhibou (C. Blanc), C. Timiris, Atar, Chinguetti, Akjoujt, Nouakchott, Beila, Ouarâne, El Djouf, Tidjikdja, Tichitt, Aouker, Boutilimit, Moudjéria, Tamchaket, Mederdra, Aleg, Bogué, Kaédi, Kiffa, Aïoun el Atrouss, Oualata, Néma, Timbédra

SENEGAL — St.Louis, Dagana, Podor, Lougu, Kébémer, Tivaouane, Cape Vert, Dakar, Thiès, Diourbel, Mbour, Fatick, Foundiougne, Kaolack, Kaffrine, Diorbivol, Matam, Sélibabi, Bakel, Kayes, Linguère, Tambacounda, Kédougou

THE GAMBIA — Banjul (Bathurst), Brikama, Basse Santa Su

GUINEA BISSAU — C. Roxo, Ziguinchor, Bissau, Bolama, Arquipelago dos Bijagos, Bafatá, Gabú

GUINEA — Boké, Telimélé, Labé, Pita, Dalaba, Mamou, Boffa, Cap Verga, Kindia, Dubréka, Conakry, Forécariah, Kambia, Dinguiraye, Dabola, Faranah, Kouroussa, Kankan, Siguiri

MALI — L. Faguibine, Tombouctou (Timbuktu), Ras el Ma, Goundam, Niafunké, Gourma-Rharous, Bamba, Bourem, Gao, Niger, Araouane, Niono, Sokolo, Ségou, Djenné, Mopti, Bandiagara, Douentza, Bamako, Kati, Koutiala, Sikasso, Bougouni, San, Massigui, Nioro du Sahel, Nara, Ballé, Bafoulabé, Satadougou, Bafing Makana, Kita

SIERRA LEONE — Port Loko, Makeni, Magburaka, Lunsar, Moyamba, Bo, Kenema, Sefadu, Kailahun, Pendembu, Segbwema, Pujehun, Bonthe, Sherbro Island, Shenge, Freetown

LIBERIA — Robertsport, Monrovia, Buchanan, Greenville (Sinoe), Harper, C. Palmas, Zwedru, Gbarnga, Totota, Timbo, Sasstown

IVORY COAST — Odienné, Touba, Séguéla, Man, Daloa, Gagnoa, Bouaflé, Yamoussoukro, Sinfra, Bouaké, Katiola, Dabakala, Bondoukou, Abengourou, Agnibilékrou, Abidjan, Grand Lahou, Sassandra, San Pédro, Tabou, Soubré, Divo, Agboville, Anyama, Bingerville, Aboisso

BURKINA FASO — Ouagadougou, Koudougou, Bobo Dioulasso, Banfora, Houndé, Léo, Tenkodogo, Ouahigouya, Tougan, Yako, Dédougou, Nouna, Gaoua

GHANA — Kumasi, Akosombo Dam, Accra, Tema, Koforidua, Enchi, Sunyani, Mampong, Kintampo, Tamale, Yendi, Navrongo, Bolgatanga, Wa, Bole, Damongo, Salaga, Cape Coast, Sekondi Takoradi, Cape Three Points, Axim, Dixcove, Winneba, Saltpond, Dunkwa, Obuasi, Oda, Asamankese, Nsuta, Tarkwa

Faranah, 1236▲, MTS. NIMBA ▲1752, Biankouma, Lola, Nzérékoré, Wologisi Mts., Yauri Bay, Gueckedou, Kissidougou, Macenta, Beyla

ATLANTIC OCEAN

Cape Verde inset

CAPE VERDE — Santo Antão, Porto Novo, Mindelo, São Vincente, São Nicolau, Sal, Boa Vista, São Tiago, Maio, Fogo, Brava, Praia

Miller Oblated Stereographic Projection West of Grenwich

1:9,000,000

© COLOUR LIBRARY BOOKS

0 100 200 300 400 500 600 KILOMETRES
0 50 100 150 200 250 300 350 400 STATUTE MILES

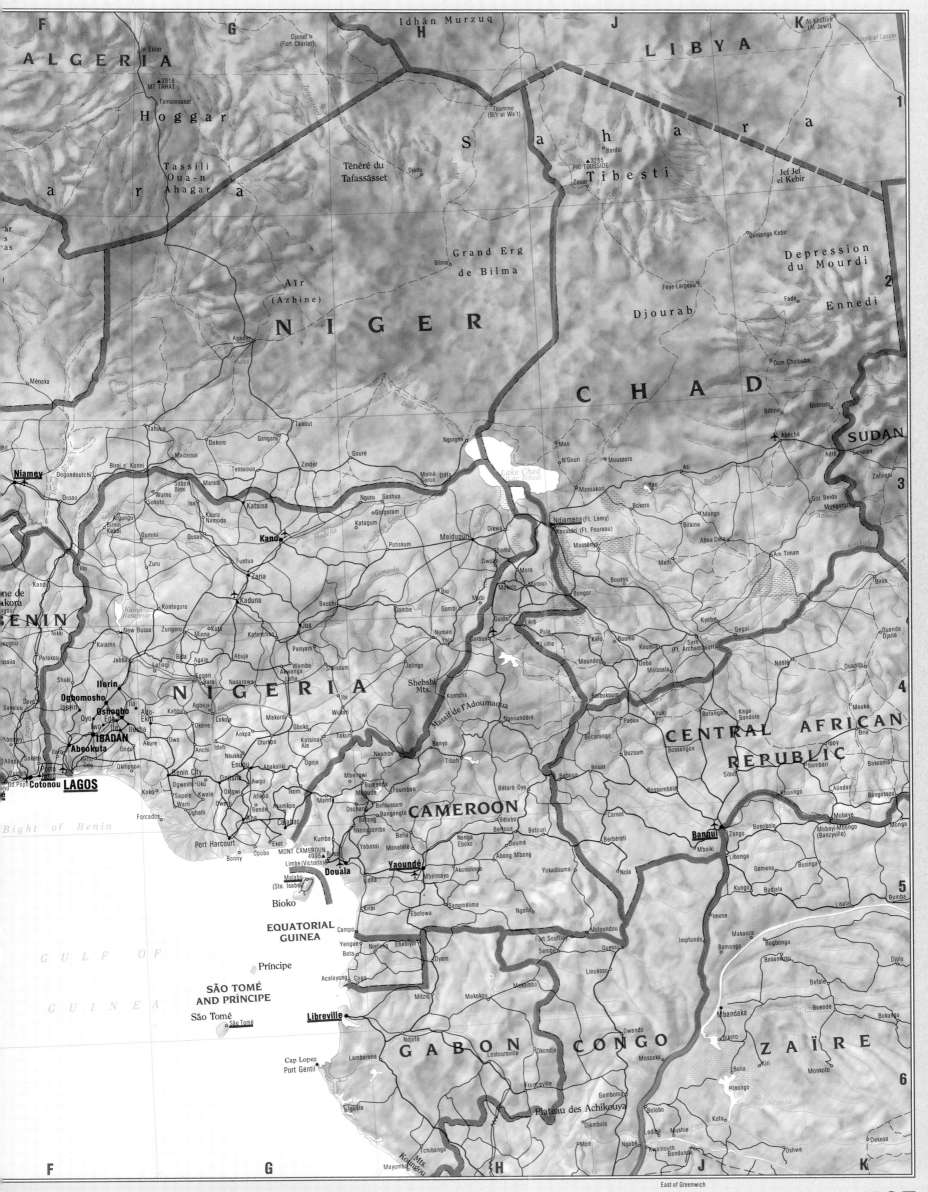

Designed and produced by E.S.R.

East of Greenwich

Miller Oblated Stereographic Projection

© COLOUR LIBRARY BOOKS

1:9,000,000

0   100   200   300   400   500   600 KILOMETRES
0   50   100   150   200   250   300   350   400 STATUTE MILES

Designed and produced by E.S.R.

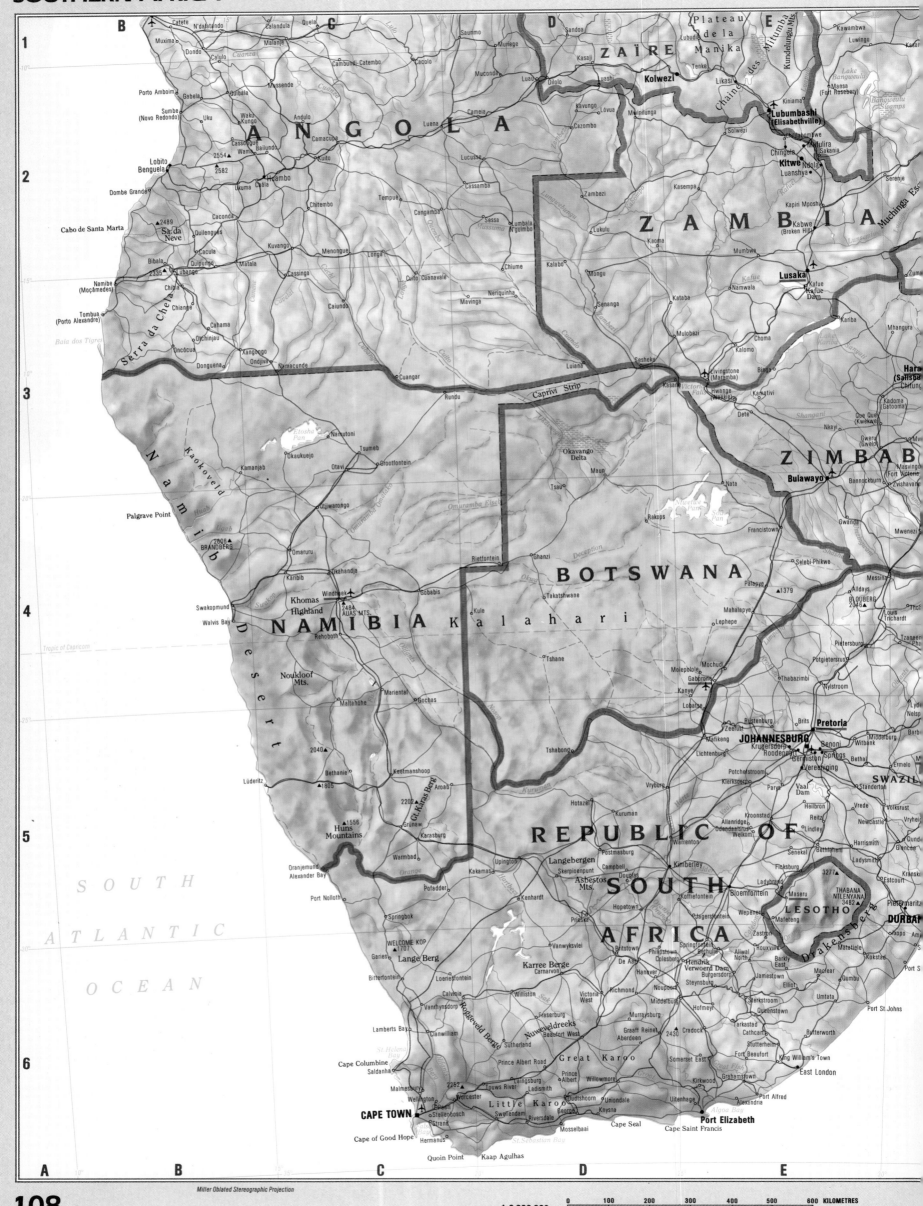

Miller Oblated Stereographic Projection

© COLOUR LIBRARY BOOKS

1:9,000,000

0 100 200 300 400 500 600 KILOMETRES
0 50 100 150 200 250 300 350 400 STATUTE MILES

F   G   H   J   K

TANZANIA

Chilumba
Songea
Masasi 945 Makondi
Tunduru Kitangari Plateau
Mecula C. Delgado
Pemba

COMOROS
Grande
Comore
Moroni
Moheli   Anjouan
Dzaoudzi
Mayotte
(France)

Tanjon'i Bobaomby
Antseranana
(Diégo-Suarez)
Nosy
Mitsio
Nosy Bé
Hell-Ville   Ambilobe   Vohimarina
(Vohémar)
Ambanja
Massif du
▲2876
Tsaratanana   Sambava

Analalava   Antsohiy   Andapa
Antalaha
Befandriana   Maroantsetra
Mahajanga   Port-   C. Masoala
Berg   Mananara
C. St. André   Soalala   Marovoay
Toraka Vestale   Nosy Boraha
Besalampy   Stampiky   Ambato-Boeny   (Sainte-Marie)
Mahabe   Maevatanana   Tsaratanana   Ambodifototra
Juan de Nova   Morafenobe   A'tomainty   Vavateniny
(France)   Fenoarivo Atsinanana
Maintirano   Antsalova   Ankazobe   A'tondrazaka
Toamasina
Tsiroanomandidy   Anjozorobe   (Tamatave)
Miarinarivo   Moramanga
Belo-Tsiribihna   Antananarivo   Andevoranto
Soavinandriana   (Tananarive)
Ambatolampy   Anosibe
an Ala   Vatomandry
Betafo   Antsirabe
Morondava   Faudriana   Marolambo
Mahabo   Ambositra   Nosy-Varika
A'tofinandrahana   Vohilava
Tsitondroina   Mananjary
Ankilabo   Manja   Fianarantsoa
Morombe   Bérorgha   Ambalavao   Ikongo
Manakara
Ambalavao   Vohipeno

INDIAN

OCEAN

MADAGASCAR

MOZAMBIQUE
MALAWI

Mzuzu   Cobue
Lundazi   Mataca
Mecula
Nkhotakota   Lichinga   Montepuez   Balama
Kasungu   Namapa
Chipata Mchinji   Maua   Muite   Lurio
Jameson (Ft. Manning)   Chipoka   Mangochi   Nacala-
Dowa   Salima   Cuamba   a-Velha
Lilongwe   Mandimba   Lalaua   Maaie
Furancungo   Ncheu Balaka   NAMULI   Iapala   Moçambique
Ulongué   Liwonde   ▲2419   Malema
Zomba   Gurue   Nampula
Blantyre   Namarroi   Mogincual
Tete   Limbe   Errego   Alto
2054   Molocue   Namaponda
Moatize   CHIPERONE   Gilé   Angoche
Mutoko   Nsanje (Port Herald)   Mocuba   Moma
Chembe   Mutarara   Namacurra
Macossa   Caia   Morela Velha   Pebane
Gorongoza   Quelimane
Nova   Muanza
Vanduzi   Chinde
Mutare   Inchope
(Umtali)   Chimoio   Buzi   Beira
Chipinge   Dombe   Nova Sofala
Chimanimani
Espungabera   Machanga
Algueirão   Nova Mambone
Massangena   Jofane   I. do Bazaruto
Madade   I. Benguérua
Vilanculos
Nova   P. S. Sebastião
Mabalane   Chigubo   Bassas
Massinga   da India
Massingir   Homoine   (France)
Panda   Inhambane
Mabalane   I. de l'Europa
Chókwe   Chibuto   (France)
Maguda   Inharrime
Xai-Xai   Manhica
Baia de Maputo
Maputo
C. de Santa Maria
Bela Vista
Makatini
Flats
Ubombo
Lake
St. Lucia
Cape Saint Lucia
Empangeni

Cabora
Bassa Dam

Morondava
Belo-Tsiribihna

Fitsitika
Toliara
(Tuléar)
Soalara   Betioky
Fianarantsoa   Farafangana
Ihosy
Vangaindrano
Ankazoabo
Betroka
Midongy
Atsimo
Bekily   Mt. de l'Ivakoany
1956
Itampolo   Ampanihy
Beampingaratra
Taolañaro
Ambovombe   (Fort Dauphin)
C. Sainte Marie   Faux Cap

Tropic of Capricorn

2

3

4

5

6   7

J   K

MAURITIUS
Port Louis
Beau Basin
Curepipe   Mahébourg
Réunion
(France)
St. Denis
St. Benoit
St. Pierre   Mascarene
Islands

L

East of Greenwich

Designed and produced by E.S.R.

109

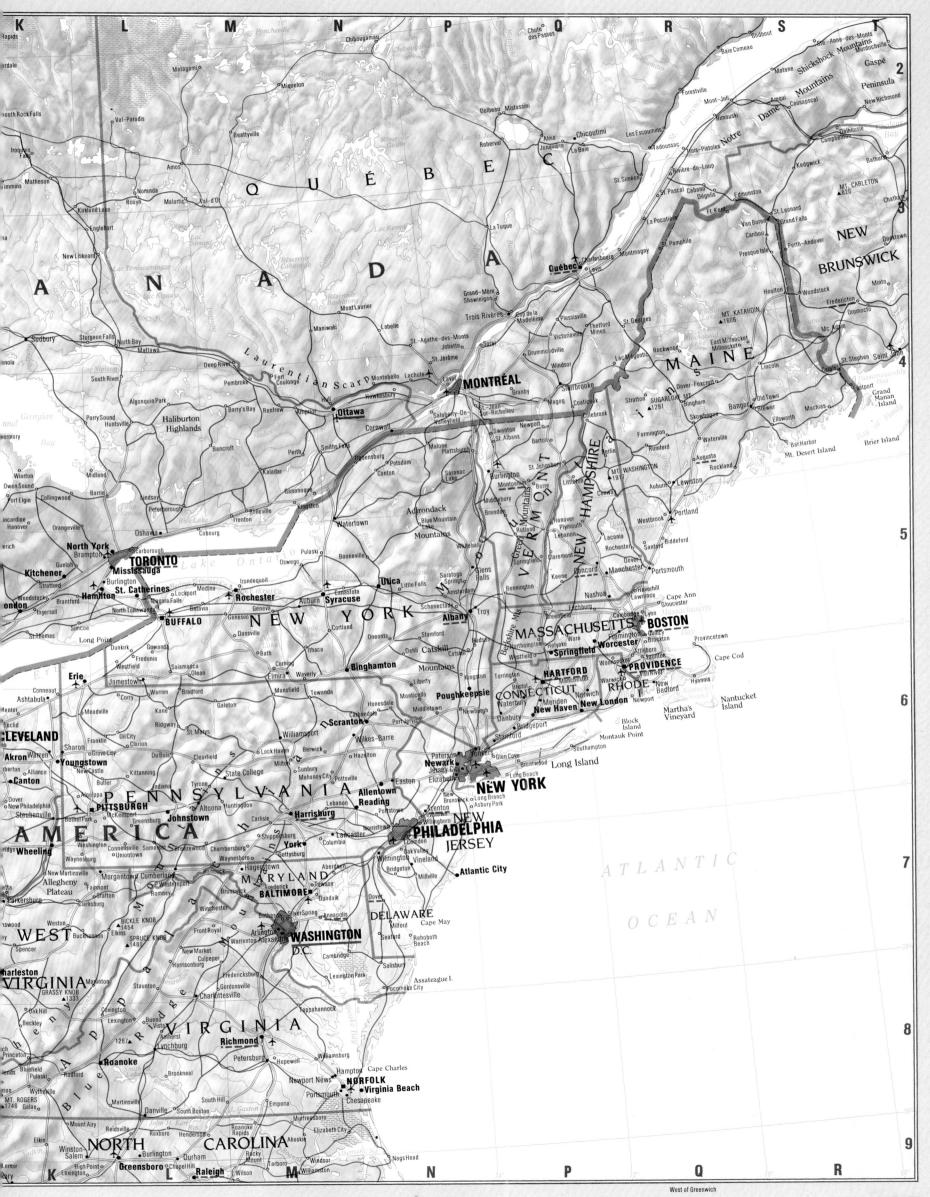

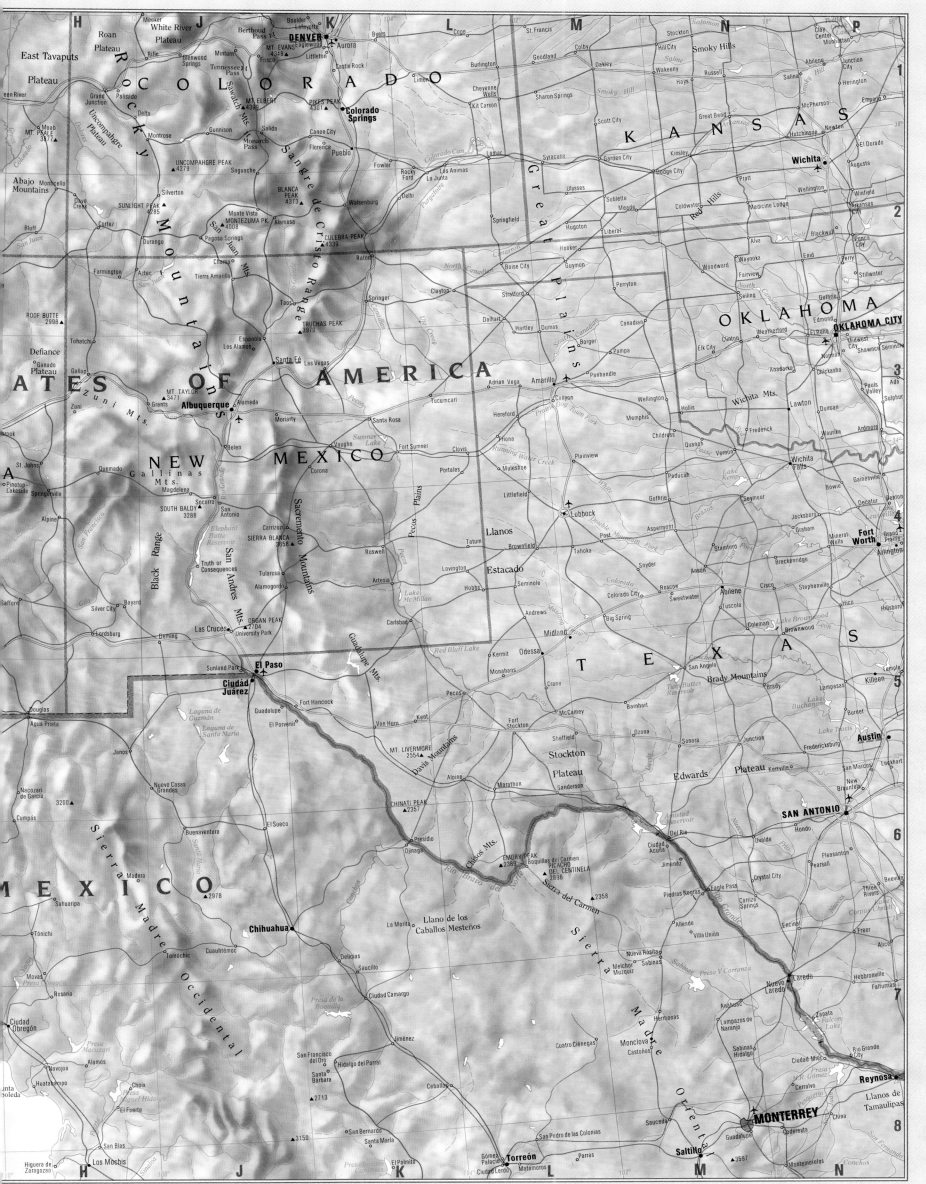

Bipolar Oblique Conic Conformal Projection

West of Greenwich

Designed and produced by E.S.R.

Bipolar Oblique Conic Conformal Projection

1:5,000,000

| 0 | 50 | 100 | 150 | 200 | 250 | 300 | 350 | 400 KILOMETRES |

| 0 | 50 | 100 | 150 | 200 | 250 STATUTE MILES |

© COLOUR LIBRARY BOOKS

MEXICO

Bipolar Oblique Conic Conformal Projection

1:6,500,000

© COLOUR LIBRARY BOOKS

0   50   100   150   200   250   300   350   400 KILOMETRES
0   50   100   150   200   250 STATUTE MILES

Bipolar Oblique Conic Conformal Projection

1:7,000,000

| 0 | 50 | 100 | 150 | 200 | 250 | 300 | 350 | 400 KILOMETRES |

| 0 | 50 | 100 | 150 | 200 | 250 STATUTE MILES |

© COLOUR LIBRARY BOOKS

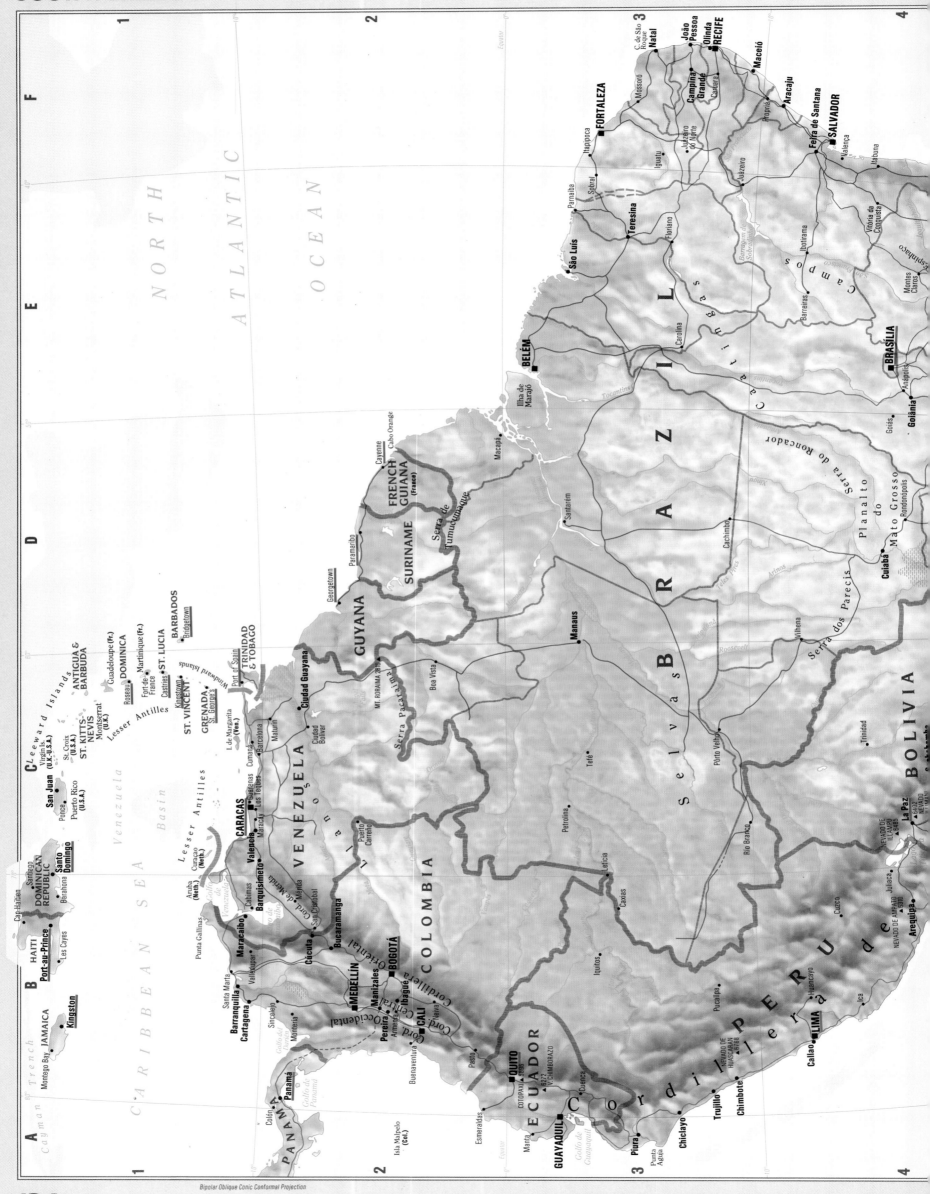

Bipolar Oblique Conic Conformal Projection

1:16,000,000

© COLOUR LIBRARY BOOKS

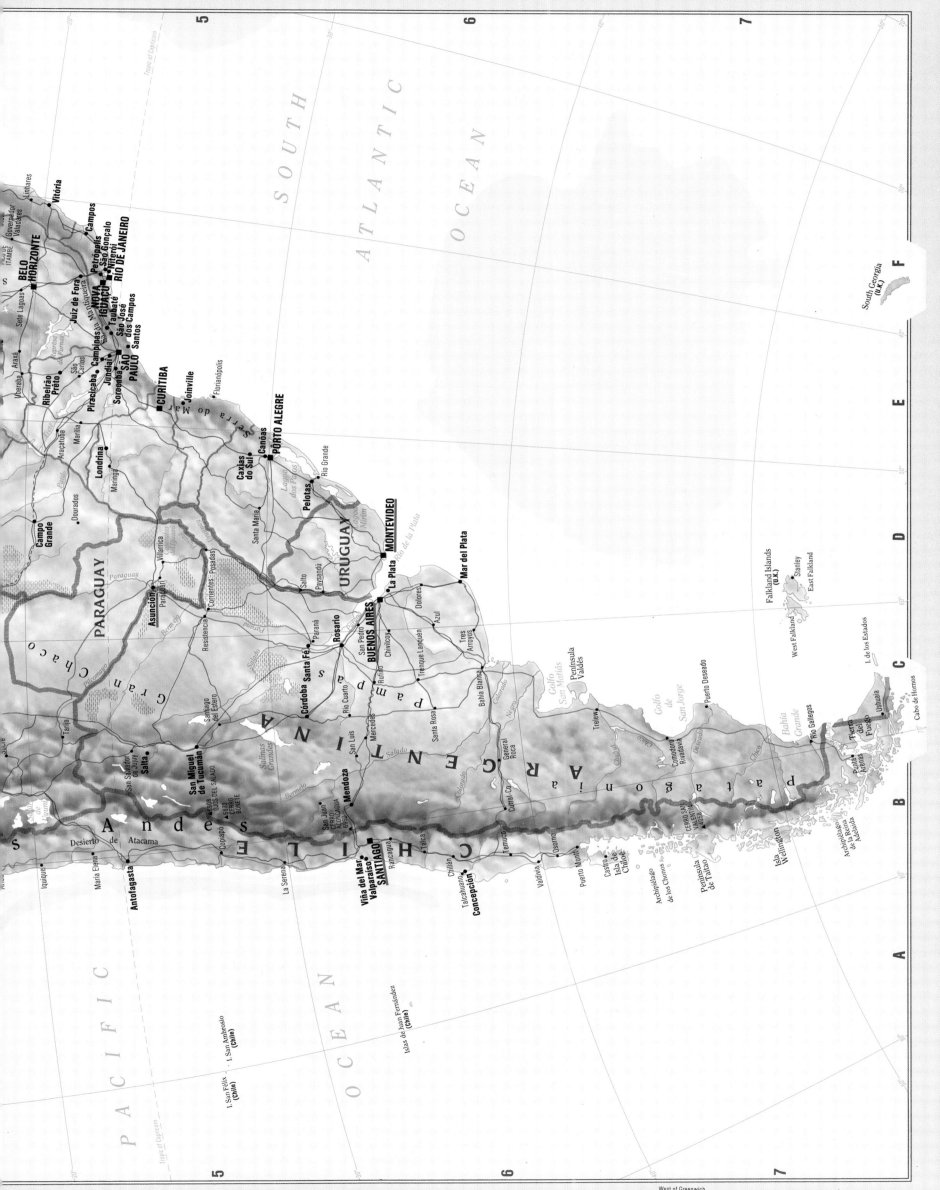

Bipolar Oblique Conic Conformal Projection

© COLOUR LIBRARY BOOKS

1:11,000,000

| 0 | 100 | 200 | 300 | 400 | 500 | 600 | 700 | 800 KILOMETRES |

| 0 | 100 | 200 | 300 | 400 | 500 STATUTE MILES |

NORTH ATLANTIC OCEAN

Paramaribo Nieuw Amsterdam Moengo Albina Iracoubo
Totness Groninge   Sinnamary
Affobakka   Saint   Kourou
CURINAME   Laurent   Cayenne
FRENCH   Roura
Grand Santi   Guisanbourg   Kaw
GUIANA   Oiapoque Cabo Caciporé   Cabo Orange
(France)
Inini   Punta Grande
de Haan Geb   Pontoetoe
Oranje Gebergte   Bienveneu
Malavate   Amapá
Kapiting   Regina
Serra   Tumucumaque   Ilha de Maracá
AMAPÁ
Merirumā   Serra do Navio
Azuari   Pôrto Grande   Ponta Grossa
Macapá
Chaves
Mouths of
Ilha Grande   Soure   Salinópolis   the Amazon
do Gurupá   Ponta de Pedras Curuçá
Oriximiná Óbidos Almeirim   Gurupá Vigia Capanema   Ilhas de São João
Faro Prainha   Melgaço BELÉM   Viseu
Juriti Curralinho Abaetetuba São José do Gurupi Turiaçu
Santarém Pombal   Igarapé Miri Mojú   Marassumé
Belterra Cametá   Mocajuba   Alcântara
Parintins   Baião   São Luís
Altamira   Tucuruí   Cajapió Viana Rosário Tutóia
Itaituba   PARÁ   Pimentel Itapecurú Mirim Araioses Parnaíba
Vila Nova   Jacundá Bacabal   Brejo Luzilândia FORTALEZA
Carajari   Serra do Gurupi Pedreiras Codó Piripiri Tianguá Ipu
Tucupé   Sobrado   Marabá   Coroatá Caxias   Sobral Baturité
São João   Barra do Presidente Dutra   Crateús
do Araguaia Imperatriz Corda MARANHÃO Teresina   Senador Pompeu
São Félix   Xambioá Colinas São Miguel   Jaguaribe   RIO GRANDE
Araguaína Paranaidji Pastos Bons do Tapuio PIAUÍ Arneiroz CEARÁ DO NORTE Natal
Serra das   Valença Várzea Grande   Iguatu
BRAZIL   Carolina Araras Balsas do Piauí Oeiras Picos Campos Sales Crato Juàzeiro Patu
Serra   Loreto Uruçuí   Floriano   Jaicós do Norte Cajazeiras PARAÍBA João Pessoa
Pau d'Arco   Couto Magalhães   Eliseu Martins Simplício Mendes Ouricuri Campina Cabo Branco
Conceção do Araguaia   São João do Piauí   Grande   RECIFE
Araguacema   Bom Jesus São Raimundo Nonato PERNAMBUCO Olinda
Pedro Afonso Lizardo Nova Remanso Rajada   Petrolina   Jaboatão
Miracema do Norte   Gilbués Redenção Juàzeiro ALAGOAS
Cristalândia   Nova Sento Sé   Maceió
Pôrto Nacional   Xique-Xique   Euclides da Cunha SERGIPE
Peixe   Natividade Formosa do Rio Prêto Senhor do Bonfim Queimadas Aracaju
BAHIA   Barra Irecê   Jacobina Tucano
Porto dos Gauchos   Taguatinga Barreiras Morro do Chapéu Serrinha
Campo de Diauarum   Angical Ibotirama Ipupiara Mundo Novo Alagoinhas
Santana   Palmeiras Feira de Santana
Mato Grosso GOIÁS São Domingos Bom Jesus da Lapa Macaúbas Ipirá
DO GROSSO   Serra Dourada Riacho de Santana Nazaré SALVADOR
Nobres   Aruanã   Cavalcante Novo Acre   Valença I. de Tinharé
Guia   Alto Coité Ceres   Niquelândia Carinhanha Jequié I. Boipeba
Cuiabá Rondonópolis   Uruaçu Sítio da Abadia Côcos Manga Brumado Ponta do Mutá
Chavantina   1678 Serra Bonita Condeúba Vitória da Itabuna
Pôrto dos Gauchos Ceres Formosa Januária Monte Azul Conquista Ilhéus
BRASÍLIA Brasília Pedra Azul
Aruanã DISTRITO Barrocão Salto da Divisa
Caiapônia Anápolis FEDERAL Rio Pardo de Minas
Paraúna Leopoldo Bulhões São Romão Ponta Santo Antônio
Goiânia Montes Claros   Jequitinhonha
Anhumas Hidrolândia Cristalina Bocaiuva   Escondido
Morrinhos Paracatu Pirapora Araçuaí Rachim
Pantanal do Rio Verde MINAS Piro de Minas Capelinha Pôrto Seguro
Táquari Pompéu Corinto PICO DE ITAMBÉ Carlos Chagas Ponta da Baleia
MATO GROSSO Araguari GERAIS Diamantina 2040 Teófilo Otôni Helvécia
DO SUL Uberlândia Patos de Minas Guanhães Campanário
Pantanal do Araguari Patrocínio Governador ESPÍRITO SANTO
Rio Negro Ituiutaba Prata Abaeté Valadares
DO SUL Ituma   São Mateus

West of Greenwich

137

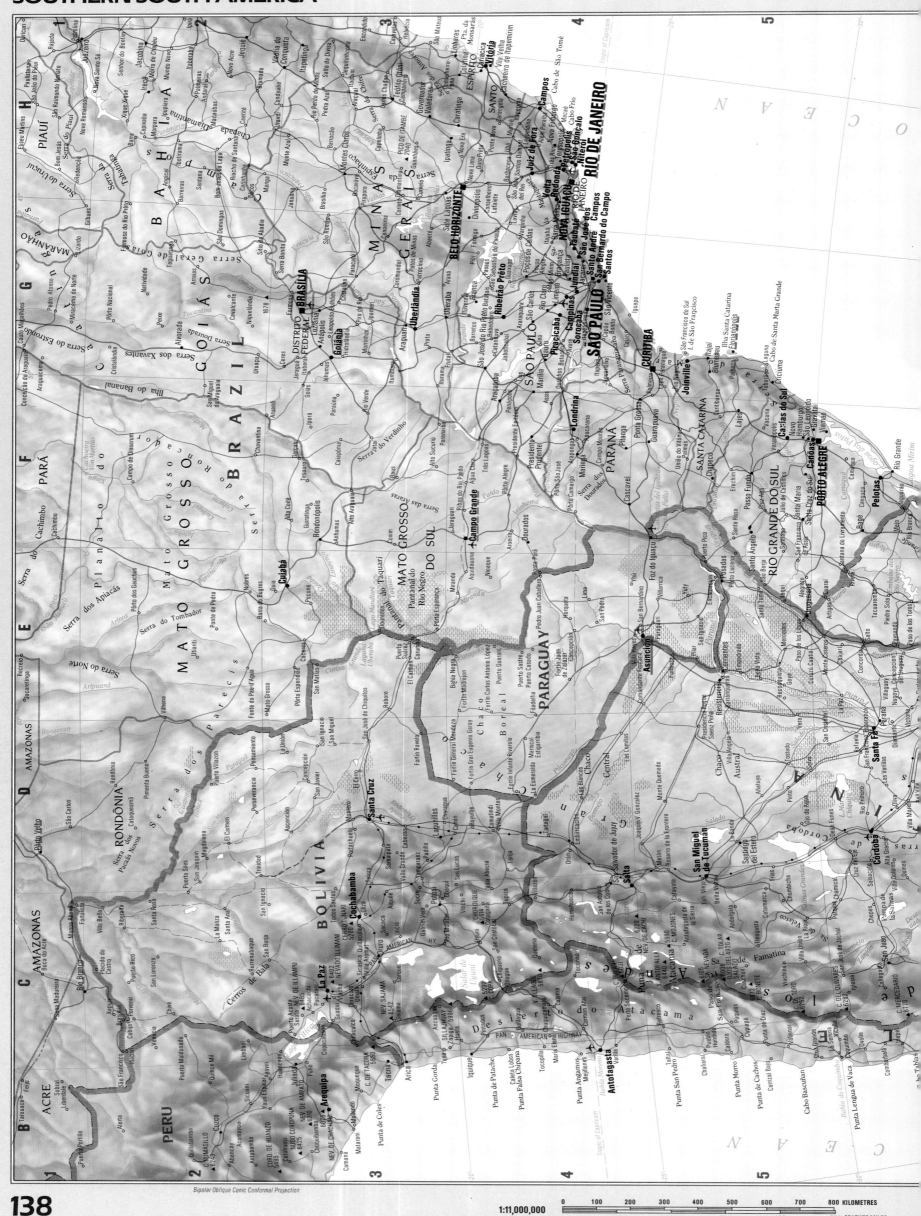

Bipolar Oblique Conic Conformal Projection

1:11,000,000

| 0 | 100 | 200 | 300 | 400 | 500 | 600 | 700 | 800 KILOMETRES |

| 0 | 100 | 200 | 300 | 400 | 500 STATUTE MILES |

© COLOUR LIBRARY BOOKS

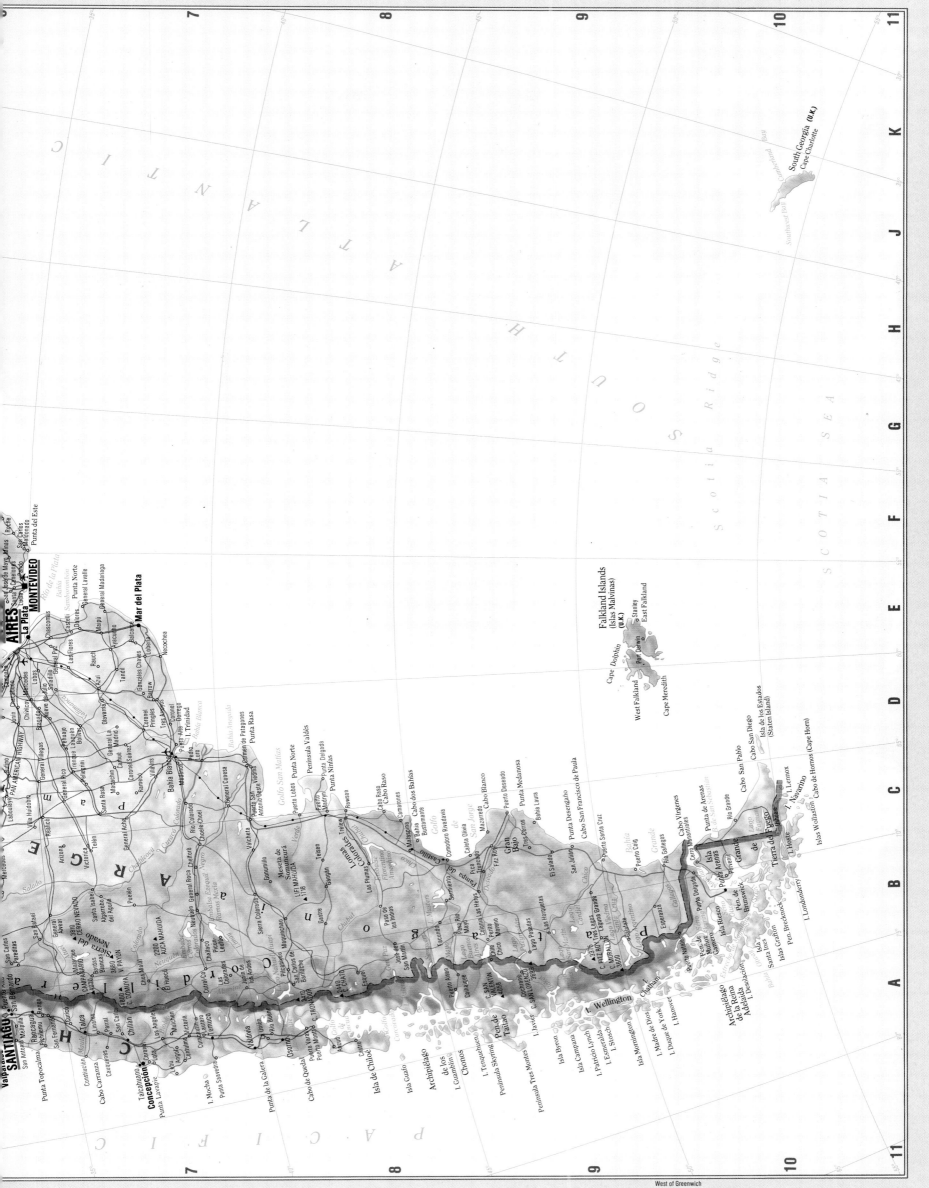

South Georgia (U.K.)
Cape Charlotte
Southwest Bay
Cumberland Bay

Falkland Islands
(Islas Malvinas)
(U.K.)
Stanley
Port Darwin
East Falkland
Cape Dolphin
West Falkland
Cape Meredith

ATLANTIC

SOUTH

Scotia Ridge

SCOTIA SEA

PACIFIC

ARGENTINA

CHILE

AIRES
La Plata
MONTEVIDEO
Mar del Plata

SANTIAGO
Valparaíso
Concepción
Talcahuano

Punta del Este
Rocha

Punta Norte
Bahía Blanca

Cabo San Diego
Isla de los Estados (Staten Island)
Cabo San Pablo
Cabo de Hornos (Cape Horn)
Islas Wollaston

Tierra del Fuego
Río Grande
Punta Arenas

PAN AMERICAN HIGHWAY

West of Greenwich

Designed and produced by E.S.R.

139

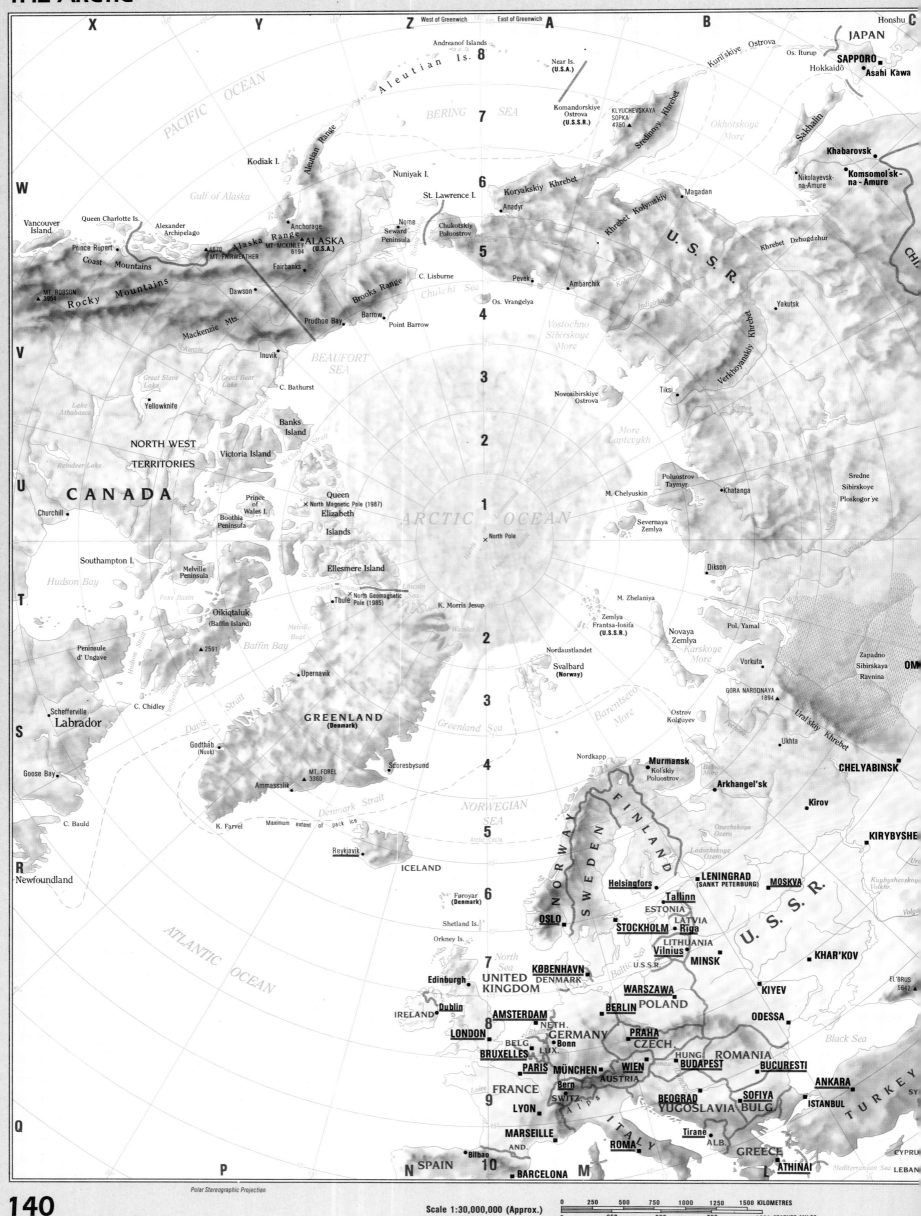

Polar Stereographic Projection

© COLOUR LIBRARY BOOKS

Scale 1:30,000,000 (Approx.)

| 0 | 250 | 500 | 750 | 1000 | 1250 | 1500 KILOMETRES |

| 0 | 250 | 500 | 750 | 1000 STATUTE MILES |

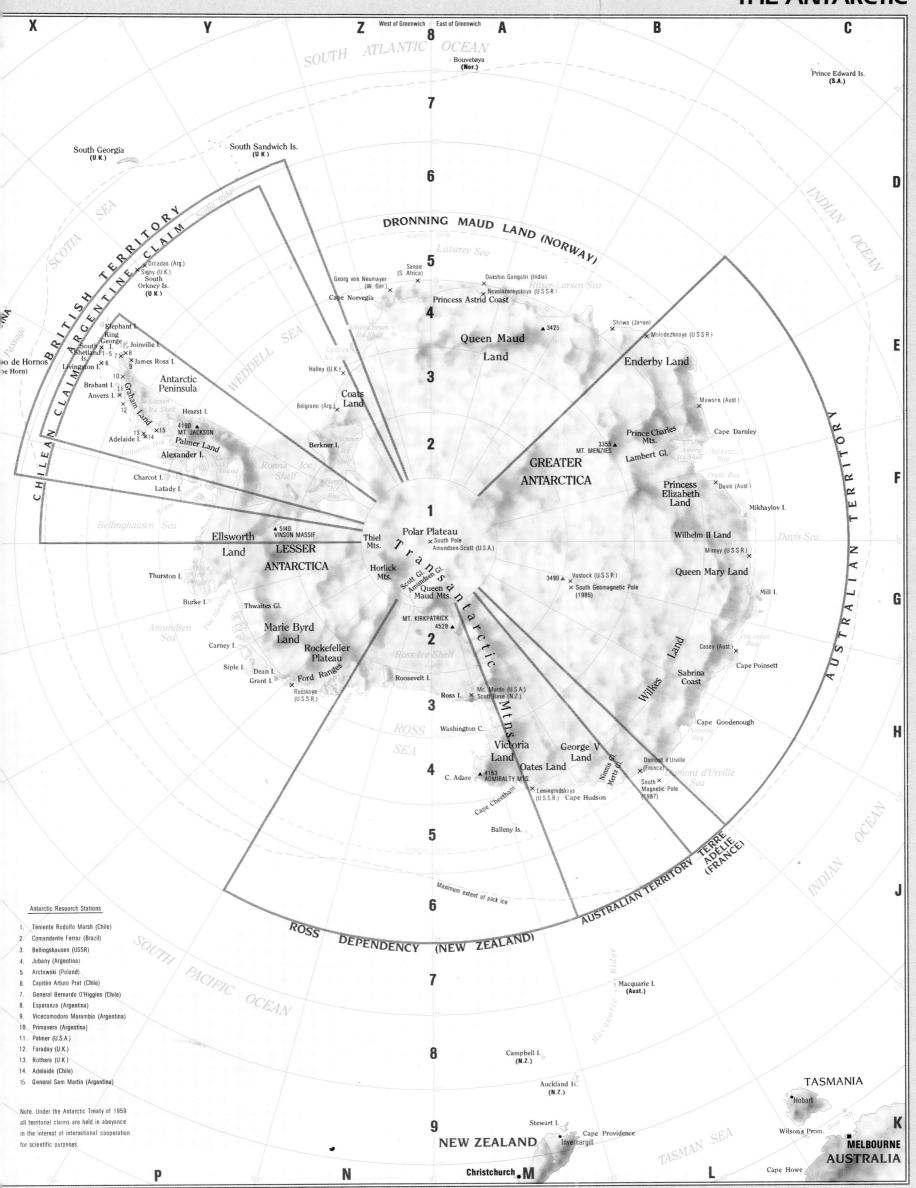

151

Name	Map	Ref
Ben MorCoigach	56	C3
Ben More *Central, U.K.*	57	D4
Ben More *Strathclyde, U.K.*	56	B4
Ben More Assynt	56	D2
Benmore, Lake	115	C6
Bennachie	56	F3
Benn Cleuch	57	E4
Bennetta, Ostrov	85	R1
Ben Nevis	57	C4
Bennington	125	P5
Benoni	108	E5
Be, Nosy	109	J2
Ben Rinnes	56	E3
Bensheim	70	C4
Benson *U.K.*	53	F3
Benson *U.K.*	126	G5
Ben Starav	57	C4
Bent	95	P8
Bentinck Island	93	J6
Bent Jbail	94	B5
Bentley	55	H3
Benton	128	F3
Benton Harbor	124	G5
Bentung	90	C5
Benue	105	G4
Ben Venue	57	D4
Ben Vorlich	57	D4
Benwee	58	C5
Benwee Head	58	C4
Ben Wyvis	56	D3
Benxi	87	N3
Beo	91	H5
Beograd	72	F3
Beppu	89	C9
Beqa	114	R9
Berat	74	E2
Berau, Teluk	114	A2
Berber	103	F4
Berbera	103	J5
Berberati	102	C7
Berck	64	D3
Berdichev	79	D6
Berdigestyakh	85	M4
Berdyansk	79	F6
Berea	124	H8
Bereeda	103	K5
Beregovo	79	C6
Berens	119	R5
Berens River	119	R5
Bere Regis	52	E4
Berettyo	73	F2
Berettyoujfalu	73	F2
Bereza	71	L2
Berezhany	71	L4
Berezhnykh, Mys	85	Q1
Berezina	78	D5
Berezino	78	D5
Berezna	79	E5
Berezniki	78	K4
Berezno	71	M3
Berezovka *Rossiyskaya S.F.S.R., U.S.S.R.*	78	K3
Berezovka *Rossiyskaya S.F.S.R., U.S.S.R.*	85	K5
Berezovka *Rossiyskaya S.F.S.R., U.S.S.R.*	85	T3
Berezovka *Ukraine S.S.R., U.S.S.R.*	79	E6
Berezovo *U.S.S.R.*	84	Ae4
Berezovo *U.S.S.R.*	85	W4
Berezovskaya	85	K5
Berg	108	C6
Berga	67	G1
Bergama	76	B3
Bergamo	68	B3
Bergeforsen	62	G5
Bergen *E. Germany*	70	E1
Bergen *Norway*	63	J6
Bergen op Zoom	64	F3
Bergerac	65	D6
Bergfors	62	H2
Bergisch-Gladbach	70	B3
Bergsviken	62	J4
Berhala, Selat	90	C6
Beringa, Ostrov	81	T4
Bering Glacier	118	G3
Beringovskiy	85	X4
Bering Sea	143	H3
Bering Strait	118	B2
Berislav	79	E6
Beris, Ra's	95	Q9
Berja	66	E4
Berkak	62	C5
Berkakit	85	L5
Berkeley *U.K.*	52	E3
Berkeley *U.S.A.*	126	A2
Berkhamsted	53	G3
Berkner Island	141	W3
Berkovitsa	73	G4
Berkshire	53	F3
Berkshire Downs	53	F3
Berkshire Mountains	125	P5
Berlevag	62	N2
Berlin *E. Germany*	70	E2
Berlin *U.S.A.*	125	Q4
Bermeja, Sierra	66	D4
Bermejo *Argentina*	138	C6
Bermejo *Argentina*	138	D4
Bermeo	66	E1
Bermillo de Sayago	66	C2
Bermuda	117	N5
Bern	68	A2
Bernau	70	E2
Bernay	64	D4
Bernburg	70	D3
Berne	68	A2
Berner Alpen	68	A2
Berneray *U.K.*	57	A4
Berneray *U.K.*	56	A3
Bernina, Piz	68	B2
Beroroha	109	J4
Berounka	70	E4
Berre, Etang de	65	F7
Berriedale	56	E2
Berriedale Water	56	E2
Berrigan	113	K6
Berringarra	112	D4
Berrouaghia	67	H4
Berry *Australia*	113	L5
Berry *France*	65	E5
Berryessa, Lake	122	C8
Berry Head	52	D4
Berry Islands	132	J1
Bershad	73	K1
Berthoud Pass	123	L8
Bertoua	105	H5
Beru	111	S2
Beruri	136	E4
Berwick	125	M6
Berwick-upon-Tweed	57	F5
Berwyn Mountains	52	D2
Berzence	72	D2
Besalampy	109	H3
Besancon	65	G5
Besar, Kai	91	J7
Besbre	65	E5
Beshneh	95	M7
Besiri	77	J4
Beskidy Zachodnie	71	H4
Beslan	79	G7
Besni	77	G4
Bessarabia	73	K2
Bessarabka	73	K2
Bessbrook	58	K4
Bessemer *Alabama, U.S.A.*	129	J4
Bessemer *Winconsin, U.S.A.*	124	F3
Bestamak *U.S.S.R.*	86	D2
Bestamak *U.S.S.R.*	79	K6
Bestobe	84	A6
Bestuzhevo	78	G3
Betafo	109	J3
Betanzos	66	B1
Betare Oya	105	H4
Bethal	108	E5
Bethanie	108	C5
Bethany	124	C6
Bethel	118	C3
Bethel Park	125	L6
Bethesda *U.K.*	54	E3
Bethesda *U.S.A.*	125	M7
Bethlehem *Israel*	94	B6
Bethlehem *South Africa*	108	E5
Bethulie	108	E6
Bethune *France*	64	D4
Bethune *France*	64	E3
Betioky	109	H4
Betpak-Dala	86	B2
Bet-Pak-Data	86	B2
Betroka	109	J4
Betsiamites	125	R2
Betsiboka	109	J3
Bettiah	92	F3
Bettyhill	56	D2
Betul	92	E4
Betwa	92	E4
Betws-y-coed	54	F3
Beuvron	65	D5
Beverley *Australia*	112	D5
Beverley *U.K.*	55	J3
Beverly Hills	126	C3
Bexhill	53	H4
Beykoz	76	C2
Beyla	104	D4
Beylul	96	F10
Beyneu	79	K6
Beypazari	76	D2
Beypinar	77	G3
Beysehir	76	D4
Beysehir Golu	76	D4
Beyton	53	H2
Beytussebap	77	K4
Bezhetsk	78	F4
Beziers	65	E7
Bezmein	95	P2
Bhadgaon	92	G3
Bhadrachalam	92	F5
Bhadrakh	92	G4
Bhadravati	92	E6
Bhagalpur	92	G3
Bhakkar	92	D2
Bhamo	93	J4
Bhandara	92	E4
Bhanrer Range	92	F4
Bharatpur *Pradesh, India*	92	F4
Bharatpur *Rajasthan, India*	92	E3
Bharuch	92	D2
Bhatinda	92	D2
Bhatpara	93	G4
Bhavnagar	92	D4
Bhawanipatna	92	F5
Bhilwara	92	D3
Bhima	92	E5
Bhiwani	92	E3
Bhopal	92	E4
Bhopalpatnam	92	F5
Bhor	92	D5
Bhubaneshwar	92	G4
Bhuj	92	C4
Bhumiphol Dam	93	J5
Bhusawal	92	E4
Bhutan	93	G3
Bia	136	D4
Biaban	95	N8
Biabanak	95	S5
Biak	114	B2
Biala Podlaska	71	K2
Bialobrzegi	71	J3
Bialowieza	71	K2
Bialystok	71	K2
Bianco	69	F6
Biankouma	104	D4
Biaro	91	H5
Biarritz	65	C7
Biasca	68	B2
Biba	102	F2
Bibai	88	H4
Bibala	106	B5
Bibby Island	119	S3
Biberach	70	C4
Bibury	53	F3
Bicester	53	F3
Bicheno	113	K7
Bickle Knob	125	L7
Bida	105	G4
Bidar	92	E5
Biddeford	125	Q5
Biddulph	55	G3
Bidean Nam Bian	57	C4
Bideford	52	C3
Bideford Bay	52	C3
Bidford-on-Avon	53	F2
Bidokht	95	P4
Bidzhan *U.S.S.R.*	88	C1
Bidzhan *U.S.S.R.*	88	C2
Biebrza	71	K2
Biel	68	A2
Bielefeld	70	C2
Biella	68	B3
Bielsko-Biala	71	H4
Bielsk Podlaski	71	K2
Bien Hoa	93	L6
Bienne	68	A2
Bienveneu	137	G3
Bienville, Lac	121	M6
Biferno	69	E5
Biga	76	B2
Bigadic	76	C3
Big Bay	114	T11
Big Belt Mountains	122	J4
Big Blue	123	R7
Bigbury Bay	52	D4
Biggar *Canada*	123	K1
Biggar *U.K.*	57	E5
Biggleswade	53	G2
Big Horn	123	K5
Big Horn Mountains	123	L5
Big Island	120	M5
Big Pine	126	C2
Big Piney	123	J6
Big Sheep Mountains	123	L4
Big Sioux	123	R5
Big Snowy Mount	122	K4
Big Spring	127	M4
Big Stone Gap	124	J8
Big Timber	123	J5
Big Trout Lake	119	T4
Bihac	72	C3
Bihar	92	G4
Bihar	92	G3
Biharamulo	107	F3
Bihoro	88	K4
Bihu	87	M6
Bijagos, Arquipelago dos	104	B3
Bijapur	92	E5
Bijar	94	H4
Bijeljina	72	E3
Bijelo Polje	72	E4
Bijie	93	L3
Bijnor	92	E3
Bikaner	92	D3
Bikin *U.S.S.R.*	88	E2
Bikin *U.S.S.R.*	88	F2
Bikoro	106	C3
Bilad Bani Bu Ali	97	P5
Bilad Ghamid	96	E6
Bilad Zahran	96	E6
Bilaspur	92	F4
Bilauktaung Range	93	J6
Bilbao	66	E1
Bilchir	85	J6
Bilecik	76	C2
Biled	73	F3
Bile Karpaty	71	G4
Bilesha Plain	107	H2
Bilgoraj	71	K3
Bili	106	E2
Bilin	93	J5
Billabalong	112	D4
Billericay	53	H3
Billingham	55	H2
Billings	123	K5
Billingshurst	53	G3
Bilma	101	H5
Bilma, Grand Erg de	101	H5
Biloela	113	L3
Bilo Gora	72	D3
Biloxi	128	H5
Biltine	102	D5
Bilugyun	93	J5
Binalud, Kuh-e	95	P3
Binatang	90	E5
Binder	87	L2
Bindloe Island	136	A7
Bindura	108	F3
Binefar	67	G2
Binga	108	E3
Bingara	113	L4
Bingerville	104	E4
Bingham	125	R4
Binghamton	125	N5
Bingley	55	H3
Bingol	77	J3
Bingol Daglari	77	J3
Binjai *Indonesia*	90	B5
Binjai *Indonesia*	90	D5
Binongko	91	G7
Bintan	90	C5
Bintuhan	90	C6
Bintulu	90	E5
Bin Xian *Heilongjiang, China*	88	A3
Bin Xian *Shaanxi, China*	93	L2
Binyang	93	L4
Bio	114	K7
Biobio	139	B7
Biograd	72	C4
Bioko	105	G5
Bir	92	E5
Bira *U.S.S.R.*	88	D1
Bira *U.S.S.R.*	88	D1
Bira *U.S.S.R.*	85	P7
Birag, Kuh-e	95	Q8
Birak	101	H3
Bir al Hisw	96	E4
Bir al War	101	H4
Birao	102	D5
Biratnagar	93	G3
Bir Butayman	77	H4
Birca	73	G4
Birch Island	122	D2
Birch Mountains	119	N4
Bird	119	S4
Bird Island	133	R7
Birdlip	53	E3
Birdum	113	G2
Birecik	77	G4
Bireun	90	B4
Bir Fardan	97	J5
Bir Ghabalou	67	H4
Bir Hadi	97	K7
Birhan	103	G5
Birikchul	84	D6
Birjand	95	P5
Birkenhead *New Zealand*	115	E2
Birkenhead *U.K.*	55	F3
Birksgate Range	112	F4
Birlad *Romania*	73	J2
Birlad *Romania*	73	J2
Birlestik	86	B2
Birmingham *U.K.*	53	F2
Birmingham *U.S.A.*	129	J4
Bir Moghrein	100	C3
Birnie Island	111	U2
Birnin Kebbi	105	F3
Birni nKonni	101	G6
Birobidzhan	88	D1
Birofeld	88	D1
Birr	59	G6
Bir, Ras el	103	H5
Birreencorragh	58	C5
Birrimbah	112	G2
Birsk	78	K4
Birtle	123	P2
Birtley	55	H2
Biryusa	84	F5
Birzai	63	L8
Biscay, Bay of	65	B6
Bischofshofen	68	D2
Biscotasi Lake	124	J3
Bisert	78	K4
Bisevo	72	D4
Bisha	96	C9
Bishah, Wadi	96	F6
Bishnupur	93	G4
Bishop	126	C2
Bishop Auckland	55	H2
Bishop Burton	55	J3
Bishop's Castle	52	D2
Bishops Falls	121	Q8
Bishop's Stortford	53	H3
Bishri, Jbel	77	H5
Biskra	101	G2
Biskupiec	71	J2
Bislig	91	H4
Bismarck Archipelago	114	D2
Bismarck Range	114	D3
Bismark	123	P4
Bismil	77	J4
Bismo	63	C6
Bisotun	94	H4
Bispfors	62	G5
Bissau	104	B3
Bissett	123	S2
Bistcho Lake	119	M4
Bistretu	73	G4
Bistrita *Romania*	73	H2
Bistrita *Romania*	73	J2
Bistritei, Muntii	73	H2
Bitburg	70	B3
Bitche	64	G4
Bitik	79	J5
Bitkine	102	C5
Bitlis	77	K3
Bitola	73	F5
Bitonto	69	F5
Bitterfontein	108	C6
Bitterroot	122	G4
Bitterroot Range	122	G4
Bitti	69	B5
Biu	105	H3
Bivolu	73	H2

Biwa-ko 89 E8
Biyad, Al 96 H5
Biyagundi 96 C9
Biysk 84 D6
Bizerta 69 B7
Bizerte 101 G1
Bjargtangar 62 S12
Bjelovar 72 D3
Bjerkvik 62 L2
Bjorklinge 63 G6
Bjorksele 62 H4
Bjorna 62 H5
Bjorneborg *Finland* 63 J6
Bjorneborg *Sweden* 63 F7
Bjornevatn 62 N2
Bjornoya 80 C2
Bjurholm 62 H5
Bjursas 63 F6
Bla Bheinn 56 B3
Black *Alaska, U.S.A.* 118 G2
Black *Arizona, U.S.A.* 127 H4
Black *Arkansas, U.S.A.* 128 G3
Black *New York, U.S.A.* 125 N5
Blackadder Water 57 F5
Blackall 113 K3
Black Bay 124 F2
Black Belt 129 J4
Blackburn 55 G3
Black Canyon City 126 F3
Blackdown Hills 52 D4
Blackfoot 122 H6
Blackford 57 E4
Black Head 59 D6
Blackhead Bay 59 D6
Blackhill 55 H3
Black Hills 123 N5
Black Isle 56 D3
Black Mesa 126 G2
Blackmill 52 D3
Black Mountain 52 D3
Black Mountains 52 D3
Blackpool 55 F3
Black Range 127 J4
Black River Falls 124 E4
Blackrock 58 K5
Black Rock Desert 122 E7
Black Sea 51 P7
Blacksod Bay 58 B4
Blackstairs Mount 59 J7
Blackstairs Mountains 59 J7
Blackthorn 53 F3
Black Volta 104 E4
Black Water 57 E4
Blackwater *Australia* 113 K3
Blackwater *Meath, Ireland* 58 J5
Blackwater *Waterford, Ireland* 59 F8
Blackwater *Essex, U.K.* 53 H3
Blackwater *Hampshire, U.K.* 53 G3
Blackwaterfoot 57 C5
Blackwater Lake 119 L3
Blackwater Reservoir *Highland, U.K.* 57 D4
Blackwater Reservoir *Tayside, U.K.* 57 E4
Blackwell 128 D2
Blackwood 112 D5
Blaenavon 52 D3
Blafjall 62 W12
Blagodarnyy 79 G6
Blagoevgrad 73 G4
Blagoveshchensk *U.S.S.R.* 78 K4
Blagoveshchensk *U.S.S.R.* 85 M6
Blagoyevo 78 H3
Blair Atholl 57 E4
Blairgowrie 57 E4
Blaka 101 H4
Blakely 129 K5
Blakeney 53 J2
Blakesley 53 F2
Blanca, Bahia 139 D7
Blanca, Costa 67 F3
Blanca Peak 127 K2
Blanca, Punta 126 E6
Blanca, Sierra 127 K4
Blanc, Cap 69 B7
Blanche Channel 114 H6
Blanche, Lake 113 H4
Blanchland 55 G2
Blanc, Mont 65 G6
Blanco 136 E7
Blanco, Cabo 139 C9
Blanco, Cape 122 B6
Blanda 62 V12
Blandford Forum 53 E4
Blanes 67 H2
Blangy 64 D4
Blankenberge 64 E3
Blanquilla, Isla 136 E1
Blantyre 107 G6
Blarney 59 E9
Blasket Islands 59 A8
Blavet 65 B5
Blaydon 55 H2
Blaye 65 C6
Bleadon 52 E3
Bleaklow Hill 55 H3
Bled 72 C2
Blekinge 63 F8
Bletchley 53 G3
Bleus, Monts 107 F2
Blida 101 F1
Bligh Water 114 R8
Blind River 124 J3
Blisworth 53 G2
Block Island 125 Q6
Bloemfontein 108 E5
Blois 65 D5
Blonduos 62 U12
Bloodvein 123 R2
Bloody Foreland 58 F2
Bloomfield 124 D6
Bloomington *Illinois, U.S.A.* 124 F6
Bloomington *Indiana, U.S.A.* 124 G7
Bloomington *Minnesota, U.S.A.* 124 D4
Bloomsbury 113 K3
Blouberg 108 E4
Blubberhouses 55 H3
Bludenz 68 B2
Bluefield 125 K8
Bluefields 132 F9
Blue Mountain Lake 125 N5
Blue Mountain Peak 132 J5
Blue Mountains 122 E5
Bluenose Lake 119 M2
Blue Ridge 129 K3
Blue Ridge Mountains 129 L3
Blue Stack 58 F3
Blue Stack Mountains 58 F3
Bluff *New Zealand* 115 B7
Bluff *U.S.A.* 127 H2
Bluff Knoll 112 D5
Bluff Point 112 C4
Bluff, Punta 126 F6
Blumenau 138 G5
Blunt 123 Q5
Blyth *Northumberland, U.K.* 55 H1
Blyth *Nottinghamshire, U.K.* 55 H3
Blyth *Suffolk, U.K.* 53 J2
Blythe 126 E4
Blythe Bridge 53 E2
Blytheville 128 H3
Bo 104 C4
Boac 91 G3
Boa Fe 136 C5
Boa Vista *Cape Verde* 104 L7
Boa Vista *Amazonas, Brazil* 136 D4
Boa Vista *Roraima, Brazil* 136 E3
Bobai 93 M4
Bobaomby, Tanjoni 109 J2
Bobbili 92 F5
Bobbio 68 B3
Bobo Dioulasso 104 E3
Bobolice 71 G2
Bobr 70 F3
Bobrinents 79 E6
Bobrka 71 L4
Bobrov 79 G5
Bobruysk 79 D5
Bobures 133 M10
Boca del Pao 136 E2
Boca do Acre 136 D5
Boca Grande 136 E2
Bocaiuva 138 H3
Boca Mavaca 136 D3
Bocaranga 102 C6
Boca Raton 129 M7
Bochnia 71 J4
Bocholt 70 B3
Bochum 70 B3
Bodalla 113 L6
Bodaybo 85 J5
Boddam 56 A2
Boden 62 J4
Bodensee 70 C5
Bodhan 92 E5
Bodmin 52 C4
Bodmin Moor 52 C4
Bodo 62 F3
Bodrum 76 B4
Bodva 71 J4
Bodza, Pasul 73 J3
Boen 65 F6
Boende 106 C3
Boffa 104 C3
Bogalusa 128 H5
Bogan 113 K5
Bogaz 76 E2
Bogazkale 76 F2
Bogazkaya 77 F2
Bogazkopru 76 F3
Bogazliyan 76 F3
Bogbonga 106 C2
Bogen 62 L2
Boggeragh Mountains 59 E8
Boghar 67 H5
Bogia 114 D2
Bognes 62 G2
Bognor Regis 53 G4
Bogo 91 G3
Bogodukhov 79 F5
Bogong, Mount 113 K6
Bogor 90 D7
Bogorodchany 71 L4
Bogorodskoye *U.S.S.R.* 78 J4
Bogorodskoye *U.S.S.R.* 85 Q6
Bogota 136 C3
Bogotol 84 D5
Bogra 93 G4
Boguchany 84 F5
Boguchar 79 G6
Bogue 100 C5
Bogue Chitto 128 G5
Boguslav 79 E6
Bo Hai 87 K4
Bohemia 70 E4
Bohmer Wald 70 E4
Bohol 91 G4
Bohol Sea 91 G4
Boiano 69 E5
Boigul 114 C3
Boipeba, Ilha 137 K6
Bois Blanc Island 124 H4
Boisdale, Loch 57 A3
Boise *U.S.A.* 122 F6
Boise *U.S.A.* 122 F6
Boise City 127 L2
Bois, Lac des 118 K2
Boissevain 123 P3
Boizenburg 70 D2
Bojana 74 E2
Bojnurd 95 N3
Boka 73 F3
Boka Kotorska 72 E4
Boke 104 C3
Bokhara 113 K4
Boknafjord 63 A7
Bokol 107 G2
Bokoro 102 C5
Boksitogorsk 78 E4
Boktor 85 P6
Bokungu 106 D3
Bolama 104 B3
Bolanos 130 H7
Bolan Pass 92 C3
Bolbec 64 D4
Bolchary 84 Ae5
Bole 104 E4
Boleslawiec 70 F3
Bolgatanga 104 E3
Bolgrad 79 D6
Boli 88 C3
Bolia 106 C3
Boliden 62 J4
Bolinao 91 F2
Bol Irgiz 79 H5
Bolivar 139 D7
Bolivar *Missouri, U.S.A.* 124 D8
Bolivar *Tennessee, U.S.A.* 128 H3
Bolivar, Cerro 133 R11
Bolivar, Pico 133 M10
Bolivia 138 C3
Boljevac 73 F4
Bolkhov 79 F5
Bollington 55 G3
Bollnas 63 G6
Bollon 113 K4
Bollstabruk 62 G5
Bolmen 63 E8
Bolobo 106 C3
Bologna 68 C3
Bologoye 78 E4
Bolotnoye 84 C5
Boloven, Cao Nguyen 93 L5
Bolsena, Lago di 69 C4
Bolsherechye 84 A5
Bolsheretsk 85 T6
Bolshevik 85 R4
Bolshevik, Ostrov 81 M2
Bolshezemelskaya Tundra 78 K2
Bolshoy Anyuy 85 U3
Bolshoy Atlym 84 Ae4
Bolshoy Balkhan, Khrebet 95 M2
Bolshoy Begichev, Ostrov 84 J2
Bolshoy Chernigovka 79 J5
Bolshoy Kavkaz 77 L1
Bolshoy Kunyak 84 A5
Bolshoy Lyakhovskiy, Ostrov 85 Q2
Bolshoy Murta 84 E5
Bolshoy Pit 84 E5
Bolshoy Porog 84 E3
Bolshoy Shantar, Ostrov 85 P5
Bolshoy Usa 78 K4
Bolshoy Yenisey 84 E6
Bolshoy Yugan 84 A5
Bolsover 55 H3
Boltana 67 G1
Bolt Head 52 D4
Bolton *Greater Manchester, U.K.* 55 G3
Bolton *Northumberland, U.K.* 57 G5
Bolu 76 D2
Bolucan 77 G3
Bolus Head 59 B9
Bolvadin 76 D3
Bolyarovo 73 J4
Bolzano 68 C2
Bom 114 D3
Boma 106 B4
Bombala 113 K6
Bombay 92 D5
Bomili 106 E2
Bom Jesus 137 J5
Bom Jesus da Lapa 137 J6
Bomlafjord 63 A7
Bomlo 63 A7
Bomongo 106 C2
Bonab 94 H3
Bonaire 133 N8
Bonaire Trench 133 N9
Bona, Mount 118 G3
Bonar Bridge 56 D3
Bonavista 121 R8
Bonavista Bay 121 R8
Bon, Cap 101 H1
Bondo 106 D2
Bondokodi 91 F7
Bondoukou 104 E4
Bone 69 A7
Bo'ness 57 E4
Bonete, Cerro 138 C5
Bone, Teluk 91 G6
Bongabong 91 G3
Bongor 102 C5
Bonham 128 D4
Bonifacio 69 B5
Bonifacio, Strait of 69 B5
Bonn 70 B3
Bonners Ferry 122 F3
Bonnetable 64 D4
Bonneval 64 D4
Bonneville 65 G5
Bonneville Salt Flats 122 H7
Bonnie Rock 112 D5
Bonny *France* 65 E5
Bonny *Nigeria* 105 G5
Bonnyrigg 57 E5
Bono 69 B5
Bonobono 91 F4
Bonorva 69 B5
Bonthe 104 C4
Bontoc 91 G2
Booligal 113 J5
Boologooro 112 C3
Boone *Iowa, U.S.A.* 124 D5
Boone *N. Carolina, U.S.A.* 129 M2
Booneville *Mississippi, U.S.A.* 128 H3
Booneville *New York, U.S.A.* 125 N5
Booroorban 113 J5
Boosaaso 103 J5
Boothia, Gulf of 120 J4
Boothia Peninsula 120 H3
Bootle 55 F3
Boot Reefs 114 C3
Bopeechee 113 H4
Boquilla, Presa de la 127 K7
Boquillas del Carmen 127 L6
Bor *Sudan* 102 F6
Bor *Turkey* 76 F4
Bor *Yugoslavia* 73 G3
Boraha, Nosy 109 J3
Borah Peak 122 H5
Boras 63 E8
Borasambar 92 F4
Borazjan 95 K7
Borba 136 F4
Borborema, Planalto da 137 K5
Borca 73 H2
Borcka 77 J2
Bordeaux 65 C6
Borden Island 120 D2
Borden Peninsula 120 K3
Borders 57 F5
Bordertown 113 J6
Bordeyri 62 U12
Bordj-Bou-Arreridj 67 J4
Bordj Bounaama 67 G5
Bordj Omar Driss 101 G3
Borensberg 63 F7
Boreray 56 A3
Borga 63 L6
Borgarnes 62 U12
Borgefjellet 62 E4
Borger 127 M3
Borgholm 63 G8
Borgo San Lorenzo 68 C4
Borgosesia 68 B3
Borgo Val di Taro 68 B3
Borgo Valsugana 68 C2
Borislav 71 K4
Borisoglebsk 79 G5
Borisov 63 Q9
Borispol 79 E5
Borja 67 F2
Borkovskaya 78 H2
Borkum 70 B2
Borlange 63 F6
Borlu 76 C3
Bormida 68 B3
Bormio 68 C2
Borneo 90 E5
Bornholm 70 F1
Bornholmsgattet 63 F9
Bornova 76 B3
Borohoro Shan 86 E3
Boroko 91 G5
Boromo 104 E3
Boronga Islands 93 H5
Borongan 91 H3
Borovichi 78 E4
Borovlyanka 84 C6
Borovsk 78 K4
Borovskoye 84 Ad6
Borrika 113 J6
Borris 59 J7
Borrisokane 59 F7
Borrisoleigh 59 G7
Borroloola 113 H2
Borrowdale 55 F2
Borshchev 73 J1
Borshchovochnyy Khrebet 85 J6
Borth 52 C2
Borujen 95 K6
Borujerd 94 J5
Borve 57 A4
Borzhomi 77 K2
Borzya 85 K7
Bosa 69 B5
Bosanski Brod 72 E3
Bosanski Novi 72 D3
Bosanski Petrovac 72 D3
Boscastle 52 C4
Bose 93 L4
Bos Gradiska 72 D3
Boshruyeh 95 N5
Bosilegrad 73 G4
Boskovice 72 E3
Bosna 72 E3
Bosnik 114 B2
Bosobolo 106 C2

Name	Page	Ref
Boso-hanto	89	H8
Bosphorus	76	C2
Bossambele	102	C6
Bossangoa	102	C6
Bossier City	128	F4
Bostan *Iran*	94	H6
Bostan *Pakistan*	92	C2
Bostanabad	94	H3
Bosten Bagrax Hu	86	F3
Boston *U.S.A.*	53	G2
Boston *U.S.A.*	125	Q5
Boston Mountains	128	E3
Botesdale	53	J2
Botev	73	H4
Botevgrad	73	G4
Bothel	55	F2
Bothnia, Gulf of	62	J5
Botna	73	K2
Botosani	73	J2
Botsmark	62	J4
Botswana	108	D4
Botte Donato	69	F6
Bottenhavet	63	H6
Bottenviken	62	K4
Bottesford	53	G2
Bottineau	123	P3
Bottisham	53	H2
Bottrop	70	B3
Botucatu	138	G4
Bouafle	104	D4
Bouake	104	D4
Bouar	102	C6
Bouarfa	100	E2
Boucant Bay	113	G1
Bouchegouf	69	A7
Bougainville	114	E3
Bougainville, Cape	112	F1
Bougainville Reef	113	K2
Bougainville Strait	114	J5
Bougaroun, Cap	101	G1
Bougie	67	J4
Bougouni	100	D6
Bougzdul	67	H5
Bouhalloufa	67	G4
Bouillon	64	F4
Bouira	67	H4
Bou Ismail	67	H4
Boujdour	100	C3
Bou Kadir	67	G4
Boulay	64	G4
Boulder	123	M8
Boulder City	126	E3
Boulogne-sur-Mer	64	D3
Boumbe I	102	C7
Boumbe II	102	C7
Boumo	102	C6
Bouna	104	E4
Boundiali	104	D4
Boung Long	93	L6
Boun Tai	93	K4
Bountiful	122	J7
Bounty Islands	111	S11
Bourail	114	W16
Bourbon-l'Archambault	65	E5
Bourbonnais *France*	65	E5
Bourbonnais *U.S.A.*	124	G6
Bourbonne-les-Bains	65	F5
Bourem	100	E5
Bourganeuf	65	D6
Bourg-en-Bresse	65	F5
Bourges	65	E5
Bourgogne	65	F5
Bourgogne, Canal de	65	E5
Bourg-Saint-Andeol	65	F6
Bourke	113	K5
Bourne	53	G2
Bournemouth	53	F4
Bou Saada	101	F1
Boussac	65	E5
Bousso	102	C5
Boutilimit	100	C5
Boves	68	A3
Bovey	52	D4
Bovey Tracy	52	D4
Bovingdon	53	G3
Bovino	69	E5
Bow	122	H2
Bowbells	123	N3
Bowen	113	K3
Bowers Bank	118	Ab9
Bowes	55	G2
Bowfell	55	F2
Bowie	128	D4
Bow Island	122	J3
Bowkan	94	H3
Bowland, Forest of	55	G2
Bowling Green *Kentucky, U.S.A.*	124	G8
Bowling Green *Ohio, U.S.A.*	124	J6
Bowman	123	N4
Bowman Bay	120	M4
Bowness	55	G2
Bowness-on-Solway	55	F2
Bowraville	113	L5
Boxford	53	H2
Bo Xian	93	N2
Boxing	87	M4
Box Tank	113	J5
Boyabat	76	F2
Boyang	87	M6
Boyarka	84	F2
Boyd Lake	119	Q3
Boyer	124	C6
Boyle	58	F5
Boyne	58	K5
Boynton Beach	129	M7
Boyuibe	138	D4
Bozburun	76	C4
Bozcaada	75	H3
Boz Daglari	76	B3
Bozdogan	76	C4
Bozeman	122	J5
Bozen	68	C2
Boze Pole	71	G1
Bozkir	76	E4
Bozkurt	76	E2
Bozoum	102	C6
Bozova	77	H4
Bozqush, Kuh-e	94	H3
Bozuyuk	76	D3
Bra	68	A3
Brabant Island	141	V6
Brabourne	53	H3
Brac	72	D4
Bracadale	56	B3
Bracadale, Loch	56	B3
Bracciano	69	D4
Bracke	62	F5
Brackley	53	F2
Bracknell	53	G3
Brad	73	G2
Bradano	69	F5
Bradda Head	54	E2
Bradenton	129	L7
Bradford *U.K.*	55	H3
Bradford *U.S.A.*	125	L6
Bradford-on-Avon	52	E3
Bradwell Waterside	53	H3
Brady	127	N5
Brady Mountains	127	N5
Brae	56	A1
Braemar	57	E3
Braemore	56	E2
Braeswick	56	F1
Braga	66	B2
Bragado	139	D7
Braganca	66	C2
Braganca Paulista	138	G4
Bragar	56	B2
Brahman Baria	93	H4
Brahmani	92	G4
Brahmapur	92	F5
Brahmaputra	93	H3
Braidwood	113	K6
Braila	73	J3
Brailsford	53	F2
Brainerd	124	C3
Braintree	53	H3
Braishfield	53	F3
Brake	70	C2
Brakel	70	C3
Brallos	75	G3
Bramdean	53	F3
Bramham	55	H3
Bramming	63	C9
Brampton *Canada*	125	L5
Brampton *U.K.*	55	G2
Bramsche	70	B2
Brancaster	53	H2
Brancaster Bay	53	H2
Branco	136	E3
Branco, Cabo	137	L5
Brandberg	108	B4
Brandbu	63	D6
Brande	63	C9
Brandenburg	70	E2
Brandesburton	55	J3
Brandon *Canada*	123	Q3
Brandon *U.S.A.*	125	P5
Brandon Bay	59	B8
Brandon Mount	59	B8
Brandon Point	59	B8
Brandval	63	E6
Branesti	73	J3
Braniewo	71	H1
Bran, Pasul	73	H3
Brantford	125	K5
Brantley	129	J5
Brantome	65	D6
Brasileia	136	D6
Brasilia *Distrito Federal, Brazil*	138	F3
Brasilia *Minas Gerais, Brazil*	138	H3
Braslav	63	M9
Brasov	73	H3
Brassey Range	91	F5
Brates, Lacul	73	K3
Bratislava	71	G4
Bratsk	84	G5
Bratslav	73	K1
Braunau	68	D1
Braunsberg	71	H1
Braunschweig	70	D2
Braunton	52	C3
Brava	104	L7
Brava, Costa	67	H2
Bravo del Norte, Rio	127	L6
Brawley	126	E4
Bray	59	K6
Bray Head	59	B9
Bray Island	120	L4
Brazil	137	G5
Brazos	128	D5
Brazzaville	106	C3
Brcko	72	E3
Brda	71	G2
Breadalbane	57	D4
Breaksea Sound	115	A6
Brean	52	D3
Brebes	90	D7
Brechfa	52	C3
Brechin	57	F4
Breckenridge *Texas, U.S.A.*	128	C4
Breckenridge *Minnesota, U.S.A.*	124	B3
Breckland	53	H2
Breclav	71	G4
Brecon	52	D3
Brecon Beacons	52	D3
Breda	64	F3
Bredon Hill	53	F3
Bredstedt	70	C1
Breezewood	125	L7
Bregenz	68	B2
Bregovo	73	G3
Breidafjordur	62	T12
Brejo	137	J4
Brekken	62	D5
Brekstad	62	C5
Bremen *U.S.A.*	129	K4
Bremen *W. Germany*	70	C2
Bremerhaven	70	C2
Bremer Range	112	E5
Bremerton	122	C4
Bremervorde	70	C2
Brendon Hills	52	D3
Brenham	128	D5
Brenig, Llyn	55	F3
Brenish	56	A2
Brenner Pass	68	C2
Breno	68	C3
Brenta	68	C3
Brentford	53	G2
Brentwood *U.K.*	53	H3
Brentwood *U.S.A.*	125	P6
Brescia	68	C3
Breskens	64	E3
Breslau	71	G3
Bressanone	68	C2
Bressay	56	A2
Bressay Sound	56	A2
Bressuire	65	C5
Brest *France*	64	A4
Brest *U.S.S.R.*	71	K2
Brestlitovsk	79	E5
Brest Litovsk	71	K2
Bretagne	64	B4
Bretcu	73	J2
Breteuil *France*	64	D4
Breteuil *France*	64	E4
Breton, Cape	121	Q8
Breton Sound	128	H6
Brett	53	H2
Brett, Cape	115	E1
Breueh	90	B4
Brevoort Island	120	P5
Brewer	125	R4
Brewster	122	E3
Brewton	129	J5
Brezhnev	78	J4
Breznice	70	E4
Brezo, Sierra del	66	D1
Bria	102	D6
Briancon	65	G6
Brianne, Llyn	52	D2
Briare	65	E5
Bribie Island	113	L4
Brichany	73	J1
Bricquebe	53	N7
Bride	54	E2
Bridestowe	52	C4
Bridgend *Mid Glamorgan, U.K.*	52	D3
Bridgend *Strathclyde, U.K.*	57	B5
Bridge of Allan	57	E4
Bridge of Gaur	57	D4
Bridge of Orchy	57	D4
Bridge of Weir	57	D5
Bridgeport *Alabama, U.S.A.*	129	K3
Bridgeport *California, U.S.A.*	126	C1
Bridgeport *Connecticut, U.S.A.*	125	P6
Bridgeport *Nebraska, U.S.A.*	123	N7
Bridgeton	125	N7
Bridgetown *Australia*	112	D5
Bridgetown *Barbados*	133	T8
Bridgetown *Canada*	121	N9
Bridgewater	121	P9
Bridgnorth	52	E2
Bridgwater	52	D3
Bridgwater Bay	52	D3
Bridlington	55	J2
Bridlington Bay	55	J2
Bridport	52	E4
Brieg	71	G3
Brienne-le-Chateau	64	F4
Brier Island	125	S4
Briey	64	F4
Brig	68	A2
Brigg	55	J3
Brighouse	55	H3
Brightlingsea	53	J3
Brighton	53	G4
Brignoles	65	G7
Brihuega	66	E2
Brikama	104	B3
Brindakit	85	P4
Brindisi	69	F5
Brinian	56	F1
Brinkley	128	G3
Brioude	65	E6
Brisbane	113	L4
Bristol *U.K.*	52	E3
Bristol *U.S.A*	125	P6
Bristol Bay	118	D4
Bristol Channel	52	D2
Bristol Lake	126	E3
Bristow	128	D3
British Columbia	118	L4
Brits	108	E5
Britstown	108	D6
Brittle, Lake	57	B3
Brive-la-Gaillarde	65	D6
Briviesca	66	E1
Brixham	52	D4
Brlik	86	C3
Brno	71	G4
Broad	129	M3
Broadback	121	L7
Broad Bay	56	B2
Broad Cairn	57	E4
Broad Haven	58	C4
Broad Hinton	53	F3
Broadhurst Range	112	E3
Broad Sound *Australia*	113	K3
Broad Sound *U.K.*	52	B3
Broadstairs	53	J3
Broads, The	53	J2
Broadus	123	M5
Broadway	53	F2
Brochel	56	B3
Brocken	70	D3
Brockenhurst	53	F4
Brock Island	120	D2
Brockman, Mount	112	D3
Brockton	125	Q5
Brod	73	F5
Broddanes	62	U12
Brodeur Peninsula	120	J3
Brodick	57	C5
Brodick Bay	57	C5
Brodnica	71	H2
Brodokalmak	84	Ad5
Brody	79	D5
Brok	71	J2
Broken Bay	113	L5
Broken Bow *Nebraska, U.S.A.*	123	Q7
Broken Bow *Oklahoma, U.S.A.*	128	E3
Broken Bow Lake	128	E3
Broken Hill *Australia*	113	J5
Broken Hill *Zambia*	107	E5
Bromberg	71	G2
Bromley	53	H3
Bromsgrove	53	E2
Bromyard	52	E2
Bronderslev	63	C8
Bronnoysund	62	E4
Bronte	69	E7
Brookfield	124	D7
Brookhaven	128	G5
Brookings *Oregon, U.S.A.*	122	B6
Brookings *S. Dakota, U.S.A.*	123	R5
Brookneal	125	L8
Brooks	122	H2
Brooks Range	118	D2
Brooksville	129	L6
Broome	112	E2
Broom, Loch	56	C3
Brora *U.K.*	56	D2
Brora *U.K.*	56	E2
Brosteni	73	G3
Broto	67	F1
Brotton	55	J2
Brou	64	D4
Brough	55	G2
Brough Head	56	E1
Brough Ness	56	F2
Broughshane	58	K3
Broughton	57	E5
Broughton in Furness	55	F2
Broughton Island	120	P4
Broughton Poggs	53	F3
Browerville	124	C3
Brow Head	59	C10
Brownfield	127	L4
Brownhills	53	F2
Browning	122	H3
Brownsville	128	D8
Brownwood	128	C5
Brownwood, Lake	127	N5
Bru	62	Y12
Bruar, The Falls of	57	E4
Bruay-en-Artois	64	E3
Bruce Bay	115	B5
Bruce, Mount	112	D3
Bruce Mountains	120	M3
Bruchsal	70	C4
Bruck	68	F1
Bruck an der Mur	68	E2
Brue	52	E3
Bruernish Point	57	A4
Bruges	64	E3
Brugg	68	B2
Brugge	64	E3
Bruhl	70	B3
Bruichladdich	57	B5
Brumado	137	J6
Brumunddal	63	D6
Brunei	90	E4
Brunette Downs	113	H2
Brunflo	62	F5
Brunico	68	C2
Brunkeberg	63	C7
Brunn	71	G4
Brunsbuttel	70	C2
Brunswick *Georgia, U.S.A.*	129	M5
Brunswick *Maine, U.S.A.*	121	N9
Brunswick *Maryland, U.S.A.*	125	M7
Brunswick *W. Germany*	70	D2
Brunswick Bay	112	E2
Brunswick, Peninsula	139	B10
Bruny Island	111	L10

Brusa	76	C2
Brush	123	N7
Brusilovka	79	J5
Brusovo	84	D4
Brussel	64	F3
Bruthen	113	K6
Bruton	52	E3
Bruxelles	64	F3
Bryan *Ohio, U.S.A.*	124	H6
Bryan *Texas, U.S.A.*	128	D5
Bryan, Mount	113	H5
Bryansk	79	E5
Bryanskoye	79	H7
Bryher	52	K5
Bryne	63	D6
Brynmawr	52	D3
Brynzeny	73	J1
Brza Palanka	73	G3
Brzava	73	F3
Brzeg	71	G3
Bua *Fiji*	114	R8
Bua *Sweden*	63	E8
Buala	114	J6
Bubanza	107	E3
Bubiyan	97	J2
Buca *Fiji*	114	R8
Buca *Turkey*	76	B3
Bucak	76	D4
Bucaramanga	136	C2
Buchach	79	D6
Buchan	56	F3
Buchanan	104	C4
Buchanan, Lake	127	N5
Buchan Gulf	120	M3
Buchannan Bay	120	L2
Bucharest	73	J3
Buchholz	70	C2
Buchlgvie	57	D4
Buchloe	70	D4
Buchon, Point	126	B3
Buchs	68	B2
Buckeye	126	F4
Buckfastleigh	52	D4
Buckhannon	125	K7
Buckhaven	57	E4
Buckie	56	F3
Buckingham	53	G3
Buckingham Bay	113	H1
Buckinghamshire	53	G3
Buckkisla	76	E4
Buckley	55	F3
Bucksburn	57	F3
Buck, The	56	F3
Bucuresti	73	J3
Bud	62	B5
Budapest	72	E2
Budardalur	62	U12
Budareyri	62	X12
Budaun	92	E3
Budduso	69	B5
Bude *U.K.*	52	C4
Bude *U.S.A.*	128	G5
Bude Bay	52	B4
Budennovsk	79	G7
Budingen	70	C3
Budir	62	Y12
Budjala	106	C2
Budleigh Salterton	52	D4
Budogoshch	78	E4
Budun	87	K1
Budungbudung	91	F6
Budu, Sabkhat al	97	J5
Buea	105	G5
Buenaventura *Colombia*	136	B3
Buenaventura *Mexico*	127	J6
Buenaventura, Bahia	136	B3
Buena Vista	125	L8
Buena Vista Lake Bed	126	C3
Buenos Aires	139	D6
Buenos Aires, Lago	139	B9
Buffalo *New York, U.S.A.*	125	L5
Buffalo *S. Dakota, U.S.A.*	123	N5
Buffalo *Texas, U.S.A.*	128	D5
Buffalo *Wyoming, U.S.A.*	123	L5
Buffalo Lake	119	M3
Buffalo Narrows	119	P4
Buftea	73	H3
Bug	71	K2
Buga	136	B3
Bugdayli	95	M2
Bugel, Tanjung	90	E7
Bugoynes	62	N2
Bugrino	78	H2
Bugsuk	91	F4
Bugulma	78	J5
Buguruslan	78	J5
Buhl	122	G6
Buhusi	73	J2
Buie, Loch	57	B4
Builth Wells	52	D2
Buin	114	G5
Buinsk	78	H5
Buin Zahra	95	K4
Buitrago del Lozoye	66	E2
Bujaraloz	67	F2
Buje	72	B3
Bujumbura	107	E3
Buk	72	D2
Buka	114	E3
Bukama	106	E4
Bukavu	107	E3
Bukhara	80	H6
Bukittinggi	90	D6
Bukk	72	F1
Bukoba	107	F3

Bukoloto	107	F2
Bula	114	A2
Bulanash	84	Ad5
Bulancak	77	H2
Bulandshahr	92	E3
Bulanik	77	K3
Bulanovo	79	K5
Bulawayo	108	E4
Buldan	76	C3
Buldana	92	E4
Buldir Island	118	Ab9
Buldurty	79	J6
Bulgan *Mongolia*	86	G2
Bulgan *Mongolia*	87	J2
Bulgaria	73	G4
Buliluyan, Cape	91	F4
Bulkeley	55	G3
Bulle	68	A2
Buller	115	C4
Bullhead City	126	E3
Bull Shoals Lake	128	F2
Bulolo	114	D3
Bulum	85	M2
Buma	114	K6
Bumba	106	D2
Buna	74	E2
Bunbeg	58	F2
Bunbury	112	D5
Bunclody	59	J7
Buncrana	58	H4
Bundaberg	113	L3
Bundoran	58	F4
Bungalaut, Selat	90	B6
Bungay	53	J2
Bungo-suido	89	D9
Bunguran Utara, Kepulauan	90	D5
Bunia	107	F2
Bunkie	128	F5
Bunratty	59	E7
Buntingford	53	G3
Buntok	90	E6
Bunyan	77	F3
Buolkalakh	85	K2
Buol Kheyr	95	K7
Buorkhaya, Guba	85	N2
Buorkhaya, Mys	85	N2
Buqayq	97	J4
Buqum, Harrat al	96	F6
Buram	102	E5
Buran	86	F2
Buraydah	96	F3
Burbage	53	F3
Burbank	126	C3
Burco	103	J6
Burdalyk	95	S2
Burdekin	113	K3
Burdur	76	D4
Burdur Golu	76	D4
Bure	53	J2
Burea	62	J4
Burentsogt	87	L2
Bureya *U.S.S.R.*	85	M7
Bureya *U.S.S.R.*	85	N6
Burg	70	D2
Burgas	73	J4
Burgdorf	68	A2
Burgeo	121	Q8
Burgersdorp	108	E6
Burgess Hill	53	G4
Burghead	56	E3
Burghead Bay	56	E3
Burgh-le-Marsh	55	K3
Burgos	66	E1
Burgsteinfurt	70	B2
Burgsvik	63	H8
Burguete	67	F1
Burhan Budai Shan	93	J1
Burhaniye	76	B3
Burhanpur	92	E4
Burias	91	G3
Burica, Punta	132	F10
Burin Peninsula	121	Q8
Buri Peninsula	96	D9
Buriram	93	K5
Burj Safita	77	G5
Burke Island	141	S4
Burketown	113	H2
Burkhala	85	R4
Burkina Faso	104	E3
Burley	122	H6
Burli	79	J5
Burlington *Canada*	125	L5
Burlington *Colorado, U.S.A.*	123	N8
Burlington *Iowa, U.S.A.*	124	E6
Burlington *N. Carolina, U.S.A.*	129	N2
Burlington *Vermont, U.S.A.*	125	P4
Burlington *Washington, U.S.A.*	122	C3
Burlton	52	E2
Burlyu-Tobe	86	D2
Burma	93	J4
Burmantovo	78	L3
Burnaby	122	C3
Burneston	55	H2
Burnet	128	C5
Burnham-on-Crouch	53	H3
Burnham-on-Sea	52	E3
Burnie	113	K7
Burnley	55	G3
Burns	122	E6
Burntwood	119	R4
Burqan	97	H2
Burqin	86	F2
Burra	113	H3
Burravoe	56	A1
Burray	56	F2

Burren, The	59	D6
Burriana	67	F3
Burrow Head	54	E2
Burrs Junction	122	F6
Burrundie	112	G1
Burry Port	52	C3
Bursa	76	C2
Bur Safaga	103	F2
Bur Said	103	F1
Bur Sudan	96	C7
Burt, Mount	112	F4
Burton Joyce	53	F2
Burton Lake	121	L7
Burton Latimer	53	G2
Burton upon Stather	55	J3
Burton-upon-Trent	53	F2
Burtrask	62	J4
Buru	91	H6
Burum	97	J9
Burundi	107	E3
Burunnoye	79	J5
Bururi	107	E3
Burwick	56	F2
Bury	55	G3
Buryatskaya A.S.S.R.	85	H6
Burylbaytal	86	C2
Burynshik	79	J6
Bury Saint Edmunds	53	H2
Busayta, Al	96	D1
Bushat	74	E2
Bushehr	95	K7
Bushimaie	106	D4
Bushmills	58	J2
Businga	106	D2
Busira	106	C3
Busk	71	L4
Buskerud	63	C6
Busko	71	J3
Busselton	112	D5
Bussol , Proliv	85	S7
Bustakh, Ozero	85	Q2
Busto Arsizio	68	B3
Busuanga	91	G3
Buta	106	D2
Butare	107	E3
Bute	57	C5
Bute, Sound of	57	C5
Butiaba	107	F2
Butler	125	L6
Butmah	77	K4
Butte	122	H5
Buttermere	55	F2
Butterworth *Malaysia*	90	C4
Butterworth *South Africa*	108	E6
Buttevant	59	E8
Button Islands	121	P5
Butuan	91	H4
Butung	91	G7
Buturlinovka	79	G5
Buulobarde	103	J7
Buurhakaba	107	H2
Buwatah	96	D4
Buxton	55	H3
Buy	78	G4
Buyba	84	E6
Buynaksk	79	H7
Buyr Nuur	87	M2
Buyuk Agri Dagi	77	L3
Buyuklacin	76	F2
Buyuk Menderes	76	C4
Buzancais	65	D5
Buzau *Romania*	73	J3
Buzau *Romania*	73	J3
Buzi	109	F3
Buzovyazy	78	K5
Buzuluk	84	Ae6
Buzuluk	79	J5
Byam Martin, Cape	120	L3
Byam Martin Island	120	F2
Byczyna	71	H3
Bydgoszcz	71	G2
Byers	123	M8
Byfleet	53	G3
Byglandsfjord	63	B7
Bykhov	79	E5
Bykovo *U.S.S.R.*	79	H6
Bykovo *U.S.S.R.*	78	H3
Byla Slatina	73	G4
Bylot Island	120	L3
Byrock	113	K5
Byron, Cape	113	L4
Byron, Isla	139	A9
Byrranga, Gory	84	E2
Byrum	63	D8
Byserovo	78	J4
Byske	62	J4
Byskealven	62	J4
Bystra	71	H4
Bystraya	85	T6
Bystrzyca Klodzka	71	G3
Bytantay	85	N3
Bytca	71	H4
Byten	71	L2
Bytom	71	H3
Bytow	71	G1
Byxelkrok	63	G8

C

Caala	106	C5
Caatingas	137	H5
Caballos Mestenos, Llano de los	127	K6

Caballeria, Cabo	67	J2
Cabanatuan	91	G2
Cabano	125	R3
Cabeza de Buey	66	D3
Cabeza Lagarto, Punta	136	B6
Cabezas	138	D3
Cabimas	136	C1
Cabinda *Angola*	106	B4
Cabinda *Angola*	106	B4
Cabo	137	L5
Cabo Colnet	126	D5
Cabo Gracias a Dios, Punta	132	F7
Cabonga, Reservoir	125	M3
Cabool	124	D8
Caboolture	113	L4
Cabora Bassa Dam	109	F3
Cabo Raso	139	C8
Caborca	126	F5
Cabot Strait	121	P8
Cabourg	64	C4
Cabourne	55	J3
Cabrach	56	E3
Cabra del Santo Cristo	66	E4
Cabrera	67	H3
Cabrera, Sierra	66	C1
Cabriel	67	F3
Cabrobo	137	K5
Cabruta	136	D2
Cacak	72	F4
Caceres *Spain*	66	C3
Caceres *Brazil*	138	E3
Caceres *Colombia*	136	B2
Cache Creek	122	C8
Cache Peak	122	H6
Cachimbo, Serra do	137	G5
Cachimbo, Serra do	137	G5
Cachi, Nevado de	138	C4
Cachoeira	138	K6
Cachoeiro de Itapemirim	138	H4
Cachos, Punta de	138	B5
Cacinci	72	D3
Cacipore, Cabo	137	G3
Cacolo	106	C5
Caconda	106	C5
Cacula	106	B5
Cadadley	103	H6
Cadale	107	J2
Cadaques	67	H1
Cadereyta	128	C8
Cader Idris	52	D2
Cadibarrawirracana, Lake	113	H4
Cadillac *Canada*	123	L3
Cadillac *U.S.A.*	124	H4
Cadi, Sierra del	67	G1
Cadiz	66	C4
Cadiz	91	G3
Cadiz, Baia de	66	C4
Cadiz, Golfo de	66	C4
Caen	64	C4
Caerdydd	52	D3
Caerfyrddin	52	C3
Caergybi	54	E3
Caernarfon	54	E3
Caernarfon Bay	54	E3
Caerphilly	52	D3
Caersws	52	D2
Caetite	137	J6
Cafayate	138	C5
Cagayan	91	G2
Cagayan de Oro	91	G4
Cagayan Islands	91	G4
Cagayan Sulu	91	F4
Cagliari	69	B6
Cagliari, Golfo di	69	B6
Caguan	136	C3
Caguas	133	P5
Cahama	106	B6
Caha Mountains	59	C9
Caherbarnagh	59	D8
Caherciveen	59	B9
Caherconlish	59	F7
Cahir	59	G8
Cahore Point	59	K7
Cahors	65	D6
Caia	109	G3
Caiaponia	138	F3
Caibarien	132	H3
Cai Be	93	L6
Caicos Islands	133	M4
Caicos Passage	133	L3
Cairndow	57	D4
Cairn Gorm	57	E3
Cairngorm Mountains	57	E3
Cairnryan	54	D2
Cairns	113	K2
Cairn Water	57	E5
Cairo *Egypt*	102	F1
Cairo *U.S.A.*	124	F8
Caiundo	106	C6
Caiwarro	113	J4
Cajamarca	136	B5
Cajapio	137	J4
Cajatambo	136	B6
Cajati	138	G4
Cajazeiras	137	K5
Cakiralan	77	F2
Cakirgol Dagi	77	H2
Cal	76	C3
Cal	103	J5
Cala	73	G2
Calabar	105	G5
Calabozo	136	D2
Calafat	73	G4
Calafate	139	B10
Calafell	67	G2

Cascavel *Ceara, Brazil* **137** K4
Cascavel *Parana, Brazil* **138** F4
Caschuil **138** C5
Caserta **69** E5
Casey **141** H5
Cashel **59** G7
Casiguran **91** G2
Casilda **138** D6
Casma **136** B5
Casnewydd **52** E3
Caspe **67** F2
Casper **123** L6
Caspian Sea **51** S7
Cass **124** J5
Cassamba **106** D5
Casse, Grande **65** G6
Cassiar Mountains **118** J3
Cassinga **106** C6
Cassino **69** D5
Cass Lake *U.S.A.* **124** C3
Cass Lake *U.S.A.* **124** C3
Cassongue **106** B5
Casteljaloux **65** D6
Castellammare del Golfo **69** D6
Castellammare, Golfo di **69** D6
Castellane **65** G7
Castellar de Santiago **66** E3
Castellar de Santisteban **66** E3
Castelli **139** E7
Castellnedd **52** D3
Castellon de la Plana **67** F3
Castellote **67** F2
Castelnaudary **65** D7
Castelo Branco **66** C3
Castelsarrasin **65** D6
Casteltermini **69** D7
Castelvetrano **69** D7
Castets **65** C7
Castilla la Nueva **66** E3
Castilla la Vieja **66** D2
Castilletes **136** C1
Castillo, Pampa del **139** C9
Castillos **139** F6
Castlebar **58** D5
Castlebay **57** A4
Castlebellingham **58** K5
Castleblayney **58** J4
Castle Bolton **55** H2
Castle Carrock **55** G2
Castleconnel **59** F7
Castledawson **58** J3
Castlederg **58** G3
Castledermot **59** J7
Castle Douglas **54** F2
Castleellis **59** K8
Castleford **55** H3
Castleisland **59** D8
Castlemaine **113** J6
Castlemartyr **59** F9
Castlepollard **58** H5
Castlerea **58** E5
Castle Rock **123** M8
Castleside **55** H2
Castleton **55** H3
Castletown *Highland, U.K.* **56** E2
Castletown *Isle of Man, U.K.* **54** E2
Castletownbere **59** C9
Castletownshend **59** D9
Castlewellan **58** L4
Castonos **127** M7
Castor **122** J1
Castres **65** E7
Castries **133** S7
Castro **139** B8
Castro Alves **137** K6
Castro del Rio **66** D4
Castropol **66** C1
Castro Urdiales **66** E1
Castro Verde **66** B4
Castrovillari **69** F6
Castuera **66** D3
Caswell Sound **115** A6
Cat **77** J3
Catacamas **132** E7
Catacaos **136** A5
Cataingan **91** G3
Catak **77** K3
Catakkopru **77** J3
Catalca **76** C2
Cataluna **67** G2
Catalzeytin **76** F2
Catamarca **138** C5
Catanduanes **91** G3
Catanduva **138** G4
Catania **69** E7
Catanzaro **69** F6
Cataqueama **136** E6
Catastrophie, Cape **113** H5
Catatumbo **133** L10
Catbalogan **91** G3
Caterham **53** G3
Catete **106** B4
Cathcart **108** E6
Cat Island **133** K2
Cato **111** N6
Catoche, Cabo **131** R7
Catria, Monte **68** D4
Catrimani *Brazil* **136** E3
Catrimani *Brazil* **136** E3
Catskill **125** P5
Catskill Mountains **125** N5
Catwick Islands **93** L6
Cauca **133** K11
Caucaia **137** K4
Caucasia **133** K11
Caucasus **77** L1
Cauit Point **91** H4
Caulkerbush **55** F1
Caungula **106** C4
Cauquenes **139** B7
Caura **133** Q11
Causapscal **125** S2
Caussade **65** D6
Cauterets **65** C7
Cauto **132** J4
Cauvery **92** E6
Cavado **66** B2
Cavaillon **65** F7
Cavalcante **138** H6
Cavally **104** D4
Cavan *Ireland* **58** H5
Cavan *Ireland* **58** H5
Cavdir **76** C4
Cavendish **53** H2
Cavite **91** G3
Caxias **136** C4
Caxias **137** J4
Caxias do Sul **138** E5
Caxito **106** B4
Cay **76** D3
Cayagzi **76** F2
Caycuma **76** E2
Cayeli **77** J2
Cayenne **137** G3
Cayeux **64** D3
Caygoren Baraji **76** C3
Cayiralan **77** F3
Cayirli **77** H3
Caykara **77** J2
Caylarbasi **77** H4
Cayman Brac **132** H5
Cayman Trench **132** F5
Caynabo **103** J6
Cayuga Lake **125** M5
Cazalla de la Sierra **66** D4
Cazma *Yugoslavia* **72** D3
Cazma *Yugoslavia* **72** D3
Cazombo **106** D5
Cazorla **66** E4
Cea **66** D1
Ceahlau **73** H2
Ceanannus Mor **58** J5
Ceara **137** K5
Ceara-Mirim **137** K5
Ceballos **127** K7
Cebollera **66** E1
Cebu *Philippines* **91** G3
Cebu *Philippines* **91** G3
Cecina **68** C4
Cedar **124** D5
Cedar City **126** F2
Cedar Creek Lake **128** D4
Cedar Falls **124** D5
Cedar Lake **119** Q5
Cedar Rapids **124** E6
Cedartown **129** K3
Cedros, Isla de **126** E6
Ceduna **113** G5
Ceelbuur **103** J7
Ceeldheer **103** J7
Ceerigaabo **103** J5
Cefalu **69** E6
Cega **66** D2
Cegled **72** E2
Ceica **73** G2
Cekerek *Turkey* **77** F2
Cekerek *Turkey* **76** F2
Celalli **77** G3
Celano **69** D4
Celaya **131** J7
Celebes **91** G6
Celebi **76** E3
Celestun **131** P7
Celikhan **77** H3
Celina **124** H6
Celje **72** C2
Celle **70** D2
Celtik **76** D3
Celyn, Llyn **52** D2
Cemaes Head **52** C2
Cemilbey **76** F2
Cemisgezek **77** H3
Cendrawasih, Teluk **91** K6
Cenga **91** H6
Cenrana **91** F6
Center **128** E5
Centinela, Picacho Del **127** L6
Cento **68** C3
Central **57** D4
Central African Republic **102** D6
Central Brahui Range **92** C3
Central, Cordillera *Colombia* **136** B3
Central, Cordillera *Dominican Republic* **133** M5
Central, Cordillera *Peru* **136** B5
Central, Cordillera *Philippines* **91** G2
Central Heights **126** G4
Centralia **122** C4
Central Makran Range **92** B3
Central, Massif **65** E6
Central Range **114** C2
Central Siberian Plateau **84** H3
Cephalonia **75** F3
Cepu **90** E7
Ceram **91** H6
Cercal **66** B4
Cerchov **70** E4
Ceres **138** G3
Ceret **65** E7
Cerignola **69** E5
Cerigo **75** G4
Cerkes **76** E2
Cerkeskoy **76** B2
Cermei **73** F2
Cermik **77** H3
Cerna *Romania* **73** G3
Cerna *Romania* **73** K3
Cerne Abbas **52** E4
Cerralvo **128** C7
Cerralvo, Isla **130** E5
Cerreto Sannita **69** E5
Cerro Azul **136** B6
Cerro de Pasco **136** B6
Cerro Machin **131** L9
Cerro Manantiales **139** C10
Cerros Colorados, Embalse **139** C7
Cervaro **69** E5
Cervati, Monte **69** E6
Cervera **67** G2
Cervera de Pisuerga **66** D1
Cervia **68** D3
Cervione **69** B4
Cesar **133** L9
Cesena **68** D3
Cesenatico **68** D3
Cesis **63** L8
Ceske Budejovice **70** F4
Cesky Brod **70** F3
Cesme **76** B3
Cessnock **113** L5
Cetate **73** G3
Cetinje **72** E4
Cetinkaya **77** G3
Cetraro **69** E6
Ceuta **66** D4
Ceva-i-Ra **111** R6
Cevennes **65** F6
Cevherli **76** F4
Cevio **68** B2
Cevizli **76** D4
Ceyhan *Turkey* **76** F4
Ceyhan *Turkey* **77** F4
Ceylanpinar **77** J4
Chaadayevka **79** H5
Chablis **65** E5
Chacabuco **139** D6
Chachani, Nevado de **138** B3
Chachapoyas **136** B5
Chachoengsao **93** K6
Chaco Austral **138** D5
Chaco Boreal **138** E4
Chaco Central **138** D4
Chad **102** C5
Chad *U.S.S.R.* **78** K4
Chadan **84** E6
Chadderton **55** G3
Chaddesley Corbett **53** E2
Chadileovu **139** C7
Chad, Lake **102** B5
Chadobets **84** F5
Chadron **123** N6
Chagai Hills **92** B3
Chagda **85** N5
Chaghcharan **95** S4
Chagny **65** F5
Chagoda **78** F4
Chagos Archipelago **82** F7
Chahah Burjah **95** R6
Chah Bahar **95** Q9
Chahbounia **67** H5
Chaho **88** B5
Chahuites **131** M9
Chaibasa **92** G4
Chai Buri **93** K5
Chaiya **93** J7
Chaiyaphum **93** K5
Chajari **138** E6
Chala **136** C7
Chalais **65** D6
Chalap Dalan **92** B2
Chala, Punta **136** B7
Chalatenango **132** C7
Chaldonka **85** K6
Chale **53** F4
Chaleur, Baie de **121** N8
Chaleur Bay **125** T3
Chalhuanca **136** C6
Chalisgaon **92** E4
Challaco **139** C7
Challacombe **52** D3
Challans **65** C5
Challis **122** G5
Chalmny Varre **78** F2
Chalna **93** G4
Chalon-sur-Marne **64** F4
Chalon-sur-Saone **65** F5
Chalus **65** D6
Chalus **95** K3
Cham **70** E4
Chama **127** J2
Chaman **92** C2
Chamba *India* **92** E2
Chamba *U.S.S.R* **84** G4
Chambal **92** E3
Chamberlain *Australia* **112** F2
Chamberlain *U.S.A.* **123** Q6
Chambersburg **125** M7
Chambery **65** F6
Chamela **130** G8
Chamical **138** C6
Chamonix **65** G6
Chamouchouane **125** P2
Champagne **64** F4
Champagnole **65** F5
Champaign **124** F6
Champflower **52** D3
Champlaine, Lake **125** P4
Champlitte **65** F5
Champoton **131** P8
Chamrajnagar **92** E6
Chamusca **66** B3
Chanaral **138** B5
Chanaran **95** P3
Chanca **66** C4
Chandalar **118** F2
Chandausi **92** E3
Chandeleur Islands **128** H6
Chandigarh **92** E2
Chandler **121** P8
Chandmani *Mongolia* **86** G2
Chandmani *Mongolia* **86** H2
Chandpur **93** H4
Chandrapur **92** E5
Chandvad **92** D4
Chanf **95** Q8
Changan **93** L2
Changane **109** F4
Changbai **88** B5
Changbai Shan **88** B4
Changchun **87** P3
Changde **93** M3
Chang-hua **87** N7
Chang Jiang **87** M5
Chang, Ko **93** K6
Changle **87** M4
Changling **87** N3
Changma **86** H4
Changnyon **87** P4
Changsan-got **87** N4
Changsha **93** M3
Changshan **87** M6
Changtai **87** M7
Changting **87** M6
Changwu **93** L1
Changxing **87** M5
Changyi **87** M4
Changzhi **87** L4
Changzhou **87** M5
Channel Islands **53** M7
Channel-Port-aux-Basques **121** Q8
Chantada **66** C1
Chanthaburi **93** K6
Chantilly **64** E4
Chantonnay **65** C5
Chantrey Inlet **120** G4
Chanute **128** E2
Chany, Ozero **84** B6
Chao **136** B5
Chao Hu **87** M5
Chao Phraya **93** K5
Chaor He **87** N2
Chaouen **100** D1
Chaoyang *China* **87** N3
Chaoyang *China* **87** N3
Chaozhou **87** M7
Chapadinha **137** J4
Chapala, Laguna de **130** H7
Chapanda **85** N5
Chapayevo **79** J5
Chapayevsk **79** H5
Chapayev-Zheday **85** K4
Chapchachi **79** H6
Chapeco **138** F5
Chapel-en-le-Frith **55** H3
Chapel Hill **129** N3
Chapeltown *Grampian, U.K.* **56** E3
Chapeltown *S. Yorkshire, U.K.* **55** H3
Chapleau **124** J3
Chaplygin **79** F5
Chapman **112** F2
Chapman, Cape **120** J4
Chapman Islands **119** P2
Chaqui **138** C3
Chara *U.S.S.R.* **85** K5
Chara *U.S.S.R.* **85** K5
Charagua **138** D3
Charak **95** M8
Charambira, Punta **136** B3
Charcot Island **141** U5
Chard **52** E4
Chardzhou **80** H6
Charente **65** C6
Chari **102** C5
Charikar **92** C1
Chariton *U.S.A.* **124** D6
Chariton *U.S.A.* **124** D6
Charkhari **92** E3
Charlemount **58** J4
Charleroi **64** F3
Charlesbourg **125** Q3
Charles, Cape **125** N8
Charles City **124** D5
Charles Island *Canada* **120** M5
Charles Island *Ecuador* **136** A7
Charleston *Illinois, U.S.A.* **124** F7
Charleston *Missouri, U.S.A.* **124** F8
Charleston *S. Carolina, U.S.A.* **129** N4
Charleston *W. Virginia, U.S.A.* **125** K7
Charlestown **58** E5
Charlestown of Aberlour **56** E3
Charleville **113** K4
Charleville-Mezieres **64** F4
Charlotte **129** M3
Charlotte Amalie **133** Q5
Charlotte, Cape **139** J10
Charlotte Harbour **129** L7
Charlottesville **125** L7
Charlottetown **121** P8
Charlton **113** J6
Charlton Island **121** L7

Congo Basin 99 E6
Conisbrough 55 H3
Coniston 55 F2
Coniston Water 54 E2
Connah's Quay 55 F3
Connaught 58 D5
Conneaut 125 K6
Connecticut *U.S.A.* 125 P6
Connecticut *U.S.A.* 125 P6
Connellsville 125 L6
Conn, Lough 58 D4
Connors Range 113 K3
Conon 56 D3
Conon Bridge 56 D3
Conrad 122 J3
Conselheiro Lafaiete 138 H4
Conselheiro Pena 138 H3
Consett 55 H2
Con Son 93 L7
Constance, Lake 70 C5
Constancia dos Baetas 136 E5
Constanta 73 K3
Constantina 66 D4
Constantine 101 G1
Constantine Bay 52 B4
Constantine, Cape 118 D4
Constantinople 76 C2
Constitucion 139 B7
Contamana 136 C5
Contas 137 J6
Contratacion 136 C2
Contrexeville 64 F4
Contulmo 139 B7
Contwoyto Lake 119 N2
Conway *Arkansas, U.S.A.* 128 F3
Conway *New Hampshire, U.S.A.* 125 Q5
Conway *S. Carolina, U.S.A.* 129 N4
Conway Bay 54 F3
Conwy 54 F3
Coober Pedy 113 G4
Cook 112 G5
Cook, Cape 122 A2
Cookeville 129 K2
Cook Inlet 118 E3
Cook Islands 143 H5
Cook, Mount 115 C5
Cook, Recif de 114 W15
Cookstown 58 J3
Cook Strait 115 E4
Cooktown 113 K2
Coolibah 112 G2
Coolidge 126 G4
Cooma 113 K6
Coomnadiha 59 C9
Coomscarrea 59 B9
Coonamble 113 K5
Coondapoor 92 D6
Coongan 112 D3
Coopers Creek 113 H4
Cooroy 113 L4
Coosa 129 J4
Coos Bay *U.S.A.* 122 B6
Coos Bay *U.S.A.* 122 B6
Cootamundra 113 K5
Cootehill 58 H4
Copacabana 138 C3
Copa, Cerro 138 C4
Cope 123 N8
Copenhagen 63 E9
Copiapo 138 B5
Copinsay 56 F2
Copkoy 76 B2
Copper 118 G3
Copper Center 118 F3
Coppermine *Canada* 119 M2
Coppermine *Canada* 119 N2
Copper Mount 122 F2
Copplestone 52 D4
Copsa Mica 73 H2
Coquet 57 G5
Coquimbo 138 B5
Coquimbo, Bahia de 138 B5
Corabia 73 H4
Coracora 136 C7
Coral Harbour 120 K5
Coral Sea Plateau 113 K2
Corantijn 136 F3
Corbeil-Essonnes 64 E4
Corbiere 53 M7
Corbieres 65 E7
Corbigny 65 E5
Corbin 124 H8
Corbones 66 D4
Corbridge 55 G2
Corby 53 G2
Corby Glen 53 G2
Corcaigh 59 E9
Corcovado, Golfo 139 B8
Corcubion 66 B1
Cordele 129 L5
Cordoba 131 L8
Cordoba *Argentina* 138 D6
Cordoba *Spain* 66 D4
Cordoba, Sierras de 138 D6
Cordova 136 B6
Cordova 118 F3
Corfe 52 D4
Corfu *Greece* 74 E3
Corfu *Greece* 74 E3
Coria 66 C2
Corigliano Calabro 69 F6
Corinda 113 H2
Corinth *Greece* 75 G4
Corinth *U.S.A.* 128 H3
Corinth, Gulf of 75 G3
Corinto *Brazil* 138 H3
Corinto *Nicaragua* 132 D8
Corixa Grande 138 E3
Cork *Ireland* 59 E9
Cork *Ireland* 59 E9
Corlay 64 B4
Corleone 69 D7
Corlu 76 B2
Cornafulla 59 F6
Corner Brook 121 Q8
Cornhill-on-Tweed 57 F4
Corning 125 M5
Corn Islands 132 F8
Cornudilla 66 E1
Cornwall *U.K.* 52 C4
Cornwall *U.K.* 125 N4
Cornwallis Island 120 H2
Cornwall Island 120 H2
Coro 136 D1
Coroata 137 J4
Corocoro 138 C3
Coromandel *Brazil* 138 G3
Coromandel *New Zealand* 115 E2
Coromandel Coast 92 F6
Coromandel Peninsula 115 E2
Corona 127 K3
Coronado, Bahia de 132 E10
Coronation Gulf 119 N2
Coronel 139 B7
Coronel Dorrego 139 D7
Coronel Pringles 139 D7
Coronel Suarez 139 D7
Corovode 75 F2
Corps 65 F6
Corpus Christi 128 D7
Corpus Christi Bay 128 D7
Corpus Christi, Lake 128 D6
Corque 138 C3
Corran 57 C4
Corraun Peninsula 58 C5
Corrib, Lough 59 D6
Corrientes *Argentina* 138 E5
Corrientes *Peru* 136 B4
Corrientes, Cabo *Colombia* 136 B2
Corrientes, Cabo *Cuba* 132 E4
Corrientes, Cabo *Mexico* 130 G7
Corrigan 128 E5
Corrigin 112 D5
Corry 125 L6
Corryvreckan, Gulf of 57 C4
Corse 69 B4
Corse, Cap 68 B4
Corsewall Point 57 C5
Corsica 69 B4
Corsicana 128 D4
Corte 69 B4
Cortegana 66 C4
Cortez 127 H2
Cortina d'Ampezzo 68 D2
Cortland 125 M5
Cortona 68 C4
Corubal 104 C3
Coruche 66 B3
Coruh 77 J2
Corum 76 F2
Corumba 138 E3
Corumba 138 G3
Corunna 66 B1
Corvallis 122 C5
Corve 52 E2
Corwen 52 D2
Cos 75 J4
Cosamaloapan 131 M8
Cosamozza 69 B4
Cosenza 69 F6
Cosiguina, Volcan 132 D8
Cosmoledo Islands 82 C7
Cosne 65 E5
Costa, Cordillera de la 133 N9
Costa Rica 132 E9
Costesti 73 H3
Cotabato 91 G4
Cotacachi 136 B3
Cotagaita 138 C4
Cotahuasi 138 B3
Cotentin 64 C4
Cotiella 67 G1
Cotonou 105 F4
Cotopaxi 136 B4
Cottage Grove 122 C6
Cottbus 70 F3
Cottingham 55 J3
Cottonwood 126 F3
Coubre, Pointe de la 65 C6
Coulommiers 64 E4
Coulonge 125 M3
Council Bluffs 124 C6
Coupar Angus 57 E4
Courantyne 136 F3
Courchevel 65 G6
Couronne, Cap 65 F7
Courtenay 122 B3
Courtmacsherry Bay 59 E9
Coutances 64 C4
Couto Magalhaes 137 H5
Coutras 65 C6
Cove 56 C3
Coventry 53 F2
Covilha 66 C2
Covington *Kentucky, U.S.A.* 124 H7
Covington *Virginia, U.S.A.* 125 L8
Cowall 57 C4
Cowan, Lake 112 E5
Cowbit 53 G2
Cowbridge 52 D3
Cowdenbeath 57 E4
Cowes 53 F4
Cowfold 53 G4
Cowlitz 122 C4
Cowra 113 K5
Coxim 138 F3
Coxs Bazar 93 H4
Coxwold 55 H2
Cozumel 131 R7
Cozumel, Isla de 131 R7
Cracow 71 H3
Cradock 108 E6
Craig 123 L7
Craigavon 58 K4
Craignure 57 C4
Crail 57 F4
Crailsheim 70 D4
Craiova 73 G3
Cramlington 55 H1
Cranborne 53 F4
Cranbrook 122 G3
Crane 127 L5
Cranleigh 53 G3
Cranstown, Kap 120 Q3
Craponne-sur-Arzon 65 E6
Crasna *Romania* 73 G2
Crasna *Romania* 73 J2
Crater Lake 122 C6
Crateus 137 J5
Crati 69 F6
Crato 137 K5
Cravo Norte 136 C2
Crawford 123 N6
Crawford Point 91 F3
Crawfordville 129 K5
Crawley 53 G3
Crazy Mountains 123 J4
Creach Bheinn 57 C4
Creag Meagaidh 57 D3
Creagorry 56 A3
Crediton 52 D4
Cree *Canada* 119 P4
Cree *U.K.* 57 D5
Cree Lake 119 P4
Creeslough 58 G2
Creetown 54 E2
Creggan 58 H3
Creggs 58 F5
Crema 68 B3
Cremona 68 B3
Crepaja 72 F3
Creran, Loch 57 C4
Cres *Yugoslavia* 72 C3
Cres *Yugoslavia* 72 C3
Crescent 122 D6
Crescent City 122 B7
Crest 65 F6
Creston 124 C6
Crestview 129 J5
Crete 75 H5
Cretin, Cape 114 D3
Creus, Cap 67 H1
Creuse 65 D5
Crevillente 67 F3
Crewe 55 G3
Crewkerne 52 E4
Crianlarich 57 D4
Criccieth 52 C2
Criciuma 138 G5
Crick 53 F2
Crickhowell 52 D3
Cricklade 53 F3
Crieff 57 E4
Criffel 55 F2
Crikvenica 72 C3
Crimea 79 E6
Cristalandia 137 H6
Cristalina 138 G3
Cristobal Colon, Pico 136 C1
Crisu Alb 73 F2
Crisu Negru 73 F2
Crisu Repede 73 G2
Crna Reka 73 F5
Crni Drim 72 F5
Croaghgorm Mountains 58 F3
Croagh Patrick 58 C5
Croatia 72 C3
Crocketford 57 E5
Crockett 128 E5
Croggan 57 C4
Crohy Head 58 F3
Croick 56 D3
Croisette, Cap 65 F7
Croke, Mount 112 D5
Croker Island 112 G1
Cromalt Hills 56 C2
Cromar 57 F3
Cromarty 56 D3
Cromarty Firth 56 D3
Cromdale, Hills of 56 E3
Cromer 53 J2
Cromwell 115 B6
Crook 55 H2
Crooked *Canada* 122 D5
Crooked *U.S.A.* 119 L4
Crooked Island 133 K3
Crooked Island Passage 133 K3
Crookham 57 F4
Crookhaven 59 C10
Crookston 124 B3
Croom 59 E7
Crosby *Isle of Man, U.K.* 54 E2
Crosby *Merseyside, U.K.* 55 F3
Crosby *U.S.A.* 124 D3
Cross 105 G4
Crossett 128 G4
Cross Fell 55 G2
Crossgar 58 L4
Cross Hands 52 C3
Crosshaven 59 F9
Cross Lake 119 R5
Crossmaglen 58 J4
Crossmolina 58 D4
Cross Sound 118 H4
Crossville 129 K3
Crotone 69 F6
Crouch 53 H3
Crowborough 53 H3
Crowle 55 J3
Crowley's Ridge 128 G3
Crowsnest Pass 119 N6
Croxton Kerrial 53 G2
Croydon *Australia* 113 J2
Croydon *U.K.* 53 G2
Crozet, Iles 142 C6
Crozier Channel 120 C2
Cruces, Punta 136 B2
Crudgington 52 E2
Crumlin 58 K3
Cruz Alta 138 F5
Cruz, Cabo 132 J5
Cruz del Eje 138 C6
Cruzeiro do Sul 136 C5
Cruz Grande *Chile* 138 B5
Cruz Grande *Mexico* 131 K9
Crymych 52 C3
Crystal City 127 N6
Crystal Falls 124 F3
Csongrad 72 F2
Csorna 72 D2
Cuamba 109 G2
Cuando 106 D6
Cuangar 106 C6
Cuango 106 C4
Cuanza 106 C4
Cuatro Cienegas 127 L7
Cuauhtemoc 127 J6
Cuautla 131 K8
Cuba 132 G4
Cubango 106 C6
Cubara 133 L11
Cubuk 76 E2
Cuchi 106 C5
Cuchilla Grande 138 E6
Cuchivero 136 D2
Cuchumatanes, Alto 132 B7
Cuckfield 53 G3
Cucuta 136 C2
Cuddalore 92 E6
Cuddapah 92 E6
Cudgwa 113 K6
Cue 112 D4
Cuellar 66 D2
Cuenca 136 B4
Cuencame 130 H5
Cuenca, Serrania de 66 E2
Cuernavaca 131 K8
Cuero 128 D6
Cuiaba *Brazil* 138 E3
Cuiaba *Brazil* 138 E3
Cuicatlan 131 L9
Cuilcagh 58 G4
Cuillin Hills 56 B3
Cuillin Sound 57 B3
Cuito 106 C6
Cuito Cuanavale 106 C6
Cuitzeo, Laguna de 131 J8
Cuiuni 136 E4
Cukai 90 C5
Cukurca 77 K4
Cu Lao Hon 93 L6
Culbertson 123 M3
Culebra Peak 127 K2
Culebra, Sierra de la 66 C2
Culiacan 130 F5
Culion 91 F3
Culiseui 137 G6
Culkein 56 C2
Cullera 67 F3
Cullin, Lough 58 D5
Cullman 129 J3
Cullybackey 58 K3
Culm 52 D4
Culmen 77 H4
Culpeper 125 L7
Cults 57 F3
Culverden 115 D5
Culworth 53 F2
Culzean Bay 57 D5
Cumacay 77 K3
Cumali 76 B2
Cumana 136 E1
Cumbal, Nevado de 136 B3
Cumberland *Kentucky, U.S.A.* 124 H8
Cumberland *W. Virginia, U.S.A.* 125 L7
Cumberland Bay 139 J10
Cumberland Mountains 129 K2
Cumberland Peninsula 120 P4
Cumberland Plateau 129 J3
Cumberland Sound 120 N4
Cumbernauld 57 E5
Cumbria 55 G2
Cumbrian Mountains 55 F2
Cumbum 92 E5
Cumina 137 F4
Cummings 122 C8
Cumnock 57 D5

Name	Page	Grid
Delaram	95	R5
Delaware *Ohio, U..S.A.*	124	J6
Delaware *Pennsylvania, U.S.A.*	125	N6
Delaware *U.S.A.*	125	N7
Delaware Bay	125	N7
Delcevo	73	G5
Delemont	68	A2
Delft	64	F2
Delfzijl	64	G2
Delgada, Punta	131	L8
Delgado, Cabo	109	H2
Delgerhaan	87	J2
Delgo	102	F3
Delhi *India*	92	E3
Delhi *India*	92	E3
Delhi *Colorado, U.S.A.*	127	L2
Delhi *New York, U.S.A.*	125	N5
Delice *Turkey*	76	E3
Delice *Turkey*	76	F2
Delicias	127	K6
Delijan	95	K4
Delingha	93	J1
Delitzsch	70	E3
Delle	65	G5
Dellys	101	F1
Delmenhorst	70	C2
Delnice	72	C3
Delray Beach	129	M7
Del Rio	127	M6
Delsbo	63	G6
Delta *Colorado, U.S.A.*	127	H1
Delta *Utah, U.S.A.*	126	F1
Delta Junction	118	F3
Delvin	58	H5
Dema	78	J5
Demanda, Sierra de la	66	E1
Demba	106	D4
Dembi Dolo	103	F6
Demer	64	F3
Demerara	136	F2
Deming	127	J4
Demini	136	E3
Demirci	76	C3
Demir Kazik	76	F4
Demirkoy	76	B2
Demmin	70	E2
Demnate	100	D2
Demopolis	129	J4
Dempo, Gunung	90	C6
Demyanskoye	84	Ae5
Denakil	103	H5
Denan	103	H6
Denau	86	B4
Denbigh	55	F3
Denbigh, Cape	118	C3
Denby Dale	55	H3
Dendang	90	D6
Dendermonde	64	F3
Dendi	103	G6
Denezhkino	84	D3
Dengkou	87	K3
Dengqen	93	J2
Den Haag	64	F2
Den Helder	64	F2
Denia	67	G3
Deniliquin	113	K6
Denio	122	E7
Denison *Iowa, U.S.A.*	124	C6
Denison *Texas, U.S.A.*	128	D4
Denison, Mount	118	E4
Denizli	76	C4
Denmark	63	B9
Denmark Strait	116	S2
Dennis Head	56	F1
Denny	57	E4
Denpasar	90	F7
Densongi	91	G6
Denta	73	F3
Denton	128	D4
D'Entrecasteaux Islands	114	E3
D'Entrecasteaux, Point	112	D5
Denver	123	M8
Deogarh	92	F4
Deoghar	92	G4
Deolali	92	D5
Deosai, Plains of	92	E2
Dep	85	M6
Deqen	93	J3
Deqing	93	M4
De Queen	128	E3
Dera Bugti	92	C3
Dera Ghazikhan	92	D2
Dera Ismail Khan	92	D2
Derajat	92	D2
Derazhno	71	M3
Derazhnya	73	J1
Derbent	79	H7
Derby *Australia*	112	E2
Derby *U.K.*	53	F2
Derbyshire	55	H3
Derekoy	76	B2
Dereli	77	H2
Derg	58	G3
Dergachi	79	F5
Derg, Lough *Donegal, Ireland*	58	G3
Derg, Lough *Tipperary, Ireland*	59	F7
De Ridder	128	F5
Derik	77	J4
Derinkuyu	76	F3
Derna	101	K2
Derong	93	J3
Derravaragh, Lough	58	H5
Derry	58	H2
Derrynasaggart Mountains	59	D9
Derryveagh Mountains	58	F2
Derudeb	103	G4
Derveni	75	G3
Derventa	72	D3
Derwent *Australia*	113	K7
Derwent *Derbyshire, U.K.*	55	H3
Derwent *N. Yorkshire, U.K.*	55	J3
Derwent Reservoir	55	H2
Derwent Water	54	E2
Derzhavinsk	84	Ae6
Desaguadero *Argentina*	138	C6
Desaguadero *Bolivia*	138	C3
Descanso	126	D4
Deschambault Lake	119	Q5
Deschutes	122	D5
Dese	103	G5
Deseado	139	C9
Desemboque	126	F5
Desengano, Punta	139	C9
Desert Center	126	E4
Desert Peak	122	H7
Des Moines *U.S.A.*	124	D6
Des Moines *U.S.A.*	124	D6
Desna	79	E5
Desolacion, Isla	139	B10
Des Plaines	124	G5
Dessau	70	E3
Destna	71	G3
Dete	108	E3
Detmold	70	C3
Detour, Point	124	G4
Detroit	124	J5
Detroit Lakes	124	C4
Deutschlandsberg	68	E2
Deva	73	G3
Devakottai	92	E7
Devdevdyak	84	H4
Devecikonagi	76	C3
Devecser	72	D2
Devegedcidi Baraji	77	H3
Develi	76	F3
Deventer	64	G2
Deveron	56	F3
Devils	127	M5
Devil's Bridge	52	D2
Devils Lake	123	Q3
Devils Paw	118	J4
Devils Tower	123	M5
Devin	73	H5
Devizes	53	F3
Devli	92	E3
Devnya	73	J4
Devoll	75	F2
Devon	52	D4
Devon Island	120	J2
Devonport	115	E2
Devrek	76	D2
Devrekani	76	E2
Devrez	76	E2
Devyatkova	84	Ae5
Dewangiri	93	H3
Dewas	92	E4
De Witt	128	G3
Dewsbury	55	H3
Dey-Dey, Lake	112	G4
Deyhuk	95	N5
Deylaman	95	J3
Deyong, Tanjung	114	B3
Deyyer	95	K8
Dez	94	J5
Dezful	94	J5
Dezhneva, Mys	118	B2
Dezhou	87	M4
Dhaka	93	G4
Dhamar	96	G9
Dhampur	92	E3
Dhamtari	92	F4
Dhanbad	92	G4
Dhandhuka	92	D4
Dhang Range	92	F3
Dhankuta	93	G3
Dhar	92	E4
Dharmapuri	92	E6
Dharmavaram	92	E6
Dharmjaygarh	92	F4
Dharwad	92	D5
Dhaulagiri	92	F3
Dhaulpur	92	E3
Dhenkanal	92	G4
Dhenousa	75	H4
Dhermatas, Akra	75	G3
Dhermi	74	E2
Dheskati	75	F3
Dhespotiko	75	H4
Dhialvos Zakinthou	75	F4
Dhidhimotikhon	75	J2
Dhikti Ori	75	H5
Dhirfis	75	G3
Dhodhekanisos	75	J4
Dhomokos	75	G3
Dhoraji	92	D4
Dhoxaton	75	H2
Dhrangadhra	92	D4
Dhrepanon, Akra	75	G3
Dhuburi	93	G3
Dhule	92	D4
Dia	75	H5
Diamante	138	D6
Diamantina *Australia*	113	H4
Diamantina *Brazil*	138	H3
Diamantina, Chapada	137	J6
Diamond Lake Junction	122	D6
Diaoling	88	B3
Diavata	75	G2
Diba al Hisn	97	N4
Dibaya	106	D4
Dibdibah, Ad	96	H2
Dibrugarh	93	H3
Dickinson	123	N4
Dickson	129	J2
Dicle	77	J4
Didcot	53	F3
Didinga Hills	103	F7
Didnovarre	62	K1
Didwana	92	D3
Die	65	F6
Diebougou	104	E3
Diefenbaker, Lake	123	L2
Diego-Suarez	109	J2
Dielette	53	N6
Dien Bien Phu	93	K4
Diepholz	70	C2
Dieppe	64	D4
Dietfurt	70	D4
Diffa	101	H6
Digby	121	N9
Digges Island	120	L5
Digne	65	G6
Digoin	65	F5
Digor	77	K2
Digul	114	C3
Diinsoor	107	H2
Dijlah, Nahr	77	K5
Dijon	65	F5
Dikakah, Ad	97	K7
Dikanas	62	G4
Dikbiyik	77	G2
Dikili	76	B3
Dikson	84	C2
Dikwa	105	H3
Dili	91	H7
Di Linh	93	L6
Dilizhan	77	L2
Dillia	101	H5
Dilling	102	E5
Dillingen	70	D4
Dillingham	118	D4
Dillon	122	H5
Dilolo	106	D5
Dimapur	93	H3
Dimashq	77	G6
Dimbelenge	106	D4
Dimbokro	104	E4
Dimbo vita	73	H3
Dimitrovgrad *Bulgaria*	73	H4
Dimitrovgrad *U.S.S.R.*	78	H5
Dimona	94	B6
Dimovo	73	G4
Dinagat	91	H3
Dinajpur	93	G3
Dinan	64	B4
Dinanagar	92	E2
Dinant	64	F3
Dinar	76	D3
Dinara Planina	72	D3
Dinard	64	B4
Dinas Head	52	C2
Dinbych	55	F3
Dinbych-y-pysgod	52	C3
Dinder	96	B10
Dindigul	92	E6
Dinek	76	E4
Dinggye	93	G3
Dingle	59	B8
Dingle Bay	59	B8
Dingle Peninsula	59	B8
Dinguiraye	104	C3
Dingwall	56	D3
Dingxi	93	K1
Dingxin	86	H3
Dingxing	87	M4
Dinh Lap	93	L4
Dinnington	55	H3
Dinosaur	123	K7
Dionard	56	D2
Diorbivol	104	C2
Diouloulou	104	B3
Diourbel	104	B3
Dipolog	91	G4
Dir	92	D1
Direction, Cape	113	J1
Dire Dawa	103	H6
Direkli	77	G3
Dirk Hartogs Island	112	C4
Dirra	102	E5
Dirranbandi	113	K4
Disappointment, Cape	122	B4
Disappointment, Lake	112	E3
Discovery Bay	113	J6
Dishna *Egypt*	103	F2
Dishna *U.S.A.*	118	D3
Disko	120	R4
Disko Bay	120	R4
Disna *U.S.S.R.*	63	M9
Disna *U.S.S.R.*	63	N9
Dispur	93	H3
Diss	53	J2
Dissen	96	E8
Distrito Federal	138	G3
Ditchling Beacon	53	G4
Ditinn	104	C3
Dittaino	69	E7
Ditton Priors	52	E2
Diu	92	D4
Divandarreh	94	H4
Divinopolis	138	G4
Divi Point	92	F5
Divisor, Serra do	136	C5
Divnoye	79	G6
Divrigi	77	H3
Dixcove	104	E5
Dixon Entrance	118	J5
Diyadin	77	K3
Diyala	94	G4
Diyarbakir	77	J4
Diza	77	L3
Dja	105	H5
Djado	101	H4
Djambala	106	B3
Djanet	101	G4
Djelfa	101	F2
Djema	102	E6
Djenne	100	E6
Djibouti	103	H5
Djibouti	103	H5
Djolu	106	D2
Djougou	105	F4
Djourab	102	C4
Djupivogur	62	X12
Djurdjura	67	J4
Djursland	63	D8
Dmitriya Lapteva, Proliv	85	Q2
Dmitrov	78	F4
Dnepr	79	E6
Dneprodzerzhinsk	79	E6
Dnepropetrovsk	79	F6
Dneprovskaya Nizmennost	79	D5
Dneprovsko-Bugskiy Kanal	71	L2
Dnestr	73	K2
Dnestrovskiy Liman	73	L2
Dno	78	E4
Doaktown	125	T3
Doba	102	C6
Dobbiaco	68	D2
Dobeln	70	E3
Dobiegniew	70	F2
Dobo	114	A3
Doboj	72	E3
Dobra	71	H3
Dobre Miasto	71	J2
Dobric	73	J4
Dobrodzien	71	H3
Dobrogea	73	K3
Dobrovolsk	71	K1
Dobrush	79	E5
Dobryanka	78	K4
Dobsina	71	J4
Dobson	115	C5
Dochart	57	D4
Docking	53	H2
Dodecanese	75	J4
Dodge City	127	M2
Dodman Point	52	C4
Dodoma	107	G4
Doetinchem	64	G3
Dofa	91	H6
Dogai Coring	93	G2
Doganbey	76	D4
Doganhisar	76	D3
Dogankent	76	F4
Dogansehir	77	G3
Doganyol	77	H3
Doganyurt	76	E2
Dog Creek	122	C2
Dogen Co	93	H2
Dog Lake	124	F2
Dogo	89	D7
Dogondoutchi	101	F6
Dogubeyazit	77	L3
Dogukardeniz Daglari	77	J2
Doha	97	K4
Doi Luang	93	K5
Dojran	73	G5
Dojransko Jezero	73	G5
Doka *Indonesia*	114	A3
Doka *Sudan*	96	B10
Dokkum	64	G2
Dokshitsy	63	M9
Dokurcun	76	D2
Dolak	114	B3
Dolak, Tanjung	91	K7
Dolanog	52	D2
Dolbeau	125	P2
Dol-de-Bretagne	64	C4
Dole	65	F5
Dolgellau	52	D2
Dolginovo	71	M1
Dolgiy, Ostrov	84	Ac3
Dolgoye	71	K4
Dolina	79	C6
Dolinsk	88	J2
Dolinskaya	79	E6
Dollar	57	E4
Dollar Law	57	E5
Dolni Kralovice	70	F4
Dolok, Tanjung	114	A3
Dolomitiche, Alpi	68	C2
Dolo Odo	103	H7
Dolores *Argentina*	139	E7
Dolores *Uruguay*	139	E6
Dolores *U.S.A.*	122	K8
Dolphin and Union Strait	119	N1
Dolphin, Cape	139	E10
Dolsk	71	G3
Domanic	76	C3
Dombas	63	C5
Dombe	109	F3
Dombe Grande	106	B5
Dombovar	72	E2
Dombrad	73	F1
Dome, Puy de	65	E6
Domett	115	D5
Domfront	64	C4
Dominica	133	S7

Dominical 132 F10
Dominican Republic 133 M5
Dominion, Cape 120 M4
Domo 103 J6
Domodossola 68 B2
Domuya, Cerro 139 B7
Don *Grampian, U.K.* 56 F3
Don *S. Yorkshire, U.K.* 55 H3
Don *U.S.S.R.* 79 G6
Donaghadee 58 L3
Donaldsville 128 G5
Donau 68 E1
Donauworth 70 D4
Don Benito 66 D3
Doncaster 55 H3
Dondo 106 B4
Dondra Head 92 F7
Donegal *Ireland* 58 F3
Donegal *Ireland* 58 G3
Donegal Bay 58 F3
Donegal Point 59 C7
Donenbay 86 D2
Doneraile 59 E8
Donetsk 79 F6
Dongan *Heilongjiang, China* 88 E2
Dongan *Hunan, China* 93 M3
Dongara 112 C4
Dongbolhai Shan 93 G2
Dongchuan 93 K3
Dongfang 93 L5
Dongfanghong 88 D2
Donggala 91 F6
Dong Hoi 93 L5
Dongjingcheng 88 B3
Dongliu 87 M5
Dongluk 86 F4
Dongning 88 C3
Dongola 102 F4
Dongping 87 M4
Dongshan 87 N5
Dongsheng 87 K4
Dongtai 87 N5
Donguena 106 B6
Dong Ujimqin Qi 87 M2
Dongxi Lian Dao 87 M5
Donington 53 G2
Doniphan 124 E8
Donji Vakuf 72 D3
Donna 62 E3
Donner Pass 122 D8
Donnington 52 E2
Dooagh 58 B5
Doon 57 D5
Doonbeg 59 C7
Doonerak, Mount 118 E2
Doon, Loch 57 D5
Doorin Point 58 F3
Dor 95 R6
Dorada, Costa 67 G2
Dora, Lake 112 E3
Dora Riparia 68 A3
Dorbiljin 86 E2
Dorchester 52 E4
Dorchester, Cape 120 L4
Dordogne 65 C6
Dordrecht 64 F3
Dore 65 E6
Dore Lake 119 P5
Dore, Mont 65 E6
Dorgali 69 B5
Dori 104 E3
Dorking 53 G3
Dormo, Ras 96 F10
Dornbirn 68 B2
Dornie 56 C3
Dornoch 56 D3
Dornoch Firth 56 D3
Dorofeyevskaya 84 C2
Dorohoi 73 J2
Dorotea 62 G4
Dorovitsa 78 H4
Dorset 52 E4
Dortdivan 76 E2
Dortmund 70 B3
Dortyol 77 G4
Doruokha 84 J2
Dorutay 77 L3
Dosatuy 85 K7
Dosso 101 F6
Dossor 79 J6
Dothan 129 K5
Douai 64 E3
Douala 105 G5
Douarnenez 64 A4
Double Mountain Fork 127 M4
Doubs 65 F5
Doubtful Sound 115 A6
Doubtless Bay 115 D1
Doue-la-Fontaine 65 C5
Douentza 100 E5
Douglas *South Africa* 108 D5
Douglas *Isle of Man, U.K.* 54 D2
Douglas *Strathclyde, U.K.* 57 E5
Douglas *Arizona, U.S.A.* 127 H5
Douglas *Georgia, U.S.A.* 129 L5
Douglas *Wyoming, U.S.A.* 123 M6
Doullens 64 E3
Doulus Head 59 B9
Doume 105 H5
Doune 57 D4
Dourada, Serra 137 H6
Dourados *Brazil* 138 E3
Dourados *Brazil* 138 F4
Dourados, Serra dos 138 F4
Douro 66 B2

Dove 55 H3
Dove Dale 55 H3
Dover *U.K.* 53 J3
Dover *Delaware, U.S.A.* 125 N7
Dover *New Hampshire, U.S.A.* 125 Q5
Dover *Ohio, U.S.A.* 125 K6
Dover-Foxcroft 125 R4
Dover, Strait of 53 J4
Dovrefjell 62 C5
Dowa 107 F5
Dowlatabad *Afghanistan* 95 R5
Dowlatabad *Afghanistan* 95 S3
Dowlatabad *Iran* 95 N7
Dowlat Yar 92 C2
Down 58 L4
Downham Market 53 H2
Downpatrick 58 L4
Downpatrick Head 58 D4
Downs, The 53 J3
Downton 53 F4
Dow Rud 94 J5
Dowshi 92 C1
Dozen 89 D7
Draa, Oued 100 D3
Drac 65 F6
Dracevo 73 F5
Drachten 64 G2
Dragalina 73 J3
Dragasani 73 H3
Dragoman 73 G4
Dragonera, Isla 67 H3
Dragon's Mouth 133 S9
Dragsfjard 63 K6
Draguignan 65 G7
Dra, Hamada du 100 D3
Drake 123 P4
Drakensberg 108 E6
Drake Passage 141 V7
Drama 75 H2
Drammen 63 H7
Drangedal 63 C7
Draperstown 58 J3
Dras 92 E2
Drau 68 E2
Drava 72 E3
Dravograd 72 C2
Drawa 70 F2
Drawsko, Jezioro 71 G2
Drayton Valley 119 N5
Dren 73 G4
Drenewydd 52 D2
Dresden 70 E3
Dresvyanka 78 K2
Dreux 64 D4
Drin 75 F2
Drina 72 E3
Drin i zi 74 E1
Drobak 63 H7
Drobin 71 H2
Drogheda 58 K5
Drogichin 71 L2
Drogobych 79 C6
Drohiczyn 71 K2
Droichead Atha 58 K5
Droichead Nua 59 J6
Droitwich 53 E2
Drokiya 73 J1
Drome 65 F6
Dromedary, Cape 113 L6
Dromore 58 K4
Dronfield 55 H3
Dronne 65 D6
Dronning Maud Land 141 Z5
Dropt 65 D6
Drovyanaya 84 A2
Drumcollogher 59 E8
Drumheller 122 H2
Drummond 122 H4
Drummond Islands 124 J3
Drummond Range 113 K3
Drummondville 125 P4
Drummore 54 E2
Drumochter, Pass of 57 D4
Drumshanbo 58 F4
Druridge Bay 55 H1
Druskininkai 71 K1
Druzhba *Kazakstan S.S.R., U.S.S.R.* 86 E2
Druzhba *Rossiyskaya, S.F.S.R., U.S.S.R.* 71 J1
Druzhina 85 R3
Drvar 72 D3
Drweca 71 H2
Dry 112 G2
Dry Bay *Canada* 121 N6
Dry Bay *U.S.A.* 118 H4
Dryden 124 D2
Drysdale, River 112 F2
Dschang 105 H4
Duab 94 J4
Dualo 91 G6
Duarte, Pico 133 M5
Duba 96 B3
Dubai 97 M4
Dubawnt Lake 119 Q3
Dubayy 97 M4
Dubbagh, Jamal Ad 96 B3
Dubbo 113 K5
Dubenskiy 79 K5
Dublin *Ireland* 59 K6
Dublin *Ireland* 59 K6
Dublin *U.S.A.* 129 L4
Dublin Bay 59 K6
Dubna 78 F4
Dubno 79 D5

Du Bois 125 L6
Dubois *Idaho, U.S.A.* 122 H5
Dubois *Wyoming, U.S.A.* 123 K6
Dubossary 79 D6
Dubreka 104 C4
Dubrovitsa 71 M3
Dubrovka *U.S.S.R.* 79 E5
Dubrovka *U.S.S.R.* 79 G6
Dubrovnik 72 E4
Dubrovskoye 84 J5
Dubuque 124 E5
Duchang 87 M6
Duchesne *U.S.A.* 123 J7
Duchesne *U.S.A.* 123 J7
Duchess 113 H3
Ducie Island 143 J5
Duck 129 J3
Ducklington 53 F3
Duck Mountain 119 Q5
Duddington 53 G2
Dudinka 84 D3
Dudley 53 E2
Duenas 66 D2
Duero 66 D2
Duffield 53 F2
Duff Islands 114 N6
Dufftown 56 E3
Dufton 55 G2
Duga Zapadnaya, Mys 85 R5
Dughaill, Loch 56 C3
Dugi Otok 72 C3
Duisburg 70 B3
Dukambiya 96 C9
Dukat 73 G4
Duk Fadiat 102 F6
Duk Faiwil 102 F6
Dukhan 97 K4
Duki Bolen 85 P6
Dukla 71 J4
Dukou 93 K3
Dulan 93 J1
Duldurga 85 J6
Duleek 58 K5
Dulga-Kyuyel 84 J4
Dulgalakh 85 N3
Dullingham 53 H2
Dull Lake 118 C3
Dulnain 56 E3
Dulovo 73 J4
Duluth 124 D3
Duma 77 G6
Dumaguete 91 G4
Dumai 90 C5
Dumaran 91 F3
Dumas *Arkansas, U.S.A.* 128 G4
Dumas *Texas, U.S.A.* 127 M3
Dumbarton 57 D5
Dumbea 114 X17
Dumbier 71 H4
Dumfries 55 F1
Dumfries and Galloway 57 E5
Dumitresti 73 J3
Dumka 93 G4
Dumlu 77 J2
Dumlupinar 76 C3
Dumoine 125 M3
Dumont d'Urville 141 K5
Dumont d'Urville Sea 141 J6
Dumyat 103 F1
Duna 72 E2
Dunaj 71 H5
Dunajec 71 J3
Dunany Point 58 K5
Dunarea 73 J3
Dunaujvaros 72 E2
Dunav 73 H4
Dunay *Moldavia S.S.R., U.S.S.R.* 73 K3
Dunay *Rossiyskaya, S.F.S.R., U.S.S.R.* 88 D4
Dunayevtsy 73 J1
Dunay, Ostrov 85 L2
Dunbar *Australia* 113 J2
Dunbar *U.K.* 57 F4
Dunblane 57 E4
Dunboyne 59 K6
Duncan *Canada* 122 C3
Duncan *U.S.A.* 128 D3
Duncan Passage 93 H6
Duncansby Head 56 E2
Dunchurch 53 F2
Dundaga 63 K8
Dundalk *Ireland* 58 K4
Dundalk *U.S.A.* 125 M7
Dundalk Bay 58 K5
Dundas 120 M2
Dundas, Lake 112 E5
Dundas Peninsula 120 D3
Dundas Strait 112 G1
Dun Dealgan 58 K4
Dundee *South Africa* 108 F5
Dundee *U.K.* 57 F4
Dundonald 57 D5
Dundonnell 56 C3
Dundrennan 54 F2
Dundrod 58 K3
Dundrum 58 L4
Dundrum Bay 58 L4
Dundwa Range 92 F3
Dunecht 57 F3
Dunedin *New Zealand* 115 C6
Dunedin *U.S.A.* 129 L6
Dunfanaghy 58 G2
Dunfermline 57 E4
Dungannon 58 J3

Dungarpur 92 D4
Dungarvan 59 G8
Dungarvan Harbour 59 G8
Dungeness 53 H4
Dungiven 58 J3
Dungloe 58 F3
Dungu 107 E2
Dungun 90 C5
Dunholme 55 J3
Dunhua 88 B4
Dunhuang 86 F3
Dunkeld 113 J6
Dunkerque 64 E3
Dunkirk 125 L5
Dunkur 103 G5
Dunkwa 104 E4
Dun Laoghaire 59 K6
Dunlavin 59 J6
Dunleer 58 K5
Dunmanus Bay 59 C9
Dunmanway 59 D9
Dunmore Town 132 J2
Dunmurry 58 K3
Dunnet Bay 56 E2
Dunnet Head 56 E2
Dunoon 57 D5
Dunragit 54 E2
Duns 57 F4
Dunseith 123 P3
Dunsford 52 D4
Dunstable 53 G3
Dunstan Mountains 115 B6
Dunster 52 D3
Duntelchaig, Loch 56 D3
Duntroon 115 C6
Dunvegan 56 B3
Dunvegan Head 56 B3
Dupang Ling 93 M3
Dupree 123 P5
Duque de York, Isla 139 A10
Du Quoin 124 F7
Duragan 76 F2
Durance 65 F7
Durand, Recif 114 Y17
Durango *Mexico* 130 G5
Durango *U.S.A.* 127 J2
Durankulak 73 K4
Durant 128 D3
Durazno 138 E6
Durazzo 74 E2
Durban 108 F6
Durcal 66 E4
Durdevac 72 D2
Durelj 87 J4
Duren 70 B3
Durg 92 F4
Durgapur *Bangladesh* 93 H3
Durgapur *India* 93 G4
Durham *U.K.* 55 H2
Durham *U.K.* 55 H2
Durham *U.S.A.* 129 N2
Durisdeer 57 E5
Durma 96 H4
Durmitor 72 E4
Durness 56 D2
Durness, Kyle of 56 D2
Durres 74 E2
Dursey Head 59 B9
Dursey Island 59 B9
Dursley 52 E3
Dursunbey 76 C3
D'Urville Island 115 D4
Dury Voe 56 B1
Dushak 95 Q3
Dushan 93 L3
Dushanbe 86 B4
Dushanzi 86 G4
Duskotna 73 J4
Dusseldorf 70 B3
Dutch Harbor 118 Ae9
Dutovo 78 K3
Duvan 78 K4
Duyun 93 L3
Duzce 76 D2
Duzkoy 77 H2
Dvinskaya Guba 78 F3
Dvorets 84 F5
Dwarka 92 C4
Dyadino 84 H5
Dyatkovo 79 E5
Dyatlovo 71 L2
Dybvad 63 D8
Dyce 56 F3
Dyer, Cape 120 P4
Dyersburg 128 H2
Dyfed 52 C3
Dyfi 52 D2
Dyje 71 G4
Dykh Tau 79 G7
Dynow 71 K4
Dyrnesvagen 62 B5
Dyulino 73 J4
Dzamin Uud 87 L3
Dzaoudzi 109 J2
Dzavhan Gol 86 G2
Dzaygil Hid 86 H2
Dzerzhinsk *Belorussiya S.S.R., U.S.S.R.* 78 D5
Dzerzhinsk *Rossiyskaya S.F.S.R., U.S.S.R.* 78 G4
Dzhalal-Abad 86 C3
Dzhalinda 85 L6
Dzhambeyty 79 J5
Dzhambul *U.S.S.R.* 86 C2
Dzhambul *U.S.S.R.* 86 C3

Dzhambul *U.S.S.R.*	79	J6
Dzhamm	85	N2
Dzhankoy	79	E6
Dzhebel *Bulgaria*	73	H5
Dzhebel *U.S.S.R.*	95	M2
Dzhelinde	84	J2
Dzhezkazgan	80	H5
Dzhirgatal	86	C4
Dzhizak	86	B3
Dzhugdzhur, Khrebet	85	P5
Dzhulfa	94	G2
Dzhungarskiy Alatau, Khrebet	86	E2
Dzhurin	79	D6
Dzhusaly	86	A2
Dzialdowo	71	J2
Dzialoszyn	71	H3
Dzilam de Bravo	131	Q7
Dzungarian Basin	86	F2
Dzuunbayan	87	L3
Dzuunbulag	87	M2

E

Eagle *Newfoundland, Canada*	121	Q7
Eagle *Yukon, Canada*	118	H2
Eagle *U.S.A.*	118	G3
Eagle Lake *Canada*	124	D2
Eagle Lake *U.S.A.*	122	D7
Eagle, Mount	59	B8
Eagle Pass	127	M6
Eagle Point	114	D4
Eaglesham	57	D5
Eagles Hill	59	B9
Eaglestone Reef	111	S4
Ealing	53	G3
Earby	55	G3
Earlsferry	57	F4
Earl Shilton	53	F2
Earlston	57	F4
Earl Stonham	53	J2
Earn	57	E4
Earn, Loch	57	D4
Earp	126	E3
Easingwold	55	H2
East Anglian Heights	53	H2
Eastbourne	53	H4
East Brent	52	E3
East Bridgford	53	G2
East Cape	115	G2
East China Sea	87	P6
East Cleddau	52	C3
East Dean	53	H4
East Dereham	53	H2
Easter Island	143	K5
Eastern Ghats	92	E6
Eastern Ross	56	D3
East Falkland	139	E10
East Germany	70	E3
East Grinstead	53	G3
East Haddon	53	F2
East Hoathly	53	H4
East Ilsley	53	F3
East Indies	142	E5
East Kilbride	57	D5
East Lake Tarbert	56	B3
Eastleigh	53	F4
East Linton	57	F4
East Loch Roag	56	B2
East London	108	E6
Eastmain *Canada*	121	L7
Eastmain *Canada*	121	M7
Eastmain-Opinaca, Reservoir	121	L7
Eastman	129	L4
East Midlands Airport	53	F2
East Millnocket	125	R4
Eastoft	55	J3
Easton *U.K.*	52	E4
Easton *U.S.A.*	125	N6
East Point *Prince Edward Island, Canada*	121	P8
East Point *Quebec, Canada*	121	P8
Eastport	125	S4
East Retford	55	J3
Eastry	53	J3
East Saint Louis	124	E7
East Siberian Sea	85	T2
East Sussex	53	H3
East Tavaputs Plateau	123	K8
Eastville	55	K3
East Wittering	53	G4
Eastwood	55	H3
Eatonton	129	L4
Eau Claire	124	E4
Ebbw Vale	52	D3
Ebe-Basa	85	M4
Ebebiyin	105	H5
Ebeltoft	63	D8
Eber Golu	76	D3
Ebersberg	70	D4
Eberswalde	70	E2
Ebinur Hu	86	E3
Eboli	69	E5
Ebolowa	105	H5
Ebrach	70	D4
Ebro	66	G2
Ecclefechan	57	E5
Eccles	55	G3
Eccleshall	52	E2
Eccleston	55	G3
Eceabat	76	B2
Ech Cheliff	100	F1
Echeng	93	M2
Echigo-sammyaku	89	G7
Echo Bay *Ontario, Canada*	124	H3

Echo Bay *NW. Territories, Canada*	119	M2
Echternach	64	G4
Echuca	113	J6
Ecija	66	D4
Eckernforde	70	C1
Eclipse Sound	120	L3
Ecmiadzin	77	L2
Ecuador	136	B4
Ed	103	H5
Ed	63	H7
Edah Wagga	112	D4
Edam	64	F2
Eday	56	F1
Ed Damazin	103	F5
Ed Damer	96	A8
Ed Debba	102	F4
Ed-Deffa	102	E1
Edderton	56	D3
Eddrachillis Bay	56	C2
Ed Dueim	103	F5
Ede *Netherlands*	64	F2
Ede *Nigeria*	105	F4
Edea	105	H5
Edehon Lake	119	R3
Edel Land	112	C4
Eden *Australia*	113	K6
Eden *Cumbria, U.K.*	55	G2
Eden *Kent, U.K.*	53	H3
Eden *U.S.A.*	123	K6
Edenderry	59	H6
Edgecumbe	115	F2
Edgeley	123	Q4
Edgell Island	121	P5
Edgemont	123	N6
Edgeoya	80	D2
Edgeworthstown	58	G5
Edhessa	75	G2
Edievale	115	B6
Edinburg	128	D7
Edinburgh	57	E5
Edirne	76	B2
Edisto	129	M4
Edith River	112	G1
Edjeleh	101	G3
Edland	63	B7
Edmond	128	D3
Edmonds	122	C4
Edmonton	119	N5
Edmunston	125	R3
Edolo	68	C2
Edremit	76	B3
Edremit Korfezi	76	B3
Edson	119	M5
Edward, Lake	107	E3
Edwardson, Cape	115	B7
Edwards Plateau	127	M5
Edzhen	85	P4
Eeklo	64	E3
Eel	122	B7
Efate	114	U12
Eferding	68	E1
Eflani	76	E2
Efyrnwy, Llyn	52	D2
Ega	63	D8
Egadi, Isole	69	D7
Egersund	63	B7
Egerton, Mount	112	D3
Eggan	105	G4
Egg Lagoon	113	J6
Egglescliffe	55	H2
Eggum	62	E2
Egham	53	G3
Eghol	114	H6
Egilsstadir	62	X12
Egiyn Gol	86	J1
Eglinton	58	H2
Eglinton Island	120	C2
Egmount, Mount	115	E3
Egremont	55	F2
Egridir	76	D4
Egridir Golu	76	D3
Egvekinot	85	Y3
Egypt	102	E2
Ehingen	70	C4
Eibar	66	E1
Eidem	62	D4
Eidfjord	63	B6
Eidi	62	Z14
Eidsvold	113	L4
Eidsvoll	63	D6
Eifel	70	B3
Eigg	57	C4
Eigg, Sound of	57	B4
Eight Degree Channel	92	D7
Eighty Mile Beach	112	E2
Eilerts de Haan Geb	137	F3
Eil, Loch	57	C4
Eilsleben	70	D2
Einbeck	70	C3
Eindhoven	64	F3
Eiriksjokull	62	U12
Eirunepe	136	D5
Eisenach	70	D3
Eisenhuttenstadt	70	F2
Eisenkappel	68	E2
Eishort, Lake	57	C3
Eisleben	70	D3
Eitorf	70	B3
Ejea de los Caballeros	67	F1
Ejido Insurgentes	130	D5
Ejin Horo Qi	87	K4
Ejin Qi	86	J3
Ejutla	131	L9
Ekenas	63	K6

Eket	105	G5
Eketahuna	115	E4
Ekhinadhes	75	F3
Ekhinos	75	H2
Ekibastuz	84	B6
Ekimchan	85	N6
Ekonda	84	G3
Eksjo	63	F8
Ekwan	121	K7
El Affroun	67	H4
Elafonisos	75	G4
El Araiche	100	D1
El Arco	126	F7
El Arish	103	F1
Elasson	75	G3
Elat	94	B7
Elazig	77	H3
El Azraq	94	C6
El Bahri, Borg	67	H4
Elba, Isole d	69	C4
El Balyana	103	F2
Elban	85	P6
El Banco	136	C2
El Barco de Avila	66	D2
El Barco de Valdeorras	66	C1
Elbasan	74	F2
El Bayadh	100	F2
Elbe	70	C2
Elbert, Mount	123	L8
Elberton	129	L3
Elbeuf	64	D4
Elbeyli	77	G4
Elbing	71	H1
Elbistan	77	G3
Elblag	71	H1
Elbrus	79	G7
El Burgo de Osma	66	E2
El Cajon	126	D4
El Callao	136	E2
El Campo	128	D6
El Carmen *Bolivia*	138	E3
El Carmen *Bolivia*	136	E6
El Centro	126	E4
El Cerro	138	D3
El Chaparro	136	D2
Elche	67	F3
Elche de la Sierra	67	F3
Eldikan	85	P4
Eldivan	76	E2
El Djazair	101	F1
El Djouf	100	D4
Eldon	124	D7
El Dorado *Arkansas, U.S.A.*	128	F4
El Dorado *Kansas, U.S.A.*	128	D2
El Dorado *Venezuela*	133	S11
Eldoret	107	G2
Elektrostal	78	F4
Elephant Butte Reservoir	127	J4
Elephant Island	141	W6
Eleskirt	77	K3
El Eulma	101	G1
Eleuthera	132	J2
Elevsis	75	G3
El Faiyum	102	F2
El Fasher	102	E5
El Fashn	102	F2
El Ferrol	66	B1
El Fuerte	127	H7
Elgepiggen	63	D5
El Geteina	103	F5
Elgin *U.K.*	56	E3
Elgin *Illinois, U.S.A.*	124	F5
Elgin *N. Dakota, U.S.A.*	123	P4
El Giza	102	F1
Elgol	57	B3
El Golea	101	F2
El Golfo de Santa Clara	126	E5
Elgon, Mont	107	F2
El Hawata	96	B10
El Hodna, Chott	67	J5
El Homra	102	F5
El Hosh	103	F5
El Huecu	139	B7
Elikon	75	G3
Elisabethville	107	E5
Eliseu Martins	137	J5
Elista	79	G6
Elizabeth *Australia*	113	H5
Elizabeth *U.S.A.*	125	N6
Elizabeth City	129	P2
Elizabeth Reef	113	M4
Elizabethton	129	L2
Elizabethtown	124	H8
Elizondo	67	F1
El Jadida	100	D2
El Jafr	94	C6
El Jebelein	103	F5
El Jerid, Chott	101	G2
Elk	122	G3
Elk	71	K2
El Kala	69	B7
El Kamlin	103	F5
Elk City	128	C3
El Khalil	94	B6
El Kharga	102	F2
Elkhart	124	H6
El Khartum	103	F4
Elkhorn	123	Q6
Elkhotovo	79	G7
Elkhovo	73	J4
Elkin	129	M2
Elkins	125	L7
Elko	122	G7
El Koran	103	H6
El Korima, Oued	100	E2

El Lagowa	102	E5
Elland	55	H3
Ellef Ringnes Island	120	F2
Ellen	55	F2
Ellendale *Australia*	112	E2
Ellendale *U.S.A.*	123	Q5
Ellen, Mount	122	J8
Ellensburg	122	D4
Ellesmere	52	E2
Ellesmere Island	120	K2
Ellesmere, Lake	115	D5
Ellesmere Port	55	G3
Ellice	119	Q2
Ellington	114	R8
Elliot	108	E6
Elliot Lake	124	J3
Elliot, Mount	113	K2
Elliston	113	H5
El Llano	132	H10
Ellon	56	F3
Ellsworth	125	R4
Ellsworth Land	141	U4
Ellwangen	70	D4
Elmadag	76	E3
Elma Dagi	76	E3
El Mahalla El Kubra	102	F1
Elmali	76	C4
El Manaqil	103	F5
El Mansura	102	F1
El Mesellemiya	103	F5
El Milk	102	E4
El Minya	102	F2
Elmira	125	M5
Elmore	113	J6
Elmshorn	70	C2
El Muglad	102	E5
El Nido	91	F3
El Obeid	102	F5
El Odaiya	102	E5
Elorza	136	D2
El Oued	101	G2
Eloy	126	G4
El Palmito	127	K8
El Pardo	66	E2
El Paso *Illinois, U.S.A.*	124	F6
El Paso *Texas, U.S.A.*	127	J5
Elphin	56	C2
El Porvenir	127	K5
El Potosi	128	B8
El Progreso	132	D7
El Puente del Arzobispo	66	D3
El Qahira	102	F1
El Qasr	102	E2
El Qunaytirah	94	B5
El Real	132	J10
El Reno	128	D3
El Ronquillo	66	C4
El Rosario	126	E5
El Sahuaro	126	F5
El Salado	139	C9
El Salto	130	G6
El Salvador	132	C8
El Sam'an de Apure	133	N11
El Sauzal	126	D5
Elsham	55	J3
El Socorro	126	F5
Elster	70	E3
Elsterwerda	70	E3
El Sueco	127	J6
El Suweis	103	F2
El Tambo	136	B4
Eltham	115	E3
El Thamad	96	B2
El Tigre	133	Q10
El Tih	96	A2
Eltisley	53	G2
El Tocuyo	133	N10
Elton *U.K.*	53	G2
Elton *U.S.S.R*	79	H6
El Tule	131	L9
El Tur	96	A2
Eluru	92	F5
Elvanfoot	57	E5
Elvas	66	C3
Elveden	53	H2
Elverum	63	D6
El Viejo	133	L11
El Vigia	136	C2
Elwy	55	F3
Ely *Cambridgeshire, U.K.*	53	H2
Ely *Mid Glamorgan, U.K.*	52	D3
Ely *Minnesota, U.S.A.*	124	E3
Ely *Nevada, U.S.A.*	126	E1
Elze	70	C2
Ema	63	M7
Emae	114	U12
Emamrud	95	M3
Emam Taqi	95	P4
Eman	63	G8
Emao	114	U12
Emba	79	K6
Embarcacion	138	D4
Embleton	55	H1
Embona	75	J4
Embrun	65	G6
Embu	107	G3
Emden	70	B2
Emerald	113	K3
Emerald Island	120	D2
Emerson	123	R3
Emet	76	C3
Emeti	114	C3
Emi	84	F6
Emigrant Pass	122	F7
Emin	86	E2

Faranah 104 C3
Farasan, Jazair 96 E8
Farcau 71 L5
Fareham 53 F4
Farewell, Cape 115 D4
Farewell Spit 115 D4
Far Falls 123 T2
Fargo 123 R4
Faridpur 93 G4
Farigh, Wadi al 101 K2
Farila 63 F6
Fariman 95 P4
Faringdon 53 F3
Farjestaden 63 G8
Farmington *Maine, U.S.A.* 125 Q4
Farmington *Missouri, U.S.A.* 124 E8
Farmington *New Mexico, U.S.A.* 127 H2
Farnborough 53 G3
Farnham 53 G3
Farnworth 55 G3
Faro 63 H8
Faro *Brazil* 137 F4
Faro *Portugal* 66 C4
Farosund 63 H8
Farquhar Islands 82 D8
Farrai 75 F3
Farranfore 59 C8
Farrar 56 D3
Farrashband 95 L7
Farsala 75 G3
Farsi 95 R5
Farsund 63 B7
Fartak, Ra's 97 L9
Farvel, Kap 116 Q3
Fasa 95 L7
Fasad 97 L7
Fasano 69 F5
Faske Bugt 70 E1
Fastov 79 D5
Fatehabad 92 E3
Fatehgarh 92 E3
Fatehpur *Rajasthan, India* 92 D3
Fatehpur *Uttar Pradesh, India* 92 F3
Fatezh 79 F5
Fatick 104 B3
Fatima 66 B3
Fatmomakke 62 F4
Fatsa 77 G2
Fatuna 111 T4
Faurei 73 J3
Fauro Vaghena 114 H5
Fausing 63 D8
Fauske 62 F3
Faux Cap 109 J5
Faversham 53 H3
Fawley 53 F4
Fawr, Fforest 52 D3
Faxafloi 62 T12
Faxalven 62 G5
Faya-Largeau 102 C4
Fayetteville *Arkansas, U.S.A.* 128 E2
Fayetteville *N. Carolina, U.S.A.* 129 N3
Fayetteville *Tennessee, U.S.A.* 129 J3
Faylaka 97 J2
Fazilka 92 D2
Fderik 100 C4
Feale 59 D8
Fear, Cape 129 P4
Feather 122 D8
Featherston 115 E4
Fecamp 64 D4
Fedorovka 84 Ad6
Fedulki 84 Ae4
Feeagh, Lough 58 C5
Fegu 87 L4
Fehmarn 70 D1
Fehmer Boelt 70 D1
Feijo 136 C5
Feilding 115 E4
Feira de Santana 137 K6
Feistritz 68 E2
Fei Xian 87 M4
Feke 77 F4
Feklistova, Ostrov 85 P5
Felahiye 77 F3
Felanitx 67 H3
Feldbach 68 E2
Feldberg 68 A2
Feldkirch 68 B2
Feldkirchen 68 E2
Felipe Carillo Puerto 131 Q8
Felix, Cape 120 G4
Felixstowe 53 J3
Felling 55 H2
Feltre 68 C2
Femer Balt 63 D9
Femund 63 D5
Fener Burun 77 H2
Fengcheng 87 M6
Fengdu 93 L3
Fenggang 93 L3
Fengjie 93 L2
Fengning 87 M3
Fengshan 93 L4
Fengtai 93 N2
Fengxian 93 N3
Fengzhen 87 L3
Fen He 87 L4
Feni Island 114 E2
Fenoarivo Atsinanana 109 J3
Fens, The 53 H2
Fenxi 87 L4
Fenyang 87 L4
Fenyi 93 M3
Feodosiya 79 F6
Feolin Ferry 57 B5
Ferbane 59 G6
Ferdows 95 P4
Fergana 86 B3
Fergus Falls 124 B3
Fergusson Island 114 E3
Ferkessedougou 104 D4
Fermanagh 58 G4
Fermo 68 D4
Fermoy 59 F8
Fernandina Beach 129 M5
Fernandina, Isla 136 A7
Fernando de Noronha, Isla 48 E5
Ferness 56 E3
Fernie 122 G3
Ferns 59 K7
Ferrai 75 J2
Ferrans 59 J6
Ferrara 68 C3
Ferrat, Cap 67 F5
Ferreira do Alentejo 66 B3
Ferrenafe 136 B5
Ferriday 128 G5
Ferrol, Peninsula de 136 B5
Ferto 68 F2
Fes 100 D2
Fessenden 123 Q4
Fetesti 73 J3
Fethaland, Point of 56 A1
Fethiye 76 C4
Fethiye Korfezi 76 C4
Fetisovo 79 J7
Fetlar 56 B1
Fetsund 63 D7
Fetzara El Hadjar 69 A7
Feurs 65 F6
Fevralskoye 85 N6
Feyzabad 92 D1
Ffestiniog 52 D2
Fianarantsoa 109 J4
Fiandberg 62 G4
Fichtel-gebirge 70 D3
Ficksburg 108 E5
Fidenza 68 C3
Fier 74 E2
Fife Ness 57 F4
Figeac 65 E6
Figline Valdarno 68 C4
Figueira da Foz 66 B2
Figueira de Castelo Rodrigo 66 C2
Figueres 67 H1
Figuig 100 E2
Figuiro dos Vinhos 66 B3
Fiji 114 Q8
Filadelfia 138 D4
Filby 53 J2
Filchner Ice Shelf 141 X3
Filey 55 J2
Filey Bay 55 J2
Filiasi 73 G3
Filiatra 75 F4
Filipow 71 K1
Filipstad 63 F7
Fillmore *California, U.S.A.* 126 C3
Fillmore *Utah, U.S.A.* 126 F1
Fimi 106 C3
Finale Emilia 68 C3
Final, Punta 126 E6
Findhorn 56 E3
Findik 77 G3
Findikli 77 J2
Findikpinari 76 F4
Findlay 124 J6
Fingoe 109 F3
Finike 76 D4
Finisterre, Cabo 66 B1
Finke *Australia* 113 G4
Finke *Australia* 113 H4
Finland 63 L6
Finland, Gulf of 63 L7
Finnmark 62 L1
Finnmarksvidda 62 K2
Finnsnes 62 M2
Finschhafen 114 D3
Finsteraarhorn 68 B2
Finstown 56 E1
Fintona 58 H4
Fionn Loch 56 C3
Fionnphort 57 B4
Firat 77 H3
Firedrake Lake 119 Q3
Firenze 68 C4
Firle Beacon 53 H4
Firozabad 92 E3
Firozpur 92 D2
Firsovo 88 J2
Firuzabad 95 L7
Firuzkuh 95 L4
Fish 108 C4
Fisher, Cape 120 K5
Fishguard 52 C3
Fismes 64 E4
Fitchburg 125 Q5
Fitful Head 56 A2
Fitsitika 109 H4
Fitzgerald 129 L5
Fitz Roy 139 C9
Fitzroy 112 F2
Fitz Roy, Cerro 139 B9
Fitzroy Crossing 112 F2
Fitzwilliam Strait 120 C2
Fiuggi 69 D5
Fiume 72 C3
Fiumicino 69 D5
Fivemiletown 58 H4
Fizi 107 E3
Fjallasen 62 J3
Fladdabister 56 A2
Flagstaff 126 G3
Flakatrask 62 H4
Flamborough 55 J2
Flamborough Head 55 J2
Flaming 70 E3
Flaming Gorge Reservoir 123 K7
Flamingo 129 M8
Flash 55 H3
Flasjon 62 F4
Flathead 122 G3
Flathead Lake 122 G4
Flathead Range 122 G3
Flattery, Cape 122 B3
Fleet 53 G3
Fleetwood 55 F3
Flekkefjord 63 B7
Flen 63 G7
Flensburg 70 C1
Flers 64 C4
Flesberg 63 C7
Fleurance 65 D7
Flims 68 B2
Flinders Island 113 K6
Flinders Reefs 113 K2
Flin Flon 119 Q5
Flint *U.K.* 55 F3
Flint *Georgia, U.S.A.* 129 K5
Flint *Michigan, U.S.A.* 124 J5
Flintham 53 G2
Flisa 63 E6
Flix 67 G2
Fliyos 76 E2
Floka 75 F4
Florac 65 E6
Florence *Italy* 68 C4
Florence *Alabama, U.S.A.* 129 J3
Florence *Arizona, U.S.A.* 126 G4
Florence *Colorado, U.S.A.* 127 K1
Florence *Oregon, U.S.A.* 122 B6
Florence *S. Carolina, U.S.A.* 129 N3
Florencia 136 B3
Florentino Ameghino, Embalse 139 C8
Flores *Brazil* 137 J5
Flores *Guatemala* 132 C6
Flores *Indonesia* 91 G7
Floreshty 79 D6
Flores, Laut 91 F7
Floresta 137 K5
Floriano 137 J5
Florianopolis 138 G5
Florida *Uruguay* 139 E6
Florida *U.S.A.* 129 L6
Florida Islands 114 K6
Florida Keys 129 M8
Florida, Straits of 129 N8
Floridia 69 E7
Florina 75 F2
Floro 63 A6
Flotta 56 E2
Flumen 67 F2
Fly 114 C3
Foca 76 B3
Foca 72 E4
Fochabers 56 E3
Focsani 73 J3
Foggia 69 E5
Fogi 91 H6
Fogo 104 L7
Fogo Island 121 R8
Fohr 70 C1
Foinaven 56 D2
Foix 65 D7
Folda 62 F3
Folegandros 75 H4
Foligno 69 D4
Folkestone 53 J3
Folkingham 53 G2
Folkston 129 L5
Follonica 69 C4
Foltesti 73 K3
Fond-du-Lac *Canada* 119 Q4
Fond du Lac *U.S.A.* 124 F5
Fonni 69 B5
Fonsagrada 66 C1
Fonseca, Golfo de 132 D8
Fontainebleau 64 E4
Fonte Boa 136 D4
Fonte do Pau-d'Agua 136 F6
Fontenay-le-Comte 65 C5
Font-Romeu 65 E7
Fontur 62 X11
Fonualei 111 U5
Fonyod 72 D2
Foraker, Mount 118 E3
Forbes 113 K5
Forcados 105 G4
Forcalquier 65 F7
Forde 63 A6
Fordham 53 H2
Fordon 71 H2
Ford Ranges 141 Q3
Fordyce 128 F4
Forecariah 104 C4
Foreland Point 52 D3
Forel, Mount 116 R2
Forest *Canada* 124 K5
Forest *U.S.A.* 128 H4
Forestier Peninsula 113 K7
Forest Park 129 K4
Forestville 125 R2
Forez, Monts du 65 E6
Forfar 57 F4
Forgandenny 57 E4
Fork 123 K5
Forks 122 B4
Forli 68 D3
Formartin 56 F3
Formby 55 F3
Formby Point 55 F3
Formentera 67 G3
Formentor, Cabo de 67 H3
Formia 69 D5
Formiga 138 G4
Formosa 87 N7
Formosa *Argentina* 138 E5
Formosa *Brazil* 138 G3
Formosa do Rio Preto 137 H6
Foroyar 62 Z14
Forres 56 E3
Forrest 112 F5
Forrest City 128 G3
Forsayth 113 J2
Forsnas 62 H3
Forsnes 62 C5
Forssa 63 K6
Forsyth *Missouri, U.S.A.* 124 D8
Forsyth *Montana, U.S.A.* 123 L4
Fort Albany 121 K7
Fortaleza *Bolivia* 136 D5
Fortaleza *Brazil* 137 K4
Fort Archambault 102 C6
Fort Beaufort 108 E6
Fort Benton 123 J4
Fort Bragg 122 C8
Fort Charlet 101 G4
Fort Chipewyan 119 N4
Fort Collins 123 M7
Fort Coulonge 125 M4
Fort-Dauphin 109 J5
Fort-de-France 133 S7
Fort de Polignac 101 G3
Fort Dodge 124 C5
Fortescue 112 D3
Fort Flatters 101 G3
Fort Foureau 105 J3
Fort Frances 124 D2
Fort Franklin 118 L2
Fort Good Hope 118 K2
Forth 57 D4
Fort Hall 107 G3
Fort Hancock 127 K5
Forth, Firth of 57 F4
Fortin Carlos Antonio Lopez 138 E4
Fortin General Mendoza 138 D4
Fortin Gral Eugenio Garay 138 D4
Fortin Infante Rivarola 138 D4
Fortin Juan de Zalazar 138 E4
Fortin Madrejon 138 E4
Fortin Ravelo 138 D3
Fort Jameson 107 F3
Fort Kent 125 R3
Fort Lamy 102 C5
Fort Lauderdale 129 M7
Fort Liard 118 L3
Fort Macleod 122 H3
Fort McMurray 119 N4
Fort McPherson 118 J2
Fort Madison 124 E6
Fort Manning 107 F5
Fort Morgan 123 N7
Fort Myers 129 M7
Fort Nelson 119 L4
Fort Norman 118 K3
Fortore 69 E5
Fort Payne 129 K3
Fort Peck 123 L3
Fort Peck Dam 123 L4
Fort Peck Reservoir 123 L4
Fort Pierce 129 M7
Fort Portal 107 F2
Fort Providence 119 M3
Fort Qu'Appelle 123 N2
Fort Randall 118 Af8
Fort Resolution 119 N3
Fortrose 56 D3
Fort Rosebery 107 E5
Fort Saint James 118 L5
Fort Saint John 119 L4
Fort Scott 124 C8
Fort Severn 120 J6
Fort Shevchenko 79 J7
Fort Simpson 119 L3
Fort Smith *Canada* 119 N3
Fort Smith *U.S.A.* 128 E4
Fort Soufflay 106 B2
Fort Stockton 127 L5
Fort Sumner 127 K3
Fort Trinquet 100 D1
Fortuna 122 B7
Fortune Bay 121 Q8
Fort Valley 129 L4
Fort Vermilion 119 M4
Fort Victoria 108 F4
Fort Walton Beach 129 J5
Fort Wayne 124 H6
Fort William 57 C4
Fort Worth 128 D4
Fort Yukon 118 F2
Forur 95 M8
Foshan 93 M4
Fosheim Peninsula 120 K2
Fosna 62 D5
Fossombrone 68 D4
Fossvellir 62 X12
Foster 113 K6

Golmarmara 76 B3
Golmud 93 H1
Golo 69 B4
Golova 76 D4
Golovanevsk 73 L1
Golovnino 88 K4
Golpayegan 95 K5
Golpazari 76 D2
Goma 107 E3
Gombe 105 H3
Gombi 105 H3
Gomel 79 E5
Gomera 100 B3
Gomez Palacio 127 L8
Gomishan 95 M3
Gonaives 133 L5
Gonam *U.S.S.R.* 85 M5
Gonam *U.S.S.R.* 85 N5
Gonave, Golfe de la 133 L5
Gonave, Ile de la 133 L5
Gonbad-e Kavus 95 M3
Gonda 92 F3
Gondal 92 D4
Gonder 103 G5
Gondia 92 F4
Gonen *Turkey* 76 B2
Gonen *Turkey* 76 B3
Gongbogyamda 93 H3
Gongolo 105 H3
Gongpoquan 86 H3
Goniadz 71 K2
Gonumillo 139 C8
Gonzales *California, U.S.A.* 126 B2
Gonzales *Texas, U.S.A.* 128 D6
Gonzales Chaves 139 D7
Goob Weyn 107 H3
Goodenough, Cape 141 J5
Goodenough Island 114 E3
Good Hope, Cape of 108 C6
Gooding 122 G6
Goodland 123 P8
Goole 55 J3
Goolgowi 113 K5
Goomen 113 L4
Goondiwindi 113 L4
Goose Bay 121 P7
Goose Creek 129 M4
Goose Lake 122 D7
Goplo, Jezioro 71 H2
Goppingen 70 C4
Gora Kalwaria 71 J3
Gorakhpur 92 F3
Gorazde 72 E4
Gorda, Punta 138 B3
Gordes 76 C3
Gordonsville 125 L7
Gore 115 B7
Gore 103 G6
Gorele 77 H2
Goresbridge 59 J7
Gorey *Ireland* 59 K7
Gorey *U.K.* 53 M7
Gorgan 95 M3
Gorgan, Rud-e 95 M3
Gorgona, Isola di 68 B4
Gorgoram 105 H3
Gori 77 L1
Gorice 75 F2
Gorinchem 64 F3
Goris 94 H2
Gorizia 68 D3
Gorka 78 H3
Gorkha 92 F3
Gorki *Belorussiya S.S.R., U.S.S.R.* 78 E5
Gorki *Rossiyskaya S.F.S.R., U.S.S.R.* 84 Ae3
Gorki *Rossiyskaya S.F.S.R., U.S.S.R.* 78 H4
Gorkiy 78 G4
Gorkovskoye Vodokhranilishche 78 G4
Gorlev 63 D9
Gorlice 71 J4
Gorlitz 70 F3
Gorlovka 79 F6
Gornji Milanovac 72 F3
Gornji Vakuf 72 D4
Gorno-Altaysk 84 D6
Gornozavodsk 88 H2
Gornyak 84 C6
Gornyy *U.S.S.R.* 79 H5
Gornyy *U.S.S.R.* 85 P6
Gorodenka 73 H1
Gorodets 78 G4
Gorodok 71 K4
Gorodovikovsk 79 G6
Goroka 114 D3
Gorokhov 71 L3
Gorong, Kepulauan 91 J6
Gorongoza 109 F3
Gorontalo 91 G5
Goroshikha 84 D3
Gorran Haven 52 C4
Gorseinon 52 C3
Gort 59 E6
Gortaclare 58 H3
Gortahork 58 F2
Gorumna Island 59 C6
Goryn 79 D5
Gorzow Wielkopolski 70 F2
Goschen Strait 114 E4
Gosforth 55 H1
Goshogawara 88 H5
Gospic 72 C3
Gosport 53 F4
Gostivar 73 F5
Gota 62 Z14
Gota Kanal 63 G7
Gotaland 63 E8
Goteborg 63 H8
Goteborg Och Bohus 63 D7
Gotene 63 E7
Gotha 70 D3
Gothenburg 63 D8
Gotland 63 H8
Goto-retto 89 B9
Gotse Delchev 73 G5
Gotska Sandon 63 H7
Gotsu 89 D8
Gottingen 70 C3
Gottwaldov 71 G4
Gouda 64 F2
Goudhurst 53 H3
Gough Island 48 F6
Gouin, Reservoir 125 N2
Goulais 124 J3
Goulburn 113 K5
Goulburn Islands 113 G1
Goundam 100 E5
Gourdon 65 D6
Goure 101 H6
Gourma-Rharous 100 E5
Gournay 64 D4
Gourock 57 D5
Govena, Mys 85 V5
Goverla 71 L4
Governador Valadares 138 H3
Governor's Harbour 132 J2
Govind Pant Sagar 92 F4
Govorovo 85 M2
Gowanbridge 115 D4
Gowanda 125 L5
Gower 52 C3
Gowna, Lough 58 G5
Goya 138 E5
Goynucek 77 F2
Goynuk *Turkey* 76 D2
Goynuk *Turkey* 77 J3
Goz Beida 102 D5
Gozne 76 F4
Gozo 74 C4
Goz Regeb 96 B8
Graaff Reinet 108 D6
Gracac 72 C3
Gradaus, Serra dos 137 G5
Grado *Italy* 68 D3
Grado *Spain* 66 C1
Gradoli 69 C4
Gradsko 73 F5
Grafham Water 53 G2
Grafton *Australia* 113 L4
Grafton *N. Dakota, U.S.A.* 123 R3
Grafton *W. Virginia, U.S.A.* 125 K7
Grafton, Islas 139 B10
Graham 128 C4
Graham Island *British Columbia, Canada* 118 J5
Graham Island *NW. Territories, Canada* 120 H2
Graham Land 141 V5
Grahamstown 108 E6
Graie, Alpi 68 A3
Graiguenamanagh 59 J7
Grain 53 H3
Grajau 137 H4
Grajewo 71 K2
Grampian 56 E3
Grampian Mountains 57 D4
Grampound 52 C4
Gramsh 75 F2
Gran 137 F3
Granada *Nicaragua* 132 E9
Granada *Spain* 66 E4
Granard 58 H5
Gran Bajo 139 C9
Granby *Canada* 125 P4
Granby *U.S.A.* 123 L7
Gran Canaria 100 B3
Gran Chaco 138 D4
Grand *Canada* 125 K5
Grand *Michigan, U.S.A.* 124 H5
Grand *Missouri, U.S.A.* 124 C6
Grand *S. Dakota, U.S.A.* 123 P5
Grand Bahama 132 H1
Grand Bois, Coteau de 124 C3
Grand Canal *China* 87 M5
Grand Canal *Ireland* 59 H6
Grand Canyon *U.S.A.* 126 F2
Grand Canyon *U.S.A.* 126 F2
Grand Cayman 132 G5
Grand Coulee 122 E4
Grand Coulee Dam 122 E4
Grande *Brazil* 138 G4
Grande *Mexico* 131 L9
Grande *Nicaragua* 132 E8
Grande, Bahia 139 C10
Grande Cache 119 M5
Grande, Cienaga 133 K10
Grande Comore 109 H2
Grande Miquelon 121 Q8
Grande O'Guapay 138 D3
Grande Prairie 119 M4
Grande, Punta 137 G3
Grande, Rio 127 M6
Grande Ronde 122 F5
Gran Desierto 126 E5
Grandes Rocques 53 M7
Grand Falls *New Brunswick, Canada* 125 S3
Grand Falls *Newfoundland, Canada* 121 Q8
Grand Forks 123 R4
Grand Island 123 Q7
Grand Isle 128 H6
Grand Junction 127 H1
Grand Lahou 104 E4
Grand Lake *New Brunswick, Canada* 128 G6
Grand Lake *Newfoundland, Canada* 121 Q8
Grand Lake *U.S.A.* 125 S3
Grand Lake O' the Cherokees 128 E2
Grand-Lieu, Lac de 65 C5
Grand Manan Island 125 S4
Grand Marais *Michigan, U.S.A.* 124 H3
Grand Marais *Minnesota, U.S.A.* 124 E3
Grand-Mere 125 P3
Grandola 66 B3
Grand Popo 105 F4
Grand Prairie 128 D4
Grand Rapids *Canada* 119 R5
Grand Rapids *Michigan, U.S.A.* 124 H5
Grand Rapids *Minnesota, U.S.A.* 124 D3
Grandrieu 65 E6
Grand Saint Bernard, Col du 68 A3
Grand Santi 137 G3
Graney, Lough 59 E7
Grangemouth 57 E4
Grange-over-Sands 55 G2
Grangesberg 63 F6
Grangeville 122 F5
Granite Peak 123 K5
Granitola, Capo 69 D7
Granna 63 F7
Granollers 67 H2
Gran Pajonal 136 C6
Gran Paradiso 68 A3
Grantham 53 G2
Grant Island 141 R4
Grant, Mount 122 E8
Grantown-on-Spey 56 E3
Grants 127 J3
Grantshouse 57 F4
Grants Pass 122 C6
Granville 64 C4
Granville Lake 119 Q4
Grasby 55 J3
Gras, Lac de 119 N3
Grasmere 55 F2
Graso 63 H6
Grasse 65 G7
Grassrange 123 K4
Grass Valley 122 D8
Grassy 113 J7
Grassy Knob 125 K7
Gratens 65 D7
Graus 67 G1
Gravatai 138 F5
Gravdal 62 E2
Gravelines 64 E3
Grave, Pointe de 65 C6
Gravesend 53 H3
Gravois, Pointe-a- 133 L5
Gray 65 F5
Grayling 124 H4
Grays 53 H3
Grays Harbor 122 B4
Graz 68 E2
Great Abaco 132 J1
Great Artesian Basin 113 J4
Great Astrolabe Reef 114 R9
Great Australian Bight 112 F5
Great Ayton 55 H2
Great Baddow 53 H3
Great Bahama Bank 132 H2
Great Bardfield 53 H3
Great Barrier Island 115 E2
Great Barrier Reef 113 K2
Great Basin 122 F7
Great Bear Lake 119 L2
Great Bend 127 N1
Great Blasket Island 59 A8
Great Budworth 55 G3
Great Cumbrae 57 D5
Great Dividing Range 113 K3
Great Driffield 55 J2
Great Dunmow 53 H3
Greater Antarctica 141 D2
Greater Antilles 132 G4
Greater Khingan Range 87 N2
Greater London 53 G3
Greater Manchester 55 G3
Great Exuma Island 132 K3
Great Falls 122 J4
Great Fish 108 E6
Great Gable 55 F2
Great Guana Cay 132 J2
Great Harwood 55 G3
Great Inagua 133 L4
Great Indian Desert 92 D3
Great Island 59 F9
Great Karas Berg 108 C5
Great Karoo 108 D6
Great Lakes 143 L3
Great Longton 55 H2
Great Malvern 52 E2
Great Mercury Island 115 E2
Great Nicobar 93 H7
Great North East Channel 114 C3
Great Ormes Head 54 F3
Great Ouse 53 H2
Great Papuan Plateau 114 C3
Great Plains 123 J2
Great Ruaha 107 G4
Great Sacandaga Lake 125 N5
Great Salt Lake 122 H7
Great Salt Lake Desert 122 H7
Great Sand Hills 123 K2
Great Sandy Desert 112 E3
Great Sankey 55 G3
Great Sea Reef 114 R8
Great Sitkin Island 118 Ac9
Great Slave Lake 119 N2
Great Smeaton 55 H2
Great Stour 53 J3
Great Sugar Loaf 59 K6
Great Torrington 52 C4
Great Victoria Desert 112 F4
Great Wall of China, The 87 L4
Great Whernside 55 H2
Great Witley 52 E2
Great Yarmouth 53 J2
Great Yeldham 53 H2
Great Zab 94 F3
Gredos, Sierra de 66 D2
Greece 75 F3
Greeley 123 M7
Greely Fjord 120 K1
Green *Kentucky, U.S.A.* 124 G8
Green *Wyoming, U.S.A.* 123 J6
Green Bay *U.S.A.* 124 G4
Green Bay *U.S.A.* 124 G4
Green Bell, Ostrov 80 H1
Greenbrier 125 K8
Greencastle 58 K4
Greeneville 129 L2
Greenfield 125 P5
Green Hammerton 55 H2
Greenhead 55 G2
Green Island 115 C6
Greenisland 58 L3
Green Islands 114 E2
Greenland 116 Q1
Greenlaw 57 F4
Greenlough 112 D4
Greenlowther 57 D5
Green Mountains 125 P5
Greenock 57 D5
Green River *Papua New Guinea* 114 C2
Green River *Utah, U.S.A.* 127 G1
Green River *Wyoming, U.S.A.* 123 K7
Greensboro 129 N2
Greensburg 125 L6
Greenstone Point 56 C3
Green Valley 126 G5
Greenville *Liberia* 104 D4
Greenville *Alabama, U.S.A.* 129 J5
Greenville *Mississippi, U.S.A.* 128 G4
Greenville *N. Carolina, U.S.A.* 129 P3
Greenville *S. Carolina, U.S.A.* 129 L3
Greenville *Texas, U.S.A.* 128 D4
Greenwood *Mississippi, U.S.A.* 128 G4
Greenwood *S. Carolina, U.S.A.* 129 L3
Greers Ferry Lake 128 F3
Gregorio 136 C5
Gregory, Lake 113 H4
Gregory Range 113 J2
Greian Head 57 A3
Greifswald 70 E1
Grein 68 E1
Greipstad 62 H2
Greiz 70 E3
Gremikha 78 F2
Gremyachinsk 78 K4
Grena 63 D8
Grenada 133 S8
Grenada *U.S.A.* 128 H4
Grenadines, The 133 S8
Grenen 63 D8
Grenfell 123 N2
Grenivik 62 V12
Grenoble 65 F6
Grenville, Cape 113 J1
Gresford 55 G3
Gresham 122 C5
Gresik 90 E7
Greta 55 H1
Gretna 55 F2
Grevena 75 F2
Greybull 123 K5
Grey Island 121 Q7
Grey Mare's Tail 57 E5
Greymouth 115 C5
Grey Range 113 J4
Greysteel 58 H2
Greystones 59 K6
Greytown 115 E4
Griefswald Bodden 70 E1
Griffin 129 K4
Griffith 113 K5
Griffith Island 120 G3
Grigoriopol 73 K2
Grimailov 71 M4
Grim, Cape 113 J7
Grimsby 55 J3
Grimsey 62 W11
Grimshaw 119 M4
Grimstad 63 C7
Grindavik 62 T13
Grindsted 63 C9
Gringley on the Hill 55 J3
Grinnell 124 D6
Grinnell Peninsula 120 G2

Name	Page	Ref.
Hamamatsu	89	F8
Hamar	63	D6
Hamata, Gebel	96	B4
Hama-Tombetsu	88	J3
Hambantota	92	F7
Hambleton	55	G3
Hamburg *U.S.A.*	124	C6
Hamburg *W. Germany*	70	D2
Hamdaman, Dasht-i	95	Q4
Hamd, Wadi al	96	C4
Hame	63	L6
Hameln	70	C2
Hamhung	87	P4
Hami	86	F3
Hamilton	113	H3
Hamilton *Bermuda*	117	N5
Hamilton *Canada*	125	L5
Hamilton *New Zealand*	115	E2
Hamilton *U.K.*	57	D5
Hamilton *Alabama, U.S.A.*	129	J3
Hamilton *Montana, U.S.A.*	122	G4
Hamilton *Ohio, U.S.A.*	124	H7
Hamilton Inlet	121	Q7
Hamim, Wadi al	101	K2
Hamina	63	M6
Hamitabat	76	D4
Hamm	70	B2
Hammar, Hawr al	94	H6
Hammarstrand	62	G5
Hammeenlinna	63	L6
Hammerdal	62	F5
Hammerfest	62	K1
Hammersley Range	112	D3
Hammond *Indiana, U.S.A.*	124	G6
Hammond *Louisiana, U.S.A.*	128	G5
Hammond *Montana, U.S.A.*	123	M5
Hamnavoe	56	A1
Hampden	115	C6
Hampshire	53	F3
Hampshire Downs	53	F3
Hampton *Arkansas, U.S.A.*	128	F4
Hampton *S. Carolina, U.S.A.*	129	M4
Hampton *Virginia, U.S.A.*	125	M8
Hamra , Al Hammadah al	101	H3
Hamrange	63	G6
Hamrin, Jebel	77	L5
Hamun-i Mashkel	92	B3
Hamur	77	K3
Hanahan	114	E3
Hanak	77	K2
Hanalei	126	R9
Hanamaki	88	H6
Hancheng	93	M1
Hancock	125	L7
Handa	89	F8
Handan	87	L4
Handeni	107	G4
Handlova	71	H4
Hanford	126	C2
Hangang	87	P4
Hangayn Nuruu	86	H2
Hanggin Houqi	87	K3
Hanggin Qi	87	K4
Hango	63	K7
Hangzhou	87	N5
Hangzhou Wan	87	N5
Hanhongor	87	J3
Hani	77	J3
Hanifah, Wadi	96	H4
Hanish al Kabir	96	F10
Haniyah, Al	94	H7
Han Jiang	87	M7
Hanko	63	K7
Hanksville	126	G1
Hanna	122	H2
Hannah Bay	121	L7
Hannibal	124	E7
Hann, Mount	112	F2
Hannover	70	C2
Hano-bukten	63	F9
Hanoi	93	L4
Hanover *Canada*	125	K4
Hanover *South Africa*	108	D6
Hanover *U.S.A.*	125	P5
Hanover, Isla	139	B10
Hanpan, Cape	114	E2
Han Pijesak	72	E3
Han Shui	93	M2
Hanson Bay	115	F6
Hanstholm	63	C8
Hantay	86	J2
Hanyuan	93	K3
Hanzhong	93	L2
Haparanda	62	L4
Happisburgh	53	J2
Hapsu	88	B5
Hapur	92	E3
Haql	96	B2
Hara	87	K2
Harad *Saudi Arabia*	97	J4
Harad *Yemen*	96	F8
Harads	62	J3
Haramachi	89	H7
Harare	108	F3
Harasis, Jiddat al	97	N7
Harbin	87	P2
Harbiye	77	G4
Harbour Breton	121	Q8
Harby	53	G2
Hardangerfjord	63	B6
Hardanger-Jokulen	63	B6
Hardangervidda	63	B6
Hardin	123	L5
Hardoi	92	F3
Hardy	128	G2
Hare Bay	121	Q7
Harer	103	H6
Harewood	55	H3
Hargeysa	103	H6
Hargigo	96	D9
Har Hu	93	J1
Harib	96	G9
Haridwar	92	E3
Harihari	115	C5
Harima-nada	89	E8
Harim, Jambal Al	97	N4
Hari-Rud	95	S4
Harjedalen	62	E5
Harlan	124	C6
Harlem	123	K3
Harleston	53	J2
Harlingen	64	F2
Harlow	53	H3
Harlowton	123	K4
Harmancik	76	C3
Harmil	96	E8
Harney Basin	122	D6
Harney Lake	122	E6
Harnosand	62	G5
Haro	66	E1
Haro, Cabo	126	G7
Haroldswick	56	A1
Harpanahalli	92	E6
Harpenden	53	G3
Harper	104	D5
Harper Passage	115	C5
Harpstedt	70	C2
Harrah, Ad	94	D6
Harran	77	H4
Harray, Loch of	56	E1
Harricanaw	125	M2
Harrietsham	53	H3
Harrington	55	F2
Harris	56	B3
Harrisburg *Illinois, U.S.A.*	124	F8
Harrisburg *Pennsylvania, U.S.A.*	125	M6
Harrismith	108	E5
Harrison	128	F2
Harrison Bay	118	E1
Harrisonburg	125	L7
Harrison, Cape	121	Q7
Harrison Lake	122	D3
Harrisonville	124	C7
Harris Ridge	140	A1
Harris, Sound of	56	A3
Harrogate	55	H3
Harrow	53	G3
Harsit	77	H2
Harstad	62	G2
Harsvik	62	D4
Hart	118	H2
Hartbees	108	D5
Hartberg	68	E2
Harteigen	63	B6
Hartford	125	P6
Harthill	57	E5
Hartkjolen	62	E4
Hartland	52	C4
Hartland Point	52	C3
Hartlepool	55	H2
Hartley	127	L3
Hartola	63	M6
Hartsville	129	M3
Hartwell Reservoir	129	L3
Hartz	108	E5
Harut	97	L8
Harvey *Australia*	112	D5
Harvey *U.S.A.*	124	G6
Harwich	53	J3
Haryana	92	E3
Harz	70	D3
Hasan Dagi	76	F3
Hashish, Ghubbat	97	P6
Haskoy	77	K2
Haslemere	53	G3
Haslingden	55	G3
Hassa	77	G4
Hassan	92	E6
Hassankeyf	77	J4
Hassela	63	L5
Hassi Habadra	101	F3
Hassleholm	63	E8
Hastings *Australia*	113	K7
Hastings *New Zealand*	115	F3
Hastings *U.K.*	53	H4
Hastings *Michigan, U.S.A.*	124	H5
Hastings *Nebraska, U.S.A.*	123	Q7
Hastveda	63	E8
Hasvik	62	K1
Haswell	55	H2
Hatanbulag	87	K3
Hatchie	128	H3
Hatfield *Hertfordshire, U.K.*	53	G3
Hatfield *S. Yorkshire, U.K.*	55	H3
Hatfield Peverel	53	H3
Hatgal	86	J1
Hathras	92	E3
Hatibah, Ra's	96	D6
Ha Tien	93	K6
Ha Tinh	93	L5
Hatip	76	E4
Hat Island	120	G4
Hato	136	A2
Hatohudo	91	H7
Hatskiy	84	D5
Hatteras, Cape	129	Q3
Hattiesburg	128	H5
Hatton	56	G3
Hattras Passage	93	J6
Hatunsaray	76	E4
Hatuoto	91	H6
Haugesund	63	A7
Haughton	53	E2
Hauhui	114	K6
Haukivesi	62	N5
Haukivuori	63	M5
Hauraha	114	K7
Hauraki Gulf	115	E2
Haut Atlas	100	D2
Hauts Plateaux	100	E2
Havana	124	E6
Havant	53	F4
Havasu	126	F3
Havasu, Lake	126	E3
Havel	70	E2
Havelock North	115	F3
Haverfordwest	52	C2
Haverhill *U.K.*	53	H2
Haverhill *U.S.A.*	125	Q5
Havoysund	62	L1
Havran	76	B3
Havre	123	K3
Havre-Saint-Pierre	121	P7
Havsa	76	B2
Havza	77	F2
Hawaii *U.S.A.*	126	R10
Hawaii *U.S.A.*	126	T11
Hawaya, Al	97	J6
Hawea, Lake	115	B6
Hawera	115	E3
Hawes	55	G2
Haweswater Reservoir	55	G2
Hawick	57	F5
Hawke	121	Q7
Hawke Bay	115	F3
Hawke, Cape	113	L5
Hawkesbury	125	N4
Hawkhurst	53	H3
Hawkinge	53	J3
Hawknest Point	133	K2
Hawnby	55	H2
Hawng Luk	93	J4
Hawra	97	J9
Hawran, Wadi	94	E5
Hawsker	55	J2
Hawthorne	126	C1
Haxby	55	H2
Hay *New South Wales, Australia*	113	J5
Hay *Northern Territory, Australia*	113	H3
Hay *Canada*	119	M3
Hayden	123	L7
Hayes	119	R4
Hayes Halvo	120	N2
Hayes, Mount	118	F3
Hayjan	96	G8
Hayl	97	N4
Hayl, Wadi al	77	H5
Haymana	76	E3
Hayrabolu	76	B2
Hay River	119	M3
Hays	96	F10
Hays	123	Q8
Haywards Heath	53	G4
Hazaran, Kuh-e	95	N7
Hazard	124	J8
Hazar Golu	77	H3
Hazaribag	92	G4
Hazaribagh Range	92	F4
Hazar Masjed, Kuh-e	95	P3
Hazel Grove	55	G3
Hazelton *Canada*	118	K4
Hazelton *U.S.A.*	125	N6
Hazen Bay	118	B3
Hazlehurst	128	G5
Hazro	77	J3
Headcorn	53	H3
Head of Bight	112	G5
Healdsburg	126	A1
Healesville	113	K6
Heanor	55	H3
Heard Islands	142	D6
Hearst	124	J2
Hearst Island	141	V5
Heart	123	P4
Heathfield	53	H4
Heathrow	53	G3
Hebbronville	128	C7
Hebden Bridge	55	G3
Hebei	87	M4
Hebel	113	K4
Heber City	122	J7
Hebi	87	L4
Hebrides, Sea of the	57	A4
Hebron *Canada*	121	P6
Hebron *Israel*	94	B6
Hebron *N. Dakota, U.S.A.*	123	N4
Hebron *Nebraska, U.S.A.*	123	R7
Hecate Strait	118	J5
Hechi	93	L4
Hechuan	93	L2
Heckington	53	G2
Hecla and Griper Bay	120	D2
Hector, Mount	115	E4
Hede	62	E5
Hedland, Port	112	D3
Hedmark	63	D6
Heerenveen	64	F2
Heerlen	64	F3
Hefa	94	B5
Hefei	87	M5
Hefeng	93	M3
Hegang	87	Q2
Hegura-jima	89	F7
Heiban	102	F5
Heide	70	C1
Heidelberg	70	C4
Heidharhorn	62	U12
Heighington	55	H2
Heilbron	108	E5
Heilbronn	70	C4
Heiligenhafen	70	D1
Heiligenstadt	70	D3
Heilong Jiang *China*	88	B2
Heilongjiang *China*	88	D1
Heimaey	62	U13
Heimdal	62	D5
Heinavesi	62	N5
Heinola	63	M6
Heinze Islands	93	J6
Hejing	86	F3
Hekimhan	77	G3
Hel	71	H1
Helagsfjallet	62	E5
Helena *Arkansas, U.S.A.*	128	G3
Helena *Montana, U.S.A.*	122	J4
Helen Island	91	J5
Helensburgh	57	D4
Helensville	115	E2
Helgoland	70	B1
Helgolander Bucht	70	B1
Heli	88	C2
Heligenblut	68	D2
Helleh	95	K7
Hellin	67	F3
Hell's Mouth	52	C2
Hell-Ville	109	J2
Helmand	95	R6
Helmond	64	F3
Helmsdale *U.K.*	56	E2
Helmsdale *U.K.*	56	E2
Helong	88	B4
Hel, Polwysep	71	H1
Helsingborg	63	E8
Helsingfors	63	L6
Helsingor	63	E8
Helsinki	63	K6
Helston	52	B4
Helvecia	137	K7
Helvellyn	55	F2
Hemel Hempstead	53	G3
Hempstead	128	D5
Hemsworth	55	H3
Henan	93	M2
Henares	66	E2
Henashi-zaki	88	G5
Henbury	113	G3
Hendek	76	D2
Henderson *Kentucky, U.S.A.*	124	G8
Henderson *N. Carolina, U.S.A.*	129	N2
Henderson *Nevada, U.S.A.*	126	E3
Henderson *Texas, U.S.A.*	128	E4
Hendersonville	129	L3
Hendorabi	95	L8
Hendota	124	F6
Hendrik Verwoerd Dam	108	E6
Hengdaohezi	88	B3
Hengduan Shan	93	J3
Hengelo	64	G2
Hengshan *Hunan, China*	93	M3
Hengshan *Shanxi, China*	87	K4
Hengshui	87	M4
Heng Xian	93	L4
Hengyang	93	M3
Henley-on-Thames	53	G3
Hennebont	65	B5
Henqam	95	M8
Henrietta Maria, Cape	121	K6
Henryetta	128	E3
Henry Ice Rise	141	W2
Henry Mountains	126	G1
Henry Point	112	D5
Henslow, Cape	114	K6
Hentiyn Nuruu	87	K2
Henty	113	K6
Henzada	93	J5
Heppner	122	E5
Hepu	93	L4
Hequ	87	L4
Heradsfloi	62	X12
Herat	95	R4
Herault	65	E7
Herbertville	115	F4
Herby	71	H3
Heredia	132	E9
Hereford *U.K.*	52	E2
Hereford *U.S.A.*	127	L3
Hereford and Worcester	52	E2
Hereke	76	C2
Heretaniwha Point	115	B5
Herford	70	C2
Herington	123	R8
Herisau	68	B2
Herlen Gol	87	L2
Herm	53	M7
Hermanas	127	M7
Herma Ness	56	B1
Hermanus	108	C6
Hermel	94	C4
Hermiston	122	E5
Hermitage	53	F3
Hermitage Bay	121	Q8
Hermit Islands	114	D2
Hermon, Mount	77	G6
Hermosillo	126	G6
Hernad	73	F1
Herne	70	B3
Herne Bay	53	J3

Name	Page	Grid
Herning	63	C8
Herrera del Duque	66	D3
Herriard	53	F3
Herrick	113	K7
Herroro, Punta	131	R8
Hersbruck	70	D4
Herschel Island	118	H2
Hertford	53	G3
Hertfordshire	53	G3
Hervey Bay	113	L3
Herzberg	70	D3
Hesdin	64	E3
Hessfjord	62	M2
Hesteyri	63	T11
Hestra	63	E8
Heswall	55	F3
Hethersett	53	J2
Hetton-le-Hole	55	H2
Heuru	114	K7
Heversham	55	G2
Hexham	55	G2
He Xian *Anhui, China*	87	M5
He Xian *Guangxi, China*	93	M4
Heydalir	62	X12
Heysham	55	G2
Heyuan	87	L7
Heywood	55	G3
Heze	93	N1
Hialeah	129	M8
Hibak, Al	97	L6
Hibaldstow	55	J3
Hibbing	124	D3
Hibernia Reef	110	F4
Hickory	129	M3
Hicks Cays	132	C6
Hico	128	C4
Hidaka-sammyaku	88	J4
Hidalgo del Parral	127	K7
Hiddensee	70	E1
Hidrolandia	138	G3
Hieflau	68	E2
Hienghene	114	W16
Hierro	100	B3
Higashi-suido	89	B8
Higham Ferrers	53	G2
Highampton	52	C4
Highbury	113	J2
Highclere	53	F3
High Force	55	G2
High Hesket	55	G2
Highland	56	C3
Highland Park	124	G5
High Level	119	M4
High Point	129	N3
High River	122	H2
High Street	55	G2
High Wycombe	53	G3
Higuera de Zaragozao	127	H8
Higuey	133	N5
Hiiumaa	63	K7
Hijar	67	F2
Hijaz	96	E6
Hikman, Barr al	97	P6
Hikone	89	F8
Hikurangi	115	E1
Hildesheim	70	C2
Hill City	123	Q8
Hillingdon	53	G3
Hillington	53	H2
Hill Island Lake	119	N3
Hillsboro *N. Dakota, U.S.A.*	123	R4
Hillsboro *Ohio, U.S.A.*	124	J7
Hillsboro *Texas, U.S.A.*	128	D5
Hillsborough	58	K4
Hilo	126	T11
Hilpsford Point	55	F2
Hilton Head Island	129	M4
Hilvan	77	H4
Hilversum	64	F2
Hima	96	G7
Himachal Pradesh	92	E2
Himalaya	92	E3
Himare	74	E2
Himatnagar	92	D4
Himeji	89	E8
Himmerland	63	C8
Himmetdede	76	F3
Hims	94	C4
Hinche	133	L5
Hinchinbrook Island	118	F3
Hinckley	53	F2
Hinderwell	55	J2
Hindhead	53	G3
Hindley	55	G3
Hindmarsh, Lake	113	J6
Hindon	53	E3
Hindubagh	92	C2
Hindu Kush	92	D1
Hindupur	92	E6
Hinganghat	92	E4
Hingoli	92	E5
Hinis	77	J3
Hinnoya	62	F2
Hinojosa del Duque	66	D3
Hintlesham	53	J2
Hinton	119	M5
Hinzir Burun	77	F4
Hirado-shima	89	B9
Hirakud Reservoir	92	F4
Hirara	89	G11
Hiratsuka	89	G8
Hirfanli Baraji	76	E3
Hirlau	73	J2
Hiroo	88	J4
Hirosaki	88	H5
Hiroshima	89	D8
Hirschberg	70	F3
Hirsova	73	J3
Hirtshals	63	C8
Hirwaun	52	D3
Hisar	92	E3
Hisma	96	C2
Hissjon	62	J5
Hit	94	F5
Hitachi	89	H7
Hitchin	53	G3
Hitoyoshi	89	C9
Hitra	62	C5
Hiu	114	T10
Hiuchi-nada	89	D8
Hiz	53	G2
Hizan	77	K3
Hjalmaren	63	G7
Hjalmar Lake	119	P3
Hjelmeland	63	B7
Hjorring	63	C8
Ho	104	F4
Hoa Binh	93	L4
Hobara	89	H7
Hobart	113	K7
Hobbs	127	L4
Hoboksar	86	F2
Hobro	63	C8
Hobyo	103	J6
Hocalar	76	C3
Hochalm Spitze	68	D2
Ho Chi Minh	93	L6
Hochstadt	70	D4
Hockley	53	H3
Hockley Heath	53	F2
Hodal	92	E3
Hodder	55	G3
Hoddesdon	53	G3
Hodge Beck	55	H2
Hodmezovasarhely	72	F2
Hodna, Monts du	67	J5
Hodnet	52	E2
Hodonin	71	G4
Hoea	126	T10
Hoeryong	88	B4
Hof	70	D3
Hofdakaupstadur	62	U12
Hofmeyr	108	E6
Hofn *Iceland*	62	T11
Hofn *Iceland*	62	X12
Hofors	63	G6
Hofsjokull	62	V12
Hofu	89	C8
Hoganas	63	E8
Hoggar	101	G4
Hogsby	63	G8
Hogsty Reef	133	L4
Hohe Rhon	70	C3
Hohe Tauern	68	D2
Hohhot	87	L3
Hoh Xil Shan	92	G1
Hoi An	93	L5
Hoima	107	F2
Hokensas	63	F7
Hokianga Harbour	115	D1
Hokitika	115	C5
Hokkaido	88	H3
Hokksund	63	C7
Hokota	89	H7
Hokou	93	K4
Hokuno	89	F8
Holarfjall	62	V12
Holbeach	53	H2
Holborn Head	56	E2
Holbrook	127	G3
Holdenville	128	D3
Holderness	55	J3
Holdrege	123	Q7
Holguin	132	J4
Holic	71	G4
Holitna	118	D3
Holjes	63	E6
Hollabrunn	68	F1
Holland	124	G5
Hollandstoun	56	F1
Hollis	128	C3
Hollywood	129	M7
Holm	62	E4
Holman Island	119	M1
Holmavik	62	U12
Holme-on-Spalding-Moor	55	J3
Holmes Chapel	55	G3
Holmes Reef	113	K2
Holmfirth	55	H3
Holms O	120	Q3
Holmsund	62	J5
Holoin Gun	86	J3
Holstebro	63	C8
Holsteinsborg	120	R4
Holsworthy	52	C4
Holt	53	J2
Holton *Canada*	121	Q7
Holton *U.S.A.*	124	C7
Holy Cross	118	D3
Holyhead	54	E3
Holyhead Bay	55	E3
Holy Island *Gwynedd, U.K.*	54	E3
Holy Island *Northumberland, U.K.*	55	H1
Holy Island *Strathclyde, U.K.*	57	C5
Holyoke *Colorado, U.S.A.*	123	N7
Holyoke *Massachusetts, U.S.A.*	125	P5
Holywell	55	F3
Holywood *Dumfries and Galloway, U.K.*	57	E5
Holywood *Down, U.K.*	58	L3
Homalin	93	H4
Hombre Muerto, Salar de	138	C5
Home Bay	120	N4
Home Hill	113	K2
Home Point	115	E1
Homer	128	F4
Homer Tunnel	115	A6
Hommelvik	62	D5
Hommersak	63	D6
Homoine	109	G4
Homs	77	G5
Honavar	92	D6
Honaz Dagi	76	C4
Hon Chong	93	K6
Hondo *Mexico*	131	Q8
Hondo *U.S.A.*	128	C6
Honduras	132	C7
Honduras, Golfo de	132	C6
Honefoss	63	D6
Honesdale	125	N6
Honey Lake	122	D7
Hong Kong	87	L7
Hongliuyuan	86	H3
Hongo	86	G2
Hongor *Mongolia*	87	L2
Hongor *Mongolia*	87	L2
Hongshui He	93	L4
Hong, Song	93	K4
Hongsong	87	P4
Honguedo Strait	121	P8
Hongxing Sichang	86	F3
Hongze	87	M5
Hongze Hu	87	M5
Honiara	114	J6
Honingham	53	J2
Honiton	52	D4
Honjo	88	G6
Hon Khoai	93	K7
Honningsvag	62	L1
Honohina	126	T11
Honokaa	126	T10
Honolulu	126	S10
Honshu	89	E7
Hood	119	N2
Hood Canal	122	C4
Hood Island	136	A7
Hood, Mount	122	D5
Hood Point	114	D4
Hood River	122	D5
Hoogeveen	64	G2
Hooghly	93	G4
Hook	53	G3
Hooker	127	M2
Hook Head	59	J8
Hook Norton	53	F3
Hooper, Cape	120	N4
Hoor	63	E9
Hoorn	64	F2
Hoover Dam	126	E2
Hopa	77	J2
Hope *Canada*	122	D3
Hope *U.K.*	55	H3
Hope *U.S.A.*	128	F4
Hopedale	121	P6
Hopelchen	131	Q8
Hope, Loch	56	D2
Hopen	80	D2
Hope Pass	115	C5
Hopetown	108	D5
Hopewell	125	M8
Hopkins Lake	112	F3
Hopkinsville	124	G8
Hoquiam	122	C4
Horasan	77	K2
Horby	63	E9
Hordaland	63	B6
Horezu	73	G3
Horley	53	G3
Horlick Mountains	141	R1
Hormoz	95	N8
Hormuz, Strait of	97	N3
Horn *Austria*	68	E1
Horn *Iceland*	62	T11
Hornavan	62	G3
Horn, Cape	139	C10
Horncastle	55	J3
Horndal	63	G6
Horndean	53	F4
Hornefors	62	H5
Hornepayne	124	H2
Horn Head	58	G2
Horn, Iles de	111	T4
Horningsham	52	E3
Horn Mountains	119	L3
Hornos, Cabo de	139	C11
Hornsea	55	J3
Horovice	70	E4
Horqin Youyi Qianqi	87	N2
Horqin Zuoyi Houqi	87	N3
Horqueta	138	E4
Horsehoe Bend	122	F6
Horsens	63	C9
Horsey	53	J2
Horsforth	55	H3
Horsham *Australia*	113	J6
Horsham *U.K.*	53	G3
Horsham Saint Faith	53	J2
Horsley	53	G3
Horsovsky Tyn	70	E4
Horten	63	D7
Horton	118	L2
Horwich	55	G3
Hosaina	103	G6
Hosap	77	K3
Hose Mountains	90	E5
Hoseynabad	94	H4
Hoshangabad	92	E4
Hoshiarpur	92	E2
Hospet	92	E5
Hospitalet	67	H2
Hossegor	65	C7
Hoste, Isla	139	C11
Hotamis	76	E4
Hotan	92	F1
Hotazel	108	D5
Hoti	91	J6
Hoting	62	G4
Hot Springs *Arkansas, U.S.A.*	128	F3
Hot Springs *S. Dakota, U.S.A.*	123	N6
Hottah Lake	119	M2
Hotte, Massif de la	133	K5
Houailou	114	W16
Houdan	64	D4
Houghton	124	F3
Houghton-le-Spring	55	H2
Houlton	125	S3
Houma *China*	93	M1
Houma *U.S.A.*	128	G6
Houmt Souk	101	H2
Hounde	104	E3
Hounslow	53	G3
Houston *Mississippi, U.S.A.*	128	H4
Houston *Texas, U.S.A.*	128	E6
Houtman Rocks	112	C4
Hova	63	F7
Hovd	86	G2
Hovd Gol	86	G2
Hove	53	G4
Hoveyzeh	94	J6
Hovingham	55	J2
Hovlya	79	G6
Hovsgol	87	K3
Hovsgol Nuur	86	J1
Howa	102	E4
Howakil	96	E9
Howard City	124	H5
Howard Lake	119	P3
Howden Moor	55	H3
Howden Reservoir	55	H3
Howe, Cape	113	K6
Howe of the Mearns	57	F4
Howitt, Mount	113	K6
Howland Island	111	T1
Howrah	93	G4
Hoxtolgay	86	F2
Hoxud	86	F3
Hoy	56	E2
Hoyanger	63	B6
Hoyerswerda	70	F3
Hoylake	55	F3
Hoyos	66	C2
Hoy Sound	56	E2
Hradeckralove	70	F3
Hron	71	H4
Hrubieszow	71	K3
Hsin-cheng	87	N7
Hsin-chu	87	N7
Hsipaw	93	J4
Huab	108	B4
Huacho	136	B6
Huachuan	88	C2
Huacrachuco	136	B5
Huade	87	L3
Huadian	87	P3
Huaibei	93	N2
Huaide	87	N3
Huai He	93	M2
Huaihua	93	M3
Huaiji	93	M4
Huainan	87	M5
Huairou	87	M3
Huaiyin	87	M5
Huajuapan de Leon	131	L9
Huallaga	136	B5
Huallanca	136	B5
Huama	88	C2
Huamachuco	136	B5
Huambo	106	C5
Huampusirpi	132	E7
Huanan	88	C2
Huancane	138	C3
Huancavelica	136	B6
Huancayo	136	B6
Huanghuan	93	N2
Huang Hai	87	N4
Huang He	87	L4
Huanghua	87	M4
Huangling	93	L1
Huangpi	93	M2
Huangshi	93	M2
Huang Xian	87	N4
Huangyan	87	N6
Huangyuan	93	K1
Huanren	87	P3
Huanta	136	C6
Huan Xian	93	L1
Huanzo, Cordillera	136	C6
Huara	138	C3
Huaral	136	B6
Huaraz	136	B5
Huarmey	136	B6
Huascaran, Nevado	136	B5
Huatabampo	127	H7
Huayin	93	M2
Huayuan	93	L3
Hubei	93	M2

Name	Page	Grid
Karymskoye	85	J6
Kas	76	C4
Kasai	106	C3
Kasaji	106	D5
Kasama	107	F5
Kasane	108	E3
Kasanga	107	F4
Kasangulu	106	C3
Kasaragod	92	D6
Kasar, Ras	96	D7
Kasba Lake	119	Q3
Kasba Tadla	100	D2
Kasempa	106	E5
Kasese	107	F2
Kashaf	95	Q3
Kashan	95	K5
Kashary	79	G6
Kashgar	86	D4
Kashi	86	D4
Kashima	89	C9
Kashin	78	F4
Kashipur	92	E3
Kashira	78	F5
Kashiwazaki	89	G7
Kashkanteniz	86	C2
Kashkarantsy	78	F2
Kashmar	95	P4
Kasimov	78	G5
Kasin	92	D2
Kasiruta	91	H6
Kaskinen	62	J5
Kasko	62	J5
Kas Kong	93	K6
Kasli	84	Ad5
Kasmere Lake	119	Q4
Kasongo	106	E3
Kasongo-Lunda	106	C4
Kasos	75	J5
Kasos, Stenon	75	J5
Kaspiyskiy	79	H6
Kassala	103	G4
Kassandra	75	G2
Kassel	70	C3
Kasserine	101	G1
Kastamonu	76	E2
Kastaneai	75	J2
Kastelli	75	G5
Kastellorizon	76	C4
Kastoria	75	F2
Kastorias, Limni	75	F2
Kastornoye	79	F5
Kastron	75	H3
Kasulu	107	F3
Kasumi	89	E8
Kasumiga-ura	89	H7
Kasungu	107	F5
Kata	84	G5
Kataba	106	E6
Katagum	105	H3
Katahdin, Mount	125	R4
Katako Kombe	106	D3
Katanning	112	D5
Katastari	75	F4
Katav Ivanovsk	78	K5
Katchall	93	H7
Katen	88	F2
Katerini	75	G2
Katha	93	J4
Katherina, Gebel	103	F2
Katherine	112	G1
Kathmandu	92	G3
Kati	100	D6
Katihar	93	G3
Katikati	115	E2
Katiola	104	D4
Katla	62	V13
Katlabukh, Ozero	73	K3
Katmai Volcano	118	E4
Kato Nevrokopion	75	G2
Katoomba	113	L5
Kato Stavros	75	G2
Katowice	71	H3
Katrineholm	63	G7
Katrine, Loch	57	D4
Katsina	105	G3
Katsina Ala	105	G4
Katsuura	89	H8
Katsuyama	89	F7
Kattavia	75	J5
Kattegat	63	D8
Kauai	126	R9
Kauai Channel	126	R10
Kauhajoki	62	K5
Kauiki Head	126	S10
Kaujuitok	120	H3
Kaulakahi Channel	126	Q9
Kaunakakai	126	S10
Kaunas	71	K1
Kaura Namoda	105	G3
Kaushany	73	K2
Kautokeino	62	K2
Kavacha	85	V4
Kavaje	74	E2
Kavak	77	G2
Kavaklidere	76	C4
Kavalerovo	88	E3
Kavali	92	E6
Kavalla	75	H2
Kavar	95	L7
Kavarna	73	K4
Kavgamis	77	H4
Kavieng	114	E2
Kavir, Dasht-e	95	M4
Kavir-e Namak	95	N4
Kavungo	106	D5
Kavusshap Daglari	77	K3
Kaw	137	G3
Kawagoe	89	G8
Kawaguchi	89	G8
Kawaihae	126	T10
Kawakawa	115	E1
Kawambwa	107	E4
Kawardha	92	F4
Kawasaki	89	G8
Kawerau	115	F3
Kawhia	115	E3
Kawhia Harbour	115	E3
Kawimbe	107	F4
Kawkareik	93	J5
Kawthaung	93	J7
Kayak Island	118	G4
Kayan	91	F5
Kaydak, Sor	79	J7
Kaye, Cape	120	H3
Kayenta	127	G2
Kayes	100	C6
Kaymaz	76	D3
Kaynar	86	D2
Kaynarca	76	D2
Kayseri	76	F3
Kayuagung	90	C6
Kazachinskoye	84	H5
Kazachye	85	P2
Kazakh	77	L2
Kazakhskiy Melkosopochnik	86	C2
Kazakhskiy Zaliv	79	J2
Kazakhstan S.S.R.	79	J6
Kazan	78	H4
Kazan Turkey	76	E2
Kazan U.S.S.R.	119	R3
Kazandzhik	95	M2
Kazan Lake	119	R3
Kazanluk	73	H4
Kazan-retto	83	N4
Kazatin	79	D6
Kazbek	77	L1
Kazerun	95	K7
Kazgorodok	84	Ae6
Kazhim	78	J3
Kazi Magomed	94	J1
Kazim Karabekir	76	E4
Kaztalovka	79	H6
Kazumba	106	D4
Kazy	95	N2
Kazym	84	Ae4
Kazymskaya	84	Ae4
Kazymskiy Mys	84	Ae4
Kea Greece	75	H4
Kea Greece	75	H4
Keady	58	J4
Keal, Loch na	57	B4
Kearny	126	G4
Keaukaha	126	T11
Keban	77	H3
Keban Baraji	77	H3
Kebemer	104	B2
Kebezen	84	D6
Kebnekaise	62	H3
Kebock Head	56	B2
Kebri Dehar	103	H6
Kech a Terara	103	G6
Kechika	118	K4
Keciborlu	76	D4
Kecil, Kai	91	J7
Kecskemet	72	E2
Kedainiai	63	K9
Kedgwick	125	S3
Kedong	87	P2
Kedougou	104	C3
Kedva	78	J3
Keel	58	B5
Keelby	55	J3
Keele	118	K3
Keele Peak	118	J3
Keeler	126	D2
Keene	125	P5
Keeper Hill	59	F7
Keetmanshoop	108	C5
Keewatin NW. Territories, Canada	119	R3
Keewatin Ontario, Canada	124	C2
Kefallinia	75	F3
Kefamenanu	91	G7
Kefken	76	D2
Keflavik	62	T12
Keglo Bay	121	N6
Kegulta	79	G6
Kehsi Mansam	93	J4
Keighley	55	H3
Keitele Kaskisuomi, Finland	62	L5
Keitele Kuopio, Finland	62	M5
Keith	56	F3
Keith Arm	119	L2
Keiyasi	114	Q8
Kekertaluk Island	120	N4
Keketa	114	C3
Kel	85	M3
Kelang	90	C5
Keld	55	G2
Keles	76	C3
Kelibia	101	H1
Kelkit Turkey	77	G2
Kelkit Turkey	77	H2
Keller Lake	119	L3
Kellett, Cape	118	K1
Kellog	84	D4
Kellogg	122	F4
Kelloselka	62	N3
Kells	58	J5
Kelme	63	K9
Kelmentsy	73	J1
Kelo	102	C6
Kelolokan	91	F5
Kelowna	122	E3
Kelsey Bay	122	B2
Kelso New Zealand	115	B6
Kelso U.K.	57	F5
Keluang	90	C5
Kelvedon	53	H3
Kem	78	E3
Kemah	77	H3
Kemaliye	77	H3
Kemalpasa	77	J2
Kemalpasar	76	B3
Kemano	118	K5
Kemer Turkey	76	C4
Kemer Turkey	76	C4
Kemer Turkey	76	D4
Kemerovo	84	D5
Kemi	62	L4
Kemijarvi Finland	62	L3
Kemijarvi Finland	62	M3
Kemijoki	62	L3
Kemmerer	123	J7
Kempen	64	F3
Kempendyayi	85	K4
Kemp, Lake	127	N4
Kemps Bay	132	H2
Kempsey	113	L5
Kempten	70	D5
Kempt, Lac	125	N3
Kempton	113	K7
Ken	92	F3
Kenadsa	100	E2
Kenai	118	E3
Kenai Mountains	118	E4
Kenai Peninsula	118	F3
Kendal	55	G2
Kendall, Cape	120	J5
Kendari	91	G6
Kendawangan	90	E6
Kendraparha	92	G4
Kendyrliki	86	F2
Kenema	104	C4
Kenete Karavastas	74	E2
Kenge	106	C3
Kengtung	93	J4
Kenhardt	108	D5
Kenilworth	53	F2
Kenitra	100	D2
Keniut	85	X4
Kenli	87	M4
Kenmare Ireland	59	C9
Kenmare Ireland	59	C9
Kenmore	57	D4
Kennacraig	57	C5
Kennebec	125	R4
Kenner	128	G5
Kennet	53	F3
Kennewick	122	E4
Kenninghall	53	J2
Kenn Reef	113	M3
Kenogami	121	K7
Keno Hill	118	H3
Kenora	124	C2
Kenosha	124	G5
Kent U.K.	53	H3
Kent U.S.A.	127	K5
Kentau	86	B3
Kentford	53	H2
Kentmere	55	G2
Kent Peninsula	119	P2
Kentucky U.S.A.	124	G8
Kentucky U.S.A.	124	H8
Kentucky Lake	124	F8
Kentwood	128	G5
Kenya	107	G2
Keokea	126	S10
Keokuk	124	E6
Keos	75	H4
Kepi	91	K7
Kepno	71	G3
Keppel Bay	113	L3
Kepsut	76	C3
Kerala	92	E6
Kerama-retto	89	H10
Keravat	114	E2
Kerch	79	F6
Kerchenskiy Proliv	79	F6
Kerema	114	D3
Keremeos	122	E3
Keren	103	G4
Kerguelen, Ile	142	D6
Keri	75	F4
Kericho	107	G3
Kerinci, Gunung	90	C6
Keriya He	92	F1
Kerki	95	S3
Kerkinitis, Limni	75	G2
Kerkira Greece	74	E3
Kerkira Greece	74	E3
Kerma	102	F4
Kermadec Islands	111	T8
Kermadec Trench	143	H6
Kerman	95	N6
Kerman Desert	95	P7
Kermen	73	J4
Kermit	127	L5
Kern	126	C2
Keros	78	J3
Kerpineny	73	K2
Kerrera	57	C4
Kerrville	127	N5
Kerry	59	C8
Kerry Head	59	C8
Kerrykeel	58	G2
Keruh	90	C4
Kerulen	87	L2
Kesalahti	63	N6
Kesan	76	B2
Kesap	77	H2
Kesennuma	88	H6
Keshvar	94	J5
Keskin	76	E3
Keski-Suomi	62	K5
Keskozero	78	E3
Keswick	55	F2
Keszthely	72	D2
Ket	84	D5
Keta	104	F4
Keta, Ozero	84	E3
Ketapang	90	D6
Ketchikan	118	J4
Kete	104	E4
Ketmen, Khrebet	86	E3
Ketoy, Ostrov	85	S7
Ketrzyn	71	J1
Kettering	53	G2
Kettle Ness	55	J2
Kettle River Range	122	E3
Kettlewell	55	G2
Kettusoja	62	N3
Keurus-selka	63	L5
Keushki	84	Ae4
Kew	133	M4
Kewanee	124	F6
Keweenaw	124	G3
Keweenaw Bay	124	G3
Keweenaw Point	124	G3
Keyano	121	M7
Keyaygyr	86	D3
Keyi	86	E3
Key Largo	129	M8
Key, Lough	58	F4
Keynsham	52	E3
Key West	129	M8
Keyworth	53	F2
Kez	78	J4
Kezhma	84	G5
Khabarovo	84	Ad3
Khabarovsk	88	E1
Khabarovsk Kray	85	P6
Khabur	94	E4
Khadki	92	D5
Khairagarh	92	F4
Khairpur Pakistan	92	C3
Khairpur Pakistan	92	D3
Khakhar	85	P5
Khalafabad	94	J6
Khalili	95	L8
Khalkhal	94	J3
Khalki	75	J4
Khalkis	75	G3
Khalmer-Yu	84	Ad3
Khalturin	78	H4
Khamar Daban, Khrebet	84	G6
Khambhat	92	D4
Khambhat, Gulf of	92	D4
Khamili	75	J5
Khamir	96	F8
Kham Keut	93	K5
Khammam	92	F5
Khamra	85	J4
Khanabad	92	C1
Khan al Baghdadi	94	F5
Khanaqin	94	G4
Khanda	84	H6
Khandela	92	E3
Khandra	75	J5
Khandwa	92	E4
Khandyga	85	P4
Khangokurt	84	Ad4
Khanh Hoa	93	L6
Khanh Hung	93	L7
Khani	85	L5
Khania	75	H5
Khaniadhana	92	E4
Khanion Kolpos	75	G5
Khanka, Ozero	88	D3
Khanpur	92	D3
Khan Shaykhun	94	C4
Khantau	86	C3
Khantayka	84	D3
Khantayskoye, Ozero	84	E3
Khanty-Mansiysk	84	Ae4
Khan Yunis	94	B6
Kharabali	79	H6
Kharagpur	93	G4
Kharalakh	85	L3
Kharan	95	N7
Kharanaq	95	M5
Kharaulakhskiy Khrebet	85	M2
Kharbur	77	J5
Kharga, El Wahat el	102	F3
Kharg Island	97	K2
Kharitah, Shiqqat al	96	H8
Khark	97	K2
Kharkov	79	F6
Kharku	97	K2
Khar Kuh	95	L6
Kharlovka	78	F2
Kharsawan	92	G4
Kharstan	85	Q2
Khartoum	103	F4
Khartoum North	103	F4
Kharutayuvam	78	K2
Khasalakh	85	M2
Khasan	88	C4

Khasavyurt 79 H7
Khash 95 Q7
Khash 95 R6
Khash, Dasht-i- 92 B2
Khashm el Girba 96 B9
Khash Rud 95 R6
Khashuri 77 K2
Khasi Hills 93 H3
Khaskovo 73 H5
Khatanga *U.S.S.R.* 84 G2
Khatanga *U.S.S.R.* 84 G2
Khatangskiy Zaliv 84 H2
Khatayakha 78 K2
Khatyrka 85 X4
Khaybar, Harrat 96 E4
Khaypudyrskaya Guba 78 K2
Khayran, Ra's al 97 P5
Khaysardakh 85 M4
Khe Bo 93 K5
Kheisia 77 J5
Khemis Miliana 67 H4
Khemisset 100 D2
Khenchela 101 G1
Khenifra 100 D2
Kherrata 67 J4
Khersan 95 K6
Kherson 79 E6
Khe Sanh 93 L5
Kheta 84 G2
Khiitola 63 N6
Khilok 85 J6
Khios *Greece* 75 H3
Khios *Greece* 75 J3
Khirbat Isriyah 77 G5
Khiva 80 H5
Khlebarovo 73 J4
Khmelnik 79 D6
Khmelnitskiy 79 D6
Khodzhakala 95 N2
Kholm *Afghanistan* 92 C1
Kholm *U.S.S.R.* 78 E4
Kholmogory 78 G3
Kholmsk 88 J2
Khomas Highland 108 C4
Khomeyn 95 K5
Khomeynishahr 95 K5
Khong 93 L6
Khongkhoyuku 85 N4
Khonj 95 L8
Khoper 79 G5
Khor *U.S.S.R.* 88 E2
Khor *U.S.S.R.* 88 E2
Khora Sfakion 75 H5
Khorat, Cao Nguyen 93 K5
Khordha 92 G4
Khordogoy 85 K4
Khoreyver 78 K2
Khorgo 84 J2
Khorinsk 84 H6
Khorod 79 E6
Khorol 88 C3
Khorovaya 84 A3
Khorramabad *Iran* 94 J5
Khorramabad *Iran* 95 N4
Khorramshahr 94 J6
Khosf 95 P5
Khosheutovo 79 H6
Khosk 95 R4
Khosrowabad 94 J6
Khotin 73 J1
Khouribga 100 D2
Khoyniki 79 D5
Khristiana 75 H4
Khroma 85 Q2
Khuff 96 G4
Khulna 93 G4
Khulo 77 K2
Khunjerab Pass 92 E1
Khunsar 95 K5
Khunti 92 G4
Khur 95 P4
Khurays 97 J4
Khurja 92 E3
Khuryan Munjan, Jazair 97 N8
Khust 79 C6
Khutu Datta 85 Q7
Khuzdar 92 C3
Khvaf 95 Q4
Khvalynsk 79 H5
Khvor 95 M5
Khvormuj 95 K7
Khvoy 94 G2
Khvoynaya 78 E4
Khwaja Muhammad, Koh-i- 92 D1
Khyber Pass 92 D2
Khyrov 71 K4
Kiamba 91 G4
Kiantajarvi 62 N4
Kiaton 75 G3
Kiberg 62 P1
Kibombo 106 E3
Kibondo 107 F3
Kibwezi 107 G3
Kibworth Harcourt 53 G2
Kicevo 73 F5
Kicking Horse Pass 119 M5
Kidal 100 F5
Kidan, Al 97 M5
Kidderminster 52 E2
Kidnappers, Cape 115 F3
Kidsgrove 55 G3
Kidwelly 52 C3
Kidyut, Wadi 97 K8
Kiel 70 D1
Kielce 71 J3
Kielder 57 F5
Kielder Forest 57 F5
Kielder Water 57 F5
Kieler Bucht 70 D1
Kieta 114 F3
Kiev 79 E5
Kiffa 100 C5
Kifissos 75 G3
Kifri 94 G4
Kigali 107 F3
Kigi 77 J3
Kiglapait, Cape 121 P6
Kigoma 107 E3
Kiholo 126 T11
Kii-sanchi 89 E9
Kii-suido 89 E9
Kikai-jima 89 B11
Kikiakki 84 C4
Kikinda 72 F3
Kikladhes 75 H4
Kikonai 88 H5
Kikori 114 C3
Kikwit 106 C3
Kil 63 E7
Kilafors 63 G6
Kilakh 97 K5
Kilauea 126 R9
Kilauea Crater 126 T11
Kilbasan 76 E4
Kilbeggan 59 H6
Kilberry 58 J5
Kilbirnie 57 D5
Kilbrannan Sound 57 C5
Kilbride *Ireland* 59 K7
Kilbride *U.K.* 57 A3
Kilbuck Mountains 118 D3
Kilchu 88 B5
Kilcock 59 J6
Kilcolgan 59 E6
Kilcormac 59 G6
Kilcoy 113 L4
Kilcullen 59 J6
Kildare *Ireland* 59 J6
Kildare *Ireland* 59 J6
Kildin, Ostrov 62 R2
Kildinstroy 62 Q2
Kilfinnane 59 F8
Kilgore 128 E4
Kilham 57 F5
Kilickaya 77 J2
Kilifi 107 G3
Kilimanjaro 107 G3
Kilinailau Islands 114 F2
Kilis 77 G4
Kiliya 79 D6
Kilkee 59 C7
Kilkeel 58 L4
Kilkelly 58 E5
Kilkenny *Ireland* 59 H7
Kilkenny *Ireland* 59 H7
Kilkhampton 52 C4
Kilkieran Bay 59 C6
Killadysert 59 D7
Killala 58 D4
Killala Bay 58 D4
Killaloe 59 F7
Killarney 59 C8
Killashandra 58 G4
Killeen 128 D5
Killenaule 59 G7
Killiecrankie 57 E4
Killiecrankie, Pass of 57 E4
Killin 57 D4
Killinek Island 121 P5
Killini 75 G4
Killorglin 59 C8
Killybegs 58 F3
Killylea 58 J4
Kilmacthomas 59 H8
Kilmallock 59 E8
Kilmaluag 56 B3
Kilmarnock 57 D5
Kilmaurs 57 D5
Kilmelford 57 C4
Kilmez 78 J4
Kilmurry 59 D7
Kilnsea 55 K3
Kiloran 57 B4
Kilosa 107 G4
Kilpisjarvi 62 J2
Kilrea 58 J3
Kilrush 59 D7
Kilsyth 57 D5
Kiltan 92 D6
Kilwa Masoko 107 G4
Kilwinning 57 F4
Kilyos 76 C2
Kimbal, Mount 118 G3
Kimbe Bay 114 E3
Kimberley *Canada* 122 G3
Kimberley *South Africa* 108 D5
Kimberley Plateau 112 F2
Kimi 75 H3
Kimito 63 K6
Kimmeridge 53 E4
Kimolos 75 H4
Kimry 78 F4
Kimvula 106 C4
Kimzha 78 G2
Kinabalu, Gunung 90 F4
Kinbasket Lake 122 F2
Kinbrace 56 E2
Kincardine *Canada* 125 K4
Kincardine *U.K.* 57 E4
Kindat 93 H4
Kinder 128 F5
Kinder Scout 55 H3
Kindersley 123 K2
Kindia 104 C3
Kindu 106 E3
Kinel 79 J5
Kinel-Cherkasy 78 J5
Kineshma 78 G4
Kingaroy 113 L4
Kingarth 57 C5
King Christian Island 120 F2
King City 126 B2
King George Island 141 W6
King George Sound 112 D5
Kinghorn 57 E4
Kingisepp 63 M7
Kingiseppa 63 K7
King Island 113 J6
King, Lake 112 D5
King Leopold Ranges 112 F2
Kingman 126 E3
Kingoonya 113 H5
Kings 126 B2
King Salmon 118 D4
Kingsbarns 57 F4
Kingsbridge 52 D4
King's Bromley 53 F2
Kingsclere 53 F3
Kingscote 113 H6
Kingscourt 58 J5
Kingsford 124 F4
Kingsley 55 H3
King's Lynn 53 H2
Kingsmill Group 111 R2
King Sound 112 E2
Kings Peak 123 J7
Kingsport 129 L2
Kingston *Australia* 113 H6
Kingston *Canada* 125 M4
Kingston *Jamaica* 132 J5
Kingston *New Zealand* 115 B6
Kingston *U.S.A.* 125 P6
Kingston Bagpuize 53 F3
Kingston-upon-Hull 55 J3
Kingston-upon-Thames 53 G3
Kingstown 133 S8
Kingsville 128 D7
Kingswood 52 E3
Kington 52 D2
Kingussie 57 D3
King William Island 120 G3
King William's Town 108 E6
Kiniama 107 E5
Kinik 76 B3
Kinloch 57 B3
Kinlochewe 56 C3
Kinloch Hourn 57 C3
Kinna 63 E8
Kinnaird Head 56 F3
Kinnegad 59 H6
Kinnerley 52 E2
Kinnert, Yam 94 B5
Kinoosao 119 Q4
Kinross 57 E4
Kinsale 59 E9
Kinsalebeg 59 G9
Kinsarvik 63 B6
Kinshasa 106 C3
Kinsley 127 N2
Kinston 129 P3
Kintampo 104 E4
Kintore 56 F3
Kintyre 57 C5
Kintyre, Mull of 57 C5
Kinuachdrachd 57 C4
Kiparissia 75 F4
Kiparissiakos Kolpos 75 F4
Kipawa, Lac 125 L3
Kipengere Range 107 F4
Kipili 107 F4
Kipini 107 H3
Kipnuk 118 C4
Kipseli 75 G3
Kirakira 114 K7
Kiraz 76 C3
Kirazli 76 B2
Kirbasi 76 D2
Kirbey 84 H3
Kircubbin 58 L4
Kirec 76 C3
Kirenga 84 H5
Kirenis 76 C4
Kirensk 84 H5
Kirgizskiy Khrebet 86 C3
Kirgiz Step 79 J6
Kiri 106 C3
Kiribati 111 S2
Kirik 77 J2
Kirikhan 77 G4
Kirikkale 76 E3
Kirillo 78 F4
Kirin 87 P3
Kirinyaga 107 G3
Kirka 76 D3
Kirkagac 76 B3
Kirk Bulag Dag 94 H3
Kirkburton 55 H3
Kirkby 55 G3
Kirkby in Ashfield 55 H3
Kirkby Lonsdale 55 G2
Kirkby Stephen 55 G2
Kirkcaldy 57 E4
Kirkcambeck 57 F5
Kirkcolm 54 D2
Kirkcudbright 54 E2
Kirkcudbright Bay 54 E2
Kirkenes 62 P2
Kirkestinden 62 H2
Kirkheaton 57 G5
Kirkintilloch 57 D5
Kirkland Lake 125 K2
Kirk Langley 53 F2
Kirklareli 76 B2
Kirklington 55 J3
Kirk Michael 54 E2
Kirkoswald 55 G2
Kirk Smeaton 55 H3
Kirksville 124 D6
Kirkton 57 F4
Kirkton of Culsalmond 56 F3
Kirkton of Largo 57 F4
Kirkuk 94 G4
Kirkwall 56 F2
Kirkwhelpington 57 F5
Kirkwood 108 E6
Kirlangic Burun 76 D4
Kirmir 76 E2
Kirov *U.S.S.R.* 78 E5
Kirov *U.S.S.R.* 78 H4
Kirova 86 D2
Kirovabad 79 H7
Kirovakan 77 L2
Kirovgrad 79 E6
Kirovo-Chepetsk 78 H4
Kirovsk *Rossiyskaya S.F.S.R., U.S.S.R.* 62 Q3
Kirovsk *Turkmeniya S.S.R., U.S.S.R.* 95 Q3
Kirovskiy 88 D3
Kirriemuir 57 F4
Kirs 78 J4
Kirsanov 79 G5
Kirsehir 76 F3
Kirtgecit 77 K3
Kirthar Range 92 C3
Kirtlington 53 F3
Kirton 55 J3
Kiruna 62 J3
Kiryu 89 G7
Kisa 63 F8
Kisamou, Kolpos 75 G5
Kisangani 106 E2
Kisar 91 H7
Kisarazu 89 G8
Kiselevsk 84 D6
Kishanganj 93 G3
Kishangarh 92 D3
Kishb, Harrat 96 E5
Kishika-zaki 89 C10
Kishinev 79 D6
Kishiwada 89 E8
Kishorganj 93 H4
Kishorn, Loch 56 C3
Kisii 107 F3
Kiska Island 118 Ab9
Kiskunfelegyhaza 72 E2
Kiskunhalas 72 E2
Kislovodsk 79 G7
Kismaayo 107 H3
Kiso-Fukushima 89 F8
Kiso-sammyaku 89 F8
Kispest 72 E2
Kissidougou 104 C4
Kissimmee 129 M7
Kisumu 107 F3
Kita 100 D6
Kitajaur 62 J3
Kitakami *Japan* 88 H6
Kitakami *Japan* 88 H6
Kitakami-sanmyaku 88 J3
Kita-kyushu 89 C9
Kitale 107 G2
Kitami 88 J4
Kitami-sammyaku 88 H6
Kitangari 107 G5
Kitay, Ozero 73 K3
Kit Carson 127 L1
Kitchener 125 K5
Kitee 62 P5
Kitgum 107 F2
Kithira *Greece* 75 G4
Kithira *Greece* 75 G4
Kithnos *Greece* 75 H4
Kithnos *Greece* 75 H4
Kitikmeot 119 N1
Kitimat 118 K5
Kitinen 62 M3
Kitkiojoki 62 K3
Kitsuki 89 C9
Kittanning 125 L6
Kittila 62 L3
Kitui 107 G3
Kitunda 107 F4
Kitwe 107 E5
Kitzbuhel 68 D2
Kitzbuheler Alpen 68 D2
Kitzingen 70 D4
Kivalo 62 L3
Kivijarvi 62 L5
Kivu, Lake 107 E3
Kiyev 79 E5
Kiyevka 88 D4
Kiyevskoye Vodokhranilishche 79 E5
Kiyikoy 76 C2
Kizel 78 K4
Kizema 78 H3
Kizilagac 77 J3
Kizilcaboluk 76 C4
Kizilcadag 76 C4
Kizilhisar 76 C4

Name	Page	Grid
Kizilirmak	76	E2
Kizil Irmak	77	F2
Kizilkaya	76	D4
Kiziloren	76	E4
Kiziltepe	77	J4
Kizlyar	79	H7
Kizyl-Arvat	95	N2
Kizyl-Atrek	95	M3
Kizyl Ayak	95	S3
Kizyl-Su	95	L2
Kjollefjord	62	M1
Kjopsvick	62	L2
Kladanj	72	E3
Kladno	70	F3
Kladovo	73	G3
Klagenfurt	68	E2
Klaipeda	63	L9
Klamath *U.S.A.*	122	B7
Klamath *U.S.A.*	122	C7
Klamath Falls	122	D6
Klamath Mountains	122	C6
Klamono	91	J6
Klaralven	63	J6
Klatovy	70	E4
Klekovaca	72	D3
Klenak	72	E3
Klerksdorp	108	E5
Klichka	85	K7
Klimovichi	79	E5
Klin	78	F4
Klinovec	70	E3
Klintsovka	79	H5
Klintsy	79	E5
Klisura	73	H4
Kljuc	72	D3
Klobuck	71	H3
Klodzka *Poland*	71	G3
Klodzko *Poland*	71	G3
Klos	75	F2
Klosterneuberg	68	F1
Klosters	68	B2
Klrovskiy	79	H6
Kluane	118	H3
Kluane Lake	118	H3
Kluczbork	71	H3
Klyevka	84	A6
Klyuchevskaya Sopka	85	U5
Klyuchi	85	U5
Klyukvinka	84	D5
Kmagta	114	J6
Kmanjab	108	B3
K2, Mount	92	E1
Knapdale	57	C5
Knaresborough	55	H2
Knife	123	N4
Knight Island	118	F3
Knighton	52	D2
Knin	72	D3
Knjazevac	73	G4
Knockadoon Head	59	G9
Knockalla Mount	58	G2
Knockanaffrin	59	G8
Knockaunapeebra	59	G8
Knocklayd	58	K2
Knockmealdown Mountains	59	G8
Knocknaskagh	59	F8
Knottingley	55	H3
Knox, Cape	118	J5
Knoxville *Iowa, U.S.A.*	124	D6
Knoxville *Tennessee, U.S.A.*	129	L3
Knoydart	57	C3
Knud Rasmussen Land	120	P2
Knutholstind	63	C6
Knutsford	55	G3
Knyazhaya Guba	62	Q3
Knyazhevo	78	G4
Knysna	108	D6
Knyszyn	71	K2
Koba	90	D6
Kobarid	72	B2
Kobayashi	89	C10
Kobberminebugt	120	R5
Kobelyaki	79	E6
Kobenhavn	63	E9
Koblenz	70	B3
Kobowre, Pegunungan	91	K6
Kobrin	71	L2
Kobroor	91	J7
Kobuk	118	D2
Kobuleti	77	J2
Kobya	85	M4
Koca *Turkey*	76	B3
Koca *Turkey*	76	C3
Koca *Turkey*	76	E2
Kocapinar	77	K3
Kocarli	76	B4
Koceljevo	72	E3
Koch Bihar	93	G3
Kochechum	84	G3
Kochegarovo	85	K5
Kocher	70	C4
Kochi	89	D9
Koch Island	120	L4
Kochkorka	86	D3
Koch Peak	122	J5
Kochumdek	84	E4
Koden	71	K3
Kodiak	118	E4
Kodiak Island	118	E4
Kodima	78	G3
Kodinar	92	D4
Kodok	103	F6
Kodomari	88	H5
Kodyma	73	L2
Kofcaz	76	B2
Koffiefontein	108	D5
Koflach	68	E2
Koforidua	104	E4
Kofu	89	G8
Koge	63	E9
Kogilnik	73	K2
Ko, Gora	88	F2
Kohat	92	D2
Kohima	93	H3
Koh-i Qaisar	95	S5
Kohtla-Jarve	63	M7
Koide	89	G7
Koi Sanjaq	94	G3
Koitere	62	P5
Koivu	62	L3
Koje	89	B8
Kojonup	112	D5
Kokand	86	B3
Kokas	91	J6
Kokchetav	84	Ae6
Kokemaenjoki	63	K6
Kokenau	91	K6
Kokkola	62	K5
Koko	105	G4
Kokoda	114	D3
Kokomo	124	G6
Kokpekty	86	E2
Koksoak	121	N6
Kokstad	108	E6
Koktas	86	C2
Kokubu	89	C10
Kokuora	85	R2
Kokura	89	C9
Kokuy	85	K6
Kok-Yangak	86	C3
Kola	62	Q2
Kolaka	91	G6
Kolar	92	E6
Kolari	62	K3
Kolarovgrad	73	J4
Kolasin	72	E4
Kolay	77	F2
Kolberg	70	F1
Kolbuszowa	71	J3
Kolchugino	78	F4
Kolda	104	C3
Kolding	63	C9
Kole	106	D3
Kolguyev, Ostrov	78	H2
Kolhapur	92	D5
Kolin	70	F3
Kolki	71	L3
Kolkuskull	62	V12
Kollabudur	62	T12
Koln	70	B3
Kolno	71	J2
Kolobrzeg	70	F1
Kologriv	78	G4
Kolombangara	114	H5
Kolomna	78	F4
Kolono	91	G6
Koloubara	72	F3
Kolozsvar	73	G2
Kolpashevo	84	C5
Kolpino	78	E4
Kolskiy Poluostrov	78	F2
Koltubanovskiy	79	J5
Koluszki	71	H3
Kolva *U.S.S.R.*	78	K3
Kolva *U.S.S.R.*	78	K2
Kolwezi	106	E5
Kolyma	85	U3
Kolymskaya Nizmennost	85	T3
Kolymskiy, Khrebet	85	T4
Komadugu Gana	105	H3
Komandorskiye Ostrova	81	T4
Komarno	71	H5
Komarom	72	E2
Komatsu	89	F7
Komering	90	C6
Komi A.S.S.R.	78	J3
Kommunarsk	79	F6
Komodo	91	F7
Komoe	104	E4
Kom Ombo	103	F3
Komoran	91	K7
Komosomolets, Ostrov	81	L1
Komotini	75	H2
Komovi	74	E1
Kompong Cham	93	L6
Kompong Chhnang	93	K6
Kompong Som	93	K6
Kompong Speu	93	K6
Kompong Sralao	93	L6
Kompong Thom	93	K6
Komrat	79	D6
Komsomolets, Zaliv	79	J6
Komsomolsk	79	E6
Komsomolskiy	79	J6
Komsomolsk-na-Amure	85	P6
Konakovo	78	F4
Koncanica	72	D3
Konch	92	E3
Konda *Indonesia*	91	J6
Konda *U.S.S.R.*	84	Ae4
Kondagaon	92	F5
Kondinin	112	D5
Kondinskoye	84	Ae5
Kondoa	107	G3
Kondon	85	P6
Kondoponga	78	E3
Konduz	92	C1
Kone	114	W16
Konevo	78	F3
Kong	104	E4
Kongan	89	J10
Kong Christian den X Land	120	W3
Kong Karls Land	80	D2
Kongolo	106	E4
Kongsberg	63	C7
Kongsvinger	63	E6
Kong Wilhelms Land	120	X2
Koniecpol	71	H3
Konigsberg	71	J4
Konigs Wusterhausen	70	E2
Konin	71	H2
Konitsa	75	F2
Koniya	89	B11
Konkamaalv	62	J2
Konkoure	104	C3
Konnern	70	D3
Konnevesi	62	M5
Konosha	78	G3
Konotop	79	E5
Konqi He	86	F3
Konskie	71	J3
Konstantinovka	79	F6
Konstantinovsk	79	G6
Konstanz	68	B2
Kontagora	105	G3
Kontcha	105	H4
Kontiomaki	62	N4
Kontum	93	L6
Kontum, Plateau du	93	L6
Konya	76	E4
Konya Ovasi	76	E3
Konzhakovskiy Kamen, Gora	78	K4
Kootenai	122	G3
Kootenay	122	F3
Kootenay Lake	122	F3
Kopaonik	73	F4
Kopasker	62	W11
Kopavogur	62	U12
Koper	72	B3
Kopervik	63	A7
Kopet Dag, Khrebet	95	N2
Kopeysk	84	Ad5
Koping	63	F7
Kopka	124	F1
Kopmanholmen	62	H5
Koppang	63	D6
Kopparberg *Sweden*	63	F7
Kopparberg *Sweden*	63	F6
Koppi *U.S.S.R.*	88	G1
Koppi *U.S.S.R.*	88	H1
Kopru	76	D4
Koprubasi	76	C3
Koprulu	76	E4
Kopruoren	76	C3
Kopychintsy	73	H1
Kor	95	L6
Kora	77	K2
Korab	72	F5
Korahe	103	H6
Koraluk	121	P6
Korana	72	C3
Korba	69	C7
Korbach	70	C3
Korbu, Gunung	90	C5
Korce	75	F2
Korcula	72	D4
Korda	84	F4
Kord Kuv	95	M3
Korea Bay	87	N4
Korea, North	87	P4
Korea, South	87	P4
Korea Strait	89	B8
Korennoye	84	H2
Korenovsk	79	F6
Korf	85	V4
Korforskiy	88	E1
Korgan	77	G2
Korgen	62	E3
Korhogo	104	D4
Korido	91	K6
Korim	91	K6
Korinthiakos Kolpos	75	G3
Korinthos	75	G4
Koriyama	89	H7
Korkinitskiy Zaliv	79	E6
Korkodon	85	T4
Korkuteli	76	D4
Korla	86	F3
Kormakiti, Akra	76	E5
Kornat	72	C4
Koro	114	R8
Korocha	79	F5
Koroglu Daglari	76	E2
Koronia, Limni	75	G2
Koronowo	71	G2
Koros	72	F2
Korosten	79	D5
Korostyshev	79	D5
Korotaikha	78	L2
Korovin Volcano	118	Ad9
Korpilombolo	62	K3
Korsakov	88	J2
Korsnas	62	J5
Korti	103	F4
Kortrijk	64	E3
Korucu	76	B3
Koryakskaya Sopka	85	U6
Koryanskiy Khrebet	85	Z5
Koryazhma	78	H3
Korzybie	71	G1
Kos *Greece*	75	J4
Kos *Greece*	75	J4
Koschagyl	79	J6
Koscian	71	G2
Koscierzyna	71	G1
Kosciusco, Mount	113	K6
Kosciusko	128	H4
Kose	77	H2
Kos Golu	76	B2
Koshiki-retto	89	B10
Kosice	71	J4
Koski	63	K6
Koslan	78	H3
Koslin	71	G1
Kosma	78	H2
Kosong	88	B6
Kosong-ni	88	B5
Kossou, Lac de	104	D4
Kossovo	71	L2
Kostajnica	72	D3
Kosti	103	F5
Kostino	84	D3
Kostomuksha	62	P4
Kostopol	71	M3
Kostroma *U.S.S.R.*	78	G4
Kostroma *U.S.S.R.*	78	G4
Kostrzyn	70	F2
Kosu-dong	89	B8
Kosva	78	K4
Kosyu	78	K2
Kosyuvom	78	K2
Koszalin	71	G1
Kota	92	E3
Kotaagung	90	C7
Kota Baharu	90	C4
Kotabaru *Indonesia*	90	E6
Kotabaru *Indonesia*	90	F6
Kota Belud	90	F4
Kotabumi	90	C5
Kota Kinabalu	90	F4
Kotala	62	N3
Kotamubagu	91	G5
Kota Tinggi	90	C5
Kotel	73	J4
Kotelnich	78	H4
Kotelnikovo	79	G6
Kotelnyy, Ostrov	85	P1
Kotikovo	88	E2
Kotka	63	M6
Kot Kapura	92	D2
Kotlas	78	H3
Kotli	92	D2
Kotlik	118	C3
Koto	85	P7
Kotor	72	E4
Kotovo	79	G5
Kotovsk *Rossiyskaya S.F.S.R., U.S.S.R.*	79	G5
Kotovsk *Ukraine S.S.R., U.S.S.R.*	79	D6
Kotri	92	C3
Kottagudem	92	F5
Kottayam	92	E7
Kotto	102	D6
Kotuy	84	G2
Kotyuzhany	73	K2
Kotzebue	118	C2
Kotzebue Sound	118	C2
Kouango	102	C6
Koudougou	104	E3
Koufonisi	75	J5
Koukajuak, Great Plain of the	120	M4
Kouki	102	C6
Koumac	114	W16
Koumenzi	86	F3
Koumra	102	C6
Koundara	104	C3
Koungou Mountains	106	B3
Kounradskiy	86	D2
Kourou	137	G2
Kouroussa	104	D3
Kousseri	105	J3
Koutiala	100	D6
Kouvola	63	M6
Kova	84	G5
Kovachevo	73	J4
Kovanlik	77	H2
Kovdor	62	P3
Kovdozero, Ozero	62	Q3
Kovel	71	L3
Kovernino	78	G4
Kovero	62	P5
Kovik Bay	121	L5
Kovno	71	K1
Kovrov	78	G4
Kovylkino	78	G5
Kowalewo	71	H2
Kowloon	87	L7
Koycegiz	76	C4
Koyda	78	G2
Koyuk	118	C3
Koyukuk	118	D3
Koyulhisar	77	G2
Koza	89	E9
Kozakli	76	F3
Kozan	77	F4
Kozani	75	F2
Kozekovo	71	M1
Kozelsk	78	F5
Kozhevnikovo	84	B5
Kozhikode	92	E6
Kozhim	78	K2
Kozhposelok	78	F3
Kozhva	78	K2
Kozlu	76	D2
Kozludere	77	G4
Kozluk	77	J3
Kozmodemyansk	78	H4

L

Labrit 65 C6
Labuha 91 H6
Labuhan 90 D7
Labuhanbajo 91 F7
Labuhanbilik 90 C5
Labytnangi 84 Ae3
Lac 74 E2
La Calzada de Calatrava 66 E3
Lacanau 65 C6
La Carlota 139 D6
La Carolina 66 E3
La Cava 67 G2
Laccadive Islands 92 D6
Laccadive Sea 92 E7
La Ceiba 132 D7
Lacepede Bay 113 H6
La Chaise-Dieu 65 E6
Lacha, Ozero 78 F3
La Charite 65 E5
La Chartre-sur-le-Loir 65 D5
La Chatre 65 D5
La Chaux-de-Fonds 68 A2
Lachin 94 H2
Lachlan 113 K5
La Chorrera 132 H10
Lachute 125 N4
La Cieneguita 126 G6
La Ciotat 65 F7
Lac la Biche 119 N5
Lac Megantic 125 Q4
La Colorada 126 G6
Laconi 69 B6
Laconia 125 Q5
La Coruna 66 B1
La Croix, Lac 124 D2
La Crosse 124 E5
La Cruz *Costa Rica* 132 E9
La Cruz *Mexico* 130 F6
Lacul Razelm 73 K3
Ladakh Range 92 E2
Ladder Hills 56 E3
La Desirade 133 S6
Ladik 77 F2
Ladismith 108 D6
Ladiz 95 Q7
Ladozhskoye Ozero 63 P6
Ladybank 57 E4
Ladybower Reservoir 55 H3
Ladybrand 108 E5
Ladysmith *Canada* 122 C3
Ladysmith *South Africa* 108 E5
Ladysmith *U.S.A.* 124 E4
Ladyzhenka 84 Ae6
Ladyzhinka 79 D6
Lae 93 K5
Laem Ngop 93 K6
La Esmeralda *Paraguay* 138 D4
La Esmeralda *Venezuela* 136 D3
La Fayette 129 K3
Lafayette *Colorado, U.S.A.* 123 M8
Lafayette *Indiana, U.S.A.* 124 G6
Lafayette *Louisiana, U.S.A.* 128 F5
La Fe 132 E3
La Ferte-Bernard 64 D4
La-Ferte-Saint-Aubin 65 D5
Laffan, Ra's 97 K4
Lafia 105 G4
Lafiagi 105 G4
La Fleche 65 C5
La Follette 129 K2
La Fria 136 C2
Laft 95 M8
La Fuente de San Esteban 66 C2
La Galite 69 B7
Lagan 63 E8
Lagarfljot 62 X12
Lagen *Norway* 63 C6
Lagen *Norway* 63 D6
Laggan 57 D3
Laggan Bay 57 B5
Laggan, Loch 57 D4
Laghouat 101 F2
Lagny 64 E4
Lagonegro 69 E5
Lago Posadas 139 B9
Lagos *Nigeria* 105 F4
Lagos *Portugal* 66 B4
Lagos de Moreno 130 J7
La Grande *Canada* 121 M7
La Grande *U.S.A.* 122 E5
La Grande 2, Reservoir 121 L7
La Grande 3, Reservoir 121 L7
La Grande 4, Reservoir 121 M7
La Grange *Georgia, U.S.A.* 129 K4
La Grange *Kentucky, U.S.A.* 124 H7
La Grange *Texas, U.S.A.* 128 D6
La Granja 66 D2
La Gran Sabana 136 E2
La Guardia 66 B2
Laguardia 66 E1
La Gudina 66 C1
La Guerche-de-Bretagne 65 C5
Laguna 138 G5
Laguna Grande 139 C9
Lagunillas *Bolivia* 138 D3
Lagunillas *Venezuela* 133 M9
Laha 87 N2
La Habana 132 F3
Lahad Datu 91 F4
Lahave 121 P9
Lahij 96 G10
Lahijan 95 J3
Lahn *W. Germany* 70 C3
Lahn *W. Germany* 70 C3
Lahore 92 D2
Lahr 70 B4
Lahti 63 L6
Laibach 72 C2
Laibin 93 L4
Lai Chau 93 K4
L'Aigle 64 D4
Laihia 62 J5
Laimbele, Mount 114 T12
Laina 75 J2
Laingsburg 108 D6
Lainioalven 62 K3
Lair 56 C3
Lairg 56 D2
Lais 90 C6
Laitila 63 J6
Laiwui 91 H6
Laixi 87 N4
Laiyang 87 N4
Laiyuan 87 L4
Laizhou Wan 87 M4
Lajes 138 F5
La Junta 127 L2
Lakatrask 62 J3
Lake Andes 123 Q6
Lakeba 114 S9
Lakeba Passage 114 S9
Lake Cargelligo 113 K5
Lake Charles 128 F5
Lake City *Florida, U.S.A.* 129 L5
Lake City *S. Carolina, U.S.A.* 129 N4
Lake District 55 F2
Lake Grace 112 D5
Lake Harbour 120 N5
Lake Havasu City 126 E3
Lake Jackson 128 E6
Lake King 112 D5
Lake Kopiago 114 C3
Lakeland 129 M6
Lake Louise 122 F2
Lake Murray 114 C3
Lakeport 122 C8
Lake Providence 128 G4
Lakeview 122 D6
Lake Wales 129 M7
Lakewood 124 K6
Lakhdaria 67 H4
Lakhpat 92 C4
Lakki 92 D2
Lakonikos Kolpos 75 G4
Laksefjorden 62 M1
Lakselv 62 L1
Lakshadweep 92 D6
Lakuramau 114 E2
Lala Musa 92 D2
Lalaua 109 G2
Laleh Zar, Kuh-e 95 N7
Lalibela 103 G5
La Libertad 132 B6
La Ligua 139 B6
Lalin 66 B1
Lalin 87 P2
La Linea 66 D4
Lalin He 88 A3
Lalitpur 92 E4
Lalla Khedidja 67 J4
La Loche 119 P4
La Loupe 64 D4
La Louviere 64 F3
La Luz 132 E8
Lalyo 102 F7
Lamag 91 F4
La Mancha 66 E3
La Manza 136 D6
Lama, Ozero 84 D3
Lamar *Colorado, U.S.A.* 127 L1
Lamar *Missouri, U.S.A.* 124 C8
Lamas 136 B5
Lamastre 65 F6
Lamballe 64 B4
Lambarene 106 B3
Lambas 114 R8
Lambay Island 59 K6
Lamberhurst 53 H3
Lambert, Cape 114 E2
Lambert Glacier 141 E4
Lamberts Bay 108 C6
Lamb Head 56 F1
Lambia 75 F4
Lambon 114 E2
Lambourn 53 F3
Lamb's Head 59 B9
Lambton, Cape 118 L1
Lame 102 B6
Lamego 66 C2
Lamenu 114 U12
Lameroo 113 J6
Lamia 75 G3
Lammermuir 57 F5
Lammermuir Hills 57 F5
Lammhult 63 F8
Lammi 63 L6
Lamon Bay 91 G3
Lamont *California, U.S.A.* 126 C3
Lamont *Wyoming, U.S.A.* 123 L6
La Morita 127 K6
La Moure 123 Q4
Lam Pao Reservoir 93 K5
Lampasas 128 C5
Lampazos de Naranjo 128 B7
Lampedusa 74 B5
Lampeter 52 C2
Lampinou 75 G3
Lampione 74 B5
Lamport 53 G2
Lampsa 62 P4
Lamu 107 H3
Lan 71 M2
Lanai 126 S10
Lanai City 126 S10
Lanark 57 D5
La Nava de Ricomalillo 66 D3
Lanbi Kyun 93 J6
Lancang 93 K4
Lancashire 55 G3
Lancaster *U.K.* 55 G2
Lancaster *Ohio, U.S.A.* 124 J7
Lancaster *Pennsylvania, U.S.A.* 125 M6
Lancaster *S. Carolina. U.S.A.* 129 M3
Lancaster Sound 120 J3
Lanciano 69 E4
Lancut 71 K3
Landau 70 C4
Landeck 68 C2
Lander 123 K6
Landerneau 64 A4
Landes 65 C6
Landi 95 R6
Landor 112 D4
Landrum 129 L3
Landsberg *Poland* 70 F2
Landsberg *W. Germany* 70 D4
Landsborough 113 J3
Land's End 52 B4
Lands End 120 B2
Landshut 70 E4
Landskrona 63 E9
Lanesborough 58 G5
Lanett 129 K4
Langa Co 92 F2
Langadhia 75 F4
Langavat, Loch 56 B2
Langdon 123 Q3
Lange Berg 108 C6
Langebergen 108 D5
Langeland 63 D9
Langelmavesi 63 L6
Langeoog 70 B2
Langesund 63 C7
Langevag 62 B5
Langfang 87 M4
Langfjord 62 B5
Lang Head 56 A1
Langhirano 68 C3
Langholm 57 E5
Langjokull 62 U12
Langkawi 93 J7
Langnau 68 A2
Langness Point 54 E2
Langogne 65 E6
Langon 65 C6
Langoya 62 F2
Langport 52 E3
Langres 65 F5
Langsa 90 B5
Langsele 62 G5
Langsett 55 H3
Lang Son 93 L4
Langtoft 55 J2
Langtrask 62 J4
Languedoc 65 E7
Langwathby 55 G2
Langzhong 93 L2
Lannemezan 65 D7
Lannion 64 B4
Lansing 124 H5
Lansjarv 62 K3
Lanslebourg 65 G6
Lanta, Ko 93 J7
Lanusei 69 B6
Lanvaux, Landes de 65 B5
Lanxi 87 P2
Lanzarote 100 C3
Lanzhou 93 K1
Laoag 91 G2
Laoang 91 H3
Lao Cai 93 K4
Laois 59 H7
Laon 64 E4
La Oroya 136 B6
Laos 90 C2
Laoye Ling 88 B3
Laoyemiao 86 F3
Lapa 138 G5
Lapalisse 65 E5
La Palma *Panama* 132 H10
La Palma *Spain* 100 B3
La Palma del Condado 66 C4
La Paragua 136 E2
La Paz *Argentina* 139 C6
La Paz *Argentina* 138 E6
La Paz *Bolivia* 138 C3
La Paz *Mexico* 130 D5
La Pedrera 136 D4
La Piedad 130 H7
La Place 128 G5
La Plant 123 P5
La Plata 139 E6
La Pocatiere 125 R3
La Pola de Gordon 66 D1
La Porte 124 G6
Lapovo 73 F3
Lappajarvi 62 K5
Lappeenranta 63 N6
Lappi 62 M3
Lapseki 76 B2
Laptev Sea 85 M1
Laptevykh, More 85 M1
Lapua 62 K5
La Puebla 67 H3
La Puntilla 136 A4
La Quiaca 138 C4
L'Aquila 69 D4
Lar 95 M8
Larache 100 D1
Larak 95 N8
La Rambla 66 D4
Laramie 123 M7
Laramie Mountains 123 M6
Laranjal 137 F4
Larantuka 91 G7
Larat *Indonesia* 114 A3
Larat *Indonesia* 114 A3
Larba 67 H4
Laredo *Spain* 66 E1
Laredo *U.S.A.* 128 C7
La Reole 65 C6
Largo *U.S.A.* 129 L7
Largo *Venezuela* 133 R10
Largoward 57 F4
Largs 57 D5
Lari 94 H2
Larino 69 E5
La Rioja 138 C5
Larisa 75 G3
Lark 53 H2
Larkana 92 C3
Larkhall 57 F4
Larlomkiny 84 A5
Larne 58 L3
La Robla 66 D1
La Roche 114 Y16
La Roche-Bernard 65 B5
La Rochelle 65 C5
La Roche-sur-Yon 65 C5
La Roda 67 E3
La Romana 133 N5
La Ronge 119 P4
Larrey Point 112 D2
Larsen Ice Shelf 141 V5
Larvik 63 D7
La Salle 124 F6
Las Animas 127 L1
Las Aves, Isla 136 D1
Las Coloradas 139 B7
Las Cruces 127 J4
La Selle 133 M5
La Serena 138 B5
La Seu d'Urgell 67 G1
Las Flores 139 E7
Lasham 53 F3
Lash-e Joveyn 95 Q6
Lashkar 92 E3
Lashkar Gah 92 B2
Las Horquetas 139 B9
La Sila 69 F6
Lasjerd 95 L4
Las Lomitas 138 D4
Las Marismas 66 C4
Las Mercedes 133 P10
Laso 63 D8
La Souterraine 65 D5
Las Palmas 100 B3
La Spezia 68 B3
Las Plumas 139 C8
Lassen Peak 122 D7
Last Mountain Lake 123 M2
Lastoursville 106 B3
Lastovo 72 D4
Las Trincheras 133 Q11
L'Astrolabe, Recifs de 114 W15
Lasva 72 D3
Las Varillas 138 D6
Las Vegas *Nevada, U.S.A.* 126 E2
Las Vegas *New Mexico, U.S.A.* 127 K3
Latacunga 136 B4
Latady Island 141 U4
Latakia 77 F5
Late 111 U5
Latefoss 63 B7
Latgale 63 M8
Latheron 56 E2
La Tina 136 B4
Latina 69 D5
Latoritsa 71 K4
La Tour-du-Pin 65 F6
Latrobe 113 K7
La Tuque 125 P3
Latur 92 E5
Latviya S.S.R. 63 K8
Lau *Sudan* 102 F6
Lau *Sudan* 102 F6
Laucola 114 S8
Lauder 57 F4
Lauderdale 57 F5
Lauenberg 70 D2
Laughlan Islands 114 E3
Lau Group 114 S8
Launceston *Australia* 113 K7
Launceston *U.K.* 52 C4
Launglon Bok Islands 93 J6
La Union *Bolivia* 138 D3
La Union *Chile* 139 B8
La Union *Colombia* 136 B3
La Union *El Salvador* 132 D8
La Union *Mexico* 131 Q9
La Union *Spain* 67 F4
Laupheim 70 C4
Laura 113 J2
La Urbana 133 P11
Laurel *Mississippi, U.S.A.* 128 H5
Laurel *Montana, U.S.A.* 123 K5
Laurencekirk 57 F4
Laurentian Scarp 125 M3
Laurentien, Plateau 121 M7
Laurenzana 69 E5

Linapacan Strait **91** F3
Linares *Chile* **139** B7
Linares *Mexico* **128** C8
Linares *Spain* **66** E3
Lincang **93** K4
Lincoln *New Zealand* **115** D5
Lincoln *U.K.* **55** J3
Lincoln *Illinois, U.S.A.* **124** F6
Lincoln *Maine, U.S.A.* **125** R4
Lincoln *Nebraska, U.S.A.* **123** R7
Lincoln City **122** B5
Lincoln Sea **140** R2
Lincolnshire **55** J3
Lincolnton **129** M3
Lindau **70** C5
Linde **85** L3
Linden *Guyana* **136** F2
Linden *U.S.A.* **129** J3
Linderodsasen **63** E9
Lindesberg **63** F7
Lindi **107** G4
Lindley **108** E5
Lindos **75** K4
Lindsay *Canada* **125** L4
Lindsay *California, U.S.A.* **126** C2
Lindsay *Montana, U.S.A.* **123** M4
Lindu Point **114** S8
Linfen **93** M1
Lingao **93** L5
Lingayen **91** G2
Lingen **70** B2
Lingfield **53** G3
Lingga **90** C6
Lingga, Kepulauan **90** C6
Lingle **123** M6
Lingling **93** M3
Lingshi **87** L4
Lingshui **93** M5
Lingsugur **92** E5
Linguere **104** B2
Ling Xian **93** M3
Lingyuan **87** M3
Lingyun **93** L4
Linhai **87** N6
Linhares **138** H3
Linhe **87** K3
Linh, Ngoc **93** L5
Linkoping **63** F7
Linkou **88** C3
Linlithgow **57** E5
Linnhe, Loch **57** C4
Linosa **74** B5
Linru **93** M2
Lins **138** G4
Linsell **63** E5
Linslade **53** G3
Lintao **93** K1
Linton *U.K.* **53** H2
Linton *U.S.A.* **123** P4
Linwu **93** M3
Linxi **87** M3
Linxia **93** K1
Linyi *China* **87** M4
Linyi *China* **87** M4
Linz *Austria* **68** E1
Linz *W. Germany* **70** B3
Linze **86** J4
Lion, Golfe du **65** F7
Liouesso **106** C2
Lipa *Philippines* **91** G3
Lipa *Yugoslavia* **72** D3
Lipari, Isola **69** E6
Lipari, Isole **69** E6
Lipenska nadrz **70** F4
Lipetsk **79** F5
Lipiany **70** F2
Lipin Bor **78** F3
Liping **93** L3
Lipkany **79** D6
Lipljan **73** F4
Lipnishki **71** L2
Lipno **71** H2
Lippe **70** C3
Lipsoi **75** J4
Lipson **75** F3
Lipu **93** M4
Lipusz **71** G1
Lira **107** F2
Lircay **136** C6
Liri **69** D5
Lisabata **91** H6
Lisala **106** D2
Lisboa **66** B3
Lisbon *Portugal* **66** B3
Lisbon *U.S.A.* **123** R4
Lisburn **58** K3
Lisburne, Cape **118** B2
Liscannor Bay **59** D7
Lisdoonvarna **59** D6
Lishi **87** L4
Lishui **87** M6
Lisichansk **79** F6
Lisieux **64** D4
Liskeard **52** C4
L'Isle-Jourdain **65** D7
Lismore *Australia* **113** L4
Lismore *Ireland* **59** G8
Lismore *U.K.* **57** C4
Liss **53** G3
Listowel **59** D8
Lit **62** F5
Litang **93** K3
Litani **137** G3
Litchfield **124** F7
Litherland **55** G3
Lithgow **113** L5
Lithinon, Akra **75** H5
Litos **66** C2
Litovko **85** P7
Little **128** E4
Little Abaco **132** J1
Little Aden **96** G10
Little Andaman **93** H6
Little Bahama Bank **132** H1
Little Barrier Island **115** E2
Little Belt Mountains **122** J4
Littleborough **55** G3
Little Bow **122** H2
Little Cayman **132** G5
Little Colorado **126** G3
Little Falls *Minnesota, U.S.A.* **124** C3
Little Falls *New York, U.S.A.* **125** N5
Littlefield **127** L4
Littlehampton **53** G4
Little Inagua Island **133** L4
Little Karoo **108** D6
Little Minch, The **56** B3
Little Missouri **123** M5
Little Nicobar **93** H7
Little Ouse **53** H2
Little Pamir **92** D1
Littleport **53** H2
Little Red **128** G3
Little Rock **128** F3
Little Rocky Mountains **123** K3
Little Scarcies **104** C4
Little Sitkin Island **118** Ab9
Little Smoky **119** M5
Little Snake **123** K7
Little South-west Miramichi **125** S3
Little Strickland **55** G2
Littleton *Colorado, U.S.A.* **123** M8
Littleton *New Hampshire, U.S.A.* **125** Q4
Little Wabash **124** F7
Little Waltham **53** H3
Litva S.S.R. **62** K9
Liulin **87** L4
Liupan Shan **93** L1
Liuyang **93** M3
Liuzhou **93** L4
Livani **63** M8
Live Oak **129** L5
Livermore **126** B2
Livermore, Mount **127** K5
Liverpool *Australia* **113** L5
Liverpool *U.K.* **55** G3
Liverpool Bay *Canada* **118** K1
Liverpool Bay *U.K.* **55** F3
Livingston *Canada* **121** N7
Livingston *U.K.* **57** E5
Livingston *Montana, U.S.A.* **123** J5
Livingston *Texas, U.S.A.* **128** E5
Livingstone **106** E6
Livingstone, Chutes de **106** B4
Livingstone Falls **106** B4
Livingstone Mountains **107** F4
Livingston Island **141** V6
Livingston, Lake **128** E5
Livno **72** D4
Livny **79** F5
Livojoki **62** M4
Livonia **124** J5
Livorno **68** C4
Liwiec **71** J2
Liwonde **107** G6
Li Xian **93** M3
Liyang **87** M5
Lizard **52** B4
Lizardo **137** H5
Lizard Point **52** B4
Ljosavatn **62** W12
Ljubinje **72** E4
Ljubisnja **72** E4
Ljubljana **72** C2
Ljungan **62** G5
Ljungby **63** E8
Ljusdal **63** G6
Ljusnan **63** F5
Llanarmon Dyffryn Ceiriog **52** D2
Llanbadarn Fynydd **52** D2
Llanbedr **52** C2
Llanberis **54** E3
Llanbrynmair **52** D2
Llandeilo **52** D3
Llandovery **52** D3
Llandrindod Wells **52** D2
Llandudno **54** F3
Llanelli **52** C3
Llanerchymedd **54** E3
Llanes **66** D1
Llanfaethlu **54** E3
Llanfair Caereinion **52** D2
Llanfairfechan **54** F3
Llanfair Talhaiarn **55** F3
Llanfyllin **52** D2
Llangefni **55** E3
Llanglydwen **52** C3
Llangollen **52** D2
Llangranog **52** C2
Llangurig **52** D2
Llanidloes **52** D2
Llanilar **52** C2
Llanos **136** D2
Llanquihue, Lago **139** B8
Llanrhystud **52** C2
Llanrwst **54** F3
Llantrisant **52** D3
Llanwenog **52** C2
Llanwrtyd Wells **52** D2
Llawhaden **52** C3
Llerena **66** C3
Lleyn Peninsula **52** C2
Lliria **67** F3
Llivia **67** G1
Llobregat **67** G2
Lloydminster **119** P5
Lluchmayor **67** H3
Llyswen **52** D2
Loa **138** C4
Loanhead **57** E5
Lobatse **108** E5
Lobau **70** F3
Loberia **139** E7
Lobez **70** F2
Lobito **106** B5
Lobos **139** E7
Lobos, Island **126** G7
Locarno **68** B2
Lochaber **57** D4
Lochailort **57** C4
Lochan Fada **56** C3
Loch Ard Forest **57** D4
Lochboisdale **57** A3
Lochearnhead **57** D4
Loches **65** D5
Lochgelly **57** E4
Lochgilphead **57** C4
Lochinver **56** C2
Lochmaben **57** E5
Lochmaddy **56** A3
Lochnagar **57** E4
Lochranza **57** C5
Loch Shin **56** D2
Lochy, Loch **57** D4
Lock **113** H5
Lockerbie **57** E5
Lockhart **128** D6
Lock Haven **125** M6
Lockport **125** L5
Locri **69** F6
Loddekopinge **63** E9
Loddon *Australia* **113** J6
Loddon *U.K.* **53** J2
Lodeve **65** E7
Lodeynoye Pole **78** E3
Lodge Grass **123** L5
Lodgepole **123** M7
Lodi *Italy* **68** B3
Lodi *U.S.A.* **126** B1
Lodingen **62** F2
Lodja **106** D3
Lodwar **107** G2
Lodz **71** H3
Loeriesfontein **108** C6
Lofoten **62** E2
Loftus **55** J2
Logan **122** J7
Logan, Mount **118** G3
Logansport *Indiana, U.S.A.* **124** G6
Logansport *Louisiana, U.S.A.* **128** F5
Loge **106** B4
Logishin **71** M2
Logone **102** C5
Logrono **66** E1
Logrosan **66** D3
Loh **114** T10
Lohardaga **92** F4
Loharu **92** E3
Lohit **93** J3
Lohja **63** L6
Lohtaja **62** K4
Loikaw **93** J5
Loimaa **63** K6
Loimijoki **63** K6
Loing **65** E5
Loi, Phu **93** K4
Loir **65** C5
Loire **65** B5
Loja *Ecuador* **136** B4
Loja *Spain* **66** D4
Lokantekojarvi **62** M3
Lokhpodgort **78** M2
Lokhvitsa **79** E5
Lokichokio **107** F2
Lokilalaki, Gunung **91** G6
Lokka **62** M3
Loknya **78** E4
Lokoja **105** G4
Lokshak **85** N6
Lokuru **114** H6
Lol **102** E6
Lola **104** D4
Lolland **63** D9
Lolo **122** G4
Loloda **91** H5
Lolo Pass **122** G4
Lolvavana, Passage **114** U11
Lom *Bulgaria* **73** G4
Lom *Norway* **63** C6
Lomami **106** D3
Lomas Coloradas **139** C8
Lomazy **71** K3
Lombarda, Serra **137** G3
Lombe **107** G4
Lombez **65** D7
Lomblen **91** G7
Lombok **90** F7
Lome **104** F4
Lomela **106** D3
Lomir **94** J2
Lomond Hills **57** E4
Lomond, Loch **57** D4
Lomonosov Ridge **140** A1
Lompobattang, Gunung **91** F7
Lompoc **126** B3
Lomza **71** K2
London *Canada* **125** K5
London *U.K.* **53** G3
Londonderry *U.K.* **58** H2
Londonderry *U.K.* **58** J3
Londonderry, Cape **112** F1
Londonderry, Isla **139** B11
Londoni **114** R8
Londrina **138** F4
Lone Pine **126** C2
Longa *Angola* **106** C5
Longa *Angola* **106** C6
Longa Island **56** C3
Long Akah **90** E5
Longa, Ostrova de **81** S2
Long Bay **129** N4
Long Beach *California, U.S.A.* **126** C4
Long Beach *New York, U.S.A.* **125** P6
Long Branch **125** P6
Longchang **93** L3
Longchuan **87** M7
Longde **93** L1
Long Eaton **53** F2
Longford *Ireland* **58** G5
Longford *Ireland* **58** G5
Longformacus **57** F5
Longframlington **57** G5
Longhoughton **55** H1
Longhua **87** M3
Longhui **93** M3
Long Island *Bahamas* **133** K3
Long Island *Canada* **121** L7
Long Island *New Zealand* **115** A7
Long Island *Papua New Guinea* **114** D3
Long Island *U.S.A.* **125** P6
Long Island Sound **125** P6
Longjiang **87** N2
Longjing **88** B4
Longlac **124** G2
Long Lake **124** G2
Longli **93** L3
Long, Loch **57** D4
Long Melford **53** H2
Longmen **87** L7
Long Mynd, The **52** E2
Longnan **87** L7
Longnawan **90** E5
Longney **52** E3
Long Point *Canada* **125** K5
Long Point *New Zealand* **115** B7
Long Preston **55** G2
Long Range **121** Q8
Long Range Mountains **121** Q7
Longreach **113** J3
Long Reef **114** E4
Longridge **55** G3
Longshan **93** L3
Longsheng **93** M3
Longs Peak **123** M7
Long Stratton **53** J2
Longton **55** G3
Longtown **57** F5
Longuyon **64** F4
Longview *Texas, U.S.A.* **128** E4
Longview *Washington, U.S.A.* **122** C4
Longwy **64** F4
Longxi **93** K2
Long Xuyen **93** L6
Longyan **87** M6
Longyao **87** L4
Lons-le-Saunier **65** F5
Looe **52** C4
Lookout, Cape **129** P3
Loongana **112** F5
Loop Head **59** C7
Lopatin **79** H7
Lopatino **79** H5
Lopatka **85** T6
Lopatka, Mys **85** T6
Lop Buri **93** K6
Lopevi **114** U12
Lopez, Cap **106** A3
Lop Nur **86** G3
Lopphavet **62** J1
Lopra **62** Z14
Lopydino **78** J3
Lora del Rio **66** D4
Lorain **124** J6
Loralai **92** C2
Lorca **67** F4
Lordegan **95** K6
Lord Howe Island **113** M5
Lordsburg **127** H4
Lore **91** H7
Lorengau **114** D2
Lorentz **91** K7
Lorenzo **136** B3
Loreto *Brazil* **137** H5
Loreto *Colombia* **136** C4
Loreto *Mexico* **126** G7
Lorica **133** K10
Lorient **65** B5
Lorillard **119** S3
Lorinci **72** E2
Lorn **57** C4
Lorne **113** J6
Lorn, Firth of **57** C4
Lorrach **70** B5
Lorraine **64** F4
Los **63** F6
Los Alamos **127** J3
Los Andes **139** B6
Los Angeles *Chile* **139** B7
Los Angeles *U.S.A.* **126** C4

Los Angeles Aqueduct 126 C3
Los Banos 126 B2
Los Blancos 138 D4
Los Filabres, Sierra de 66 E4
Losinj 72 C3
Los Mochis 127 H8
Los Pedraches 66 D3
Los Roques 136 D1
Lossie 56 E3
Lossiemouth 56 E3
Los Teques 136 D1
Los Testigos 133 R9
Lost Trail Pass 122 H5
Lostwithiel 52 C4
Lot 65 D6
Lota 139 B7
Lotfahad 95 P3
Lothian 57 E5
Lotta 62 N2
Lottorp 63 G8
Lo-tung 87 N7
Lotzen 71 J1
Loudeac 64 B4
Loudun 65 D5
Louga 104 B2
Loughborough 53 F2
Loughbrickland 58 K4
Lougheed Island 120 E2
Loughor 52 C3
Loughrea 59 E6
Loughsalt Mount 58 G2
Lough Swilly 58 G2
Louhans 65 F5
Louisa 124 J7
Louisiade Archipelago 114 T10
Louisiana 128 F5
Lou Island 114 D2
Louis Trichardt 108 E4
Louisville Kentucky, U.S.A. 124 H7
Louisville Mississippi, U.S.A. 128 H4
Loukhi 62 Q3
Loule 66 B4
Loup 123 Q7
Lourdes 65 C7
Louth Ireland 58 K5
Louth U.K. 55 K1
Louvain 64 F3
Louviers 64 D4
Lovanger 62 J4
Lovat 78 E4
Lovberga 62 F5
Lovech 73 H4
Loveland 123 M7
Lovell 123 K5
Lovere 68 C3
Loviisa 63 M6
Lovington 127 L4
Lovisa 63 M6
Lovnas 62 F4
Lovosice 70 F3
Lovua 106 D5
Low, Cape 120 J5
Lower Arrow Lake 122 E3
Lower Hut 115 E4
Lowestoft 53 J2
Lowicz 71 H2
Lowther Hills 57 E5
Lowther Island 120 G3
Loyal, Loch 56 D2
Loyaute, Iles 114 X16
Loyma 78 H3
Loyne, Loch 57 C3
Lozarevo 73 J4
Lozere, Mont 65 E6
Loznica 72 E3
Lozovaya 79 F6
Lualaba 106 E3
Luan 93 N2
Luanda 106 B4
Luang Prabang 93 K5
Luangwa 107 F5
Luan He 87 M4
Luanjing 87 K4
Luanping 87 M3
Luanshya 107 E5
Luapula 107 E5
Luarca 66 C1
Luashi 106 D5
Luau 106 D5
Lubalo 106 C4
Lubanas Ezers 62 M8
Lubang Islands 91 G3
Lubango 106 B5
Lubartow 71 K3
Lubawa 71 H2
Lubben 70 E3
Lubbock 127 M4
Lubeck 70 D2
Lubefu 106 D3
Lubenka 79 J5
Lubero 107 E3
Lubie, Jezioro 70 F2
Lubien 71 H2
Lublin 71 K3
Lubny 79 E5
Lubosalma 62 P5
Lubsko 70 F3
Lubtheen 70 D2
Lubudi 106 E4
Lubuklinggau 90 C6
Lubumbashi 107 E5
Lubutu 106 E3
Lucan 59 K6
Lucano, Appennino 69 E5
Lucaya 129 N7

Lucca 68 C4
Lucea 132 H5
Luce Bay 54 E2
Lucedale 128 H5
Lucena Philippines 91 G3
Lucena Spain 66 D4
Lucena del Cid 67 F2
Lucenec 71 H4
Lucera 69 E5
Lucerne 68 B2
Luchow 70 D2
Luckau 70 E3
Luckenwalde 70 E2
Lucknow 92 F3
Lucon 65 C5
Lucrecia, Cabo 133 K4
Lucusse 106 D5
Luda 87 N4
Ludensheid 70 B3
Ludford 55 J3
Ludgvan 52 B4
Ludhiana 92 E2
Ludington 124 G5
Ludlow U.K. 52 E2
Ludlow U.S.A. 126 D3
Ludogorie 73 J4
Ludus 73 H2
Ludvika 63 F6
Ludwigsburg 70 C4
Ludwigshafen 70 B4
Ludwigslust 70 D2
Ludza 63 M8
Luebo 106 D4
Luena 106 C5
Luepa 136 E2
Lueyang 93 L2
Lufeng 87 M7
Lufkin 128 E5
Luga 63 N7
Lugano 68 B2
Lugano, Lago di 68 B3
Lugela 109 G3
Lugenda 109 G2
Lugg 52 E2
Lugnaquilla 59 K7
Lugo Italy 68 C3
Lugo Spain 66 C1
Lugoj 73 F3
Lugovoy 86 C3
Lugton 57 D5
Luiana 106 D6
Luichart, Loch 56 D3
Luik 64 F3
Luimneach 59 E7
Luing 57 D4
Luinne Bheinn 57 C3
Luiro 62 M3
Luiza 106 D4
Lujan 139 C6
Lujiang 87 M5
Lukashkin Yar 84 B4
Lukeville 126 F5
Lukovit 73 H4
Lukovo 72 F5
Lukow 71 K3
Lukoyanov 78 G4
Lukulu 106 D5
Lulea 62 K4
Lulealven 62 J3
Luleburgaz 76 B2
Lulo 106 C4
Lulong 87 M4
Lulonga 106 C2
Luluabourg 106 D4
Lulworth Cove 53 E4
Lumbala Nguimbo 106 D5
Lumberton 129 N3
Lumbovka 78 G2
Lumbrales 66 C2
Lumbreras 66 E1
Lumbres 64 E3
Lumijoki 62 L4
Lumphanan 57 F3
Lumsden 115 B6
Lumut, Tanjung 90 D6
Lunan 93 K4
Lunan Bay 57 F4
Lunayyir, Harrat 96 C4
Lunberger Heide 70 C2
Lund 63 E9
Lundar 123 Q2
Lundazi 107 F5
Lundy 52 C3
Lune 55 G2
Luneburg 70 D2
Lunel 65 F7
Luneville 64 G4
Lungga 114 K6
Lungwebungu 106 D5
Luni 92 D3
Luninets 71 M2
Lunsar 104 C4
Lunsemfwa 107 E5
Luntai 86 E3
Luobei 88 C2
Luobuzhuang 86 F4
Luocheng 93 L4
Luodian 93 L3
Luoding 93 M4
Luo He 93 L1
Luohe 93 M2
Luotian 93 N2
Luoyang 93 M2

Luqu 93 K2
Lure 65 G5
Lurgan 58 K4
Lurio Mozambique 109 G2
Lurio Mozambique 109 H2
Lusaka 107 E6
Lusambo 106 D3
Lusancay Islands 114 E3
Lushi 93 M2
Lush, Mountain 112 F2
Lushoto 107 G3
Lushui 93 J3
Lusignan 65 D5
Lusk 123 M6
Luspebryggan 62 H3
Lussac-les-Chateaux 65 D5
Lut, Bahrat 94 B6
Lut, Dasht-e 95 P6
Lut-e Zangi Ahmad 95 P7
Luthrie 57 E4
Luton 53 G3
Lutong 90 E5
Lutsk 79 D5
Lutterworth 53 F2
Luukkonen 63 N6
Luuq 107 H2
Luverne 124 B5
Luwingu 107 E5
Luwuk 91 G6
Luxembourg 64 F4
Luxembourg 64 G4
Luxeuil 65 G5
Luxi 93 J4
Luxor 103 F2
Luza U.S.S.R. 78 H3
Luza U.S.S.R. 78 H3
Luzern 68 B2
Luzhou 93 L3
Luziania 138 G3
Luzilandia 137 J4
Luzon 91 G2
Luzon Strait 91 G1
Lvov 71 L4
Lvovka 84 B5
Lwowek 71 G2
Lyadova 73 J1
Lyakhovskiye Ostrova 85 Q2
Lyall, Mount 122 G3
Lyallpur 92 D2
Lyapin 78 L3
Lybster 56 E2
Lyck 71 K2
Lyckele 62 H4
Lydd 53 H4
Lyddan Ice Rise 141 Y4
Lydenburg 108 F5
Lydford 52 C4
Lydney 52 E3
Lyell Range 115 D4
Lyman 123 J7
Lyme Bay 52 D4
Lyme Regis 52 E4
Lymington 53 F4
Lymm 55 G3
Lyna 71 J1
Lynchburg 125 L8
Lynd 113 J2
Lyndon 112 D3
Lyne 57 F5
Lyness 56 E2
Lyngdal 63 B7
Lyngseidet 62 J1
Lynher 52 C4
Lynn 125 Q5
Lynn Canal 118 H4
Lynn Lake 119 Q4
Lynton 52 D3
Lynx Lake 119 P3
Lyon France 65 F6
Lyon U.K. 57 D4
Lyon Inlet 120 K4
Lyon, Loch 57 D4
Lyonnais, Monts du 65 F6
Lyra Reef 114 E2
Lyskovo 78 H4
Lysva 78 K4
Lytham Saint Annes 55 F3
Lythe 55 J2
Lyttelton 115 D5
Lytton 122 D2
Lyubashevka 73 L2
Lyubcha 71 M2
Lyubertsy 78 F4
Lyubeshov 71 L3
Lyubimets 73 J5
Lyuboml 71 L3
Lyubotin 79 F6
Lyudinovo 79 E5
Lyushcha 71 M2

M

Maaia 109 H2
Maam Cross 59 C6
Maan 94 B6
Maanqiao 86 F3
Maanselka 62 N5
Maanshan 87 M5
Maarianhamina 63 G6
Maarrat an Numan 94 C4
Maas 64 F3
Maaseik 64 F3
Maasin 91 G3
Maastricht 64 F3

Maba 91 H5
Mabalane 109 F4
Mabar 96 G9
Mablethorpe 55 K5
Macachin 139 D7
Macae 138 H4
McAdam 125 S4
McAlester 128 E3
McAllen 128 C7
McAllister, Mount 113 K5
MacAlpine Lake 119 Q2
Macapa 137 G3
Macara 136 B4
McArthur 113 H2
Macau 137 K5
Macaubas 138 J6
Macauley Islands 111 T8
McBeth Fjord 120 N4
McBride 119 L5
McCamey 127 L5
McCammon 122 H6
McCarthy 118 G3
Macclesfield 55 G3
McClintock Channel 119 Q1
McClintock Range 112 F2
McClure Strait 120 C3
McComb 128 G5
McCook 123 P7
McCreary 123 Q2
McDermitt 122 F7
Macdonnell Ranges 113 G3
Macduff 56 F3
Maceio 137 K5
Maceio, Punta da 137 K4
Macenta 104 D4
Macerata 68 D4
McGehee 128 G4
Macgillycuddy's Reeks 59 C9
Macha 85 K5
Machachi 136 B4
Machakos 107 G3
Machala 136 B4
Machanga 109 G4
Macharioch 57 C5
Machias 125 S4
Machichaco, Cap 66 E1
Machilipatnam 92 F5
Machiques 136 C2
Machir Bay 57 B5
Machynlleth 52 D2
Macin 73 K3
McIntosh 123 P5
Macka 77 H2
Mackay 113 K3
Mackay, Cape 120 D2
Mackay, Lake 112 F3
MacKay Lake 119 N3
McKean Island 111 U2
McKeesport 125 L6
Mackenzie Australia 113 K3
Mackenzie Canada 118 J2
Mackenzie Bay Antarctic 141 E5
Mackenzie Bay Canada 118 H2
Mackenzie King Island 120 D2
Mackenzie Mountains 118 H3
Mackinac, Straits of 124 H4
McKinley, Mount 118 E3
McKinney 128 D4
Macklin 123 K1
McLaughlin 123 P5
Maclean Strait 120 F2
Maclear 108 E6
McLeod, Lake 112 C3
Macmillan 118 J3
McMillan, Lake 127 K4
McMinnville Oregon, U.S.A. 122 C5
McMinnville Tennessee, U.S.A. 129 K3
McMurdo 141 M3
Macomb 124 E6
Macomer 69 B5
Macon 65 F5
Macon Georgia, U.S.A. 129 L4
Macon Missouri, U.S.A. 124 D7
Macossa 109 F3
McPherson 128 D1
Macquarie 113 K5
Macquarie Harbour 113 K7
Macquarie Island 141 L8
McRae 129 L4
Macroom 59 E9
McTavish Arm 119 M2
Macuspana 131 N9
Macuzari, Presa 127 H7
McVicar Arm 119 L2
Mad 122 C7
Madaba 94 B6
Madade 109 F4
Madagascar 109 J3
Madang 114 D3
Madaoua 101 G6
Madaripur 93 H4
Madawaska 125 M4
Maddalena, Isola di 69 B5
Maddaloni 69 E5
Maddy, Loch 56 A3
Madeira Brazil 136 E5
Madeira Portugal 100 B2
Madelia 124 C5
Maden Turkey 77 H3
Maden Turkey 77 J2
Madera Mexico 127 H6
Madera U.S.A. 126 B2
Madetkoski 62 M3
Madhubani 92 G3
Madhya Pradesh 92 E4

Name	Page	Grid
Madidi	136	D6
Madinat ash Shab	96	G10
Madingo-Kayes	106	B3
Madingou	106	B3
Madin Jadid	77	H5
Madison *Indiana, U.S.A.*	124	H7
Madison *Montana, U.S.A.*	122	J5
Madison *Nebraska, U.S.A.*	123	R7
Madison *S. Dakota, U.S.A.*	123	R5
Madison *Winsconin, U.S.A.*	124	F5
Madisonville *Kentucky, U.S.A.*	124	G8
Madisonville *Texas, U.S.A.*	128	E5
Madiun	90	E7
Mado Gashi	107	G2
Madoi	93	J2
Madona	63	M8
Madrakah, Ra's	97	N7
Madras *India*	92	F6
Madras *U.S.A.*	122	D5
Madre de Dios	136	D6
Madre de Dios, Isla	139	A10
Madre, Laguna *Mexico*	128	D8
Madre, Laguna *U.S.A.*	128	D7
Madre Occidental, Sierra	127	H6
Madre Oriental, Sierra	127	L7
Madre, Sierra	91	G2
Madrid	66	E2
Madridejos	66	E3
Madrigalejo	66	D3
Madrona, Sierra	66	D3
Madura *Australia*	112	F5
Madura *Indonesia*	90	E7
Madurai	92	E7
Madura, Selat	90	E7
Madzharovo	73	H5
Maebashi	89	G7
Maerus	73	H3
Maesteg	52	D3
Maestra, Sierra	132	J4
Maevatanana	109	J3
Maewo	114	U11
Mafa	91	H5
Mafeteng	108	E5
Mafia Island	107	G4
Mafikeng	108	E5
Mafra	66	B3
Mafraq	94	C3
Maga	114	S8
Magadan	85	S5
Magadan Oblast	85	V3
Magadi	107	G3
Magallanes, Estrecho de	139	B10
Magangue	136	C2
Magara	76	E4
Magarida	114	D4
Magburaka	104	C4
Magdagachi	85	M6
Magdalena *Bolivia*	136	E6
Magdalena *Colombia*	136	C2
Magdalena *Mexico*	126	F7
Magdalena *Mexico*	126	G5
Magdalena *Mexico*	130	H7
Magdalena, Isla	130	C5
Magdalena, Llano de la	130	D5
Magdalen Islands	121	P8
Magda Plateau	120	K3
Magdeburg	70	D2
Magdelena	127	J3
Magee, Island	58	L3
Magelang	90	E7
Magellan, Strait of	139	B10
Magenta, Lake	112	D5
Mageroya	62	L1
Maggiore, Lago	68	B3
Maghagha	102	F2
Magharee Islands	59	B8
Maghera	58	J3
Magherafelt	58	J3
Magheramorne	58	L3
Magilligan Point	58	J2
Magina	66	E4
Maglic	72	E4
Maglie	69	G5
Magnolia	128	F4
Magoe	109	F3
Magog	125	P4
Magpie	121	P7
Magro	67	F3
Magude	109	F5
Maguse Lake	119	R3
Maguse Point	119	S3
Magwe	93	H4
Mahabad	94	G3
Mahabe	109	J3
Mahabharat Range	92	G3
Mahabo	109	H4
Mahaddayweyne	107	J2
Mahadeo Hills	92	E4
Mahagi	107	F2
Mahajanga	109	J3
Mahakam	90	F5
Mahalapye	108	E4
Mahallat	95	K5
Mahanadi	92	F4
Mahanoy City	125	M6
Mahao	88	A4
Maharashtra	92	E5
Maharlu, Daryacheh-ye	95	L7
Maha Sarakham	93	K5
Mahavavy	109	J3
Mahbubnagar	92	E5
Mahdah	97	M4
Mahdia *Guyana*	136	F2
Mahdia *Tunisia*	101	H1
Mahe	92	E6
Mahebourg	109	L7
Mahenge	107	G4
Mahesana	92	D4
Mahi	92	D4
Mahia Peninsula	115	G3
Mahmudabad *India*	92	F3
Mahmudabad *Iran*	95	L3
Mahmudia	73	K3
Mahmudiye	76	D3
Mahnomen	124	B3
Mahon	67	J3
Mahrah, Al	97	K8
Mahukona	126	T10
Mahuva	92	D4
Maicao	136	C1
Maiche	65	G5
Maicuru	137	G4
Maidenhead	53	G3
Maidi	91	H5
Maidstone	53	H3
Maiduguri	105	H3
Maihar	92	F4
Maijdi	93	H4
Maikala Range	92	F4
Main *U.K.*	58	K3
Main *W. Germany*	70	C4
Main Barrier Range	113	J5
Main Channel	125	K4
Mai-Ndombe, Lac	106	C3
Maine *France*	64	C4
Maine *U.S.A.*	125	R4
Maine Soroa	101	H6
Maingkwan	93	J3
Mainland *Orkney Is., U.K.*	56	E2
Mainland *Shetland Is., U.K.*	56	A1
Maintirano	109	H3
Mainua	62	M4
Mainz	70	C4
Maio	104	L7
Maipu	139	E7
Maiquetia	133	P9
Maira	68	A3
Maisi, Cabo	133	K4
Maiskhal	93	H4
Maitland *New South Wales, Australia*	113	L5
Maitland *S. Australia, Australia*	113	H5
Maiz, Islas del	132	F8
Maizuru	89	E8
Majagual	136	C2
Majene	91	F6
Maji	103	G6
Majiang	93	L3
Majin	87	M6
Majorca	67	H3
Maka *Senegal*	104	C3
Maka *Solomon Is.*	114	K6
Makale	91	F6
Makambako	107	F4
Makanza	106	C2
Makarikha	78	K2
Makarova	84	D2
Makarska	72	D4
Makaryev	78	G4
Makassar	91	F7
Makassar, Selat	91	F6
Makat	79	J6
Makatini Flats	109	F5
Makay, Massif du	109	J4
Makeni	104	C4
Makenu	126	S10
Makeyevka	79	F6
Makhachkala	79	H7
Makharadze	77	K2
Makhmur	94	F4
Makhyah, Wadi	97	J8
Maki	91	J6
Makinsk	84	A6
Makkah	96	D6
Makkovik	121	Q6
Makkovik, Cape	121	Q6
Makogai	114	R8
Makokou	106	B2
Makondi Plateau	107	G5
Makov	71	H4
Makra	75	H4
Makrai	92	E4
Makran	92	B3
Makri	75	H2
Makronisi	75	H4
Maksatikha	78	F4
Maksim	78	K3
Maksimovka	88	F2
Makteir	100	C4
Maku	94	G2
Makurazaki	89	C10
Makurdi	105	G4
Makushin Volcano	118	Ae9
Mala	62	M4
Malabang	91	G4
Malabar Coast	92	D6
Malabo	105	G5
Malacca, Strait of	90	C5
Malacky	71	G4
Mala Fatra	71	H4
Malaga *Colombia*	136	C2
Malaga *Spain*	66	D4
Malagarasi	107	F3
Malahide	59	K6
Malaita	114	K6
Malakal	103	F6
Malakanagiri	92	F5
Malakand	92	D2
Malakula	114	T12
Malang	90	E7
Malanje	106	C4
Malao	114	T11
Mala, Punta	136	B2
Malaren	63	G7
Malargue	139	C7
Malartic	125	L2
Malaspina	139	C8
Malaspina Glacier	118	G4
Malatya	77	H3
Malatya Daglari	77	H3
Malavate	137	G3
Malavi	94	H5
Malawi	107	F5
Malawi, Lake	107	F5
Malaybalay	91	H4
Malayer	94	J4
Malay Peninsula	90	C5
Malaysia	90	D5
Malazgirt	77	K3
Malbork	71	H1
Malchin *E. Germany*	70	E2
Malchin *Mongolia*	86	G2
Malcolm's Point	57	B4
Malden	124	F8
Maldives	82	F6
Maldon	53	H3
Maldonado	139	F6
Maldonado, Punta	131	K9
Male	82	F6
Malea, Akra	75	G4
Malegaon	92	D4
Male Karpaty	71	G4
Malema	109	G2
Malemba-Nkulu	106	E4
Maleme	75	G5
Maler Kotla	92	E2
Malesherbes	64	E4
Maleta	84	H6
Malevangga	114	H5
Malgobek	79	G7
Malgomaj	62	G4
Malhat	77	K5
Malheur	122	F6
Malheur, Lake	122	E6
Mali	100	E5
Mali Hka	93	J3
Mali Kanal	72	E3
Mali Kyun	93	J6
Malimba, Mont	107	E4
Malin *Ireland*	58	H2
Malin *U.S.S.R.*	79	D5
Malin Beg	58	E3
Malindi	107	H3
Malin Head	58	H2
Malin More	58	E3
Malka	85	T6
Malkachan	85	S5
Malkapur	92	E4
Malkara	76	B2
Malkinia	71	K2
Malko Turnovo	73	J5
Mallaig	57	C4
Mallawi	102	F2
Mallorca	67	H3
Mallow	59	E8
Mallwyd	52	D2
Malm	62	D4
Malmberget	62	J3
Malmedy	64	G3
Malmesbury *South Africa*	108	C6
Malmesbury *U.K.*	53	E3
Malmo	63	E9
Malmohus	63	E9
Malmyzh	78	J4
Malo	114	T11
Malolo	114	Q8
Malone	125	N4
Malorita	71	L3
Malo Strait	114	T11
Maloy	62	A6
Maloyaroslavets	78	F4
Malozemelskaya Tundra	84	Ab3
Malpartida de Caceres	66	C3
Malpas	55	G3
Malpelo, Isla	134	A2
Malta	74	C5
Malta *U.S.A.*	123	L3
Malta Channel	74	C4
Maltahohe	108	C4
Maltby	55	H3
Maltepe	76	C2
Malton	55	J2
Malu	73	J3
Maluku	91	H6
Maluku, Laut	91	H5
Malung	63	E6
Maluu	114	K6
Malvan	92	D5
Malvern	128	F3
Malvern Hills	52	E2
Malvinas, Islas	139	E10
Malykay	85	K4
Malyy Anyuy	85	U3
Malyy Lyakhovskiy, Ostrov	85	Q2
Malyy Taymyr, Ostrov	81	M2
Malyy Yenisey	84	F6
Mama	85	J5
Mamankhalinka	79	J6
Mamanuca Group	114	Q8
Mamaru	137	F4
Mambasa	107	E2
Mamberamo	114	B2
Mamburao	91	G3
Mamers	64	D4
Mamfe	105	G4
Mamlyutka	84	Ae6
Mamonovo	71	H1
Mamore	138	D3
Mamore Forest	57	D4
Mamoria	136	D5
Mamou	104	C3
Mampong	104	E4
Mamry, Jezioro	71	J1
Mamuju	91	F6
Man *India*	92	F3
Man *Ivory Coast*	104	D4
Mana	63	C7
Mana *Fr. Guiana*	137	G3
Mana *U.S.A.*	126	R9
Manacapuru	136	E4
Manacapuru, Lago de	136	E4
Manacor	67	H3
Manadir, Al	97	M5
Manado	91	G5
Managua	132	D8
Managua, Laguna de	132	D8
Manakara	109	J4
Manakhah	96	F9
Manambolo	109	H3
Manam Island	114	D2
Mananara *Madagascar*	109	J4
Mananara *Madagascar*	109	J3
Mananjary	109	J4
Manantavadi	92	E6
Manaoba	114	K6
Manapire	136	D2
Manapouri	115	A6
Manapouri, Lake	115	A6
Manas	93	H3
Manau	114	D3
Manaus	136	F4
Manavgat	76	D4
Manbij	94	C3
Mancha Real	66	E4
Manchester *U.K.*	55	G3
Manchester *Connecticut, U.S.A.*	125	P6
Manchester *Kentucky, U.S.A.*	124	J8
Manchester *New Hampshire, U.S.A.*	125	Q5
Manchester *Tennessee, U.S.A.*	129	J3
Mancora	136	A4
Mand	95	K7
Mandab, Bab el	103	H5
Mandal *Afghanistan*	95	Q5
Mandal *Norway*	63	B7
Mandala, Puncak	91	L6
Mandalay	93	J4
Mandalgovi	87	K2
Mandali	94	G5
Mandal-Ovoo	87	J3
Mandan	123	P4
Mandaon	91	G3
Mandar, Teluk	91	F6
Mandasawu, Poco	91	G7
Mandav Hills	92	D4
Mandeville	132	J5
Mandi	92	E2
Mandiore, Lago	138	E3
Mandla	92	F4
Mandoudhion	75	G3
Mandurah	112	D5
Manduria	69	F5
Mandvi	92	C4
Mandya	92	E6
Manea	53	H2
Manevichi	71	L3
Manfredonia	69	E5
Manfredonia, Golfo di	69	F5
Manga	138	J6
Mangakino	115	E3
Mangalia	73	K4
Mangalore	92	D6
Mangaon	92	D5
Mangapehi	115	E3
Manggautu	114	J7
Mangin Range	93	J4
Mangkalihat, Tanjung	91	F5
Manglares, Punta	136	B3
Mangochi	107	G5
Mangoky	109	H4
Mangole	91	H6
Mangonui	115	D1
Mangoro	109	J3
Mangotsfield	52	E3
Mangral	92	D4
Manguari	136	D4
Mangueira, Lagoa	138	F6
Mangui	87	N1
Manguinha, Pontal do	137	K6
Mangut	85	J7
Mangyshlak	79	J7
Mangyshlak, Poluostrov	79	J7
Mangyshlakskiy Zaliv	79	J7
Manhan	86	G2
Manhattan	123	R8
Manhica	109	F5
Manicore	136	E5
Manicouagan	121	N7
Manicouagan, Reservoir	121	N7
Manifah	97	J3
Manika, Plateau de la	106	E4
Manila	91	G3
Manipa, Selat	91	H6
Manipur	93	H4
Manisa	76	B3
Man, Isle of	54	E2
Manistee *U.S.A.*	124	G4
Manistee *U.S.A.*	124	H4

Manistique	124	G4	Maranguape	137	K4	Marlborough *Australia*	113	K3	Masan	89	B8
Manitoba	119	R4	Maranhao	137	H5	Marlborough *Guyana*	136	F2	Masasi	107	G5
Manitoba, Lake	123	Q2	Maranhao Grande, Cachoeira	137	F4	Marlborough *U.K.*	53	F3	Masaya	132	D8
Manitou Falls	123	T2	Maran, Koh-i-	92	C3	Marlin	128	D5	Masbate *Philippines*	91	G3
Manitou Island	124	J4	Maranon	136	C4	Marlinton	125	K7	Masbate *Philippines*	91	G3
Manitoulin	124	J4	Marans	65	C5	Marlow	53	G3	Mascara	100	F1
Manitowoc	124	G4	Marari	136	D5	Marmagao	92	D5	Mascarene Islands	109	L7
Maniwaki	125	N3	Marasesti	73	J3	Marmande	65	D6	Masela	91	H7
Manizales	136	B2	Marassume	137	H4	Marmara *Turkey*	76	B2	Maseru	108	E5
Manja	109	H4	Marateca	66	B3	Marmara *Turkey*	76	B2	Mashabih	96	C4
Manjra	92	E5	Marathokambos	75	J4	Marmara Denizi	76	C2	Masham	55	H2
Mankato	124	C4	Marathon *Canada*	124	G2	Marmaraereglisi	76	B2	Mashan *Guangxi, China*	93	L4
Mankono	104	D4	Marathon *Florida, U.S.A.*	129	M8	Marmara Golu	76	C3	Mashan *Heilongjiang, China*	88	C3
Mankovka	73	L1	Marathon *Texas, U.S.A.*	127	L5	Marmara, Sea of	76	C2	Mashhad	95	P3
Manna	90	C6	Marau Point	115	G3	Marmaris	76	C4	Mashike	88	H4
Mannar	92	E7	Maravovo	114	J6	Marmblada	68	C2	Mashiz	95	N7
Mannar, Gulf of	92	E7	Marbella	66	D4	Marmelos	136	E5	Mashkid	95	R8
Mannheim	70	C4	Marble Bar	112	D3	Marne	64	E4	Masi	62	K2
Manning, Cape	120	B2	Marble Canyon	126	G2	Maro	102	C3	Masilah, Wadi al	97	J9
Manning Strait	114	J5	Marburg	70	C3	Maroantsetra	109	J3	Masi-Manimba	106	C3
Manningtree	53	J3	Marcelino	136	D4	Marolambo	109	J4	Masindi	107	F2
Mannu	69	B6	March	53	H2	Marondera	109	F3	Masirah	97	P6
Manoa Abuna	136	D5	Marche *Belgium*	64	F3	Maroni	137	G3	Masirah, Khalij	97	N7
Manokwari	91	J6	Marche *France*	65	D5	Maros	91	F6	Masirah, Khawr al	97	P6
Manolas	75	F3	Marchena	66	D4	Marotiri Islands	115	E1	Masiri	95	K6
Manonga	107	F3	Marchena, Isla	136	A7	Maroua	105	H3	Masisi	107	E3
Manono	107	E4	Mar Chiquita, Lago	138	D6	Marovoay	109	J3	Masjed Soleyman	94	J6
Manorbier	52	C3	Marcigny	65	F5	Marowyne	137	G3	Mask, Lough	58	D5
Manorcunningham	58	G3	Marcus Baker, Mount	118	F3	Marple	55	G3	Maskutan	95	P8
Manorhamilton	58	F4	Marcus Island	83	P4	Marquette	124	G3	Maslen Nos	73	J4
Manoron	93	J6	Mardan	92	D2	Marquise	64	D3	Masoala, Cap	109	K3
Manosque	65	F7	Mar del Plata	139	E7	Marquises, Iles	143	J5	Mason Bay	115	A7
Manouane, Reservoir	121	M7	Mardin	77	J4	Marra, Jebel	102	D5	Mason City	124	D5
Mano-wan	89	G7	Mare	114	Y16	Marrakech	100	D2	Ma, Song	93	K4
Manpojin	87	P3	Mareeba	113	K2	Marrakesh	100	D2	Masqat	97	P5
Manra	111	U2	Maree, Loch	56	C3	Marrak Point	120	R5	Massa	68	C3
Manresa	67	G2	Mareeq	103	J7	Marrawah	113	J7	Massachusetts	125	P5
Mansa	107	E5	Mareuil	65	D6	Marree	113	H4	Massachusetts Bay	125	Q5
Mansehra	92	D2	Margai Caka	92	G1	Marresale	84	Ae3	Massakori	102	C5
Mansel Island	120	L5	Marganets	79	E6	Marrupa	109	G2	Massa Marittima	68	C4
Mansfield *U.K.*	55	H3	Margaret, Cape	120	H3	Marsa Alam	96	B4	Massangena	109	F4
Mansfield *Louisiana, U.S.A.*	128	F5	Margaret River	112	F2	Marsabit	107	G2	Massape	137	J4
Mansfield *Ohio, U.S.A.*	124	J6	Margarita, Isla de	136	E1	Marsala	69	D7	Massava	84	Ad4
Mansfield *Pennsylvania, U.S.A.*	125	M6	Margaritovo	88	E4	Marsden *Australia*	113	K5	Massenya	102	C5
Mansfield Woodhouse	55	H3	Margate	53	J3	Marsden *U.K.*	55	H3	Massigui	100	D6
Mansle	65	D6	Margeride, Monts de la	65	E6	Marseille	65	F7	Massillon	124	K6
Manson Creek	118	L4	Margita	73	F3	Mar, Serra do	138	G5	Massinga	109	G4
Mansoura	67	J4	Margo, Dasht-i	95	R6	Marsfjallet	62	G3	Massingir	109	F4
Manston	53	J3	Marguerite	121	N7	Marshall *Minnesota, U.S.A.*	124	C4	Masteksay	79	H6
Mansurlu	77	F4	Marguerite Bay	141	V5	Marshall *Missouri, U.S.A.*	124	D7	Masterton	115	E4
Manta	136	A4	Mari	114	C3	Marshall *Texas, U.S.A.*	128	E4	Mastikho, Akra	75	J3
Mantalingajan, Mount	91	F4	Maria Elena	138	C4	Marshall Bennett Islands	114	E3	Mastuj	92	D1
Mantaro	136	B6	Maria, Golfo de Ana	132	H4	Marshall Islands	143	G4	Masturah	96	D5
Mantecal	136	D2	Maria Madre, Isla	130	F7	Marshalltown	124	D5	Masuda	89	C8
Mantes	64	D4	Maria Magdalena, Isla	130	F7	Marshchapel	55	K3	Masulch	94	J3
Mantiqueira, Serra da	138	G4	Marianas Islands	83	N5	Marshfield	124	E4	Masurai, Bukit	90	C6
Mantova	68	C3	Marianas Trench	142	F4	Marsh Island	128	G6	Masvingo	108	F4
Mantsala	63	L6	Marian Lake	119	M3	Marske-by-the-Sea	55	H2	Masyaf	94	C4
Mantta	63	L5	Marianna *Arkansas, U.S.A.*	128	G3	Marsta	63	G7	Mat	74	F2
Mantua	68	C3	Marianna *Florida, U.S.A.*	129	K5	Martaban	93	J5	Mataboor	91	K6
Mantyharju	63	M6	Marianske Lazne	70	E4	Martaban, Gulf of	93	J5	Mataca	109	G2
Manua	111	V4	Marias	122	J3	Martapura	90	E6	Matachel	66	C3
Manuel	131	K6	Marias, Islas	130	F7	Martes, Sierra	67	F3	Matad	87	M2
Manui	91	G6	Mariato, Punta	132	G11	Marthaguy	113	K5	Matadi	106	B4
Manu Island	114	C2	Maria van Diemen, Cape	115	D1	Martha's Vineyard	125	Q6	Matafome	66	B3
Manujan	95	N8	Mariazell	68	E2	Martigny	68	A2	Matagalpa	132	E8
Manukau	115	E2	Marib	96	G9	Martigues	65	F7	Matagami *Ontario, Canada*	125	M2
Manukau Harbour	115	E2	Maribor	72	C2	Martin *Poland*	71	H4	Matagami *Quebec, Canada*	125	M2
Manulla	58	D5	Maridi	102	E7	Martin *Spain*	67	F2	Matagami, Lac	125	M1
Manus Islands	114	D2	Marie Byrd Land	141	S3	Martin *S. Dakota, U.S.A.*	123	P6	Matagorda Bay	128	D6
Manya	78	L3	Marie Galante	133	S7	Martin *Tennessee, U.S.A.*	128	H2	Matagorda Island	128	D6
Manyas	76	B2	Mariehamn	63	H6	Martinavas	53	N6	Matakana Island	115	F2
Manych Gudilo, Ozero	79	G6	Marienbad	70	E4	Martinborough	115	E4	Matakaoa Point	115	G2
Manyoni	107	F4	Marienburg	71	H1	Martinique	133	S7	Matala	106	C5
Manzanares	66	E3	Mariental	108	C4	Martinique Passage	133	S7	Matale	92	F7
Manzanillo *Cuba*	132	J4	Marienwerder	71	H2	Martin Lake	129	K4	Matam	104	C2
Manzanillo *Mexico*	130	G8	Mariestad	63	E7	Martin Point	118	G1	Matamata	115	E2
Manzanillo, Punta	136	B2	Marietta *Georgia, U.S.A.*	129	K4	Martinsberg	68	E1	Matamoros *Mexico*	128	D8
Manzariyeh	95	K4	Marietta *Ohio, U.S.A.*	125	K7	Martinsville	125	L8	Matamoros *Mexico*	127	L8
Manzhouli	87	M2	Marigot	133	S7	Martock	52	E4	Matane	125	S2
Manzini	109	F5	Mariinsk	84	D5	Marton *New Zealand*	115	E4	Mata Negra	136	E2
Manzya	84	F5	Marina di Carrara	68	C3	Marton *U.K.*	55	J3	Matanzas	132	G3
Mao	102	C5	Marina di Leuca	69	G6	Martorell	67	G2	Matapan, Cape	75	G4
Maoershan	88	A3	Marina di Monasterace	69	F6	Martos	66	E4	Matapedia	125	S2
Maoke, Pegunungan	91	K6	Marinette	124	G4	Martre, Lac La	119	M3	Matara	92	F7
Maoming	93	M4	Maringa	106	D2	Martuk	79	K5	Mataram	90	F7
Mapai	109	F4	Maringa	138	F4	Martuni	79	H7	Matarani	138	B3
Mapam Yumco	92	F2	Marion *Illinois, U.S.A.*	124	F8	Martyn	78	K2	Mataranka	112	G1
Mapire	133	Q11	Marion *Indiana, U.S.A.*	124	H6	Martze	136	D4	Mataro	67	H2
Maple Creek	123	K3	Marion *Ohio, U.S.A.*	124	J6	Marudi	90	E5	Matata	115	F2
Mappi *Indonesia*	91	K7	Marion *S. Carolina, U.S.A.*	129	N3	Marugame	89	D8	Matatiele	108	E6
Mappi *Indonesia*	91	K7	Marion *Virginia, U.S.A.*	125	K8	Marum, Mount	114	U12	Mataura *New Zealand*	115	B6
Maprik	114	C2	Marion, Lake	129	M4	Marunga	114	E2	Mataura *New Zealand*	115	B7
Mapuera	136	F4	Marion Reefs	113	L2	Marungu	107	E4	Matawai	115	F3
Maputo	109	F5	Maripa	136	D2	Marv Dasht	95	L7	Matay	86	D2
Maqdam, Ras	96	C7	Marisa	91	G5	Marvejols	65	E6	Matcha	86	B4
Maqna	96	B2	Mariscal Estigarribia	138	D4	Marvine, Mount	122	J8	Matehuala	131	J6
Maqueda	66	D2	Maritimes, Alpes	65	G6	Marwar	92	D3	Matera	69	F5
Maquinchao	139	C8	Maritsa	73	H4	Mary	95	Q3	Mateszalka	73	G2
Maraba	137	H5	Marivan	94	H4	Maryborough	113	L4	Mateur	101	G1
Maracaibo	136	C1	Mariy A.S.S.R.	78	H4	Maryevka	84	Ae6	Matfors	62	G5
Maracaibo, Lago de	136	C2	Marjamaa	63	L7	Maryland	125	M7	Matheson	125	K2
Maraca, Ilha de	137	G3	Marjayoun	94	B5	Maryport	55	F2	Mathis	128	D6
Maracay	136	D1	Marka	96	E7	Mary, Puy	65	E6	Mathry	52	B3
Maradah	101	J3	Marka	107	H2	Marystown	121	Q8	Mathura	92	E3
Maradi	101	G6	Markam	93	J3	Marysville *California, U.S.A.*	126	B1	Mati	91	H4
Maragheh	94	H3	Market Deeping	53	G2	Marysville *Kansas, U.S.A.*	123	R8	Matlock	55	H3
Marajo, Baia de	137	H4	Market Drayton	52	E2	Maryvale	113	L4	Mato, Cerro	133	Q11
Marajo, Ilha de	137	H4	Market Harborough	53	G2	Maryville *Missouri, U.S.A.*	124	C6	Mato Grosso	136	F6
Maralal	107	G2	Markethill	58	J4	Maryville *Tennessee, U.S.A.*	129	L3	Mato Grosso do Sul	138	E3
Maramasike	114	K6	Market Rasen	55	J3	Marzo, Cabo	132	J11	Mato Grosso, Planalto do	138	E3
Maramba	106	E6	Market Weighton	55	J3	Masagua	132	B7	Matra	72	E2
Maran	90	C5	Markha	85	K4	Masai Steppe	107	G3	Matrah	97	P5
Marand	94	G2	Markham	114	D3	Masaka	107	F3	Matrosovo	71	J1
						Masally	94	J2	Matruh	102	E1

Name	Page	Grid
Matsubara	89	J10
Matsue	89	D8
Ma-tsu Lieh-tao	87	M6
Matsumae	88	H5
Matsumoto	89	F7
Matsusaka	89	F8
Matsuyama	89	D9
Mattagami	121	K8
Mattancheri	92	E7
Mattawa	125	L3
Matterhorn *Switzerland*	68	A3
Matterhorn *U.S.A.*	122	G7
Matthews Peak	107	G2
Matthew Town	133	L4
Matti, Sabkhat	97	K10
Mattoon	124	F7
Matty Island	120	G3
Matua, Ostrov	85	S7
Matuku	114	R9
Maturin	136	E2
Matyushkinskaya	84	B5
Mau	92	F3
Maua	109	G2
Maubara	91	H7
Maubeuge	64	E3
Maubin	93	J5
Maubourguet	65	D7
Mauchline	57	D5
Maud	56	F3
Maues	136	F4
Mauganj	92	F4
Maui	126	S10
Maula	62	L4
Maule	139	B7
Mauleon-Licharre	65	C7
Maumere	91	G7
Maumtrasna	58	C5
Maumturk Mountains	59	C5
Maun	108	D4
Mauna Kea	126	T11
Mauna Loa	126	T11
Maungmagan Islands	93	J6
Maunoir, Lac	118	L2
Maures	65	G7
Mauriac	65	E6
Maurice, Lake	112	G4
Mauritania	100	C5
Mauritius	109	L7
Mauron	64	B4
Mauston	124	E5
Mautern	68	E2
Mavinga	106	D6
Mawbray	55	F2
Mawhai Point	115	G3
Mawlaik	93	H4
Mawson	141	E5
Maxaila	109	F4
Maxmo	62	K5
Maya	85	N5
Mayaguana Island	133	L3
Mayaguana Passage	133	L3
Mayaguez	133	P5
Mayak *China*	86	F2
Mayak *U.S.S.R.*	71	H1
Mayak *U.S.S.R.*	79	K5
Mayamey	95	M3
Mayas, Montanas	132	C6
Maybole	57	D5
May, Cape	125	N7
Maychew	96	D10
Maydh	103	J5
Mayenne *France*	64	C4
Mayenne *France*	65	C5
Mayero	84	G3
Mayfaah	97	H9
Mayfield *U.K.*	53	H3
Mayfield *U.S.A.*	124	F8
May, Isle of	57	F4
Maykop	79	G7
Maykor	78	K4
Maymakan *U.S.S.R.*	85	N5
Maymakan *U.S.S.R.*	85	P5
Maymyo	93	J4
Mayn	85	W4
Maynooth	59	J6
Mayo *Argentina*	139	B9
Mayo *Canada*	118	H3
Mayo *Ireland*	58	D5
Mayo *Mexico*	130	E4
Mayor Island	115	F2
Mayor, Pic	67	H3
Mayotte	109	J2
May Pen	132	J6
Mayraira Point	91	G2
Mayrata	75	F3
Maysville	124	J7
Mayumba	106	A3
Mayuram	92	E6
Mayville	123	R4
Mayyun Island	96	F10
Mazalat	73	H4
Mazamari	136	C6
Mazamet	65	E7
Mazar	92	E1
Mazar-e Sharif	92	C1
Mazarete	67	E2
Mazarredo	139	C9
Mazarron	67	F4
Mazarsu	86	C3
Mazaruni	136	F2
Mazatenango	132	B7
Mazatlan	130	F6
Mazdaj	95	K5
Mazeikiai	63	K8
Mazgirt	77	H3
Mazhur, Irq al	96	G3
Mazidagi	77	J4
Mazinan	95	N3
Mazirbe	63	K8
Mazury	71	J2
Mbabane	108	F5
Mbaiki	102	C7
Mbala	107	F4
Mbalavu	114	S8
Mbale	107	F2
Mbalmayo	105	H5
Mbalo	114	K6
Mbandaka	106	C2
MBanza Congo	106	B4
Mbanza-Ngungu	106	B4
Mbarara	107	F3
Mbengwi	105	G4
Mbeya	107	F4
Mbouda	105	H4
Mbour	104	B3
Mbout	100	C5
Mbuji-Mayi	106	D4
Mchinji	107	F5
MClintock	119	S4
Meade *Alaska, U.S.A.*	118	D1
Meade *Kansas, U.S.A.*	127	M2
Meadie, Loch	56	D2
Mead, Lake	126	E2
Meadow Lake	119	P5
Meadville	125	K6
Mealhada	66	B2
Meana	95	Q3
Meath	58	J5
Meaux	64	E4
Mebula	91	G7
Mecca	96	D6
Mechelen	64	F3
Mecheria	100	E2
Mechigmen	118	A2
Mechigmen Zaliv	118	A2
Mecidie	76	B2
Mecitozu	76	F2
Mecklenburger Bucht	70	D1
Mecsek	72	E2
Mecufi	109	H2
Mecula	109	G2
Medak	92	E5
Medan	90	B5
Medanos	139	D7
Medanosa, Punta	139	C9
Medea	101	F1
Medellin	136	B2
Medelpad	62	G5
Medenine	101	H2
Mederdra	100	B5
Medford	122	C6
Medgidia	73	K3
Medicine Bow Mountains	123	L7
Medicine Bow Peak	123	L7
Medicine Hat	123	J3
Medicine Lodge	127	N2
Medina *Saudi Arabia*	96	D4
Medina *N. Dakota, U.S.A.*	123	Q4
Medina *New York, U.S.A.*	125	L5
Medinaceli	66	E2
Medina del Campo	66	D2
Medina de Rioseco	66	D2
Medina Sidonia	66	D4
Medina Terminal Canal	125	L5
Medinipur	93	G4
Mediterranean Sea	98	D3
Medjerda, Monts de la	69	B7
Medkovets	73	G4
Mednyy, Ostrov	81	T4
Medoc	65	C6
Medole	68	C3
Medvezhl, Ostrova	85	U2
Medvezhyegorsk	78	E3
Medvyeditsa	78	F4
Medway	53	H3
Medyn	78	F5
Medynskiy Zavorot, Poluostrov	78	K2
Meeberrie	112	D4
Meechkyn, Kosa	85	Y3
Meekatharra	112	D4
Meeker	123	L7
Meerut	92	E3
Meeteetse	123	K5
Mega	91	J6
Megalo Khorio	75	J4
Megalopolis	75	G4
Megara	75	G3
Megeve	65	G6
Megget Reservoir	57	E5
Meghalaya	93	H3
Megion	84	B4
Megisti	76	C4
Megra *U.S.S.R.*	78	F3
Megra *U.S.S.R.*	78	G2
Mehamn	62	M1
Mehndawal	92	H3
Mehran	94	H5
Meig	56	D3
Meighen Island	120	G2
Meiktila	93	J4
Meiningen	70	D3
Meira	66	C1
Meissen	70	E3
Mei Xian	87	M7
Mejez El Bab	69	B7
Mejillones	138	B4
Mekambo	106	B2
Mekele	103	G5
Meknes	100	D2
Mekong	93	L6
Mekong, Mouths of the	93	L7
Mela	62	U12
Melaka	90	C5
Melambes	75	H5
Melanesia	142	F4
Melawi	90	E6
Melbourne *Australia*	113	J6
Melbourne *U.S.A.*	129	M6
Melbourne Island	119	Q2
Melbu	62	F2
Melchor Muzquiz	127	M7
Melenki	78	G4
Meleuz	78	K5
Melfi *Chad*	102	C5
Melfi *Italy*	69	E5
Melfort	119	Q5
Melgaco	137	G4
Melhus	62	D4
Melilla	100	E1
Melipilla	139	B6
Melita	123	P3
Melito di Porto Salvo	69	E7
Melitopol	79	F6
Melk	68	E1
Melksham	53	E3
Mellegue, Oued	101	G1
Mellerud	63	E7
Melle-sur-Bretonne	65	C5
Melling	55	G2
Mellish Reef	113	M2
Mellte	52	D3
Melnik	70	F3
Melo	138	F6
Melolo	91	G7
Melozitna	118	E2
Melrhir, Chott	101	G2
Melrose	124	C4
Melsungen	70	C3
Meltaus	62	L3
Melton Mowbray	53	G2
Melun	64	E4
Melut	103	F5
Melvern Lake	124	C7
Melville	123	N2
Melville Bugt	120	P2
Melville, Cape	113	J1
Melville Hills	118	L2
Melville Island *Australia*	112	G1
Melville Island *Canada*	120	D2
Melville, Kap	120	P2
Melville, Lake	121	Q7
Melville Peninsula	120	K4
Melvin, Lough	58	F4
Melykut	72	E2
Melyuveyem	85	W4
Memba	109	H2
Memberamo	91	K6
Memboro	91	F7
Memel	63	L9
Memmingen	70	D4
Mempawah	90	D5
Memphis *Tennessee, U.S.A.*	128	H3
Memphis *Texas, U.S.A.*	127	M3
Mena	128	E3
Menai Bridge	55	E3
Menaka	101	F5
Mendawai	90	E6
Mende	65	E6
Mendi	114	C3
Mendip Hills	52	E3
Mendocino, Cape	122	B7
Mendoza	138	C6
Menemen	76	B3
Menen	64	E3
Menfi	69	D7
Mengcheng	93	N2
Mengcun	87	M4
Mengen	76	E2
Mengene Dagi	77	L3
Menggala	90	D6
Menghai	93	K4
Mengjiagang	88	C2
Mengjiawan	87	K4
Mengla	93	K4
Mengshan	93	M4
Mengyin	87	M4
Meniet	101	F3
Menihek, Lac	121	N7
Meningie	113	H6
Menkya	78	L3
Menominee *U.S.A.*	124	G4
Menominee *U.S.A.*	124	G4
Menomonee Falls	124	F5
Menongue	106	C5
Menorca	67	J3
Mentawai, Kepulauan	90	B6
Mentawai, Selat	90	B6
Mentok	90	D6
Menton	68	A4
Mentor	125	K6
Menyamya	114	D3
Menzel Bourguiba	69	B7
Meon	53	F4
Meppel	64	G2
Meppen	70	B2
Mequinenza	67	G2
Merabellou, Kolpos	75	H5
Merak	90	D7
Merano	68	C2
Merauke	91	L7
Mercan Dagi	77	H3
Mercato Saraceno	68	D4
Merced	126	B2
Mercedario, Cerro	138	B6
Mercedes *Argentina*	139	C6
Mercedes *Argentina*	139	E6
Mercedes *Argentina*	138	E5
Mercedes *Uruguay*	138	E6
Mercimek	77	F4
Mercimekkale	77	J3
Mercurea	73	G3
Mercury Bay	115	E2
Mercy, Cape	120	P5
Mere	52	E3
Meredith, Cape	139	D10
Meredoua	100	F3
Mere Lava	114	U11
Mereworth	53	H3
Mergenovo	79	J6
Mergui	93	J6
Mergui Archipelago	93	J6
Meribah	113	J5
Meric	76	B2
Merida *Mexico*	131	Q7
Merida *Spain*	66	C3
Merida *Venezuela*	136	C2
Merida, Cordillera de	136	C2
Meriden	125	P6
Meridian	128	H4
Merig	114	T11
Merir	91	J5
Meriruma	137	G3
Merkys	63	L9
Mermaid Reef	112	D2
Merowe	103	F4
Merredin	112	D5
Merrick	57	D5
Merrill	124	F4
Merrillville	124	G6
Merrimack	125	Q5
Merritt	122	D2
Merritt Island	129	M6
Merriwa	113	L5
Mersa Fatma	96	E9
Mersea Island	53	H3
Merseburg	70	D3
Merse, The	57	F5
Mersey	55	G3
Merseyside	55	G3
Mersin	76	F4
Mersing	90	C5
Mersrags	63	K8
Merthyr Tydfil	52	D3
Mertola	66	C4
Mertvyy Kultuk, Sor	79	J6
Mertz Glacier	141	K5
Merzifon	76	F2
Merzig	70	B4
Mesa	126	G4
Mesaras, Kolpos	75	H5
Meschede	70	C3
Meselefors	62	G4
Meshik	118	D4
Meshraer Req	102	E6
Mesolongion	75	F3
Messina *Italy*	69	E6
Messina *South Africa*	108	F4
Messina, Stretto di	69	E6
Messingham	55	J3
Messini	75	F4
Messiniakos Kolpos	75	F4
Messo	84	B3
Messoyakha	84	B3
Mesta	75	H2
Mestiya	77	K1
Mestre	68	D3
Mesudiye	77	G2
Meta	136	D2
Metan	138	D5
Metapan	132	C7
Metaponto	69	F5
Metema	103	G5
Meteran	114	E2
Methven *New Zealand*	115	C5
Methven *U.K.*	57	E4
Methwin, Mount	112	E4
Metkovic	72	D4
Metlika	72	C3
Metropolis	124	F8
Metsovon	75	F3
Metu	103	G6
Metz	64	G4
Meulaboh	90	B5
Meureudu	90	B4
Meurthe	64	G4
Meuse	64	F3
Mexborough	55	H3
Mexia	128	D5
Mexicali	126	E4
Mexico	130	H6
Mexico *U.S.A.*	124	E7
Mexico City	131	K8
Mexico, Gulf of	117	K6
Meydancik	77	K2
Meydan e Gel	95	M7
Meydani, Ra's e	95	P9
Meymaneh	94	S4
Meymeh	95	K5
Meynypilgyno	85	X4
Meyrueis	65	E6
Mezdra	73	G4
Mezen *U.S.S.R.*	78	G2
Mezen *U.S.S.R.*	78	H2
Mezenc, Mont	65	F6
Mezenskaya Guba	78	G2
Mezenskiy	84	F2
Mezhdurechensk	84	D6
Mezhdusharskiy, Ostrov	80	D3
Mezhgorye	71	K4

Name	Page	Ref
Mezotur	72	F2
Mezquital	130	G6
Mezzana	68	C2
Mhangura	108	F3
Mhow	92	E4
Miahuatlan	131	L9
Miajadas	66	D3
Miami *Arizona, U.S.A.*	126	G4
Miami *Florida, U.S.A.*	129	M8
Miami *Ohio, U.S.A.*	124	H7
Miami Beach	129	M8
Mianabad	95	N3
Miandowab	94	H3
Mianeh	94	H3
Miang, Pou	93	K5
Mianwali	92	D2
Mianyang	93	K2
Miarinarivo *Madagascar*	109	J3
Miarinarivo *Madagascar*	109	J3
Miass	84	Ad5
Miastko	71	G1
Micang Shan	93	L2
Michalovce	71	J4
Michelson, Mount	118	G2
Michigan	124	H5
Michigan City	124	G6
Michigan, Lake	124	G5
Michipicoten	124	H3
Michipicoten Island	124	H3
Michurinsk	79	G5
Mickle Fell	55	G2
Mickleton	53	F2
Micronesia	142	F4
Micurin	73	J4
Middelburg *Netherlands*	64	E3
Middelburg *South Africa*	108	E5
Middelburg *South Africa*	108	E6
Middle Andaman	93	H6
Middle Barton	53	F3
Middlebury	125	P4
Middlefart	63	C9
Middlemarch	115	C6
Middlesboro	124	J8
Middlesbrough	55	H2
Middleton *Greater Manchester, U.K.*	55	G3
Middleton *Strathclyde, U.K.*	57	B4
Middleton Cheney	53	F2
Middle Tongue	55	G2
Middleton-on-the-Wolds	55	J3
Middleton Reef	113	M4
Middletown *U.K.*	52	D2
Middletown *New York, U.S.A.*	125	N6
Middletown *Ohio, U.S.A.*	124	H7
Middlewich	55	G3
Mid Glamorgan	52	D3
Midhurst	53	G4
Midi	96	F8
Midland *Canada*	125	L4
Midland *Michigan, U.S.A.*	124	H5
Midland *Texas, U.S.A.*	127	M5
Midleton	59	F9
Midongy Atsimo	109	J4
Midsomer Norton	52	E3
Midwest	123	L6
Midwest City	128	D3
Midyan	96	B3
Midyat	77	J4
Mid Yell	56	A1
Midzor	73	G4
Miechow	71	J3
Miedwie, Jezioro	70	F2
Miedzyrzecz	70	F2
Mielec	71	J3
Miena	113	K7
Mieres	66	D1
Mieso	103	H6
Mieszkowice	70	F2
Miford Sound	115	A6
Mighan	95	P6
Miguel Aleman, Presa	131	L8
Miguel Alves	137	J4
Miguel Hidalgo, Presa	127	H7
Mihaliccik	76	D3
Mihara	89	D8
Miharu	89	H7
Mihrad, Al	97	L6
Miida	96	E9
Mijares	67	F2
Mikha Tskhakaya	77	J1
Mikhaylova	84	D1
Mikhaylovgrad	73	G4
Mikhaylov Island	141	F6
Mikhaylovka *U.S.S.R.*	88	C4
Mikhaylovka *U.S.S.R.*	79	G5
Mikindani	107	G5
Mikkeli *Finland*	63	M6
Mikkeli *Finland*	63	M6
Mikolajki	71	J2
Mikonos	75	H4
Mikri Prespa, Limni	75	F2
Mikulov	71	G4
Mikun	78	J3
Mikuni	89	F7
Mikuni-sammyaku	89	G7
Mikura-jima	89	G9
Milaca	124	D4
Milagro	136	B4
Milan *Italy*	68	B3
Milan *U.S.A.*	128	H3
Milano	68	B3
Milas	76	B4
Milazzo	69	E6
Milbank	123	R5
Mildenhall	53	H2
Mildurra	113	J5
Mile	93	K4
Mileh Tharthar	94	F5
Miles	113	L4
Miles City	123	M4
Milford *U.K.*	58	G2
Milford *U.S.A.*	125	N7
Milford Haven	52	B3
Milford Sound	115	A6
Milgun	112	D4
Milh, Bahr al	94	F5
Miliana	101	F1
Miliane, Oued	69	C7
Milk	123	L3
Millas	65	E7
Millau	65	E6
Milledgeville	129	L4
Mille Lacs, Lac des	124	E2
Mille Lacs Lake	124	D3
Miller	123	Q5
Millerovo	79	G6
Millers Flat	115	B6
Millford	58	J4
Millington	128	H3
Mill Island *Antarctic*	141	G5
Mill Island *Canada*	120	L5
Millisle	58	L3
Millnocket	125	R4
Millom	55	F2
Millport	57	D5
Mills Lake	119	M3
Milltown	58	K2
Milltown Malbay	59	D7
Millville	125	N7
Millwood Lake	128	F4
Milngavie	57	D5
Milogradovo	88	E4
Milolii	126	T11
Milos *Greece*	75	H4
Milos *Greece*	75	H4
Milowka	71	H4
Milparinka	113	J4
Milpillas	131	K9
Milton *New Zealand*	115	B7
Milton *Florida, U.S.A.*	129	J5
Milton *Pennsylvania, U.S.A.*	125	M6
Milton Abbot	52	C4
Milton Ernest	53	G2
Milton Keynes	53	G2
Miluo	93	M3
Milwaukee	124	G5
Mimizan	65	C6
Mimon	70	F3
Mina Abd Allah	97	J2
Minab	95	N8
Mina de San Domingos	66	C4
Minahassa Peninsula	91	G5
Minamata	89	C9
Minas *Indonesia*	90	C5
Minas *Uruguay*	139	E6
Mina Saud	97	J2
Minas Gerais	138	G3
Minas, Sierra de las	132	C7
Minatitlan	131	M8
Minbu	93	H4
Minch, The	56	C2
Mincio	68	C3
Mindanao	91	G4
Mindelo	104	L7
Minden *U.S.A.*	128	F4
Minden *W. Germany*	70	C2
Mindoro	91	G3
Mindoro Strait	91	G3
Mindra	73	G3
Minehead	52	D3
Mine Head	59	G9
Mineola	128	E4
Mineral Wells	128	C4
Minerva Reefs	111	T6
Minervino Murge	69	F5
Minfeng	92	F1
Mingechaur	79	H7
Mingela	113	K2
Minglanilla	67	F3
Mingshui *Gansu, China*	86	H3
Mingshui *Heilongjiang, China*	87	P2
Mingulay	57	A4
Minicoy	92	D7
Minigwal	112	E4
Min Jiang	93	K3
Minle	86	J4
Minna	105	G4
Minneapolis	124	D4
Minnedosa	123	Q2
Minnesota *U.S.A.*	124	C3
Minnesota *U.S.A.*	124	C4
Minnitaki Lake	124	E1
Mino	66	B1
Minorca	67	J3
Minot	123	P3
Minsk	78	D5
Minsk Mazowiecki	71	J2
Minsterley	52	E2
Mintlaw	56	F3
Minto	125	S3
Minto Inlet	119	M1
Minto, Lac	121	L6
Minturn	123	L8
Minusinsk	84	E6
Minwakh	97	J8
Min Xian	93	K2
Minyar	78	K4
Miquelon	125	M2
Mira *Italy*	68	D3
Mira *Portugal*	66	B4
Mirabad	95	Q6
Miracema do Norte	137	H5
Miraflores	136	C2
Miraj	92	D5
Miramichi Bay	121	N8
Miramont	65	D6
Miram Shah	92	D2
Miranda *Brazil*	138	E4
Miranda *Brazil*	138	E4
Miranda de Ebro	66	E1
Miranda do Douro	66	C2
Mirande	65	D7
Mirandela	66	C2
Mirandola	68	C3
Mirapinima	136	E4
Miravci	73	G5
Mirbat, Ra's	97	M8
Mirbut	97	M8
Mirear Island	96	B5
Mirebeau	65	D5
Mirgorod	79	E6
Miri	90	E5
Miri Hills	93	H3
Mirimire	136	D1
Mirim, Lagoa	138	F6
Mirjaveh	95	Q7
Mirnyy *Antarctic*	141	G5
Mirnyy *U.S.S.R.*	85	J4
Mironovo	84	H5
Mirpur Khas	92	C3
Mirriam Vale	113	L3
Mirtoa Sea	75	G4
Mirtoon Pelagos	75	G4
Miryang	89	B8
Mirzapur	92	F3
Misgar	92	D1
Mishan	88	C3
Mi-shima	89	C8
Mishkino	78	K4
Misima Island	114	T10
Misool	91	J6
Misratah	101	J2
Missinaibi	121	K7
Mission *Canada*	122	C3
Mission *U.S.A.*	123	P6
Mission Viejo	126	D4
Mississauga	125	L5
Mississippi *U.S.A.*	128	G4
Mississippi *U.S.A.*	128	G5
Mississippi Delta	128	H6
Missoula	122	G4
Missouri *U.S.A.*	124	D7
Missouri *U.S.A.*	124	E7
Missouri, Coteau de	123	P4
Mistassibi	121	M8
Mistassini *Canada*	125	P2
Mistassini *Canada*	125	P2
Mistassini, Lac	121	M7
Mistelbach	68	F1
Mistretta	69	E7
Mitatib	96	C9
Mitchell *Australia*	113	J2
Mitchell *Australia*	113	K4
Mitchell *U.S.A.*	123	Q6
Mitchell, Mount	129	L3
Mitchelstown	59	F8
Mithankot	92	D3
Mithimna	75	J3
Mitilini	75	J3
Mito	89	H7
Mitre	111	R4
Mitrofanovskaya	78	K3
Mitsio, Nosy	109	J2
Mitsiwa	103	G4
Mitsiwa Channel	96	D9
Mittelland Kanal	70	B2
Mittelmark	70	E2
Mitumba, Chaine des	107	E4
Mitwaba	107	E4
Mitzic	106	B2
Mixteco	131	K8
Miyah, Wadi al	77	H5
Miyake-jima	89	G8
Miyake-shoto	89	G11
Miyako	88	H6
Miyako-jima	89	G11
Miyakonojo	89	C10
Miyaly	79	J6
Miyazaki	89	C10
Miyazu	89	E8
Miyoshi	89	D8
Mizdah	101	H2
Mizen Head *Cork, Ireland*	59	C10
Mizen Head *Wicklow, Ireland*	59	K7
Mizhi	87	L4
Mizil	73	J3
Mizoram	93	H4
Mizpe Ramon	94	B6
Mjolby	63	F7
Mjosa	63	D6
Mljet	72	D4
Moa *Cuba*	133	K4
Moa *Indonesia*	91	H7
Moab	127	H1
Moa Island	114	C4
Moala	114	R9
Moate	59	G6
Moatize	109	F3
Moba	107	E4
Mobaye	102	D7
Mobayi-Mbongo	106	D2
Moberly	124	D7
Mobile	129	H5
Mobile Bay	129	H5
Mobridge	123	P5
Mobutu Sese Seko, Lake	107	F2
Moca	114	S9
Mocajuba	137	G4
Mocambique	109	H3
Mocamedes	106	B6
Mocha, Isla	139	B7
Mochudi	108	E4
Mocimboa da Praia	109	H2
Moctexuma	127	H6
Moctezuma	131	K7
Mocuba	109	G3
Modder	108	E5
Modena *Italy*	68	C3
Modena *U.S.A.*	126	F2
Modesto	126	B2
Modica	69	E7
Modigliana	68	C3
Modling	68	F1
Modowi	91	J6
Moe	113	K6
Moelv	63	D6
Moengo	137	G2
Moffat	57	E5
Moffat Peak	115	B6
Mogadishu	103	J2
Mogadouro	66	C2
Mogdy	85	N6
Mogilev	78	E5
Mogilev-Podolskiy	79	D6
Mogi-Mirim	138	G4
Mogincual	109	H3
Moglice	75	F2
Mogocha	85	L6
Mogoi	91	J6
Mogok	93	J4
Mogollon Plateau	126	G3
Mogotoyevo, Ozero	85	R2
Mogoyn	86	H2
Mogoytuy	85	J6
Moguer	66	C4
Mohacs	72	E2
Mohaka	115	F3
Mohall	123	P3
Mohammadabad	95	Q6
Mohammadia	100	F1
Mohawk	125	N5
Moheli	109	H2
Mohill	58	G5
Mohoro	107	G4
Moi	63	B7
Moidart	57	C4
Moimenta da Beira	66	C2
Moindou	114	W16
Mointy	86	C2
Mo i Rana	62	F3
Moisie	121	N7
Moissac	65	D6
Moissala	102	C6
Mojave	126	C3
Mojave Desert	126	D3
Moji	89	C9
Mojones, Cerro	138	C5
Moju	137	H4
Mokai	115	E3
Mokelumne	122	D8
Moknine	101	H1
Mokohinau Island	115	E1
Mokokchung	93	H3
Mokolo	105	H3
Mokpo	87	P5
Mokra Gora	72	F4
Molaoi	75	G4
Molat	72	C3
Mold	55	F3
Moldavia	73	J2
Moldaviya S.S.R.	79	D6
Molde	62	B5
Moldova	73	J2
Moldova Noua	73	F3
Moldoveanu	73	H3
Moldovita	73	H2
Mole *Devon, U.K.*	52	D4
Mole *Surrey, U.K.*	53	G3
Molepolole	108	E4
Molfetta	69	F5
Molina de Aragon	67	F2
Molina de Segura	67	F3
Moline	124	E6
Molkom	63	E7
Mollakendi	77	H3
Mollaosman	77	K3
Mollendo	138	B3
Molln	70	D2
Molnlycke	63	E8
Molodechno	71	M1
Molodezhnaya	141	D5
Molodo *U.S.S.R.*	85	L3
Molodo *U.S.S.R.*	85	L3
Mologa	78	F4
Molokai	126	S10
Moloma	78	H4
Molotov	78	K4
Moloundou	105	J5
Molsheim	64	G4
Molson Lake	119	R5
Moluccas	91	H6
Moma *Mozambique*	109	R3
Moma *U.S.S.R.*	85	Q3
Mombasa	107	G3
Mombetsu	88	J3
Momboyo	106	C3

Nandyal	92	E5	Nastved	63	D9	Necochea	139	E7	Neufchateau *Belgium*	64	F4
Nanfeng	87	M6	Nata	108	E4	Nedong	93	H3	Neufchateau *France*	64	F4
Nanga Eboko	105	H5	Natagaima	136	B3	Nedstrand	63	A7	Neufchatel	64	D4
Nangahpinoh	90	E6	Natal *Brazil*	137	K5	Needles *Canada*	122	E3	Neufelden	68	D1
Nanga Parbat	92	D1	Natal *Indonesia*	90	B5	Needles *U.S.A.*	126	E3	Neumunster	70	C1
Nangatayap	90	E6	Natanz	95	K5	Needles Point	115	E2	Neunkirchen *Austria*	68	F2
Nangong	87	M4	Natara	85	L3	Needles, The	53	F4	Neunkirchen *W.Germany*	70	B4
Nan Hai	83	K5	Natashquan	121	P7	Neepawa	123	Q2	Neuquen *Argentina*	139	C7
Nanjing	87	M5	Natchez	128	G5	Neergaard Lake	120	L3	Neuquen *Argentina*	139	C7
Nanking	87	M5	Natchitoches	128	F5	Nefedovo	84	A5	Neuruppin	70	E2
Nan, Mae Nam	93	K5	Natewa Bay	114	R8	Nefta	101	G2	Neuse	129	P3
Nanning	93	L4	National City	126	D4	Neftechala	94	J2	Neusiedler See	68	F2
Nanortalik	116	Q2	Natitingou	105	F3	Neftegorsk	79	J5	Neuss	70	B3
Nanpan Jiang	93	K4	Natividade	137	H6	Neftekamsk	78	J4	Neustadt	70	C5
Nanpara	92	F3	Natori	89	H6	Nefyn	52	C2	Neustettin	71	G2
Nanpi	87	M4	Natron, Lake	107	G3	Nefza	69	B7	Neustrelitz	70	E2
Nanping	87	M6	Nattavaara	62	J3	Negele	103	G6	Neu-Ulm	70	D4
Nansei-shoto	89	H10	Natuna Besar	90	D5	Negev	94	B6	Nevada *Missouri, U.S.A.*	124	C8
Nansen Sound	120	H1	Natuna, Kepulauan	90	D5	Negoiu	73	H3	Nevada *U.S.A.*	122	F8
Nanshan Islands	90	E4	Naturaliste, Cape	112	D5	Negombo	92	E7	Nevada, Sierra *Argentina*	138	C5
Nansha Qundao	90	E4	Naturaliste Channel	112	C4	Negotin	73	G3	Nevada, Sierra *Spain*	66	E4
Nantais, Lac	121	M5	Nauen	70	E2	Negrais, Cape	93	H5	Nevada, Sierra *U.S.A.*	126	C2
Nantes	65	C5	Naueyi Akmyane	63	K8	Negra, Punta	136	A5	Nevado, Cerro	139	C7
Nantong	87	N5	Naujoji Vilnia	71	L1	Negritos	136	A4	Nevado, Sierra del	139	C7
Nantua	65	F5	Naul	58	K5	Negro *Argentina*	139	C7	Nevel	78	E4
Nantucket Island	125	Q6	Naumburg	70	D3	Negro *Amazonas, Brazil*	136	E4	Nevelsk	88	H2
Nantucket Sound	125	Q6	Naungpale	93	J5	Negro *Santa Catarina, Brazil*	138	F5	Nevers	65	E5
Nantwich	55	G3	Nauru	111	Q2	Negro *Uruguay*	138	F6	Neve, Sierra da	106	B5
Nant-y-moch Reservoir	52	D2	Naurzum	84	Ad6	Negros	91	G3	Nevesinje	72	E4
Nanuku Passage	114	S8	Nausori	114	R9	Negru Voda	73	K4	Nevezis	63	L9
Nanuku Reef	114	S8	Nautanwa	92	F3	Nehavand	94	J4	Nevinnomyssk	79	G7
Nanumanga	111	S3	Nautla	131	L7	Nehbandan	95	Q6	Nevis, Loch	57	C4
Nanumea	111	S3	Nauzad	95	S5	Nehe	87	N2	Nevsehir	76	F3
Nanusa, Kepulauan	91	H5	Navadwip	93	G4	Nehoiasu	73	J3	Nevyansk	84	Ad5
Nanyang	93	M2	Navahermosa	66	D3	Neijiang	93	K3	New	125	K8
Nanyuki	107	G2	Naval	91	G3	Nei Mongol Zizhiqu	87	L3	New Abbey	55	F2
Nao, Cabo de la	67	G3	Navalcarnero	66	D2	Neisse *Poland*	70	F3	New Albany	124	H7
Naococane, Lake	121	M7	Navalmoral de la Mata	66	D3	Neisse *Poland*	71	G3	New Alresford	53	F3
Naousa	75	G2	Navalpino	66	D3	Neiteyugansk	84	A4	Newark *New Jersey, U.S.A.*	125	N6
Napa	126	A1	Navan	58	J5	Neiva	136	B3	Newark *Ohio, U.S.A.*	124	J6
Napabalana	91	G6	Navarin, Mys	85	X4	Neixiang	93	M2	Newark-on-Trent	55	J3
Napalkovo	84	A2	Navarino, Isla	139	C11	Nekemte	103	G6	New Bedford	125	Q6
Napas	84	C5	Navarra	67	F1	Neksikan	85	R4	New Bedford River	53	H2
Nape	93	L5	Navars	67	G2	Nekso	63	H9	New Bern	129	P3
Napier	115	F3	Navasota	128	D5	Nelidovo	78	E4	Newberry	129	M3
Naples *Italy*	69	E5	Navassa Island	133	K5	Neligh	123	Q6	Newbiggin	55	G2
Naples *U.S.A.*	129	M7	Navax Point	52	B4	Nelkan	85	P5	Newbiggin-by-the-Sea	55	H1
Napo	136	C4	Navenby	55	J3	Nellore	92	E6	Newbigging	57	E5
Napoleon	124	H6	Naver, Loch	56	D2	Nelma	88	G2	New Braunfels	128	C6
Napoletano, Appennino	69	E5	Navia *Spain*	66	C1	Nelson *Canada*	122	F3	Newbridge	59	J6
Napoli	69	E5	Navia *Spain*	66	C1	Nelson *New Zealand*	115	D4	New Britain	114	E3
Napoli, Golfo di	69	E5	Naviti	114	Q8	Nelson *U.K.*	55	G3	New Brunswick *Canada*	121	N8
Naqadeh	94	G3	Navlya	79	E5	Nelson, Cape *Australia*	113	J6	New Brunswick *U.S.A.*	125	N6
Nar	53	H2	Navojoa	127	H7	Nelson, Cape *Papua New Guinea*	114	D3	Newbuildings	58	H3
Nara *Japan*	89	E8	Navolato	130	G5	Nelson Lagoon	118	Af8	Newburgh *U.K.*	57	E4
Nara *Mali*	100	D5	Navpaktos	75	F3	Nelspruit	108	F5	Newburgh *U.S.A.*	125	N6
Nara *Pakistan*	92	C4	Navplion	75	G4	Nema	100	D5	Newbury	53	F3
Naracoorte	113	J6	Navrongo	104	E3	Neman	78	C4	New Bussa	105	F4
Naran	87	L2	Navsari	92	D4	Neman	71	K1	Newby Bridge	55	G2
Narasapur	92	F5	Navua	114	R9	Nemira	73	J2	New Castle	125	K6
Narat	86	E3	Nawabshah	92	C3	Nemirov	73	K1	Newcastle *Australia*	113	L5
Narathiwat	93	K7	Nawada	92	G4	Nemiscau	121	L7	Newcastle *South Africa*	108	E5
Narayanganj	93	H4	Nawah	92	C2	Nemours	64	E4	Newcastle *U.K.*	58	L4
Narberth	52	C3	Nawasif, Harrat	96	F6	Nemun	63	J9	Newcastle *Indiana, U.S.A.*	124	H7
Narbonne	65	E7	Naws, Ra's	97	M8	Nemuro	88	K4	Newcastle *Wyoming, U.S.A.*	123	M6
Narborough Island	136	A7	Nawton	55	J2	Nemuro-kaikyo	88	K4	Newcastle Emlyn	52	C2
Narcea	66	C1	Naxos *Greece*	75	H4	Nemuy	85	P5	Newcastle-under-Lyme	55	G3
Nardin	95	M3	Naxos *Greece*	75	H4	Nenagh	59	F7	Newcastle-upon-Tyne	55	H2
Narew *Poland*	71	J2	Nayagarh	92	G4	Nenana	118	F3	Newcastle Waters	113	G2
Narew *Poland*	71	K2	Nayau	114	S8	Nene	53	G2	Newcastle West	59	D8
Narince	77	H4	Nay Band	95	L8	Nen Jiang	87	P1	Newchurch	52	D2
Narken	62	K3	Nay Band	95	N5	Nenjiang	87	P2	New Cumnock	57	D5
Narkher	92	E4	Nayoro	88	J3	Nenthead	55	G2	Newdegate	112	D5
Narli	77	G4	Nazare	137	K6	Neokhorion	75	F3	New Delhi	92	E3
Narmada	92	E4	Nazareth *Israel*	94	B5	Neon Karlovasi	75	J4	Newell, Lake	122	J2
Narman	77	J2	Nazareth *Peru*	136	B5	Neosho *Kansas, U.S.A.*	124	C7	New England Range	113	L5
Narnaul	92	E3	Nazarovo	84	E5	Neosho *Missouri, U.S.A.*	124	C8	Newenham, Cape	118	C4
Narodnaya, Gora	84	Ad3	Nazas	130	G5	Nepa *U.S.S.R.*	84	H5	Newfoundland *Canada*	121	P6
Naro-Fominsk	78	F4	Nazca	136	C6	Nepa *U.S.S.R.*	84	H5	Newfoundland *Canada*	121	Q8
Narowal	92	D2	Naze	89	B11	Nepal	92	F3	New Galloway	57	D5
Narpes	62	J5	Nazerat	94	B5	Nephi	126	G1	New Georgia	114	H6
Narrabri	113	K5	Naze, The	53	J3	Nephin Beg Range	58	C4	New Georgia Island	114	H6
Narrandera	113	K5	Nazik	94	G2	Nera	69	D4	New Glasgow	121	P8
Narrogin	112	D5	Nazik Golu	77	K3	Nerac	65	D6	New Guinea	114	C2
Narromine	113	K5	Nazilli	76	C4	Nerchinsk	85	K6	New Halfa	96	B9
Narsimhapur	92	E4	Nazmiye	77	H3	Neretva	72	D4	New Hampshire	125	Q5
Narsinghgarh	92	E4	Nazwa	97	N5	Neriquinha	106	D6	New Hampton	124	D5
Nart	87	M3	Nazyvayevsk	84	A5	Neris	63	L9	New Hanover	114	E2
Nartabu	91	J6	Ncheu	107	F5	Nermete, Punta	136	A5	Newhaven	53	H4
Naruko	88	H6	Ndalatando	106	B4	Neryuktey-1-y	85	K4	New Haven	125	P6
Narva	63	N7	Ndele	102	D6	Neryuvom	84	Ad3	New Iberia	128	G5
Narvik	62	G2	Ndeni	114	N7	Nes	63	C6	Newick	53	H4
Naryan Mar	78	J2	Ndjamena	102	C5	Nesbyen	63	C6	New Ireland	114	E2
Narymskiy Khrebet	86	E2	Ndjote	106	B3	Neskaupstadur	62	Y12	New Jersey	125	N6
Naryn *Rossiyskaya S.F.S.R., U.S.S.R.*	84	F6	Ndola	107	E5	Nesna	62	E3	New Kandla	92	D4
Naryn *U.S.S.R.*	86	C3	Nea	62	D5	Nesscliffe	52	E2	New Liskeard	125	L3
Naryn *U.S.S.R.*	86	D3	Nea Filippias	75	F3	Ness, Loch	56	D3	New London	125	P6
Nasarawa	105	G4	Neagh, Lough	58	K3	Nesterov *Rossiyskaya S.F.S.R., U.S.S.R.*	71	K3	Newman, Mount	112	D3
Naseby	115	C6	Neah Bay	122	B3				New Market	125	L7
Nashua	125	Q5	Neale, Lake	112	G3	Nesterov *Ukraine S.S.R., U.S.S.R.*	71	K1	Newmarket *Ireland*	59	D8
Nashville	129	J2	Nea Moudhania	75	G2	Nesterovo	84	H6	Newmarket *U.K.*	53	H2
Nasice	72	E3	Neapolis *Greece*	75	F2	Neston	55	F3	Newmarket-on-Fergus	59	E7
Nasielsk	71	J2	Neapolis *Greece*	75	H5	Nestos	75	H2	New Martinsville	125	K7
Nasijarvi	63	K6	Nea Psara	75	G3	Nesvizh	71	M2	New Meadows	122	F5
Nasik	92	D5	Near Islands	118	Aa9	Netanya	94	B5	New Mexico	127	J3
Nasir	103	F6	Neath	52	D3	Netherlands	64	F2	Newmill	57	F5
Nasir, Buhayrat	103	F3	Nebine	113	K4	Neto	69	F6	Newmilns	57	D5
Nasorolevu	114	R8	Nebit Dag	95	M2	Nettilling Lake	120	M4	New Milton	53	F4
Nasrabad	95	K4	Neblina, Pico da	136	D3	Nettleham	55	J3	Newnan	129	K4
Nass	118	K4	Nebraska	123	N7	Netzahualcoyotl, Presa	131	N9	New Orleans	128	G5
Nassau	129	P8	Nebraska City	124	C6	Neubrandenburg	70	E2	New Philadelphia	125	K6
Nasser, Lake	103	F3	Nebrodi, Monti	69	E7	Neuchatel	68	A2	New Pitsligo	56	F3
Nassjo	63	F8	Nechako	118	L5	Neuchatel, Lac de	68	A2	New Plymouth	115	E3
Nastapoka Islands	121	L6	Nechi	133	K11	Neckar	70	C4	Newport *Ireland*	58	C5

Name	Page	Ref
Norwich *U.S.A.*	125	Q6
Noshiro	88	G5
Noshul	78	H3
Nosok	84	C2
Nosop	108	D5
Nosovshchina	78	F3
Nosratabad	95	P7
Nossen	70	E3
Noss Head	56	E2
Noss, Island of	56	A2
Nosy-Varika	109	J4
Notec	71	G2
Noto	69	E7
Notodden	63	C7
Noto-hanto	89	F7
Notre Dame Bay	121	Q8
Notre Dame Mountains	121	N8
Nottingham	53	F2
Nottingham Island	120	L5
Nottinghamshire	55	H3
Notukeu Creek	123	L3
Nouadhibou	100	B4
Nouadhibou, Ras	100	B4
Nouakchott	100	B5
Noukloof Mountains	108	C4
Noumea	114	X17
Noup Head	56	E1
Noupoort	108	D6
Nouvelle-Caledonie	114	W16
Nouvelle Caledonie	114	W16
Nouvelle-France, Cap de	120	M5
Novabad	86	C4
Nova Bana	71	H4
Nova Cruz	137	K5
Nova Era	138	H3
Nova Friburgo	138	H4
Nova Iguacu	138	H4
Nova Lima	138	H4
Nova Mambone	109	G4
Novara	68	B3
Nova Remanso	137	J5
Nova Scotia	121	P8
Nova Sento Se	137	J5
Nova Sofala	109	F4
Nova Vanduzi	109	F3
Nova Varos	72	E4
Novaya Kakhovka	79	E6
Novaya Katysh	84	Ae5
Novaya Kazanka	79	H6
Novaya Novatka	84	G5
Novaya Odessa	79	E6
Novaya Sibir , Ostrov	85	R1
Novaya Tevriz	84	B5
Novaya Vodolaga	79	F6
Novaya Zemlya	84	Ab2
Novayo Ushitsa	73	J1
Nove Mesto	70	G4
Nove Zamky	71	H4
Novgorod	78	E4
Novgorod Serverskiy	79	E5
Novigrad	72	C3
Novikovo	88	J2
Novi Ligure	68	B3
Novi Pazar	72	F4
Novi Sad	72	E3
Novo Acre	137	J6
Novoaleksandrovsk	79	G6
Novoalekseyevka	79	K5
Novoanninskiy	79	G5
Novoarchangelsk	73	L1
Novo Aripuana	136	E5
Novobogatinskoye	79	J6
Novocheboksarsh	78	H4
Novocherkassk	79	G6
Novodolinka	84	A6
Novodvinsk	78	G3
Novograd-Volynskiy	79	D5
Novogrudok	71	L2
Novo Hamburgo	138	F5
Novoilinovka	85	P6
Novokazalinsk	86	A2
Novokhopersk	79	G5
Novokiyevskiy Uval	85	M6
Novokocherdyk	84	Ad6
Novokuybyshevsk	79	H5
Novokuznetsk	84	D6
Novolazareyskaya	141	A4
Novoletovye	84	G2
Novo Milosevo	72	F3
Novomitino	84	Ae5
Novomoskovsk *U.S.S.R.*	78	F5
Novomoskovsk *U.S.S.R.*	79	F6
Novopavlovka	84	H6
Novopokrovskaya	79	G6
Novopolotsk	63	N9
Novo Redondo	106	B5
Novo-Rokrovka	88	E3
Novoromanovo	84	C6
Novorossiysk	79	F7
Novorzhev	63	N8
Novo Sagres	91	H7
Novo Sergeyeva	79	J5
Novoshakhtinsk	79	F6
Novosibirsk	84	C4
Novosibirskiye Ostrova	85	Q1
Novospasskoye	79	H5
Novoukrainka	79	E6
Novo Uzensk	79	H5
Novo-Vyatsk	78	H4
Novoyeniseysk	84	E5
Novozhilovskaya	78	J3
Novozybkov	79	E5
Novska	72	D3
Novy Jicin	71	G4
Novyy	84	H2
Novyy Bor	78	J2
Novyy Bug	79	E6
Novyy Oskol	79	F5
Novyy Port	84	A3
Novyy Uzen	79	J7
Nowbaran	95	J4
Nowe	71	H2
Nowen Hill	59	D9
Nowgong	93	H3
Nowitna	118	E3
Nowograd	70	F2
Nowogrod	71	J2
Nowra	113	L5
Now Shahr	95	K3
Nowshera	92	D2
Nowy Sacz	71	J4
Nowy Targ	71	J4
Noyon *France*	64	E4
Noyon *Mongolia*	86	J3
Nozay	65	C5
Nsanje	107	G6
Nsukka	105	G4
Nsuta	104	E4
Ntem	105	H5
Ntwetwe Pan	108	E4
Nuba, Lake	102	F3
Nuba Mountains	102	F5
Nubian Desert	103	F3
Nubiya	102	E4
Nubiya, Es Sahra en	103	F3
Nudo Coropuna	136	C7
Nueces	128	C6
Nueltin Lake	119	R3
Nueva Florida	133	N10
Nueva Rosita	127	M7
Nueva San Salvador	132	C8
Nueve de Julio	139	D7
Nuevitas	132	J4
Nuevo, Bajo	132	H7
Nuevo Casas Grandes	127	J5
Nuevo Churumuco	130	J8
Nuevo Laredo	128	C7
Nugaruba Islands	114	E2
Nugget Point	115	B7
Nugrus, Gebel	96	B4
Nuhaka	115	F3
Nuh, Ra's	95	R9
Nui	111	S3
Nuits-Saint-Georges	65	F5
Nu Jiang	93	J3
Nukhayb	94	F5
Nukiki	114	H5
Nukualofa	111	T6
Nukufetau	111	S3
Nukuhu	114	D3
Nukulaelae	111	S3
Nukumanu Islands	111	N2
Nukunau	111	S2
Nukunono	111	U3
Nukus	51	U7
Nullarbor	112	G5
Nullarbor Plain	112	F5
Numan	105	H4
Numata	89	G7
Numazu	89	G8
Numedal	63	C6
Numfor	114	B2
Numto	84	A4
Nuneaton	53	F2
Nunivak Islands	116	C2
Nunligran	85	Y4
Nunney	52	E3
Nuomin He	87	N2
Nuoro	69	B5
Nupani	114	M7
Nuqdah, Ra's an	97	P6
Nuqrah	96	E4
Nur	95	K3
Nura	86	C2
Nurabad	95	K6
Nur Daglari	77	G4
Nure	68	B3
Nurek	86	B4
Nurhak	77	G4
Nurhak Dagi	77	G3
Nuristan	92	D1
Nurmes	62	N5
Nurnberg	70	D4
Nurri	69	B6
Nurzec	71	K2
Nusaybin	77	J4
Nusayriyah, Jebel al	77	G5
Nushagak Bay	118	D4
Nu Shan	93	J3
Nushki	92	C3
Nutak	121	P6
Nuugaatsiaq	120	R3
Nuuk	120	R5
Nuupas	62	M3
Nuwara	92	F7
Nuweveldreeks	108	D6
Nuyakuk, Lake	118	D4
Nuyts, Point	112	D6
Nuzayzah	77	H5
Nyahururu	107	G2
Nyainqentanglha Shan	92	G3
Nyaksimvol	84	Ad4
Nyala	102	D5
Nyamboyto	84	C3
Nyandoma	78	G3
Nyang	93	H3
Nyanza	107	E3
Nyasa, Lake	107	F5
Nyashabozh	78	J2
Nyaungu	93	H4
Nyayba	85	N2
Nyborg	63	D9
Nybster	56	E2
Nyeri	107	G3
Nyerol	103	F6
Nyima	93	G2
Nyirbator	73	G2
Nyiregyhaza	73	F2
Nyiru, Mont	107	G2
Nykarleby	62	N4
Nykobing *Denmark*	63	C8
Nykobing *Denmark*	63	D9
Nykoping	63	G7
Nylstroom	108	E4
Nymagee	113	K5
Nymburk	70	F3
Nynashamn	63	G7
Nyngan	113	K5
Nyong	105	H5
Nyons	65	F6
Nyrany	70	E4
Nyrud	62	N2
Nysa	71	G3
Nysh	85	Q6
Nyshott	63	N6
Nystad	63	J6
Nytva	78	K4
Nyuk, Ozero	62	P4
Nyuksenitsa	78	G3
Nyunzu	107	E4
Nyurba	85	K4
Nyurolskiy	84	B5
Nyuya	85	J4
Nyvrovo	85	Q6
Nzambi	106	B3
Nzega	107	F3
Nzerekore	104	D4
Nzeto	106	B4
Nzo	104	D4

O

Name	Page	Ref
Oadby	53	F2
Oahe Dam	123	P5
Oahe, Lake	123	P5
Oahu	126	S10
Oakdale	126	B2
Oakengates	52	E2
Oakes	123	Q4
Oakford	52	D4
Oakham	53	G2
Oak Hill	125	K8
Oakington	53	H2
Oakland *California, U.S.A.*	126	A2
Oakland *Nebraska, U.S.A.*	123	R7
Oak Lawn	124	G6
Oakley	123	P8
Oakover	112	E3
Oakridge	122	C6
Oak Ridge	129	K2
Oak Valley	125	N7
Oamaru	115	C6
Oa, Mull of	57	B5
Oates Land	141	L4
Oatlands	113	K7
Oaxaca	131	L9
Ob	84	Ae3
Oban	57	D4
Oberammergau	70	D5
Oberhausen	70	B3
Oberlin	123	P8
Obidos *Brazil*	137	F4
Obidos *Portugal*	66	B3
Obihiro	88	J4
Obi, Kepulauan	91	H6
Obilnoye	79	G6
Obion	128	H2
Obninsk	78	F4
Obo	102	E6
Obock	103	H5
Obok-tong	88	B5
Oborniki	71	G2
Oboyan	79	F5
Obozerskiy	78	G3
Obregon, Presa	127	H6
Obruk	76	D3
Obryvistoye	85	Q7
Observatoire, Caye de l'	111	N6
Obskaya Guba	84	A3
Obuasi	104	E4
Ocala	129	L6
Ocana *Colombia*	136	C2
Ocana *Spain*	66	E3
Occidental, Cordillera *Colombia*	136	B3
Occidental, Cordillera *Peru*	136	B6
Occidental, Grand Erg	100	F2
Oceanside	126	D4
Ocejon, Pic	66	E2
Ochamchire	77	J1
Ochil Hills	57	E4
Ochiltree	57	D5
Ock	53	F3
Ockelbo	63	G6
Ocmulgee	129	L5
Ocna Mures	73	G2
Oconee	129	L4
Ocotlan	130	H7
Ocracoke Island	129	Q3
Ocreza	66	C3
Ocsa	72	E2
Oda	89	D8
Oda	104	E4
Odadhraun	62	W12
Oda, Jebel	103	G3
Odate	88	H5
Odawara	89	G8
Odda	63	B6
Odemira	66	B4
Odemis	76	B3
Odendaalsrus	108	E5
Odense	63	D9
Oder	70	F2
Oderhaff	70	F2
Oderzo	68	D3
Odeshog	63	F7
Odessa *U.S.A.*	127	L5
Odessa *U.S.S.R.*	79	E6
Odesskoye	84	A6
Odienne	104	D4
Odmarden	63	L6
Odorheiu Secuiesc	73	H2
Odra	70	F2
Odzaci	72	E3
Oeiras	137	J5
Oekussi	91	G7
Oelrichs	123	N6
Oena, Wadi	103	F2
Oenpelli Mission	113	G1
Of	77	J2
Ofanto	69	E5
Offaly	59	G6
Offenbach	70	C3
Offenburg	70	B4
Offord D'Arcy	53	G2
Ofidhousa	75	J4
Ofotfjord	62	G2
Ofunato	88	H6
Oga	88	G6
Ogaden	103	H6
Ogaki	89	F8
Ogasawara-shoto	83	N4
Ogbomosho	105	F4
Ogden	122	J7
Ogdensburg	125	N4
Ogea	114	S9
Ogeechee	129	M4
Ogho	114	H5
Ogi	89	G7
Ogilvie Mountains	118	H3
Oginskiy, Kanal	71	L2
Ogle Point	120	G4
Oglethorpe, Mount	129	K3
Oglio	68	C3
Ognon	65	F5
Ogoamas, Gunung	91	G5
Ogoja	105	G4
Ogoki	121	J7
Ogooue	106	B3
Ogoron	85	M6
Ogosta	73	G4
Ograzden	73	G5
Ogre	63	L8
Ogurchinskiy, Ostrov	79	J8
Oguz	77	H3
Oguzeli	77	G4
Ogwashi-Uku	105	G4
Ohai	115	A6
Ohakune	115	E3
Ohata	88	H5
Ohau, Lake	115	B6
O'Higgins, Lago	139	B9
Ohingaiti	115	E3
Ohio *Kentucky, U.S.A.*	124	F8
Ohio *U.S.A.*	124	J6
Ohre	70	D2
Ohre	70	E3
Ohrid	73	F5
Ohridska Jezero	72	F5
Ohura	115	E3
Oiapoque *Brazil*	137	G3
Oiapoque *Brazil*	137	G3
Oikiqtaluk	120	L3
Oil City	125	L6
Oise	64	E4
Oita	89	C9
Oituz, Pasul	73	J2
Oiwake	88	H4
Ojinaga	127	K6
Ojo de Agua	138	D5
Ojos del Salado	138	C5
Oka *U.S.S.R.*	78	G4
Oka *U.S.S.R.*	84	G6
Okaba	114	B3
Okahandja	108	C4
Okahukura	115	E3
Okaihau	115	D1
Okanagan Lake	122	E3
Okanogan *U.S.A.*	122	E3
Okanogan *U.S.A.*	122	D2
Okara	92	D2
Okarem	95	M2
Okaukuejo	108	C3
Okavango	108	D3
Okavango Delta	108	D3
Okaya	89	G7
Okayama	89	D8
Okazaki	89	F8
Okeechobee, Lake	129	M7
Okehampton	52	C4
Okene	105	G4
Oketo	88	J4
Okha	85	Q6
Okhota	85	Q5
Okhotsk	85	Q5
Okhotskoye More	85	R5
Okhotsk, Sea of	85	R5

198

Name	Page	Grid
Peski *Kazakhstan S.S.R., U.S.S.R.*	84	Ae6
Pesqueira *Brazil*	137	K5
Pesqueria *Mexico*	127	N8
Pestovo	78	F4
Petah Tiqwa	94	B5
Petajavesi	62	L5
Petalcalco, Bahia	130	H9
Petalioi	75	H4
Petalion, Kolpos	75	H4
Petaluma	126	A1
Petatlan	131	J9
Petauke	107	F5
Peterborough *Australia*	113	H5
Peterborough *Canada*	125	L4
Peterborough *U.K.*	53	G2
Peterhead	56	G3
Peterlee	55	H2
Petermann Ranges	112	F3
Peter Pond Lake	119	P4
Petersburg *Alaska, U.S.A.*	118	J4
Petersburg *Virginia, U.S.A.*	125	M8
Petersfield	53	G3
Peterstow	52	E3
Petite Kabylie	67	J4
Petite Miquelon	121	Q8
Petit Mecatina, Riviere du	121	P7
Petitot	119	L4
Petkula	62	M3
Peto	131	Q7
Petoskey	124	H4
Petra Velikogo, Zaliv	88	C4
Petre Bay	115	F6
Petrila	73	G3
Petrodvorets	63	N7
Petrolandia	137	K5
Petrolina *Amazonas, Brazil*	136	D4
Petrolina *Pernambuco, Brazil*	137	J5
Petropavlovsk	84	Ae6
Petropavlovsk-Kamchatskiy	85	T6
Petropolis	138	H4
Petrovac	72	E4
Petrovsk	79	H5
Petrovskoye	78	K5
Petrovsk-Žabaykalskiy	84	H6
Petrozavodsk	78	E3
Petsamo	62	P2
Petteril	55	G2
Petukhovo	84	Ae5
Petworth	53	G4
Peureula	90	B5
Pevek	85	W3
Pewsey, Vale of	52	F3
Peza	78	H2
Pezenas	65	E7
Pezinok	71	G4
Pezmog	78	J3
Pfaffenhofen	70	D4
Pfarrkirchen	70	E4
Pforzheim	70	C4
Phalaborwa	108	F4
Phalodi	92	D3
Phaltan	92	D5
Phangan, Ko	93	K6
Phangnga	93	J7
Phan Rang	93	L6
Phan Thiet	93	L6
Phatthalung	93	K7
Phenix City	129	K4
Phet Buri	93	J6
Phetchabun, Thiu Khao	93	K5
Philadelphia *Mississippi, U.S.A.*	128	H4
Philadelphia *Pennsylvania, U.S.A.*	125	N6
Philip	123	P5
Philip Island	111	Q7
Philippeville	64	F3
Philippines	91	G2
Philippine Sea	91	G1
Philipstown	108	D6
Phillipsburg	123	Q8
Philpots Island	120	L2
Phnom Penh	93	K6
Phoenix	126	F4
Phoenix Islands	111	U2
Phong Saly	93	K4
Phong Tho	93	K4
Phu Cuong	93	L6
Phu Dien Chau	93	L5
Phuket	93	J7
Phuket, Ko	93	J7
Phulabani	92	F4
Phu Ly	93	L4
Phuoc Le	93	L6
Phu Tho	93	L4
Phyajoki	62	L4
Piacenza	68	B3
Piana	69	B4
Pianosa, Isola	69	C4
Piatra Neamt	73	J2
Piaui	137	J5
Piaui, Serra do	137	J5
Piave	68	D3
Piaya	90	F7
Piazza Armerina	69	E7
Pibor	103	F6
Pibor Post	103	F6
Pic	124	G2
Picardie	64	E4
Picayune	128	H5
Pichilemu	139	B6
Pickering	55	J2
Pickering, Vale of	55	J2
Pickle Lake	121	J7
Pico	69	D5
Picos	137	J5
Pico Truncado	139	C9
Picton	115	L4
Picun-Leufu	139	C7
Pidalion, Akra	76	F5
Pidurutalagala	92	F7
Piedecuesta	136	C2
Piedrabuena	66	D3
Piedrahita	66	D2
Piedralaves	66	D2
Piedras Negras	127	M6
Piedra Sola	138	E6
Pielavesi	62	M5
Pielinen	62	N5
Pierowall	56	F1
Pierre	123	P5
Pietarsaari	62	K5
Pietermaritzburg	108	F5
Pietersburg	108	E4
Pietrosu	73	H2
Pieve di Cadore	68	D2
Pigadhia	75	J5
Piggott	128	G2
Pihtipudas	62	L5
Pijijiapan	131	N10
Pikes Peak	123	M8
Pikeville	124	J8
Pikhtovka	84	C5
Pila	71	G2
Pilar	138	E5
Pilaya	138	D4
Pilcaniyeu	139	B8
Pilcomayo	138	D4
Pili	75	J4
Pilibhit	92	E3
Pilica	71	H3
Pilion	75	G3
Pilos	75	F4
Pilot Point	118	D4
Pilsen	70	E4
Pimenta Bueno	136	E6
Pimentel	137	G4
Pina	67	F2
Pinang *Malaysia*	90	C4
Pinang *Malaysia*	90	C4
Pinarbasi *Turkey*	76	E2
Pinarbasi *Turkey*	77	G3
Pinar del Rio	132	F3
Pinarhisar	76	B2
Pinawa	123	S2
Pincher Creek	122	H3
Pindare	137	H4
Pindhos Oros	75	F3
Pindi Gheb	92	D2
Pine Bluff	128	F3
Pine Bluffs	123	M7
Pine City	124	D4
Pine Creek	112	G1
Pine Creek Lake	128	E3
Pinedale	123	K6
Pine Falls	119	R5
Pinega *U.S.S.R.*	78	G3
Pinega *U.S.S.R.*	78	G3
Pine Island Bay	141	T4
Pine Pass	119	L5
Pine Point	119	N3
Pine Ridge	123	N6
Pinerolo	68	A3
Pines, Lake O' the	128	E4
Pinetop-Lakeside	127	H3
Pineville	124	J8
Pingbian	93	K4
Pingdingshan	93	M2
Pingelly	112	D5
Pingeyri	62	T12
Pingguo	93	L4
Pingjiang	93	M3
Ping, Mae Nam	93	J5
Pingquan	93	L1
Pingtan Dao	87	M6
Ping-tung	87	N7
Pingwu	93	K2
Pingxiang *Guangxi, China*	93	L4
Pingxiang *Jiangxi, China*	93	M3
Pingyang	87	N6
Pingyao	87	L4
Pingyi	87	M4
Pingyin	87	M4
Pinhao	66	C2
Pinhel	66	C2
Pini	90	B5
Pinios *Greece*	75	F4
Pinios *Greece*	75	F3
Pinnes, Akra	75	H2
Pinos, Point	126	B2
Pinotepa Nacional	131	L9
Pinrang	91	F6
Pins, Ile des	114	X17
Pinsk	71	M2
Pintados	138	C4
Pinta, Isla	136	A7
Pinto	138	D5
Pinyug	78	H3
Pioche	126	E2
Piombino	69	C4
Pioner, Ostrov	81	L2
Pionerskiy *U.S.S.R.*	84	Ad4
Pionerskiy *U.S.S.R.*	71	J1
Piotrkow Trybunalski	71	H3
Piove di Sacco	68	D3
Piperi	75	H3
Pipestone	124	B5
Pipmudcan, Reservoir	125	Q2
Piracicaba	138	G4
Piracuruca	137	J4
Piraeus	75	G4
Pirahmet	77	H2
Piraievs	75	G4
Piranhas *Amazonas, Brazil*	136	E5
Piranhas *Sergipe, Brazil*	137	K5
Piranshahr	77	L4
Pirapora	138	H3
Pirara	136	F3
Pirgos *Greece*	75	F4
Pirgos *Greece*	75	H5
Pirimapun	114	B3
Pirineos	67	F1
Pirin Planina	73	G5
Piripiri	137	J4
Pirmasens	70	B4
Pirna	70	E3
Piro do Rio	138	G3
Pirot	73	G4
Pir Panjal Range	92	D2
Piru	91	H6
Piryatin	79	E5
Piryi	75	H3
Pisa	68	C4
Pisco	136	B6
Piscopi	75	J4
Pisek	70	F4
Pishan	92	E1
Pishin	95	Q8
Pishin-Lora	92	C3
Pistayarvi, Ozero	62	P4
Pisticci	69	F5
Pistilfjordur	62	X11
Pistoia	68	C4
Pisuerga	66	D1
Pit	122	D7
Pita	104	C3
Pitanga	138	E4
Pitcairn Island	143	J5
Pitea	62	J4
Pitealven	62	H4
Pitesti	73	H3
Pithiviers	64	E4
Pitkyaranta	78	E3
Pitlochry	57	E4
Pitlyar	84	Ae3
Pitt Island *Canada*	118	K5
Pitt Island *New Zealand*	115	F7
Pittsburg	124	C8
Pittsburgh	125	K6
Pittsfield	124	E7
Pitt Strait	115	F7
Piui	138	G4
Piura	136	A5
Pjorsa	62	N2
Pjorsa	62	V12
Placentia Bay	121	Q8
Placer	91	G3
Placerville	126	B1
Placido do Castro	136	D6
Plackoviea	73	G5
Plainview	127	M3
Plaka	75	H2
Plakenska Planina	73	F5
Plampang	91	F7
Plana	70	E4
Planeta Rica	133	K10
Plankinton	123	Q6
Plant City	129	L7
Plaquemine	128	G5
Plasencia	66	C2
Plastun	88	F3
Platani	69	D7
Plata, Rio de la	139	E6
Plati	75	G2
Plato	136	C2
Platte	123	R7
Platteville	124	E5
Plattling	70	E4
Plattsburgh	125	P4
Plattsmouth	124	C6
Plauen	70	E3
Plav	72	E4
Playa Azul	130	H8
Pleasanton	128	C6
Pleihari	90	E6
Pleiku	93	L6
Plenty, Bay of	115	F2
Plentywood	123	M3
Plesetsk	78	G3
Plessisville	125	Q3
Pleszew	71	G3
Pletipi Lake	121	M7
Pleven	73	H4
Plitra	75	G4
Pljevlja	72	E4
Plock	71	H2
Plockenstein	70	E4
Ploermel	65	B5
Ploiesti	73	J3
Plomb du Cantal	65	E6
Plombieres	65	G5
Ploner See	70	D1
Plonsk	71	J2
Ploty	70	F2
Plovdiv	73	H4
Plumpton	55	G2
Plym	52	C4
Plymouth *Devon, U.K.*	52	C4
Plymouth *Montserrat, U.K.*	133	R6
Plymouth *Indiana, U.S.A.*	124	G6
Plymouth *New Hampshire, U.S.A.*	125	Q5
Plymouth Sound	52	C4
Plynlimon	52	D2
Plyussa *U.S.S.R.*	63	N7
Plyussa *U.S.S.R.*	63	N7
Plzen	70	E4
Pniewy	71	G2
Po *Burkina Faso*	104	E3
Po *Italy*	68	C3
Pobeda, Gora	85	R3
Pobedy, Pik	86	D3
Pobiedziska	71	G2
Pobla de Segur	67	G1
Pocatello	122	H6
Pocatky	70	F4
Pochep	79	E5
Pochinok	78	E5
Pochutla	131	L10
Pocomoke City	125	N7
Pocone	138	E3
Pocos de Caldas	138	G4
Podcherye	78	K3
Po della Pila, Bocche del	68	D3
Podgorica	72	E4
Podgornoye	84	C5
Podkamennaya Tunguska	84	E4
Podlaska, Nizina	71	K2
Podolsk	78	F4
Podor	104	C2
Podporozhye	78	E3
Pofadder	108	C5
Poggibonsi	68	C4
Pohang	89	B7
Pohjois-Karjala	62	N5
Pohorela	71	J4
Pohorje	72	C2
Poiana Teiului	73	J2
Poinsett, Cape	141	H5
Pointe-a-Pitre	133	S6
Pointe-Noire	106	B3
Point Etienne	100	B4
Point Fortin	133	S9
Point Hope	118	B2
Point Lake	119	N2
Point Pleasant	124	J7
Poipet	93	K6
Poitiers	65	D5
Poitou	65	C5
Poix	64	D4
Pokataroo	113	K4
Pokhara	92	F3
Pokka	62	L2
Pokrovka *Kirgiziya S.S.R., U.S.S.R.*	86	D3
Pokrovka *Rossiyskaya S.F.S.R., U.S.S.R.*	88	C4
Pokrovsk	85	M4
Pokrovskoye	84	Ae5
Polacca Wash	126	G3
Pola de Laviana	66	D1
Polan	95	Q9
Polana	71	H4
Poland	71	G2
Polar Plateau	141	A1
Polati	76	E3
Pole Khatun	95	Q3
Pol-e Safid	95	L3
Polesie Lubelskie	71	K3
Polessk	71	J1
Polesye	79	D5
Polgar	73	F2
Poliaigos	75	H4
Policastro, Golfo di	69	E6
Poligny	65	F5
Poligus	84	E4
Polikastron	75	G2
Polikhnitos	75	J3
Polillo Islands	91	G3
Polis	76	E5
Polisan, Tanjung	91	H5
Politovo	78	H3
Poliyiros	75	G2
Polkyko	84	F2
Pollachi	92	E6
Pollino, Monte	69	F6
Polmak	62	N2
Polmont	57	E5
Polna	63	N7
Polnovat	84	Ae4
Polonnoye	79	D5
Polotsk	63	N9
Polperro	52	C4
Polski Trumbesh	73	H4
Poltava	79	E6
Poltavka	84	A6
Poltsamaa	63	L7
Polunochnoye	84	Ad4
Poluostrov Shirokostan	85	P2
Poluy	84	Ae3
Polyanovo	84	Ae4
Polyarnik	85	Y3
Polyarnyy	62	Q2
Polynesia	143	H4
Polyuc	131	Q8
Pombal *Para, Brazil*	137	G4
Pombal *Paraiba, Brazil*	137	K5
Pombal *Portugal*	66	B3
Pomerania	70	E2
Pomona	126	D3
Pomorskie, Pojezierze	70	F2
Pomorskiy Proliv	78	H2
Pompano Beach	129	M7
Pompeyevka	88	C1
Pomyt	84	Ae4
Ponca City	128	D2
Ponce	133	P5
Ponce de Leon Bay	129	M8
Poncheville, Lac	125	M1

Pondicherry **92** E6
Pond Inlet **120** L3
Pondo **114** E2
Ponerihouen **114** W16
Ponferrada **66** C1
Pongoma **78** E2
Ponnaiyar **92** E6
Ponnani **92** E6
Pono **114** A3
Ponomarevka **78** J5
Ponoy *U.S.S.R.* **78** F2
Ponoy *U.S.S.R.* **78** G2
Pons **65** C6
Pont **57** G5
Ponta de Pedras **137** G4
Ponta Grossa **138** F5
Pont-a-Mousson **64** G4
Ponta Pora **138** E4
Pontardulais **52** C3
Pontarlier **65** G5
Pontchartrain, Lake **128** G5
Ponte de Barca **66** B2
Ponte de Pedra **137** F6
Pontedera **68** C4
Ponte de Sor **66** B3
Pontefract **55** H3
Ponteland **55** H1
Ponte Nova **138** H4
Ponterwyd **52** D2
Pontevedra **66** B1
Ponthierville **106** E3
Pontiac **124** J5
Pontianak **90** D6
Pontivy **64** B4
Pont-l'Abbe **65** A5
Pontoetoe **137** F3
Pontois **64** E4
Pontremoli **68** B3
Pontrilas **52** E3
Ponts **67** G2
Pontypool **52** D3
Pontypridd **52** D3
Ponziane, Isole **69** D5
Poole **53** F4
Poole Bay **53** F4
Poolewe **56** C3
Pooley Bridge **55** G2
Poona **92** D5
Poopo, Lago **138** C3
Poor Knights Islands **115** E1
Popayan **136** B3
Popigay *U.S.S.R.* **84** H2
Popigay *U.S.S.R.* **84** J2
Poplar Bluff **124** E8
Poplarville **128** H5
Popocatepetl, Volcan **131** K8
Popokabaka **106** C4
Popoli **69** D4
Popomanaseu, Mount **114** K6
Popondetta **114** D3
Porbandar **92** C4
Porcher Island **118** J5
Porcuna **66** D4
Porcupine **118** G2
Pordenone **68** D3
Pordim **73** H4
Pore **136** C2
Porec **72** B3
Pori **63** J6
Porirua **115** E4
Porjus **62** H3
Porkhov **63** N8
þorlakshofn **62** U13
Porlamar **136** E1
Porlock **52** D3
Porlock Bay **52** D3
Pornic **65** B5
Porog *U.S.S.R.* **78** F3
Porog *U.S.S.R.* **78** K3
Poronaysk **85** Q7
Poros *Greece* **75** G4
Poros *Greece* **75** G4
Porosozero **78** E3
Porozhsk **78** J3
Porozovo **71** L2
Porpoise Bay **141** J5
Porrentury **68** A2
Porsangen **62** L1
Porsanger-halvoya **62** L1
Porsgrunm **63** C7
þorshofn **62** X11
Porsuk **76** D3
Porsuk Baraji **76** D3
Porsyakha **84** A3
Portachuelo **138** D3
Portadown **58** K4
Portaferry **58** L4
Portage **124** F5
Portage la Prairie **119** R5
Portal **123** N3
Port Alberni **122** B3
Port Albert **113** K6
Portalegre **66** C3
Portales **127** L3
Port Alfred **108** E6
Port Alice **122** A2
Port Angeles **122** C3
Port Antonio **132** J5
Portarlington **59** H6
Port Arthur *Australia* **113** K7
Port Arthur *U.S.A.* **128** F6
Port Askaig **57** B5
Port Augusta **113** H5
Port-au-Prince **133** L5
Port Austin **124** J4
Portavogie **58** M4
Port-Berge **109** J3
Port Blair **93** H6
Portboil **53** N7
Port Burwell **121** P5
Port Cartier **121** N7
Port Chalmers **115** C6
Port Charlotte **129** L7
Port Clarence **118** B2
Port Clinton **124** J6
Port Coquitlam **122** C3
Port Darwin **139** E10
Port-de-Paix **133** L5
Port Dickson **90** C5
Portel **66** C3
Port Elgin **125** K4
Port Elizabeth **108** E6
Port Ellen **57** C5
Port Erin **54** E2
Porterville **126** C2
Port-Eynon **52** C3
Port Francqui **106** D3
Port Gentil **106** A3
Port Glasgow **57** F4
Port Harcourt **105** G5
Port Hardy **118** K5
Porthcawl **52** D3
Port Heiden **118** D4
Port Herald **107** G6
Porthleven **52** B4
Porthmadog **52** C2
Porth Neigwl **52** C2
Port Huron **124** J5
Port Il'ich **94** J2
Portimao **66** B4
Port Isaac **52** C4
Port Isaac Bay **52** C4
Portishead **52** E3
Port Jackson **113** L5
Port Jervis **125** N6
Port Kaituma **136** F2
Port Kembla **113** L5
Port Kenney **113** G5
Portknockie **56** F3
Port Lairge **59** H8
Portland *Australia* **113** J6
Portland *New Zealand* **115** E1
Portland *Indiana, U.S.A.* **124** H6
Portland *Maine, U.S.A.* **125** Q5
Portland *Oregon, U.S.A.* **122** C5
Portland Bay **113** J6
Portland, Bill of **52** E4
Portland, Cape **113** K7
Portland, Isle of **52** E4
Portland Point **132** J6
Portland Promontory **121** L6
Port Laoise **59** H6
Port Lavaca **128** D6
Port-Leucate **65** E7
Port Lincoln **113** H5
Portlock Reefs **114** C3
Port Loko **104** C4
Port Louis **109** L7
Port McArthur **113** H2
Port Macquarie **113** L5
Port Menier **121** P8
Port Moresby **114** D3
Portnacroish **57** C4
Portnahaven **57** B5
Port Nelson **119** S4
Port Nolloth **108** C5
Portnyagino, Ozero **84** H2
Porto **66** B2
Porto Alegre **138** F4
Porto Alexandre **106** B6
Porto Amboim **106** B5
Porto Camargo **138** F4
Porto d'Ascoli **69** D4
Porto dos Gauchos **137** F6
Porto Esperanca **138** E3
Porto Esperidiao **138** E3
Portoferraio **69** C4
Port-of-Spain **136** E1
Porto Grande **137** G3
Portogruaro **68** D3
Porto Lucena **138** F5
Portom **62** J5
Portomaggiore **68** C3
Porto Nacional **138** H6
Porto Novo *Benin* **105** F4
Porto Novo *Cape Verde* **104** L7
Port Orford **122** B6
Porto San Stefano **69** C4
Porto Sao Jose **138** F4
Porto Seguro **137** K7
Porto Socompa **138** C4
Porto Tolle **68** D3
Porto Torres **69** B5
Porto-Vecchio **69** B5
Porto Velho **136** E5
Portoviejo **136** A4
Portpatrick **54** D2
Port Pegasus **115** A7
Port Phillip Bay **113** J6
Port Pirie **113** H5
Portraine **59** K6
Portreath **52** B4
Portree **56** B3
Portrush **58** J2
Port Said **103** F1
Port Saint Joe **129** K6
Port Saint Johns **108** E6
Port-Saint-Louis **65** F7
Port Sandwich **114** T12
Port Saunders **121** Q7
Port Shepstone **108** F6
Portskerra **56** E2
Portsmouth *U.K.* **53** F4
Portsmouth *New Hampshire, U.S.A.* **125** Q5
Portsmouth *Ohio, U.S.A.* **124** J7
Portsmouth *Virginia, U.S.A.* **125** M8
Portsoy **56** F3
Port Stephens **113** L5
Portstewart **58** J2
Port Sudan **103** G4
Port Talbot **52** D3
Porttipahdan tekojarvi **62** M2
Port Townsend **122** C3
Portugal **66** B3
Portuguesa **136** D2
Portumna **59** F6
Port Washington **124** G5
Port William **54** E2
Porvenir *Bolivia* **136** D6
Porvenir *Chile* **139** B10
Porvoo **63** L6
Posadas **138** E5
Posen **71** G2
Poshekhonye Volodarsk **78** F4
Posht-e Badam **95** M5
Poso **91** G6
Posof **77** K2
Post **127** M4
Postavy **63** M9
Poste Weygand **100** F4
Postmasburg **108** D5
Postojna **72** C3
Posusje **72** D4
Posyet **88** C4
Potamia **75** F4
Potamos **75** G4
Potapovo **84** D3
Potchefstroom **108** E5
Poteau **128** E3
Potenza **69** E5
Potes **66** D1
Potgietersrus **108** E4
Poti **77** J1
Potiskum **105** H3
Potlogi **73** H3
Potnarvin **114** U13
Potomac **125** M7
Potosi **138** C3
Potsdam *U.S.A.* **125** N4
Potsdam *W. Germany* **70** E2
Pott **114** V15
Potters Bar **53** G3
Pottstown **125** N6
Pottsville **125** M6
Pouebo **114** W16
Poughkeepsie **125** P6
Poulaphouca Reservoir **59** J6
Poulter **55** H3
Poulton-le-Fylde **55** G3
Poundstock **52** C4
Pouso Alegre **138** G4
Pouzauges **65** C5
Povenets **78** E3
Poverty Bay **115** G3
Povorino **79** G5
Povungnituk **121** L6
Povungnituk Bay **121** L6
Powder **123** M5
Powell **123** K5
Powell, Lake **126** F2
Powell River **122** B3
Power Head **59** F9
Powys **52** D2
Poya **114** W16
Poyang Hu **87** M6
Poyraz **77** H3
Poysdorf **68** F1
Poytya **63** K6
Pozanti **76** F4
Pozarevac **73** F3
Poza Rica **131** L7
Pozharskoye **88** E2
Poznan **71** G2
Pozoblanco **66** D3
Pozohondo **67** F3
Pozzuoli **69** E5
Prabumulih **90** D6
Prachin Buri **93** K6
Prachuap Khiri Khan **93** J6
Praded **71** G3
Pradelles **65** E6
Prades **65** E7
Prague **70** F3
Praha **70** F3
Prahova **73** H3
Praia **104** L7
Prainha *Amazonas, Brazil* **136** E5
Prainha *Para, Brazil* **137** G4
Prairie Dog Town Fork **127** L3
Prairie du Chien **124** E5
Prairies, Coteau des **124** C5
Prairie Village **124** C7
Prapat **90** B5
Prasonisi, Akra **75** J5
Prasto **63** E9
Prata **138** G3
Prato **68** C4
Pratt **127** N2
Pravets **73** G4
Pravia **66** C1
Predazzo **68** C2
Predcal **73** H3
Predeal, Pasul **73** H3
Predivinsk **84** E5
Predlitz **68** D2
Premer **113** K5
Premuda **72** C3
Prenai **71** K1
Prentice **124** E4
Prenzlau **70** E2
Preobrazhenka **84** H5
Preparis **93** H6
Preparis North Channel **93** H5
Preparis South Channel **93** H6
Prerov **71** G4
Prescot **55** G3
Prescott *Arizona, U.S.A.* **126** F3
Prescott *Arkansas, U.S.A.* **128** F4
Prescott Island **120** G3
Preseli, Mynydd **52** C3
Preservation Inlet **115** A7
Presevo **73** F4
Presho **123** Q6
Presidencia Roque Saenz Pena **138** D5
Presidente Dutra **137** J4
Presidente Epitacio **138** F4
Presidente Prudente **138** E4
Presidio **127** K6
Preslav **73** J4
Presnovka **84** Ae6
Presov **71** J4
Prespansko Jezero **75** F2
Presque Isle **125** S3
Pressburg **71** G4
Prestatyn **55** F3
Presteigne **52** D2
Preston *U.K.* **55** G3
Preston *Minnesota, U.S.A.* **124** D5
Preston *Missouri, U.S.A.* **124** D8
Prestonburg **124** J8
Prestonpans **57** F5
Prestwick **57** F4
Pretoria **108** E5
Preveza **75** F3
Prey Veng **93** L6
Pribilof Islands **118** Ad8
Pribinic **72** D3
Pribram **70** F4
Price **126** G1
Price, Cape **93** H6
Prichard **129** H5
Priego **66** E2
Priego de Cordoba **66** D4
Prieska **108** D5
Priest Lake **122** F3
Priest River **122** F3
Prievidza **71** H4
Prignitz **70** D2
Prijedor **72** D3
Prikaspiyskaya Nizmennost **79** J6
Prilep **73** F5
Priluki *Rossiyskaya S.F.S.R., U.S.S.R.* **78** G3
Priluki *Ukraine S.S.R., U.S.S.R.* **79** E5
Primavera **141** V6
Primorsk *Azerbaydzhan S.S.R., U.S.S.R.* **79** H7
Primorsk *Ukraine, S.S.R., U.S.S.R.* **79** F6
Primorsk *U.S.S.R.* **79** H6
Primorsk *U.S.S.R.* **63** N6
Primorskiy Kray **88** E3
Primorsko **73** J4
Primorsko-Akhtarsk **79** F6
Primrose Lake **119** P5
Prince Albert *Canada* **119** P5
Prince Albert *South Africa* **108** D6
Prince Albert Peninsula **119** N1
Prince Albert Road **108** D6
Prince Albert Sound **119** N1
Prince Alfred, Cape **120** B3
Prince Charles Island **120** L4
Prince Charles Mountains **141** E4
Prince Edward Island **121** P8
Prince Edward Islands **142** C6
Prince George **119** L5
Prince Gustav Adolph Sea **120** E2
Prince of Wales, Cape *Canada* **121** M5
Prince of Wales, Cape *U.S.A.* **118** B2
Prince of Wales Island *Australia* **114** C4
Prince of Wales Island *Canada* **120** G3
Prince of Wales Island *U.S.A.* **118** J4
Prince of Wales Strait **119** M1
Prince Patrick Island **120** B2
Prince Regent Inlet **120** H3
Prince Rupert **118** J5
Princes Risborough **53** G3
Princess Astrid Coast **141** A4
Princess Charlotte Bay **113** J1
Princess Elizabeth Land **141** F4
Princess Marie Bay **120** L2
Princethorpe **53** F2
Princeton *Canada* **122** D3
Princeton *Illinois, U.S.A.* **124** F6
Princeton *Kentucky, U.S.A.* **124** G8
Princeton *Missouri, U.S.A.* **124** D6
Princeton *W. Virginia, U.S.A.* **125** K8
Prince William Sound **118** F3
Principe **105** G5
Prineville **122** D5
Prins Karls Forland **80** C2
Prinzapolca **132** E8
Priozersk **63** P6
Pripet Marshes **79** D5
Pripyat **71** M2
Pristina **73** F4
Pritzwalk **70** E2
Privas **65** F6
Privolzhskaya Vozvyshennost **79** H5

Name	Page	Grid
Quixada	137	K4
Qu Jiang	93	L2
Qujing	93	K3
Qulban Layyah	94	H7
Qumarleb	93	J2
Qumbu	108	E6
Qunayfidhah, Nafud	96	G4
Quoin Point	108	C6
Quorn	113	H5
Quorndon	53	F2
Quru Gol Pass	94	G2
Qus	103	F2
Quseir	103	F2
Qutiabad	94	J4
Qutu	96	E7
Quzhou	87	M6

R

Name	Page	Grid
Raab *Austria*	68	E2
Raab *Hungary*	72	D2
Raahe	62	L4
Raakkyla	62	N5
Raanes Peninsula	120	J2
Raanujarvi	62	L3
Raasay	56	B3
Raasay, Sound of	56	B3
Rab	72	C3
Raba	72	D2
Raba *Indonesia*	91	F7
Raba *Poland*	71	H4
Rabastens	65	D7
Rabat *Morocco*	100	D2
Rabat *Turkey*	77	J2
Rabaul	114	E2
Rabi	114	S8
Rabigh	96	D5
Rabor	95	N7
Rabyanah, Ramlat	101	K4
Race, Cape	121	R8
Rach Gia	93	L6
Raciborz	71	H3
Racine	124	G5
Rackwick	56	E2
Racoon	124	C5
Racoon Mountains	129	J3
Rada	96	G9
Radauti	73	H2
Radcliff	124	H8
Radde	88	C1
Radekhov	71	L3
Radford	125	K8
Radisson	121	L7
Radna	73	F2
Radnice	70	E4
Radnor Forest	52	D2
Radom	71	J3
Radomsko	71	H3
Radomyshl	79	D5
Radovis	73	G5
Radstadt	68	D2
Radstock	52	E3
Radstock, Cape	113	G5
Radzyn Podlaski	71	K3
Rae	119	M2
Rae Bareli	92	F3
Rae Isthmus	120	J4
Raetihi	115	E3
Rafaela	138	D6
Rafai	102	D6
Rafalovka	71	L3
Rafha	96	F2
Rafsanjan	95	M6
Raga	102	E6
Ragged Cays	133	K3
Raghtin More	58	H2
Raglan Harbour	115	E2
Ragusa *Italy*	69	E7
Ragusa *Yugoslavia*	72	E4
Rahad	96	B10
Rahat, Harrat	96	E5
Rahimyar Khan	92	D3
Rahuri	92	D5
Raichur	92	E5
Raigarh *Madhya Pradesh, India*	92	F4
Raigarh *Orissa, India*	92	F5
Rainbow City	129	J4
Rainham	53	H3
Rainier, Mount	122	D4
Rainy	124	C2
Rainy Lake	124	D2
Raippaluoto	62	J5
Raipur	92	F4
Raisduoddarhaldde	62	J2
Raistakka	62	N3
Rajada	137	J5
Rajahmundry	92	F5
Rajang	90	E5
Rajanpur	92	D3
Rajapalaiyam	92	E7
Rajapur	92	D5
Rajasthan	92	D3
Rajasthan Canal	92	D3
Rajgarh	92	E4
Rajgrod	71	K2
Rajkot	92	D4
Rajmahal Hills	93	G4
Raj Nandgaon	92	F4
Rajpipla	92	D4
Rajshahi	92	G4
Rakaia	115	C5
Rakan, Ra's	97	K3
Rakbah, Sahl	96	E5
Raketskjutfalt	62	J2
Rakhes	75	G3
Rakhov	79	C6
Rakhovo	71	L4
Rakitnoye	88	E3
Rakkestad	63	D7
Rakops	108	D4
Rakov	71	M2
Rakusha	79	J6
Rakvere	63	M7
Raleigh	129	N3
Rama	132	E8
Ramallah	94	B6
Ramasaig	56	B3
Rambi	114	S8
Rambouillet	64	D4
Rambutyo Island	114	D2
Ramdurg	92	E5
Rameco	139	D7
Rame Head	52	C4
Rameswaram	92	E7
Ramgarh	92	F4
Ramhormoz	95	J6
Ram, Jambal	96	B2
Ramor, Lough	58	H5
Ramos	130	G5
Ramos Island	114	K6
Rampart	118	E2
Rampur	92	E3
Ramree	93	H5
Ramsbottom	55	G3
Ramsele	62	G5
Ramsey *Cambridgeshire, U.K.*	53	G2
Ramsey *Essex, U.K.*	53	J3
Ramsey *Isle of Man, U.K.*	54	E2
Ramsey Bay	54	E2
Ramsey Island	52	B3
Ramsgate	53	J3
Ramsjo	63	F5
Ramtha	94	C5
Ramu	114	C3
Ramvik	62	G5
Ranau	90	F4
Rancagua	139	J6
Rance	64	B4
Rancha Cordova	126	B1
Ranchi	92	G4
Rancho California	126	D4
Randalstown	58	K3
Randazzo	69	E7
Randers	63	D8
Randolph	123	R6
Randsfjord	63	D6
Ranea	62	K4
Ranfurly	115	C6
Rangas, Tanjung	91	F6
Rangiora	115	D5
Rangitaiki	115	F3
Rangitata	115	C5
Rangkasbitung	90	D7
Rangkul	86	C4
Rangoon	93	J5
Rangpur	93	G3
Rangsang	90	C5
Ranibennur	92	E6
Raniganj	93	G4
Ranken	113	H3
Rankin Inlet *Canada*	119	S3
Rankin Inlet *Canada*	119	S3
Rankins Springs	113	K5
Rannoch Moor	57	D4
Rannoch, Loch	57	D4
Ranon	114	U12
Ranongga	114	H5
Ransiki	91	J6
Ranskill	55	H3
Rantau *Kalimantan, Indonesia*	90	F6
Rantau *Sumatera, Indonesia*	90	C5
Rantauprapat	90	B5
Rantoul	124	F6
Ranya	94	G3
Raohe	88	D2
Raon-l'Etape	64	G4
Raoul	111	T7
Rapallo	68	B3
Raper, Cape	120	N4
Rapid City	123	N5
Rapla	63	L7
Rapli	92	F3
Rapness	56	F1
Rappahannock	125	M7
Rapperswil	68	B2
Rapsani	75	G3
Rapulo	136	D6
Rapur	92	E6
Ras al Ayn	77	J4
Ras al Khafji	97	J2
Ra's al Khaymah	97	M4
Rasa, Punta	139	D8
Ras Dashen	96	D10
Raseiniai	63	K9
Ras el Ma	100	E5
Ras en Naqb	94	B6
Rashad	102	F5
Rasharkin	58	K3
Rashid	102	F1
Rasht	95	J3
Rask	95	Q8
Raska	72	F4
Raso, Cabo	139	C8
Rason, Lake	112	E4
Rasshua, Ostrov	85	S7
Rasskazovo	79	G5
Rassokha	84	H2
Rastenburg	71	J1
Rastigaissa	62	M1
Rasul	95	M8
Ratangarh	92	D3
Rat Buri	93	J6
Rathangan	59	J6
Rathcoole	59	K6
Rathdowney	59	G7
Rathdrum	59	K7
Rathen	56	F3
Rathenow	70	E2
Rathfriland	58	K4
Rathkeale	59	E7
Rathlin Island	58	K2
Rathlin Sound	58	K2
Rathluirc	59	E8
Rathmore	59	D8
Rathnew	59	K7
Rathoath	59	K5
Ratibor	71	H3
Ratisbon	70	E4
Rat Islands	118	Ab9
Ratlam	92	E4
Ratnagiri	92	D5
Ratnapura	92	F7
Ratno	79	C5
Raton	127	K2
Ratta	84	C4
Rattray	57	E4
Rattray Head	56	G3
Rattvik	63	F6
Ratzeburg	70	D2
Ratz, Mount	118	J4
Rauch	139	E7
Rauchua	85	V3
Raudales	131	N9
Raudhatain	97	H2
Raufarhofn	62	X11
Raufoss	63	D6
Raukumara Range	115	F3
Raul Leoni, Represa	133	R11
Rauma	63	J6
Raung, Gunung	90	F7
Raurkela	92	F4
Rausu	88	K3
Ravansar	94	H4
Ravar	95	N6
Rava Russkaya	79	C5
Ravenglass	55	F2
Ravenna	68	D3
Ravenscar	55	J2
Ravensthorpe	112	E5
Ravenstonedale	55	G2
Ravenswood	125	K7
Ravensworth	55	H2
Ravi	92	D2
Ravno	72	E3
Rawa	93	J3
Rawah	77	J5
Rawaki	111	U2
Rawalpindi	92	D2
Rawandiz	94	G3
Rawcliffe	55	J3
Rawdah	77	J5
Rawicz	71	G3
Rawlinna	112	F5
Rawlins	123	L7
Rawmarsh	55	H3
Rawson	139	C8
Rawtenstall	55	G3
Ray	53	F3
Rayachoti	92	E6
Rayadurg	92	E6
Rayagarha	92	F5
Rayakoski	62	N2
Ray, Cape	121	Q8
Rayen	95	N7
Rayeskiy	78	J5
Rayleigh	53	H3
Raymondville	128	D7
Ray Mountains	118	E2
Razan	94	J5
Razan	94	J4
Razdelnaya	79	E6
Razdolnoye	88	C4
Razgrad	73	J4
Razmak	92	C2
Raznas Ezers	63	M8
Raz, Pointe du	64	A4
Reading *U.K.*	53	G3
Reading *U.S.A.*	125	N6
Realico	139	D7
Rea, Lough	59	E6
Rearsby	53	F2
Reawick	56	A2
Reay	56	E2
Rebecca, Lake	112	E5
Rebi	91	J7
Reboly	62	P5
Rebrikha	84	C6
Rebrovo	73	G4
Rebun-to	88	H3
Recanati	68	D4
Recea	73	G3
Recherche, Archipelago of the	112	E5
Rechitsa	79	E5
Rechna Doab	92	D2
Recife	137	L5
Recklinghausen	70	B3
Recknitz	70	E2
Reconquista	138	E5
Recreio	136	F5
Red *Canada*	123	R2
Red *U.S.A.*	128	F5
Redalen	63	D6
Red Bay	121	Q7
Redbird	123	M6
Red Bluff	122	C7
Red Bluff Lake	127	L5
Redcar	55	H2
Redcliffe	113	L4
Red Cloud	123	Q7
Red Deer *Canada*	122	G2
Red Deer *Canada*	122	H1
Red Deer *Canada*	123	J2
Red Deer *Saskatchewan, Canada*	119	Q5
Redding	122	C7
Redditch	53	F2
Redencao	137	J5
Redfield	123	Q5
Redhakhol	92	F4
Redhill	53	G3
Red Hills	127	N2
Red Lake *Canada*	123	S2
Red Lake *Canada*	123	T2
Red Lake *U.S.A.*	124	C3
Red Lake *U.S.A.*	123	R4
Red Lodge	123	K5
Redmond	122	D5
Redon	65	B5
Redondela	66	B1
Redondo	66	C3
Red Rock	124	F2
Redruth	52	B4
Red Sea	103	G3
Red Tank	113	K5
Red Wharf Bay	54	E3
Red Wing	124	D4
Redwood City	126	A2
Reed City	124	H5
Reedsport	122	B6
Ree, Lough	58	G5
Reetton	115	C5
Refahiye	77	H3
Refresco	138	C5
Rega	70	F2
Regen	70	E4
Regensburg	70	E4
Reggane	100	F3
Reggio di Calabria	69	E6
Reggio nell Amelia	68	C3
Regina *Brazil*	137	G3
Regina *Canada*	123	M2
Reguengos de Monsaraz	66	C3
Rehna	70	D2
Rehoboth	108	C4
Rehoboth Beach	125	N7
Rehovot	94	B6
Reidh, Rubha	56	C3
Reidsville	129	N2
Reiff	56	C2
Reigate	53	G3
Reighton	55	J2
Reims	64	F4
Reina Adelaida, Archipielago de la	139	B10
Reindeer Lake	119	Q4
Reine	62	E3
Reinga, Cape	115	D1
Reinheimen	62	B5
Reinosa	66	D1
Reitz	108	E5
Relizane	100	F1
Remada	101	H2
Rembang	90	E7
Remeshk	95	P8
Remiremont	65	G4
Remontnoye	79	G6
Remoulins	65	F7
Remscheid	70	B3
Rena *Norway*	63	D6
Rena *Norway*	63	D6
Renaix	64	E3
Renard Islands	114	E4
Rendova Island	114	H6
Rendsburg	70	C1
Renfrew *Canada*	125	M4
Renfrew *U.K.*	57	D5
Rengat	90	D6
Rengo	139	B6
Renish Point	56	B3
Renk	103	F5
Renmark	113	J5
Renmin	87	P2
Rennell Island	114	K7
Rennes	64	C4
Reno *Italy*	68	C3
Reno *U.S.A.*	122	E8
Reo	91	G7
Repetek	95	R2
Repolovo	84	Ae4
Republican	123	R7
Repulse Bay *Australia*	113	K3
Repulse Bay *Canada*	120	J4
Requena *Peru*	136	C5
Requena *Spain*	67	F3
Rere	114	K6
Resadiye *Turkey*	76	B4
Resadiye *Turkey*	77	G2
Resen	73	F5
Resia, Passo de	68	C2
Resistencia	138	E5
Resita	73	F3
Resolution Island *Canada*	121	P5
Resolution Island *New Zealand*	115	A6
Resolution Lake	121	P6
Restigouche	125	S3
Retalhuleu	132	B7

Rethel 64 F4
Rethimnon 75 H5
Retiche, Alpi 68 C2
Retsag 72 E2
Retuerta de Bullaque 66 D3
Reunion 109 L7
Reus 67 G2
Reuss 68 B2
Reut 73 J2
Reutlingen 70 C4
Revel 65 D7
Revelstoke 122 E2
Reventador, Volcan 136 B4
Revillagigedo Island 118 J5
Revillagigedo, Islas 130 D8
Rewa 92 F4
Rewari 92 E3
Rexburg 122 J6
Reyes, Point 122 C9
Reyhanli 77 G4
Rey, Isla del 132 H10
Reykjaheidi 62 W12
Reykjahhd 62 W12
Reykjanesta 62 T13
Reykjavik 62 U12
Reynivellir *Iceland* 62 U12
Reynivellir *Iceland* 62 W12
Reynosa 128 C7
Rezekne 63 M8
Rhatikon Pratigau 68 B2
Rhayader 52 D2
Rheda-Wiedenbruck 70 C3
Rhee 53 G2
Rhein 70 B3
Rheine 70 B2
Rhewl 55 F3
Rhiconich 56 D2
Rhine 64 G4
Rhinelander 124 F4
Rhino Camp 107 F2
Rhir, Cap 100 D2
Rho 68 B3
Rhode Island 125 Q6
Rhodes 75 J4
Rhodopi Planina 73 G4
Rhondda 52 D3
Rhone 65 F7
Rhoose 52 D3
Rhosneigr 55 E3
Rhuddlan 55 F3
Rhum 57 B3
Rhum, Sound of 57 B4
Rhydaman 52 C3
Rhyl 55 F3
Rhynie 56 F3
Riachao do Jacuipe 138 K6
Riacho de Santana 138 J6
Riano 66 D1
Riansares 66 E3
Riau, Kepulauan 90 C5
Riaza 66 E2
Ribadeo 66 C1
Ribadesella 66 D1
Ribas do Rio Pardo 138 F4
Ribat 95 R5
Ribatejo 66 B3
Ribble 55 G2
Ribe 63 C9
Ribeirao Preto 138 G4
Ribeiro do Pombal 137 K6
Riberac 65 D6
Riberalta 136 D6
Ribnica 72 C3
Ribnitz-Damgarten 70 E1
Riccall 55 H3
Rice Lake *Canada* 125 L4
Rice Lake *U.S.A.* 124 E4
Richard Collinson Inlet 119 N1
Richards Island 118 H2
Richardson 128 D4
Richardson Mountains 118 H2
Richelieu 125 P4
Richfield 126 F1
Richland 122 E4
Richlands 125 K8
Richmond *Australia* 113 J3
Richmond *New Zealand* 115 D4
Richmond *South Africa* 108 D6
Richmond *Greater London, U.K.* 53 G3
Richmond *North Yorkshire, U.K.* 55 H2
Richmond *Indiana, U.S.A.* 124 H7
Richmond *Kentucky, U.S.A.* 124 H8
Richmond *Virginia, U.S.A.* 125 M8
Richmond Range 115 D4
Rickmansworth 53 G3
Ricla 67 F2
Ricobayo, Embalse de 66 D2
Ridgecrest 126 D3
Ridgeland 129 M4
Ridgway 125 L6
Riding Mountain 123 P2
Ridsdale 57 F5
Ried 68 D1
Rienza 68 C2
Riesa 70 E3
Riesco, Isla 139 B10
Rietfontein 108 D4
Rieti 69 D4
Rifle 123 L8
Rifstangi 62 W11
Riga 63 L8
Riga, Gulf of 63 K8
Rigan 95 P7
Rigistan 92 B2
Rigolet 121 Q7
Rihab, Ar 94 G6
Rihand 92 F4
Riiser-Larsen Sea 141 B5
Rijeka 72 C3
Rika 71 K4
Rika, Wadi al 96 G5
Rimah, Wadi al 96 E3
Rimal, Ar 97 L6
Rimavska Sobota 71 J4
Rimbo 63 H7
Rimini 68 D3
Rimna 73 J3
Rimnicu Sarat 73 J3
Rimnicu Vilcea 73 H3
Rimouski 125 R2
Rinca 91 F7
Rinchinlhumbe 86 H1
Ringe 63 D9
Ringebu 63 D6
Ringgold Isles 114 S8
Ringkobing 63 C8
Ringkobing Fjord 63 C9
Ringmer 53 H4
Ringselet 62 L3
Ringvassoy 62 H2
Ringwood 53 F4
Rinia 75 H4
Rinjani, Gunung 90 F7
Rinns Point 57 B5
Riobamba 136 B4
Rio Branco *Brazil* 136 D5
Rio Branco *Uruguay* 138 F6
Rio Bravo 128 D8
Rio Bueno 139 B8
Rio Caribe 136 E1
Rio Claro 136 E1
Rio Colorado 139 D7
Rio Cuarto 138 D6
Rio de Janeiro *Brazil* 138 H4
Rio de Janeiro *Brazil* 138 H4
Rio de Oro, Baie de 100 B4
Rio Gallegos 139 C10
Rio Grande *Argentina* 139 C10
Rio Grande *Brazil* 138 F6
Rio Grande *U.S.A.* 130 H6
Rio Grande City 128 C7
Rio Grande de Santiago 130 G7
Rio Grande do Norte 137 K5
Rio Grande do Sul 138 F5
Riohacha 136 C1
Rio Hato 132 G10
Rio Lagartos 131 Q7
Riom 65 E6
Riom-es-Montagnes 65 E6
Rio Mulatos 138 C3
Rionegro 136 C2
Rio Negro *Brazil* 138 G5
Rio Negro *Spain* 66 C1
Rio Negro, Embalse del 138 E6
Rio Negro, Pantanal do 138 E3
Rioni 77 J1
Rio Pardo de Minas 138 H3
Rio Primero 138 D6
Rio Sao Goncalo 138 H4
Riosucio *Colombia* 136 B2
Riosucio *Colombia* 136 B2
Rio Verde 138 F3
Ripley *Ohio, U.S.A.* 124 J7
Ripley *Tennessee, U.S.A.* 128 H3
Ripley *W. Virginia, U.S.A.* 125 K7
Ripoll 67 H1
Ripon 55 H2
Ripponden 55 H3
Risca 52 D3
Rishiri-to 88 H3
Rishon le Zion 94 B6
Risle 64 D4
Risor 63 C7
Risoyhamn 62 F2
Ritchie's Archipelago 93 H6
Ritter, Mount 122 E9
Ritzville 122 E4
Riva 68 C3
Rivas 132 E9
Rivera 138 E6
River Falls 124 D4
Riverina 113 K5
Riversdale 108 D6
Riverside 126 D4
Riverton *Australia* 113 H5
Riverton *Canada* 123 R2
Riverton *New Zealand* 115 B7
Riverton *U.S.A.* 123 K6
Riviere-du-Loup 125 R3
Rivoli 68 A3
Riwaka 115 D4
Riwoqe 93 J2
Riyan 97 J9
Rize 77 J2
Rizhskiy Zaliv 63 K8
Rizokarpaso 76 F5
Rjukan 63 C7
Rjuven 63 B7
Roa 66 E2
Road Town 133 Q5
Roan Fell 57 F5
Roanne 65 F5
Roanoke *N. Carolina, U.S.A.* 129 P2
Roanoke *U.S.A.* 125 L8
Roanoke *U.S.A.* 125 L8
Roanoke Rapids 129 P2
Roan Plateau 123 K8
Robat 95 R6
Robat Karim 95 K4
Robat Thand 95 Q7
Robel 70 E2
Robert Brown, Cape 120 K4
Roberton 57 E5
Robertsbridge 53 H4
Robertsfors 62 J4
Robert S. Kerr Reservoir 128 E3
Robertson Range 112 E3
Robertsport 104 C4
Roberval 125 P2
Robinson 124 G7
Robinson Ranges 112 D4
Robleda 66 C2
Robledollano 66 D3
Robles La Paz 136 C1
Roblin 123 P2
Robore 138 E3
Rob Roy Island 114 H5
Robson, Mount 119 M5
Roca, Cabo da 66 B3
Roca Partida, Isla 130 C8
Roca Partida, Punta 131 M8
Roccella Ionica 69 F6
Rocha 139 F6
Rocha da Gale, Barragem 66 C4
Rochdale 55 G3
Rochechouart 65 D6
Rochefort 65 C6
Rochelle 124 F6
Rochester *Kent, U.K.* 53 H3
Rochester *Northumberland, U.K.* 57 F5
Rochester *New Hamshire, U.S.A.* 125 Q5
Rochester *New York, U.S.A.* 125 M5
Rochester *Winconsin, U.S.A.* 124 D4
Rochford 53 H3
Rochfortbridge 59 H6
Rock 124 F5
Rockefeller Plateau 141 R3
Rock Falls 124 F6
Rockford 124 F5
Rockglen 123 L3
Rockhampton 113 L3
Rockingham *Australia* 112 D5
Rockingham *U.S.A.* 129 N3
Rockingham Bay 113 K2
Rock Island 124 E6
Rockland *Maine, U.S.A.* 125 R4
Rockland *Michigan, U.S.A.* 124 F3
Rock Springs *Montana, U.S.A.* 123 L4
Rock Springs *Wyoming, U.S.A.* 123 K7
Rockwood 125 R4
Rocky Ford 127 L1
Rocky Mount 129 P3
Rocky Mountain House 119 N5
Rocky Mountains 116 G3
Rocroi 64 F4
Rodberg 63 C6
Rodby 63 D9
Rodeby 63 F8
Rodel 56 B3
Roden 52 E2
Rodez 65 E6
Rodhos *Greece* 75 J4
Rodhos *Greece* 75 K4
Rodi Garganico 69 E5
Roding 53 H3
Rodinga 113 G3
Rodna 73 H2
Rodnei, Muntii 73 H2
Rodney, Cape *New Zealand* 115 E2
Rodney, Cape *U.S.A.* 118 B3
Rodonit, Kep i 74 E2
Rodosto 76 B2
Roebuck Bay 112 E2
Roermond 64 F3
Roeselare 64 E3
Roes Welcome Sound 120 J5
Rogachev 79 E5
Rogaland 63 B7
Rogatin 71 L4
Rogers 128 E2
Rogers, Mount 125 K8
Roggeveld Berge 108 D6
Rogliano 68 B4
Rognan 62 F3
Rogozno 71 G2
Rohri 92 C3
Rohtak 92 E3
Rois Bheinn 57 C3
Rojas 139 D6
Rojo, Cabo *Mexico* 131 L7
Rojo, Cabo *U.S.A.* 133 P6
Rokan 90 C5
Rokel 104 C4
Rokiskis 63 L9
Rolla 124 E8
Rolleston 113 K3
Roma *Australia* 113 K4
Roma *Italy* 69 D5
Roma *Sweden* 63 H8
Romain, Cape 129 N4
Romaine 121 P7
Romaldkirk 55 G2
Roman 73 J2
Romang 91 H7
Romania 73 G3
Romano, Cape 129 M8
Romanovka 85 J6
Romans-sur-Isere 65 F6
Romanzof, Cape 118 B3
Romao 136 E4
Romblon 91 G3
Rome *Italy* 69 D5
Rome *U.S.A.* 129 K3
Romerike 63 D6
Romilly 64 E4
Romney 125 L7
Romny 79 E5
Romo 63 C9
Romorantin 65 D5
Romsey 53 F4
Rona 56 C3
Ronay 56 A3
Roncador, Cayos 132 G8
Roncador, Serra do 137 G6
Ronco 68 D3
Ronda *India* 92 E1
Ronda *Spain* 66 D4
Rondane 63 C6
Ronda, Sierra de 66 D4
Ronde 63 D8
Rondeslottet 63 C6
Rondonia *Brazil* 136 E6
Rondonia *Brazil* 136 E6
Rondonopolis 138 F3
Ronge, Lac La 119 Q4
Rong Jiang 93 L4
Rong, Kas 93 K6
Rongshui 93 L3
Rong Xian 93 M4
Ronne 63 H9
Ronneby 63 F8
Ronne Entrance 141 U4
Ronne Ice Shelf 141 V3
Ronse 64 E3
Roodepoort 108 E5
Roof Butte 127 H2
Roosendaal 64 F3
Roosevelt 136 E5
Roosevelt Island 141 P3
Roosevelt, Mount 118 K4
Ropcha 78 J3
Roper 113 G1
Ropi 62 J2
Roquefort 65 C6
Rora Head 56 E2
Roraima 136 E3
Roraima, Mount 136 E2
Roros 62 D5
Rorvik 62 D4
Rosa, Cap 69 B7
Rosalia, Punta 126 E6
Rosa, Monte 68 A3
Rosario 137 J4
Rosario *Argentina* 138 D6
Rosario *Mexico* 130 G6
Rosario *Mexico* 127 H7
Rosario de la Frontera 138 D5
Rosarito 126 F6
Roscoe 127 M4
Roscommon *Ireland* 58 F5
Roscommon *Ireland* 58 F5
Roscrea 59 G7
Roseau 133 S7
Roseberth 113 H4
Rosebery 113 K7
Rosebud 122 H2
Roseburg 122 C6
Rosedale Abbey 55 J2
Rosehearty 56 F3
Rose Island 111 V4
Rosenburg 128 E6
Rosenheim 70 E5
Rose Point 118 J5
Roses 67 H1
Roses, Golfo de 67 H1
Roseto d'Abruzzi 69 D4
Rosetown 123 K2
Rosetta 102 F1
Roshkhvar 95 P4
Rosiori de Vede 73 H3
Rositsa 73 H4
Roskilde 63 E9
Roslavl 78 E5
Ross *New Zealand* 115 C5
Ross *U.K.* 57 G5
Rossall Point 55 F3
Rossano 69 F6
Rossan Point 58 E3
Rosscarbery Bay 59 D9
Ross Dependency 141 P7
Rossel Island 114 E4
Rosses Bay 58 F2
Rosses Point 58 E4
Rosses, The 58 F3
Ross Ice Shelf 141 N2
Rossington 55 H3
Ross Island 141 M3
Rossiyskaya S.F.S.R. 78 E4
Rosslare Harbour 59 K8
Ross-on-Wye 52 E3
Rossosh 79 F5
Ross River 118 J3
Ross Sea 141 N3
Rost 62 E3
Rostaq 95 L8
Rostock 70 E1
Rostonsolka 62 J2
Rostov 78 F4
Rostov-na-Donu 79 F6
Rostrevor 58 K4
Roswell *Georgia, U.S.A.* 129 K3
Roswell *New Mexico, U.S.A.* 127 K4
Rotemo 63 B7
Rotenburg 70 C2
Rothaargebirge 70 C3
Rothbury 57 G5

204

205

Sandon 53 E2
San Dona di Piave 68 D3
Sandoway 93 H5
Sandown 53 F4
Sandoy 62 Z14
Sandpoint 122 F3
Sandray 57 A4
Sandsele 62 G4
Sandstone *Australia* 112 D4
Sandstone *U.S.A.* 124 D3
Sandusky *U.S.A.* 124 J6
Sandusky *U.S.A.* 124 J6
Sandvig 70 F1
Sandvika 62 E5
Sandviken 63 G6
Sandwich 53 J3
Sandy 53 G2
Sandy Cape 113 L3
Sandy Lake 119 S5
Sandy Point 93 H6
San Esteban, Isla de 126 F6
San Felipe *Chile* 139 B6
San Felipe *Mexico* 126 E5
San Felipe *Mexico* 131 J7
San Felipe *Venezuela* 136 D1
San Felix, Isla 135 A5
San Fermin, Punta 126 E5
San Fernando *Chile* 139 B6
San Fernando *Mexico* 128 C8
San Fernando *Mexico* 128 C8
San Fernando *Philippines* 91 G2
San Fernando *Spain* 66 C4
San Fernando *Trinidad and] Tobago* 133 S9
San Fernando de Apure 136 D2
San Fernando de Atabapo 136 D3
Sanford *Florida, U.S.A.* 129 M6
Sanford *Maine, U.S.A.* 125 Q5
Sanford *N. Carolina, U.S.A.* 129 N3
Sanford, Mount 118 G3
San Francisco *Argentina* 138 D6
San Francisco *California, U.S.A.* 126 A2
San Francisco *New Mexico, U.S.A.* 127 H4
San Francisco, Cabo de 136 A3
San Francisco de Assis 138 E5
San Francisco del Oro 127 K7
San Francisco de Macoris 133 M5
San Francisco de Paula, Cabo 139 C9
San Francisco Javier 67 G3
San Francisco, Paso de 138 C5
San Gabriel, Punta 126 F6
Sangan 95 P4
Sangar 85 M4
Sang Bast 95 P3
Sangeang 91 F7
Sanggau 90 E5
Sangha 106 C2
Sangihe 91 H5
Sangihe, Kepulauan 91 H5
San Gil 136 C2
San Giovanni in Fiore 69 F6
Sangkhla Buri 93 J6
Sangli 92 D5
Sangmelima 105 H5
Sangonera 67 F4
San Gorgonio Peak 126 D3
Sangowo 91 H5
Sangre de Cristo Range 127 K1
Sangro 69 E4
Sangue 137 F6
Sanguesa 67 F1
San Guiseppe Iato 69 D7
San Hipolito, Punta 126 F7
Sanibel Island 129 L7
San Ignacio *Bolivia* 138 D3
San Ignacio *Bolivia* 136 D6
San Ignacio *Mexico* 126 F7
San Ignacio *Paraguay* 138 E5
Sanikiluaq 121 L6
San Ildefonso, Cape 91 G2
San Javier 138 D3
Sanjbod 94 J3
Sanjo 89 G7
San Joaquin *Bolivia* 136 E6
San Joaquin *U.S.A.* 126 B2
San Joaquin Valley 126 B2
San Jorge *Colombia* 133 K10
San Jorge *Solomon Is.* 114 J6
San Jorge, Bahia de 126 F5
San Jorge, Golfo de *Argentina* 139 C9
San Jorge, Golfo de *Spain* 67 G2
San Jose *Costa Rica* 132 E10
San Jose *Philippines* 91 G3
San Jose *Spain* 67 E4
San Jose *California, U.S.A.* 126 B2
San Jose *New Mexico, U.S.A.* 127 J3
San Jose de Amacuro 136 E2
San Jose de Buenavista 91 G3
San Jose de Chiquitos 138 D3
San Jose de Gracia 126 F7
San Jose de Jachal 139 C6
San Jose del Cabo 130 E6
San Jose de Mayo 139 E6
San Jose, Isla 130 D5
San Juan 131 M8
San Juan *Argentina* 138 C6
San Juan *Argentina* 138 C6
San Juan *Dominican Republic* 133 M5
San Juan *Mexico* 127 N8
San Juan *Nicaragua* 132 E8
San Juan *Peru* 136 B7
San Juan *Puerto Rico, U.S.A.* 133 P5
San Juan *Utah, U.S.A.* 127 H2

San Juan Bautista 67 G3
San Juan Bautista, Cabo 126 F6
San Juan del Norte 132 F9
San Juan del Norte, Bahia de 132 F9
San Juan de los Morros 136 D2
San Juan del Rio 131 K7
San Juanico, Punta 126 F7
San Juan Islands 122 C3
San Juan Mountains 127 J2
San Julian 139 C9
Sankt Blasjon 62 F4
Sankuru 106 D3
San Lazaro, Cabo 130 C5
San Lazaro, Sierra de 130 E6
San Lorenzo 136 D6
San Lorenzo, Cabo 136 A4
San Lorenzo, Cerro 139 B9
San Lorenzo de El Escorial 66 D2
San Lorenzo de la Parrilla 66 E3
San Lorenzo, Isla 126 F6
Sanlucar de Barrameda 66 C4
Sanlucar la Mayor 66 C4
San Lucas *Bolivia* 138 C4
San Lucas *Mexico* 130 E6
San Lucas, Cabo 130 E6
San Luis 132 C6
San Luis *Argentina* 139 C6
San Luis *Venezuela* 133 N9
San Luis Obispo 126 B3
San Luis Potosi 131 J6
San Luis Rio Colorado 126 E4
Sanluri 69 B6
San Manuel 126 G4
San Marco, Capo 69 B6
San Marcos *Mexico* 131 K9
San Marcos *U.S.A.* 128 D6
San Marcos, Island 126 F7
San Marino 68 D4
San Marino 68 D4
San Martin *Bolivia* 136 E6
San Martin *Colombia* 136 C3
San Martin de Valdeiglesias 66 D2
San Martin, Lago 139 B9
San Mateo 136 E2
San Matias 138 E3
San Matias, Golfo 139 D8
Sanmenxia 93 M2
San Miguel *Bolivia* 138 D3
San Miguel *Bolivia* 138 D3
San Miguel *El Salvador* 132 C8
San Miguel de Allende 131 J7
San Miguel de Tucuman 138 C5
San Miguel do Araguaia 137 G6
San Miguel Island 126 B3
San Miguelito 132 H10
Sanming 87 M6
Sannicandro Garganico 69 E5
San Nicolas 138 D6
San Nicolas, Bahia de 136 B7
San Nicolas Island 126 C4
Sannikova, Proliv 85 Q2
Sanok 71 K4
San Pablo 91 G3
San Pablo, Cabo 139 C10
San Pablo de Loreto 136 C4
San Pablo, Punta 126 E7
San Pedro 104 D5
San Pedro *Argentina* 139 E6
San Pedro *Mexico* 130 D6
San Pedro *Paraguay* 138 E4
San Pedro *U.S.A.* 126 G4
San Pedro Channel 126 C4
San Pedro de las Colonias 127 L8
San Pedro de Lloc 136 B5
San Pedro Martir, Sierra 126 E5
San Pedro, Punta 138 B5
San Pedros 130 G6
San Pedros de Macoris 133 N5
San Pedro, Sierra de 66 C3
San Pedro Sula 132 C7
San Pietro, Isola di 69 B6
Sanquhar 57 E5
San Quintin, Bahia de 126 E5
San Rafael *Argentina* 139 C6
San Rafael *Colombia* 136 C1
San Rafael *U.S.A.* 126 A2
San Remo 68 A4
San Salvador *Bahamas* 133 K2
San Salvador *El Salvador* 132 C8
San Salvador de Jujuy 138 C4
San Salvador, Isla 136 A7
San Sebastian 67 F1
San Sebastian Bahia de 139 C10
San Sebastiao, Ponta 109 G4
Sansepolcro 68 D4
San Severo 69 E5
San Silvestre 133 M10
Sanski Most 72 D3
Santa Ana *Bolivia* 136 D6
Santa Ana *El Salvador* 132 C7
Santa Ana *Mexico* 126 G5
Santa Ana *U.S.A.* 126 C3
Santa Ana Island 114 L7
Santa Barbara 126 C3
Santa Barbara *Honduras* 132 C7
Santa Barbara *Mexico* 127 K7
Santa Barbara Channel 126 B3
Santa Catalina, Gulf of 126 D4
Santa Catalina, Isla 130 D5
Santa Catalina Island 126 C4
Santa Catarina 138 F5
Santa Catarina, Ilha 138 G5
Santa Clara 132 H3
Santa Coloma de Farnes 67 H2
Santa Coloma de Gramanet 67 H2

Santa Comba Dao 66 B2
Santa Comba de Rossas 66 C2
Santa Cruz *Argentina* 139 B10
Santa Cruz *Bolivia* 138 D3
Santa Cruz *U.S.A.* 126 A2
Santa Cruz de la Palma 100 B3
Santa Cruz de Moya 67 F3
Santa Cruz de Tenerife 100 B3
Santa Cruz do Sul 138 F5
Santa Cruz, Isla *Ecuador* 136 A7
Santa Cruz, Isla *Mexico* 130 D5
Santa Cruz Island 126 C3
Santa Cruz Islands 114 N7
Santa Elena 136 E3
Santa Elena, Cabo 132 E9
Santa Eulalia del Rio 67 G3
Santafe 66 E4
Santa Fe *Argentina* 138 D6
Santa Fe *Panama* 132 G10
Santa Fe *U.S.A.* 127 K3
Sant Agata di Militello 69 E6
Santai *Sichuan, China* 93 L2
Santai *Xinjiang Uygur Zizhiqu, China* 86 E3
Santa Ines, Isla 139 B10
Santa Isabel *Argentina* 139 C7
Santa Isabel *Equatorial Guinea* 105 G5
Santa Isabel *Solomon Is.* 114 J5
Santa Lucia 139 E6
Santa Lucia Range 126 B2
Santa Luzia 137 K5
Santa Margarita, Isla 130 D5
Santa Maria *Brazil* 138 F5
Santa Maria *Mexico* 127 J6
Santa Maria *Mexico* 127 K8
Santa Maria *U.S.A.* 126 B3
Santa Maria *Vanuatu* 114 T11
Santa Maria *Venezuela* 133 P11
Santa Maria, Cabo de *Mozambique* 109 F5
Santa Maria, Cabo de *Portugal* 66 C4
Santa Maria di Leuca, Capo 69 G6
Santa Maria, Isla 136 A7
Santa Maria, Laguna de 127 J5
Santa Marta 136 C1
Santa Marta, Cabo de 106 B5
Santa Marta Grande, Cabo de 138 G5
Santa Maura 75 F3
Santa Monica 126 C3
Santan 91 F6
Santana 137 J6
Santana do Ipanema 137 K5
Santana do Livramento 138 E6
Santander *Colombia* 136 B3
Santander *Spain* 66 E1
Sant Antioco 69 B6
Santarem *Brazil* 137 G4
Santarem *Spain* 66 B3
Santaren Channel 132 H3
Santa Rita 136 C1
Santa Rosa *Argentina* 139 C6
Santa Rosa *Argentina* 139 D7
Santa Rosa *Bolivia* 136 D6
Santa Rosa *Brazil* 138 F5
Santa Rosa *California, U.S.A.* 126 A1
Santa Rosa *New Mexico, U.S.A.* 127 K3
Santa Rosa de Cabal 136 B3
Santa Rosa de Copan 132 C7
Santa Rosa Island 126 B4
Santa Rosalia 126 F7
Santa Rosa Range 122 F7
Santa Teresa Gallura 69 B5
Santa Vitoria do Palmar 139 F6
Santa Ynez 126 B3
Santee 129 M4
Santerno 68 C3
Sant Eufemia, Golfo di 69 F6
Santhia 68 B3
Santiago *Brazil* 138 F5
Santiago *Chile* 139 B6
Santiago *Dominican Republic* 133 M5
Santiago *Panama* 132 G10
Santiago *Peru* 136 B4
Santiago, Cerro 132 G10
Santiago de Chuco 136 B5
Santiago de Compostela 66 B1
Santiago de Cuba 133 K4
Santiago del Estero 138 D5
Santiago do Cacem 66 B3
Santiago Ixcuintla 130 G7
Santiago Papasquiaro 130 G5
San Tiburcio 130 J5
Santo Amaro 137 K6
Santo Andre 138 G4
Santo Angelo 138 F5
Santo Antao 104 L7
Santo Antonio do Ica 136 D4
Santo Domingo *Dominican Republic* 133 N5
Santo Domingo *Mexico* 126 E5
Santo Domingo de la Calzada 66 E1
Santo Domingo de los Colorados 136 B4
Santorini 75 H4
Santos 138 G4
Santos Dumont *Amazonas, Brazil* 136 D5
Santos Dumont *Minas Gerais, Brazil* 138 H4
Santo Tomas 126 D5
Santo Tome 138 E5
San Valentin, Cerro 139 B9
San Vicente de la Barquera 66 D1
San Vicente del Caguan 136 C3

San Vincent 132 C8
San Vincente 91 G2
San Vito, Capo 69 D6
Sanyati 108 E3
Sanyshand 87 L3
Sao Borja 138 E5
Sao Bras de Alportel 66 C4
Sao Carlos *Rondonia, Brazil* 136 E5
Sao Carlos *Sao Paulo, Brazil* 138 G4
Sao Domingos 137 H6
Sao Felix 137 G5
Sao Francisco *Acre, Brazil* 136 D6
Sao Francisco *Bahia, Brazil* 137 K5
Sao Francisco do Sul 138 G5
Sao Francisco, Ilha de 138 G5
Sao Joao do Rei 138 H4
Sao Joao do Araguaia 137 H5
Sao Joao do Piaui 137 J5
Sao Joao, Ilhas de 137 H4
Sao Jose 136 D4
Sao Jose do Gurupi 137 H4
Sao Jose do Rio Preto 138 G4
Sao Jose dos Campos 138 G4
Sao Leopoldo 138 F5
Sao Lourenco 138 E3
Sao Luis 137 J4
Sao Manuel 136 F5
Sao Marcos 138 G3
Sao Marcos, Baia de 137 J4
Sao Maria da Boa Vista 137 K5
Sao Mateus 138 K7
Sao Miguel dos Campos 137 K5
Sao Miguel do Tapuio 137 J5
Saona, Isla 133 N5
Saone 65 F5
Sao Nicolau 104 L7
Sao Paulo *Brazil* 138 G4
Sao Paulo *Brazil* 138 G4
Sao Paulo de Olivenca 136 D4
Sao Pedro do Sul 66 B2
Sao Raimundo Nonato 137 J5
Sao Romao 138 G3
Sao Roque, Cabo de 137 K5
Sao Sebastiao do Paraiso 138 G4
Sao Tiago 104 L7
Sao Tome 105 G5
Sao Tome 105 G5
Sao Tome and Principe 105 G5
Sao Tome, Cabo de 138 H4
Saouda, Qornet es 77 G5
Saoura, Oued 100 E2
Sao Vicente 138 G4
Sao Vicente, Cabo de 66 B4
Sao Vincente 104 L7
Sapai 75 H2
Sapanca 76 D2
Sapanca Golu 76 D2
Sape 91 F7
Sapele 105 G4
Sapientza 75 F4
Saposoa 136 B5
Sapporo 88 H4
Sapri 69 E5
Sapulut 90 F5
Saqqez 94 H3
Sarab 94 H3
Sara Buri 93 K6
Saragossa 67 F2
Saraguro 136 B4
Sarajevo 72 E4
Sarakhs 95 Q3
Sarakli 75 G2
Saraktash 79 K5
Saralzhin 79 J6
Saranac Lake 125 P4
Sarande 74 E3
Saran, Gunung 90 E6
Saranpaul 84 Ad4
Saransk 78 H5
Sarapul 78 J4
Sarapul'skoye 88 F1
Sarasota 129 L7
Sarata 73 K2
Saratoga 126 A2
Saratoga Springs 125 P5
Saratov 79 H5
Saravan 95 R8
Saravane 93 L5
Sarawak 90 E5
Saray *Turkey* 76 B2
Saray *Turkey* 77 L3
Saraychik 79 J6
Saraykent 76 F3
Saraykoy *Turkey* 76 C4
Saraykoy *Turkey* 76 F3
Sarayonu 76 E3
Sarbaz 95 Q8
Sarbisheh 95 P5
Sarcham 94 J3
Sarda 92 F3
Sardarshahr 92 D3
Sardegna 69 B5
Sardinia 69 B5
Sardis Lake 128 H3
Sareks 62 G3
Sar-e Pol 92 C1
Sar-e Yazd 95 M6
Sargans 68 B2
Sargodha 92 D2
Sarh 102 C6
Sari 95 L3
Saria 75 J5
Sarickaya 76 D2
Sarigol 76 C3
Sarikamis 77 K2

Name	Page	Ref
Seremban	90	C5
Serengeti Plain	107	F3
Serenje	107	F5
Seret	71	L4
Sergach	78	H4
Sergelen	87	K2
Sergeyevka	88	D4
Sergino	84	Ae4
Sergipe	137	K6
Seria	90	E5
Serian	90	E5
Serifos *Greece*	75	H4
Serifos *Greece*	75	H4
Serik	76	D4
Seringapatum Reef	112	E1
Serio	68	B3
Sermata, Kepulauan	91	H7
Sermiligaarsuk	120	S5
Sernovodsk *U.S.S.R.*	78	J5
Sernovodsk *U.S.S.R.*	88	K4
Sernur	78	H4
Seroglazovka	79	H6
Serov	84	Ad5
Serpa	66	C4
Serpent's Mouth	136	E2
Serpukhov	78	F5
Serra Bonita	138	G3
Serracapriola	69	E5
Serra do Navio	137	G3
Serrai	75	G2
Serrana Bank	132	G7
Serranilla Bank	132	H7
Serra Talhada	137	K5
Serrat, Cap	69	B7
Serres	65	F6
Serrinha	137	K6
Serta	66	B3
Sertania	137	K5
Serui	91	K6
Seruyan	90	E6
Servia	75	G2
Serxu	93	J2
Se San	93	L6
Sese Island	107	F3
Seshachalam Hills	92	E6
Sesheke	106	D6
Sesia	68	B3
Se Srepok	93	L6
Sessa	106	D5
Sestri Levante	68	B3
Sestroretsk	63	N6
Sesupe	71	K1
Set	93	L5
Setana	88	G4
Sete	65	E7
Sete Lagoas	138	H3
Setermoen	62	H2
Setesdal	63	C7
Setif	101	G1
Seto	89	F8
Settat	100	D2
Settle	55	G2
Setubal	66	B3
Setubal, Baia de	66	B3
Seul, Lac	119	S5
Seumayan	90	B5
Seurre	65	F5
Sevan, Ozero	77	L2
Sevastopol	79	E7
Seven	55	J2
Seven Heads	59	E9
Seven Hogs, The	59	B8
Sevenoaks	53	H3
Seven Sisters	118	K4
Severac-le-Chateau	65	E6
Severn *Canada*	121	J6
Severn *U.K.*	52	E3
Severnaya Dvina	78	G3
Severnaya Sosva	84	Ad4
Severnaya Zemlya	81	M1
Severn, Mouth of the	52	E3
Severnyy	78	H2
Severodonetsk	79	F6
Severodvinsk	78	F3
Severomorsk	62	Q2
Severo Osetinsk A.S.S.R.	79	G7
Severouralsk	84	Ad4
Severskiy Donets	79	G6
Sevier	122	H8
Sevier Lake	122	H8
Sevilla *Colombia*	136	B3
Sevilla *Spain*	66	D4
Seville	66	D4
Sevola	71	L4
Sevre Nantaise	65	C5
Sevre Niortaise	65	C5
Sevsk	79	E5
Sewa	104	C4
Seward *Alaska, U.S.A.*	118	F3
Seward *Nebraska, U.S.A.*	123	R7
Seward Peninsula	118	C2
Seyah Kuh, Kavir-e	95	L5
Seyakha	84	A2
Seychelles	82	D7
Seydisehir	76	D4
Seydisfjordur	62	Y12
Seyhan	76	F4
Seyitgazi	76	D3
Seym	79	E5
Seymchan	85	S4
Seymour *Australia*	113	K6
Seymour *Indiana, U.S.A.*	124	H7
Seymour *Texas, U.S.A.*	127	N4
Sezanne	64	E4
Sfax	101	H2
Sfintu Gheorghe	73	H3
Sfintu Gheorghe, Bratul	73	K3
s'Gravenhage	64	F2
Sgurr na Lapaich	56	C3
Shaam	97	N4
Shaanxi	93	L2
Shabunda	106	E3
Shadad, Namakzar-e	95	P6
Shadrinsk	84	Ad5
Shadwan	96	A3
Shaftesbury	53	E3
Shagany, Ozero	73	K3
Shagonar	84	E6
Shag Point	115	C6
Shahabad	92	E3
Shahbandar	92	C4
Shahdab	95	N6
Shahdol	92	F4
Shah Fuladi	92	C2
Shahgarh	92	C3
Shahhat	101	K2
Shahjahanpur	92	E3
Shahpur	92	D2
Shahpura *Madhya Pradesh, India*	92	F4
Shahpura *Rajasthan, India*	92	D3
Shahrabad	95	N3
Shahrak	95	S5
Shahr-e Babak	95	M6
Shahr-e Kord	95	K5
Shahr Rey	95	K4
Shah Rud	95	J3
Shajapur	92	E4
Shakhauz	94	G2
Shakhs, Ras	96	E9
Shakhty	79	G6
Shakhunya	78	H4
Shaki	105	F4
Shakotan-misaki	88	H4
Shaktoolik	118	C3
Shalamzar	95	K5
Shaler Mountains	119	N1
Shalfleet	53	F4
Shalkhar, Ozero	79	J5
Shaluli Shan	93	J2
Shama, Ash	94	D6
Shamary	78	K4
Shambe	102	F6
Shamil	95	N8
Shamiyah	94	D4
Sham, Jambal	97	N5
Shammar	96	E3
Shand	95	R6
Shandan	86	J4
Shandong	87	M4
Shangani	108	E3
Shanghang	87	M7
Shangqiu	93	N2
Shangrao	87	M6
Shang Xian	93	L2
Shangzhi	87	P2
Shanklin	53	F4
Shannon *Ireland*	59	E7
Shannon *New Zealand*	115	E4
Shannon, Mouth of the	59	C7
Shantarskiye Ostrova	85	P5
Shantou	87	M7
Shanxi	93	M1
Shan Xian	93	N2
Shanyin	87	L4
Shaoguan	93	M4
Shaowu	87	M6
Shaoxing	87	N6
Shaoyang	93	M3
Shap	55	G2
Shapinsay	56	F1
Shapkina	78	J2
Shaqra	96	G4
Sharanga	78	H4
Sharbithat, Ra's	97	N8
Shari	88	K4
Shari, Buhayrat	77	L5
Shark Bay	112	C4
Sharlauk	95	M2
Sharlyk	79	J5
Sharmah	96	B2
Sharm el Sheikh	96	B3
Sharon	125	K6
Sharon Springs	127	M1
Sharqi, Al Hajar ash	97	P5
Sharqi, Jazair esh	94	C5
Sharqi, Jebel esh	77	G6
Sharqiyah, Ash	97	P5
Sharqiya, Sahra Esh	103	F2
Sharurah	96	H8
Sharwayn, Ra's	97	K9
Sharya	78	H4
Shashe	108	E4
Shashemene	103	G6
Shashi	93	M2
Shasta Lake	122	C2
Shasta, Mount	122	C7
Shatsk	78	G5
Shatura	78	F4
Shaubak	94	B6
Shaunavon	123	K3
Shaw	55	G3
Shawano	124	F4
Shawbury	52	E2
Shawinigan	125	P3
Shawnce	128	D3
Sha Xi	87	M6
Sha Xian	87	M6
Shaybara	96	C4
Shaytanovka	78	K3
Shchara	71	L2
Shchekino	78	F5
Shchelyayur	78	J2
Shcherbakovo	85	U3
Shchigry	79	F5
Shchirets	71	K4
Shchors	79	E5
Shchuchin	71	L2
Shchuchinsk	84	A6
Shchuchye	84	Ad5
Shebalino	84	D6
Shebekino	79	F5
Sheberghan	92	C1
Sheboygan	124	G5
Shebshi Mountains	105	H4
Shebunino	88	H2
Sheelin, Lough	58	H5
Sheenjek	118	G2
Sheep Haven	58	G2
Sheep's Head	59	C9
Sheerness	53	H3
Sheffield *Alabama, U.S.A.*	129	J3
Sheffield *Texas, U.S.A.*	127	M5
Sheffield *U.K.*	55	H3
Shegmas	78	H3
Shekhupura	92	D2
Sheki	79	H7
Shelagskiy	85	W2
Shelagskiy, Mys	85	V2
Shelburne	121	N9
Shelburne Bay	113	J1
Shelby *Montana, U.S.A.*	122	J3
Shelby *N. Carolina, U.S.A.*	129	M3
Shelbyville *Indiana, U.S.A.*	124	H7
Shelbyville *Tennessee, U.S.A.*	129	J3
Shelikhova, Zaliv	85	T5
Shelikof Strait	118	E4
Shell Creek Range	122	G8
Shelly	122	H6
Shelton	122	C4
Sheltozero	78	F3
Shemakha	79	H7
Shemonaikha	84	C6
Shenandoah *Iowa, U.S.A.*	124	C6
Shenandoah *Virginia, U.S.A.*	125	L7
Shendam	105	G4
Shendi	103	F4
Shenge	104	C4
Shenkursk	78	G3
Shenton, Mount	112	E4
Shenyang	87	N3
Shepetovka	79	D5
Shepherd Bay	120	H4
Shepherd Islands	114	U12
Shepparton	113	K6
Sheppey, Isle of	53	H3
Shepshed	53	F2
Shepton Mallet	52	E3
Sheragul	84	G6
Sherard, Cape	120	K3
Sherborne	52	E4
Sherbro	104	C4
Sherbro Island	104	C4
Sherbrooke	125	Q4
Sherburne Reef	114	D2
Sherburn in Elmet	55	H3
Shereik	96	A7
Sheridan *Arkansas, U.S.A.*	128	F3
Sheridan *Wyoming, U.S.A.*	123	L5
Sheringham	53	J2
Sherlovaya Gora	85	K6
Sherman	128	D4
's-Hertogenbosch	64	F3
Shetland	56	A1
Shetland Islands	56	A1
Shetpe	79	J7
Shevchenko	79	J7
Shewa Gimira	103	G6
Sheya	85	K4
Sheyang	87	N5
Sheyenne	123	Q4
Shiant Islands	56	B3
Shiant, Sound of	56	B3
Shiashkotan, Ostrov	85	S7
Shibam	97	J9
Shibata	89	G7
Shibecha	88	K4
Shibetsu *Japan*	88	J3
Shibetsu *Japan*	88	K4
Shibin el Kom	102	F1
Shibotsu-jima	88	L4
Shibushi	89	C10
Shickshock Mountains	125	S2
Shiel Bridge	56	C3
Shieldaig	56	C3
Shiel, Loch	57	C4
Shihan, Wadi	97	L8
Shihezi	86	F3
Shiikh	103	J6
Shijiazhuang	87	L4
Shikarpur	92	C3
Shikoku	89	D9
Shikoku-sanchi	89	D9
Shikong	87	K4
Shikotan-to	88	L4
Shikotsu-ko	88	H4
Shildon	55	H2
Shilega	78	G3
Shiliguri	93	G3
Shilka *U.S.S.R.*	85	K6
Shilka *U.S.S.R.*	85	L6
Shillingstone	52	E4
Shillong	93	H3
Shilovo	78	G5
Shimabara	89	C9
Shimada	89	G8
Shimanovsk	85	M6
Shimian	93	K3
Shimizu	89	G8
Shimoda	89	G8
Shimoga	92	E6
Shimonoseki	89	C9
Shinano	89	G7
Shinas	97	N4
Shindand	95	R5
Shin Falls	56	D3
Shingu	89	E9
Shinjo	88	H6
Shinness	56	D2
Shinshar	77	G5
Shinyanga	107	F3
Shiogama	89	H6
Shiono-misaki	89	E9
Shiosawa	89	G7
Shiping	93	K4
Shipley	55	H3
Shippensburg	125	M6
Shippigan Island	121	P8
Shipston-on-Stour	53	F2
Shipton	55	H2
Shipton-under-Wychwood	53	F3
Shipunovo	84	C6
Shirakawa	89	H7
Shirane-san *Japan*	89	G8
Shirane-san *Japan*	89	G7
Shiraz	95	L7
Shire	107	F6
Shirebrook	55	H3
Shiretoko-misaki	88	K3
Shiriya-saki	88	H5
Shir Kuh	95	M6
Shirten Holoy Gobi	86	H3
Shirvan	95	N3
Shishaldin Volcano	118	Af9
Shivpuri	92	E3
Shivwits Plateau	126	F2
Shiwan Dashan	93	L4
Shiyan	93	M2
Shizhu	93	L3
Shizugawa	88	H6
Shizuishan	87	K4
Shizuoka	89	G8
Shkoder	74	E1
Shkumbin	74	E2
Shmidta, Ostrov	81	L1
Shobara	89	D8
Shokalskogo, Ostrov	84	A2
Shorapur	92	E5
Shorawak	95	S6
Shoreham-by-Sea	53	G4
Shorkot	92	D2
Shoshone	122	G6
Shoshone Mountains	122	F8
Shoshoni	123	K6
Shostka	79	E5
Shouguang	87	M4
Shouning	87	M6
Showa	141	C5
Showak	96	B9
Shozhma	78	G3
Shpikov	73	K1
Shpola	79	E6
Shrankogl	68	C2
Shreveport	128	F4
Shrewsbury	52	E2
Shrewton	53	F3
Shrigonda	92	D5
Shropshire	52	E2
Shrule	59	D5
Shuab, Ra's	97	P9
Shuanghezhen	87	P3
Shuangliao	87	N3
Shuangyashan	87	Q2
Shubar-Kuduk	79	K6
Shubra el-Khema	102	F1
Shucheng	87	M5
Shuga	84	B6
Shuicheng	93	K3
Shuikou	87	M6
Shujaabad	92	D3
Shulan	87	P3
Shumagin Islands	118	Af9
Shumen	73	J4
Shumerlya	78	H4
Shungnak	118	D2
Shuqrah	96	G10
Shura	77	K4
Shurab	95	K5
Shurab	95	N5
Shusf	95	Q6
Shush	94	J5
Shushenskoye	84	E6
Shushtar	94	J5
Shuswap Lake	122	E2
Shuya	78	G4
Shuya	89	G7
Shwebo	93	J4
Shwegyin	93	J5
Shweli	93	J4
Shyok	92	E2
Siahan Range	92	B3
Siah Koh	95	S5
Sialkot	92	D2
Siargao	91	H4
Siau	91	H5
Siauliai	63	K9
Sibenik	72	C4
Siberut	90	B6
Siberut, Selat	90	B6
Sibi	92	C3
Sibirskaya Nizmennost	84	G2

Name	Plate	Grid
Sibirtsevo	88	D3
Sibiryakovo, Ostrov	84	B2
Sibiti	106	B3
Sibiu	73	H3
Sibolga	90	B5
Sibsagar	93	H3
Sibsey	55	K3
Sibu	90	E5
Sibut	102	C6
Sibutu	91	F5
Sibutu Passage	91	F5
Sibuyan	91	G3
Sibuyan Sea	91	G3
Sicasica	138	C3
Sichuan	93	K2
Sichuan Pendi	93	L3
Sicie, Cap	65	F7
Sicilia	69	D7
Sicilian Channel	69	C7
Sicily	69	D7
Sicuani	136	C6
Sidatun	88	E3
Sideby	63	J5
Sidheros, Akra	75	J5
Sidhirokastron	75	G2
Sidi Akacha	67	G4
Sidi Barram	102	E1
Sidi Bel Abbes	100	E1
Sidi Ifni	100	C3
Sidi Kacem	100	D2
Sidima	88	E1
Sidlaw Hills	57	E4
Sidmouth	52	D4
Sidmouth, Cape	113	J1
Sidney *Canada*	122	C3
Sidney *Montana, U.S.A.*	123	M4
Sidney *Ohio, U.S.A.*	124	H6
Sidon	94	B5
Sidorovsk	84	C3
Siedlce	71	K2
Siegen	70	C3
Siemiatycze	71	K2
Siem Reap	93	K6
Siena	68	C4
Sieniawa	71	K3
Sierpc	71	H2
Sierra Colorada	139	C8
Sierra Leone	104	C4
Sierra Vista	127	G5
Sierre	68	A2
Sifnos	75	H4
Sifton Pass	118	K4
Sigatoka *Fiji*	114	Q8
Sigatoka *Fiji*	114	Q9
Sigean	65	E7
Sighetu Marmatiei	73	G2
Sighisoara	73	H2
Sigli	90	B4
Siglufjordur	62	V11
Sigmaringen	70	C4
Signy	141	W6
Sigovo	84	D4
Sigtuna	63	G7
Siguenza	66	E2
Siguiri	104	D3
Sigulda	63	L8
Siikajoki	62	L4
Siikavuopio	62	J2
Siilinjarvi	62	M5
Siin	88	E2
Siipyy	63	J5
Siirt	77	J4
Sikar	92	E3
Sikasso	100	D6
Sikeston	124	F8
Sikhote Alin	88	E3
Sikinos	75	H4
Sikkim	93	G3
Sil	66	C1
Sila	97	K4
Silchar	93	H4
Sile	76	C2
Silesia	71	G3
Silgarhi	92	F3
Silifke	76	E4
Siligir	84	J3
Siling Co	93	G2
Silistra	73	J3
Silivri	76	C2
Siljan	63	F6
Silkeborg	63	C8
Sillajhuay	138	C3
Sillan, Lough	58	J4
Sillon de Talbert	64	B4
Siloam Springs	128	E2
Silom	114	E2
Silopi	77	K4
Silovayakha	78	L2
Silsbee	128	E5
Silute	63	J9
Silvan	77	J3
Silver Bay	124	E3
Silver City	127	H4
Silvermines Mountains	59	F7
Silver Spring	125	M7
Silverstone	53	F2
Silverton *U.K.*	52	D4
Silverton *U.S.A.*	127	J2
Simanggang	90	E5
Simard, Lac	125	L3
Simareh Karkheh	94	H5
Simav *Turkey*	76	C3
Simav *Turkey*	76	C2
Simayr	96	E8
Simcoe	125	K5
Simcoe, Lake	125	L4
Simeonovgrad	73	H4
Simeulue	90	B5
Simferopol	79	E7
Simi	75	J4
Simiti	136	C2
Simitli	73	G5
Simla	92	E2
Simleu Silvaniei	73	G2
Simmern	70	B3
Simojarvi	62	M3
Simojoki	62	L4
Simonka	71	J4
Simplicio Mendes	137	J5
Simplon Pass	68	B2
Simpson Bay	119	N2
Simpson Desert	113	H3
Simpson Peninsula	120	J4
Simrishamn	63	F9
Simsor	77	J3
Simushir, Ostrov	85	S7
Sinabang	90	B5
Sinabung	90	B5
Sinac	72	C3
Sinafir	96	B3
Sinaia	73	H3
Sinai Peninsula	103	F2
Sinaloa	130	F4
Sinanaj	74	E2
Sinaxtla	131	L9
Sincan *Turkey*	76	E3
Sincan *Turkey*	77	G3
Since	133	K10
Sincelejo	136	B2
Sinclair's Bay	56	E2
Sind	92	E3
Sinda	88	F1
Sindal	63	D8
Sindangbarang	90	D7
Sindel	73	J4
Sindhuli Garhi	92	G3
Sindirgi	76	C3
Sindominic	73	H2
Sindor	78	J3
Sind Sagar Doab	92	D2
Sinegorye	78	J4
Sinelnikovo	79	F6
Sines	66	B4
Sines, Cabo de	66	B4
Sinetta	62	L3
Sinfra	104	D4
Singa	103	F5
Singapore	90	C5
Singaraja	90	F7
Sing Buri	93	K6
Singida	107	F3
Singitikos, Kolpos	75	G2
Singkang	91	G6
Singkawang	90	D5
Singkep	90	C6
Singleton	53	G4
Singleton, Mount	112	G3
Singosan	87	P4
Siniatsikon	75	F2
Siniscola	69	B5
Sinj	72	D4
Sinjai	91	G7
Sinjajevina	72	E4
Sinjar	77	J4
Sinkat	103	G4
Sinnamary	137	G2
Sinnes	63	B7
Sinni	69	F5
Sinnicolau Mare	72	F2
Sinoe	104	D4
Sinoe, Lacul	73	K3
Sinop	76	F2
Sinpo	88	B5
Sinpung-dong	88	B5
Sintang	90	E5
Sint Maarten	133	R5
Sinton	128	D6
Sintra	66	B3
Sinu	136	B2
Sinuiju	87	N4
Sinyavka	71	M2
Sinyaya	63	N8
Siocon	91	G4
Siofok	72	E2
Sion	68	A2
Sionascaig, Loch	56	C2
Sion Mills	58	H3
Sioule	65	E5
Sioux City	124	B5
Sioux Falls	123	R6
Sioux Lookout	119	S5
Sipalay	91	G4
Siping	87	N3
Sip Song Chau Thai	93	K4
Sipul	114	D3
Sipura	90	B6
Siquia	132	E8
Siquijor	91	G4
Sira *India*	92	E6
Sira *Norway*	63	B7
Sir Abu Nuayr	97	M4
Siracusa	69	E7
Sirajganj	93	G4
Sir Alexander, Mount	119	M5
Siran	77	H2
Sir Bani Yas	97	L4
Sir Edward Pellew Group	113	H2
Siret *Romania*	73	J2
Siret *Romania*	73	J2
Sirhan, Wadi	94	D6
Siri Kit Dam	93	K5
Sirik, Tanjung	90	E5
Sir James McBrien, Mount	118	R3
Sirjan, Kavir-e	95	L6
Sirk	95	N8
Sirna	75	J4
Sirnal	77	K4
Sirohi	92	D4
Siros *Greece*	75	H4
Siros *Greece*	75	H4
Sirri	95	M9
Sirr, Nafud as	96	G4
Sirsa	92	D3
Sir Sanford, Mount	122	F2
Sirsi	92	D6
Sirte	101	J2
Sirte, Gulf of	101	J2
Sirvan	77	K3
Sisak	72	D3
Sisaket	93	K5
Sisophon	93	K6
Sisseton	123	R5
Sissonne	64	E4
Sistan	95	P8
Sistan, Daryacheh-ye-	95	Q6
Sisteron	65	F6
Sistig-Khem	84	F6
Sistranda	62	C5
Sitamau	92	E4
Sitapur	92	F3
Sitges	67	G2
Sithonia	75	G2
Sitia	75	J5
Sitian	86	F3
Sitidgi Lake	118	J2
Sitio da Abadia	138	H6
Sitka	118	H4
Sittang	93	J5
Sittingbourne	53	H3
Sittwe	93	H4
Situbondo	90	E7
Siuri	93	G4
Siuruanjoki	62	M4
Sivas	77	G3
Sivasli	76	C3
Siverek	77	H4
Siverskiy	63	P7
Sivrice	77	H3
Sivrihisar	76	D3
Sivrihisar Daglari	76	D3
Sivuk	85	Q6
Siwa	102	E2
Siwalik Range	92	F3
Siwan	92	F3
Si Xian	87	M5
Sixmilebridge	59	E7
Sixpenny Handley	53	E4
Siya	78	G3
Siyal Islands	96	C5
Sizin	84	F6
Sjælland	63	D9
Sjorup	63	C8
Skadarsko Jezero	74	E1
Skadovsk	79	E6
Skafta	62	V13
Skagafjordur	62	V12
Skagaflos	62	T12
Skagen	63	D8
Skagerak	63	C8
Skagit	122	D3
Skagway	118	H4
Skaill	56	F2
Skala-Podolskaya	73	J1
Skanderborg	63	C8
Skanor	63	E9
Skansholm	62	G4
Skantzoura	75	H3
Skara	63	E7
Skaraborg	63	E7
Skarbak	63	C9
Skard	62	V12
Skardu	92	E1
Skarnes	63	D6
Skattkarr	63	E7
Skaudvile	63	K9
Skaulo	62	J3
Skawina	71	H4
Skeena	118	K5
Skeena Mountains	118	K4
Skegness	55	K1
Skeidararsandur	62	W13
Skelda Ness	56	A2
Skelleftea	62	J4
Skelleftealven	62	H4
Skelmersdale	55	G3
Skelton	55	J2
Skerpioenpunt	108	D5
Skerries	58	K5
Skerries, The	54	E3
Skhiza	75	F4
Ski	63	D7
Skiathos	75	G3
Skibbereen	59	D9
Skiddaw	55	F2
Skidegate	118	J5
Skidel	71	L2
Skien	63	C7
Skierniewice	71	J3
Skiftet Kihti	63	J6
Skikda	101	G1
Skipton	55	G3
Skiropoula	75	H3
Skiros *Greece*	75	H3
Skiros *Greece*	75	H3
Skive	63	C8
Skjakerhatten	62	E4
Skjalfandafljot	62	W12
Skjalfandi	62	W11
Skjern	63	C9
Skjervoy	62	J1
Sklad	85	L2
Skoghall	63	E7
Skole	71	K4
Skomer Island	53	B3
Skopelos *Greece*	75	G3
Skopelos *Greece*	75	G3
Skopelos Kaloyeroi	75	H3
Skopin	79	F5
Skopje	73	F4
Skopun	62	Z14
Skorodum	84	A5
Skorovatn	62	E4
Skovde	63	E7
Skovorodino	85	L6
Skowhegan	125	R4
Skreia	63	D6
Skudeneshavn	63	D6
Skulgam	62	H2
Skull	59	C9
Skulyany	73	J2
Skuodas	63	J8
Skutec	70	F4
Skutskar	63	G6
Skvira	79	D6
Skwierzyna	70	F2
Skye	56	B3
Skyring, Peninsula	139	B9
Skyring, Seno	139	B10
Slagelse	63	D9
Slagnas	62	H4
Slamannan	57	E5
Slamet, Gunung	90	D7
Slane	58	J5
Slaney	59	J8
Slapin, Loch	57	B3
Slatina	73	H3
Slave	119	N4
Slave Lake	119	N4
Slavgorod *Rossiyskaya S.F.S.R., U.S.S.R.*	84	B6
Slavgorod *Ukraine S.S.R., U.S.S.R.*	79	F6
Slavo	85	Q6
Slavyanka	88	C4
Slavyansk	79	F6
Slavyansk-na-Kubani	79	F6
Slawno	71	G1
Slawoborze	70	F2
Slea	55	J3
Sleaford	53	G2
Sleat, Sound of	57	C3
Sleetmute	118	D3
Sleights	55	J2
Slidell	128	H5
Slieve Anieren	58	G4
Slieveanorra	58	K2
Slieveardagh Hills	59	G7
Slieve Aughty Mountains	59	E6
Slieve Beagh	58	H4
Slieve Bloom Mountains	59	G6
Slieve Callan	59	D7
Slieve Car	58	C4
Slieve Donard	58	L4
Slieve Elva	59	D6
Slieve Gamph	58	E4
Slieve Kimalta	59	F7
Slieve League	58	E3
Slieve Mish Mountains	59	C8
Slieve Miskish	58	C9
Slieve Na Calliagh	58	H5
Slieve Rushen	58	G4
Slieve Snaght	58	H2
Sligo *Ireland*	58	E4
Sligo *Ireland*	58	F4
Sligo Bay	58	E4
Slioch	56	C3
Slipper Island	115	E2
Sliven	73	J4
Slobodchikovo	78	H3
Slobodka	73	K2
Slobodskoy	78	J4
Slobodzeya	73	K2
Slobozia *Romania*	73	H3
Slobozia *Romania*	73	J3
Slonim	71	L2
Slot, The	114	J6
Slough	53	G3
Sluch	79	D5
Slunj	72	C3
Slupsk	71	G1
Slussfors	62	G4
Slutsk	79	D5
Slyne Head	59	B6
Slyudyanka	84	G6
Smaland	63	F8
Smallwood Reservoir	121	P7
Smcanli	76	D3
Smederevo	73	F3
Smela	79	E6
Smethwick	53	E2
Smidovich	88	D3
Smiltene	63	M8
Smirnykh	85	Q7
Smith Arm	118	L2
Smith Bay *Canada*	120	L2
Smith Bay *U.S.A.*	118	E1
Smithfield *N. Carolina, U.S.A.*	129	N3
Smithfield *Utah, U.S.A.*	122	J7

Srinagar **92** D2
Sroda **71** G2
Sroda Slaska **71** G3
Stack, Loch **56** D2
Stade **70** C2
Stadhampton **53** F3
Stadthagen **70** C2
Staffin **56** B3
Stafford **53** E2
Staffordshire **53** F2
Staines **53** G3
Staintondale **55** J2
Stakhanov **79** F6
Stalac **73** F4
Stalham **53** J2
Stalingrad **79** G6
Stalybridge **55** G3
Stamford *Australia* **113** J3
Stamford *Connecticut, U.S.A.* **125** P6
Stamford *New York, U.S.A.* **125** N5
Stamford *Texas, U.S.A.* **127** N4
Stamford *U.K.* **53** G2
Stamford Bridge **55** J3
Stamfordham **57** G5
Stampiky **109** J3
Stamsund **62** E2
Standerton **108** E5
Standish *U.K.* **55** G3
Standish *U.S.A.* **124** J4
Stanford **123** J4
Stanford-le-Hope **53** H3
Stanger **108** F5
Stanhope **55** G2
Stanislav **71** L4
Stanke Dimitrov **73** G4
Stanley *Durham, U.K.* **55** H2
Stanley *Falkland Islands, U.K.* **139** E10
Stanley *U.S.A.* **123** N3
Stanley *Zaire* **107** E2
Stanley Mission **119** Q4
Stanleyville **106** E2
Stann Creek **132** C6
Stanos **75** F3
Stanovoye Nagorye **85** J5
Stanovoy Khrebet **85** L5
Stansted **53** H3
Stanthorpe **113** L4
Stanton **53** H2
Stapleford **53** F3
Stara Planina **73** G4
Staraya Russa **78** E4
Staraya Vorpavla **84** Ae4
Stara Zagora **73** H4
Starcross **52** D4
Stargard **70** F2
Starikovo **85** R2
Starke **129** L6
Starkville **128** H4
Starmyri **62** X12
Starnberg **70** D5
Starnberger See **70** D5
Staroaleyskoye **84** C6
Starobelsk **79** F6
Starodub **79** E5
Starodubskoye **88** J2
Starogard **71** H2
Starokazachye **73** K2
Starokonstantinov **79** D6
Starominskaya **79** F6
Starosielce **71** K2
Start Bay **52** D4
Start Point *Devon, U.K.* **52** D4
Start Point *Orkney Is., U.K.* **56** F1
Stary Sacz **71** J4
Staryy Oskol **79** F5
Staryy Sambor **71** K4
State College **125** M6
Staten Island **139** D10
Statesboro **129** M4
Statesville **129** M3
Staunton *U.K.* **52** E3
Staunton *U.K.* **52** E3
Staunton *U.S.A.* **125** L7
Staunton on Wye **52** E2
Stavanger **63** A7
Staveley *Cumbria, U.K.* **55** G2
Staveley *Derbyshire, U.K.* **55** H3
Staveley *N. Yorkshire, U.K.* **55** H2
Stavelot **64** F3
Stavropol **79** G6
Stavropolskaya Vozvyshennost **79** G6
Stawiski **71** K2
Staxton **55** J2
Steensby Inlet **120** L3
Steensby Peninsula **120** J3
Steens Mountain **122** E6
Steenstrups Glacier **120** Q2
Steeping **55** K3
Steere, Mount **112** D3
Stefanesti **73** J2
Stefansson Island **120** E3
Stege **63** E9
Steigerwald **70** D4
Steinbach **123** R3
Steinhuder Meer **70** C2
Steinkjer **62** D4
Stellenbosch **108** C6
Steller, Mount **118** G3
Stenay **64** F4
Stendal **70** D2
Stenhousemuir **57** E4
Stenness **56** A1
Stenness, Loch of **56** E2
Stentrask **62** H3
Stepan **71** M3
Stepanakert **94** H2
Stephens, Cape **115** D4
Stephenville *Canada* **121** Q8
Stephenville *U.S.A.* **128** C4
Stepnogorsk **84** A6
Stepnyak **84** A6
Sterkstroom **108** E6
Sterlibashevo **78** K5
Sterling *Colorado, U.S.A.* **123** N7
Sterling *Illinois, U.S.A.* **124** F6
Sterling Heights **124** J5
Sterlitamak **78** K5
Steshevskaya **78** F3
Stettin **70** F2
Steubenville **125** K6
Stevenage **53** G3
Stevens Point **124** F4
Stevenston **57** D5
Stewart **118** H3
Stewart Island **115** A7
Stewart Islands **111** P3
Stewarton **57** D5
Stewartstown **58** J3
Steynsburg **108** E6
Steyr **68** E1
St-Gildas, Pointe de **65** B5
Stibb Cross **52** C4
Stickford **55** K3
Stikine **118** J4
Stikine Mountains **118** K4
Stilis **75** G3
Stillwater *Minnesota, U.S.A.* **124** D4
Stillwater *Oklahoma, U.S.A.* **128** D2
Stilo, Punta **69** F6
Stinchar **57** D5
Stip **73** G5
Stirling *Australia* **113** G3
Stirling *U.K.* **57** E4
Stirling Range **112** D5
Stjernoya **62** K1
Stjordal **62** D5
Stockach **70** C5
Stockbridge **53** F3
Stockerau **68** F1
Stockholm *Sweden* **63** H7
Stockholm *Sweden* **63** H7
Stockport **55** G3
Stocksbridge **55** H3
Stockton *California, U.S.A.* **126** B2
Stockton *Kansas, U.S.A.* **123** Q8
Stockton Heath **55** G3
Stockton-on-Tees **55** H2
Stockton Plateau **127** L5
Stode **62** G5
Stoer, Point of **56** C2
Stoke Ferry **53** H2
Stoke-on-Trent **55** G3
Stokesley **55** H2
Stokes Point **113** J7
Stokhod **71** L3
Stokkseyri **62** U13
Stokmarknes **62** F2
Stolbovoy, Ostrov **85** P2
Stolbtsy **71** M2
Stolica **71** J4
Stolin **79** D5
Stolp **71** G1
Stolsheimen **63** B6
Stone **53** E2
Stonehaven **57** F4
Stonehouse *Gloucestershire, U.K.* **52** E3
Stonehouse *Strathclyde, U.K.* **57** E5
Stony **118** D3
Stora **63** C8
Stora Lulevatten **62** H3
Storavan **62** H4
Storby **63** H6
Stord **63** A7
Store Balt **63** D9
Store Heddinge **63** E9
Storen **62** D5
Storjord **62** F3
Storlien **62** E5
Storm Bay **113** K7
Storm Lake **124** C5
Stornoway **56** B2
Storozhevsk **78** J3
Storozhinets **73** H1
Storr, The **56** B3
Storsjon **62** F5
Storslett **62** J2
Storsteinfjellet **62** G2
Stort **53** H3
Storuman *Sweden* **62** G4
Storuman *Sweden* **62** G4
Stosch, Isla **139** A9
Stour *Dorset, U.K.* **53** E4
Stour *Suffolk, U.K.* **53** H3
Stourbridge **53** E2
Stourport-on-Severn **52** E2
Stowmarket **53** J2
Stow-on-the-Wold **53** F3
Stoyba **85** N6
Stozac **72** E4
Strabane **58** H3
Strachur **57** C4
Stradbroke **53** J2
Strait of Belle Isle **121** Q7
Strakonice **70** E4
Stralsund **70** E1
Strand **108** C6
Stranda **62** B5
Strandhill **58** E4
Strangford **58** L4
Strangford Lough **58** L4
Strangnas **63** G7
Stranorlar **58** G3
Stranraer **54** D2
Strasbourg **64** G4
Strasheny **73** K2
Strasswalchen **68** D2
Stratfield Mortimer **53** F3
Stratford *Canada* **125** K5
Stratford *New Zealand* **115** E3
Stratford *U.S.A.* **127** L2
Stratford-upon-Avon **53** F2
Strathaven **57** D5
Strathblane **57** D5
Strathbogie **56** F3
Strath Carron **56** D3
Strathclyde **57** D5
Strath Dearn **56** E3
Strath Earn **57** E4
Strath Halladale **56** E2
Strathmore *Canada* **122** H2
Strathmore *Highland, U.K.* **56** D2
Strathmore *Tayside, U.K.* **57** F4
Strath Naver **56** D2
Strath of Kildonan **56** E2
Strath Oykel **56** D2
Strath Spey **56** E3
Strathy Point **56** D2
Stratos **75** F3
Stratton *U.K.* **52** C4
Stratton *U.S.A.* **125** Q4
Straubing **70** E4
Straumnes **62** T11
Straumsjoen **62** F2
Strausberg **70** E2
Strawberry Mountains **122** E5
Strawberry Reservoir **122** J7
Streaky Bay *Australia* **113** G5
Streaky Bay *Australia* **113** G5
Streator **124** F6
Strehaia **73** G3
Strela **70** E4
Strelka-Chunya **84** G4
Stretford **55** G3
Stretton **53** G2
Streymoy **62** Z14
Strezhevoy **84** B4
Strimasund **62** F3
Strimon **75** G2
Strimonikos, Kolpos **75** G2
Strokestown **58** F5
Strolka **84** E5
Stroma **56** E2
Stromboli, Isola **69** E6
Stromness **56** E2
Stromsburg **123** R7
Stromstad **63** D7
Stromsund **62** F5
Stroms Vattudal **62** F4
Strongoli **69** F6
Stronsay **56** F1
Stronsay Firth **56** F1
Strontian **57** C4
Strood **53** H3
Stropkov **71** J4
Stroud **52** E3
Struer **63** C8
Struga **72** F5
Strugi Krasnye **63** N7
Struma **73** G4
Strumble Head **52** B2
Strumica **73** G5
Stryama **73** H4
Stryn **63** B6
Stryy **79** C6
Strzyzow **71** J4
Stuart *Florida, U.S.A.* **129** M7
Stuart *Nebraska, U.S.A.* **123** Q6
Stuart Island **118** C3
Stuart Lake **118** L5
Stuart, Mount **122** D4
Stung Treng **93** L6
Stura **68** A3
Sturgeon **125** K3
Sturgeon Bay **124** G4
Sturgeon Falls **125** L3
Sturgeon Lake **124** E1
Sturgis **123** N5
Sturovo **71** H5
Sturry **53** J3
Sturt Desert **113** J4
Sturton by Stow **55** J3
Stutterheim **108** E6
Stuttgart *U.S.A.* **128** G3
Stuttgart *W. Germany* **70** C4
Stykkisholmur **62** T12
Styr **71** L3
Suakin **103** G4
Suakin Archipelago **96** D7
Suavanao **114** J5
Subashi **94** J4
Subay, Irq **96** F6
Subei **86** H4
Subi **90** D5
Subiaco **69** D5
Sublette **127** M2
Subotica **72** E2
Suceava **73** J2
Sucha **71** H4
Suchedniow **71** J3
Suck **59** F6
Sucre **138** C3
Suda **78** F4
Sudan **102** E5
Sudbury *Canada* **125** K3
Sudbury *Derbyshire, U.K.* **53** F2
Sudbury *Suffolk, U.K.* **53** H2
Sudety **70** F3
Sudirman, Pegunungan **91** K6
Sudr **96** A2
Sud, Recif du **114** X17
Suduroy **62** Z14
Sudzha **79** F5
Sue **102** E6
Suess Land **120** W3
Suez **103** F2
Suez Canal **103** F1
Suez, Gulf of **103** F2
Suffolk **53** H2
Sufian **94** G2
Sugarloaf Mount **125** Q4
Sugla Golu **76** D4
Sugoy **85** T4
Suhait **87** J4
Suhar **97** N4
Suhbaatar **87** K1
Suhut **76** D3
Suibin **88** C2
Suichuan **93** M3
Suide **87** L4
Suidong **88** D2
Suifenhe **88** C3
Suifen He **88** C4
Suihua **88** A2
Suileng **88** A2
Suining **93** L2
Suiping **93** M2
Suir **59** G8
Suixi **93** M4
Sui Xian **93** M2
Suizhong **87** N3
Suj **87** K3
Sukabumi **90** D7
Sukhinichi **78** F5
Sukhona **78** G3
Sukhumi **79** G7
Sukkertoppen **120** R5
Sukkertoppen Iskappe **120** R4
Sukkur **92** C3
Sukma **92** F5
Sukon **91** G6
Sukpay **88** F2
Sukpay Datani **88** F2
Suksun **78** K4
Sukumo **89** D9
Sulaiman Range **92** C3
Sula, Kepulauan **91** H6
Sulakyurt **76** E2
Sulawesi **91** G6
Sulawesi, Laut **91** G5
Sulaymaniyah **94** G4
Sulby **54** E2
Sulejow **71** H3
Sulina **73** K3
Sulina, Bratul **73** K3
Sulingen **70** C2
Sulitjelma **62** G3
Sullana **136** A4
Sullivan **124** E7
Sullivan Lake **122** J2
Sullom Voe **56** A1
Sullorsuaq **120** R3
Sully **65** E5
Sulmona **69** D4
Sulphur *Oklahoma, U.S.A.* **128** D3
Sulphur *Texas, U.S.A.* **128** E4
Sulphur Springs **128** E4
Sultandagi **76** D3
Sultanhani *Turkey* **76** E3
Sultanhani *Turkey* **77** F3
Sultanhisar **76** C4
Sultanpur **92** F3
Sulu Archipelago **91** G4
Suluklu **76** E3
Sulu Sea **91** F4
Suly **84** Ae6
Sulz **70** C4
Sulzberger Bay **141** P3
Sumar **94** G5
Sumarokovo **84** D4
Sumatera **90** C6
Sumba **91** F7
Sumbar **95** H2
Sumbawa **91** F7
Sumbawabesar **91** F7
Sumbawanga **107** F4
Sumbe **106** B5
Sumburgh **56** A2
Sumburgh Head **56** A2
Sumedang **90** D7
Sumenep **90** E7
Sumgait **79** H7
Summan, As *Saudi Arabia* **96** H3
Summan, As *Saudi Arabia* **97** J5
Summer Isles **56** C2
Summer Lake **122** D6
Summerside **121** P8
Summit Lake **118** L4
Sumner Lake **127** K3
Sumperk **71** G4
Sumprabum **93** J3
Sumter **129** M4
Sumy **79** E5
Sunamganj **93** H3
Sunart, Loch **57** C4
Sunaynah **97** M5
Sunaysilah **77** J5
Sunbury **125** M6
Sunchon **87** P5

Name	Page	Grid
Wittenberg	70	E3
Wittenberge	70	D2
Wittingen	70	D2
Witti Range	90	F5
Wittstock	70	E2
Witu	107	H3
Witu Islands	114	D2
Wkra	71	J2
Wladyslawowo	71	H1
Wloclawek	71	H2
Wlodawa	71	K3
Wloszczowa	71	H3
Wodzislaw	71	J3
Wodzislaw Slaski	71	H3
Woitape	114	D3
Wokam	91	J7
Woken	88	C2
Woking	53	G3
Wokingham	53	G3
Wolds, The	55	J3
Wolf	124	F4
Wolf Point	123	M3
Wolfsberg	68	E2
Wolfsburg	70	D2
Wolf, Volcan	136	A7
Wolin	70	F2
Wollaston, Cape	119	M1
Wollaston, Islas	139	C11
Wollaston Lake	119	Q4
Wollaston Peninsula	119	M2
Wollongong	113	L5
Wologisi Mountains	104	C4
Wolomin	71	J2
Wolstenholme, Cape	120	L5
Wolsztyn	70	G2
Wolverhampton	53	E2
Wolverton	53	G2
Wolviston	55	H2
Wombourne	53	E2
Wombwell	55	H3
Wondoola	113	J2
Wonju	87	P4
Wonosobo	90	D7
Wonsan	87	P4
Wonthaggi	110	L9
Wood	123	L3
Woodbourne	115	D4
Woodbridge	53	J2
Woodburn	113	L4
Woodhall Spa	55	J3
Woodland	126	B1
Woodlark Island	114	E3
Woodlark Islands	114	E3
Woodroffe, Mount	112	G4
Woodside	113	K6
Woods, Lake	113	G2
Woods, Lake of the	124	C2
Woods Point	113	K6
Woodstock Australia	113	J3
Woodstock New Brunswick, Canada	125	S3
Woodstock Ontario, Canada	125	K5
Woodstock U.K.	53	F3
Woodville New Zealand	115	E4
Woodville U.S.A.	128	E5
Woodward	128	C2
Woody Head	115	E2
Wooler	57	F5
Woonsocket	125	Q6
Wooramel	112	C4
Woore	52	E2
Wooton Wawen	53	F2
Wootton Bassett	53	F3
Worcester South Africa	108	C6
Worcester U.K.	52	E2
Worcester U.S.A.	125	Q5
Worgl	68	D2
Workington	55	F2
Worksop	55	H3
Worland	123	L5
Worms	70	C4
Worms Head	52	C3
Worth	70	C4
Worthing	53	G4
Wotu	91	G6
Wowoni	91	G6
Wragby	55	J3
Wrangel Island	116	B1
Wrangell	118	J4
Wrangle	55	K3
Wrath, Cape	56	C2
Wray	123	N7
Wreake	53	G2
Wreck Reef	113	M3
Wrecsam	55	G3
Wrexham	55	G3
Wrington	52	E3
Wroclaw	71	G3
Wronki	71	G2
Wrottesley, Cape	120	B3
Wroxham	53	J2
Wrzesnia	71	G2
Wubin	112	D5
Wubu	87	L4
Wuchang	87	P3
Wuchuan	87	L3
Wudayah	96	H8
Wudinna	113	H5
Wudu	93	K2
Wufeng	93	M2
Wugang	93	M3
Wuhai	87	K4
Wuhan	93	M2
Wuhu	87	M5
Wu Jiang	93	L3

Name	Page	Grid
Wukari	105	G4
Wuliang Shan	93	K4
Wuliaru	91	J7
Wulin	88	B3
Wumeng Shan	93	K3
Wundsiedel	70	E3
Wuning	93	M3
Wunstorf	70	C2
Wuntho	93	J4
Wuping	87	M6
Wuppertal	70	B3
Wurarga	112	D4
Wurmsee	70	D5
Wurno	105	G3
Wurzburg	70	C4
Wurzen	70	E3
Wushi	86	D3
Wutonggou	86	H3
Wuvulu Island	114	C2
Wuxi Jiangsu, China	87	N5
Wuxi Sichuan, China	93	L2
Wuxing	87	N5
Wuxuan	93	L4
Wuyiling	88	B1
Wuying	88	B1
Wuyuan	87	K3
Wuzhi Shan	93	M5
Wuzhou	93	M4
Wye Derbyshire, U.K.	55	H3
Wye Gwent, U.K.	52	E3
Wylye	53	E3
Wymondham	53	J2
Wynard	123	M2
Wynbring	113	G5
Wyndham Australia	112	F2
Wyndham New Zealand	115	B7
Wynne	128	G3
Wyoming	123	K6
Wyoming Peak	122	J6
Wyre	55	G3
Wyre Forest	52	E2
Wyrzysk	71	G2
Wysokie	71	K3
Wyszogrod	71	J2
Wytheville	125	K8

X

Name	Page	Grid
Xaafuun	103	K5
Xaafuun, Raas	103	K5
Xai-Xai	109	F5
Xambioa	137	H5
Xangongo	106	C6
Xanten	70	B3
Xanthi	75	H2
Xapuri	136	D6
Xarardheere	103	J7
Xavantes, Serra dos	137	H6
Xegil	86	D3
Xenia	124	J7
Xiachengzi	88	C3
Xiaguan	93	K3
Xiahe	93	K1
Xiamen	87	M7
Xian	87	L4
Xian	93	L2
Xianfeng	93	L3
Xiangfang	93	M2
Xiang Jiang	93	M3
Xiangquan He	92	F2
Xiangtan	93	M3
Xiangyang	88	A3
Xianning	93	M3
Xian Xian	87	M4
Xianyang	93	L2
Xiaobai	88	B2
Xiao Hinggan Ling	87	P1
Xiaojiahe	88	D2
Xiao Shui	93	M3
Xicotepec	131	L7
Xieng Khouang	93	K5
Xifeng	93	L3
Xigaze	93	G3
Xiji	88	A2
Xi Jiang	93	M4
Xilin Guangxi, China	93	L4
Xilin Heilongjiang, China	88	B2
Xilin Hot	87	M3
Xilokastron	75	G3
Ximiao	86	H3
Xin Barag Youqi	87	M2
Xin Barag Zuoqi	87	M2
Xinchang	87	N6
Xinfeng Guangdong, China	87	L6
Xinfeng Jiangxi, China	87	L7
Xingan	93	M3
Xingcheng	87	N3
Xinglong Hebei, China	87	M3
Xinglong Heilongjiang, China	87	P1
Xinglongzhen	88	A2
Xingtai	87	L4
Xingtang	87	L4
Xingu	137	G4
Xingwen	93	K3
Xingxingxia	86	H3
Xinhua	93	M3
Xining	93	K1
Xinjiang	93	M1
Xinjiang Uygur Zizhiqu	92	F1
Xinjin	87	N4
Xinlin	87	M3
Xinmin	87	P2
Xinpu	87	M5
Xintai	87	M4

Name	Page	Grid
Xinwen	87	M4
Xinxiang	93	M1
Xinyang	93	M2
Xinyi Guangdong, China	93	M4
Xinyi Jiangsu, China	87	M5
Xinyi He	87	M5
Xinyuan	86	E3
Xinzhou	87	L4
Xiqing Shan	93	K2
Xique-Xique	137	J6
Xisha Qundao	93	M5
Xi Ujimqin Qi	87	M3
Xiushan	93	L3
Xixia	93	M2
Xixiang	93	L2
Xizang Gaoyuan	92	F2
Xizang Zizhiqu	92	F2
Xochimilco	131	K8
Xpujil	131	Q8
Xuanwei	93	K3
Xuchang	93	M2
Xuddur	107	H2
Xuefeng Shan	93	M3
Xunke	87	P2
Xuru Co	92	G2
Xushui	87	M4
Xuwen	93	M4
Xuyong	93	L3
Xuzhou	93	N2

Y

Name	Page	Grid
Yaan	93	K2
Yabassi	105	G5
Yablanitsa	73	H4
Yablis	132	F7
Yablonitse, Pereval	71	L4
Yablonov	71	L4
Yablonovyy Khrebet	85	J6
Yabrai Yanchang	86	J4
Yabrud	77	G6
Yabuyanos	136	C4
Yada	84	A3
Yadgir	92	E5
Yadkin	129	M2
Yadua	114	R8
Yaeyama-shoto	89	F11
Yafran	101	H2
Yagan	86	J3
Yagodnoye	85	R4
Yagodnyy	84	Ae5
Yahuma	106	D2
Yahyali	76	F3
Yaizu	89	G8
Yakacik	77	G4
Yakapinar	77	F4
Yakima U.S.A.	122	D4
Yakima U.S.A.	122	D4
Yako	104	E3
Yakoruda	73	G4
Yakovlevka	88	D3
Yakrik	86	E3
Yaksha	78	K3
Yakumo	88	H4
Yaku-shima	89	C10
Yakutat	118	H4
Yakutsk	85	M4
Yakutskaya A.S.S.R.	85	M3
Yala	93	K7
Yalak	77	G3
Yalcizcam	77	K2
Yalinca	77	K4
Yalinga	102	D6
Yalkubul, Punta	131	Q7
Yallourn	113	K6
Yalong Jiang	93	K3
Yalova	76	C2
Yalpug	73	K2
Yalpug, Ozero	73	K3
Yalta	79	E7
Yaltushkov	73	J1
Yalu	87	P3
Yalu He	87	N2
Yalutorovsk	84	Ae5
Yalvac	76	D3
Yamagata	89	H6
Yamaguchi	89	C8
Yamal, Poluostrov	84	Ae2
Yaman Dagi	77	G3
Yambering	104	C3
Yambio	102	E7
Yambol	73	J4
Yamdena	91	J7
Yamethin	93	J4
Yamgort	78	L3
Yamin, Puncak	91	K6
Yamma Yamma, Lake	113	J4
Yamoussoukro	104	D4
Yampa	123	L7
Yamparaez	138	D3
Yampol	73	K1
Yam, Ramlat	96	G8
Yamsk	85	S5
Yamuna	92	E3
Yamunanagar	92	E2
Yamyshevo	84	B6
Yamzho Yumco	93	H3
Yana	85	P2
Yanam	92	F5
Yanan	93	L1
Yanaul	78	J4
Yanbual Bahr	96	D4
Yancheng	87	N5
Yanchi	87	K4

Name	Page	Grid
Yanchuan	87	L4
Yande	114	V16
Yandrakinot	118	A3
Yandun	86	F3
Yangarey	78	L2
Yangchun	93	M4
Yanghe	87	M5
Yangjiang	93	M4
Yangquan	87	L4
Yangshan	93	M4
Yangshuo	93	M4
Yangtze	93	L2
Yangyang	88	B6
Yangzhou	87	M5
Yanina	75	F3
Yanisyarvi, Ozero	62	P6
Yankton	123	R6
Yanqi	86	F3
Yanshou	88	B3
Yantai	87	N4
Yantra	73	H4
Yanxing	88	C2
Yanzhou	87	M4
Yao	102	C5
Yaoquanzi	86	H4
Yaounde	105	H5
Yaoxiaolong	88	A1
Yapen	91	K6
Yapen, Selat	91	K6
Yap Islands	91	K4
Yaprakali	76	E2
Yaqui	127	H6
Yar U.K.	53	F4
Yar U.S.S.R.	78	J4
Yaraka	113	J3
Yaransk	78	H4
Yarashev	73	J1
Yardley Hastings	53	G2
Yare	53	J2
Yarenga	78	H3
Yarensk	78	H3
Yariga-take	89	F7
Yarim	96	G9
Yarimca	76	C2
Yaritagua	136	D2
Yarkant He	92	E1
Yarkovo	84	Ae5
Yarlung Zangbo Jiang	93	H3
Yarma	76	E4
Yarmolintsy	73	J1
Yarmouth	121	N9
Yarongo	84	Ae3
Yaroslavl	78	F4
Yarraloola	112	D3
Yarra Yarra Lakes	112	D4
Yarroto	84	A3
Yarrow	57	E5
Yar Sale	84	A3
Yarsomovy	84	A4
Yartsevo U.S.S.R.	84	D4
Yartsevo U.S.S.R.	78	E4
Yarty	52	D4
Yarumal	136	B2
Yary	84	Ae3
Yasawa	114	Q8
Yasawa Group	114	Q8
Yaselda	71	L2
Yashbum	96	H9
Yashiro-jima	89	D9
Yashkul	79	H6
Yasin	92	D1
Yasinya	71	L4
Yasnaya Polyana	88	F3
Yass	113	K5
Yasuj	95	K6
Yasun Burun	77	G2
Yata	136	D6
Yatagan	76	C4
Yate	114	X17
Yates Center	128	E2
Yates Point	115	A6
Yathkyed Lake	119	R3
Yatsushiro	89	C9
Yatta Plateau	107	G3
Yatton	52	E3
Yauri Espinar	136	C6
Yavatmal	92	E4
Yavi, Cerro	136	D2
Yavlenka	84	Ae6
Yavorov	71	K4
Yavr	62	N2
Yavu	77	G3
Yavuzeli	77	G4
Yawatahama	89	D9
Yawng-hwe	93	J4
Yawri Bay	104	C4
Ya Xian	93	L5
Yaxley	53	G2
Yaya	84	D5
Yaygin	77	J3
Yayla	77	J3
Yayladagi	77	G5
Yazd	95	M6
Yazd-e Khvast	95	L6
Yazihan	77	H3
Yazoo City	128	G4
Yazovir Dimitrov	73	H4
Ybbs	68	E1
Ydseram	105	H3
Ye	93	J5
Yealmpton	52	C4
Yecheng	92	E1
Yecla	67	F3
Yedinka	88	G2

Place	Page	Ref
Yedinsty	79	D6
Yedoma *U.S.S.R.*	78	G3
Yedoma *U.S.S.R.*	78	J2
Yedondin	85	J6
Yeeda River	112	E2
Yefira	75	G3
Yefremov	79	F5
Yegorova, Mys	88	F3
Yegoryevsk	78	F4
Yei	102	F7
Yeijo, Cerro	136	B4
Yekaterininka	78	L3
Yekaterinoslavka	85	M6
Yekhegnadzor	77	L3
Yelabuga	78	J4
Yelantsy	84	H6
Yelets	79	F5
Yeletskiy	78	L2
Yelizarovo	84	Ae4
Yelizavety, Mys	85	Q6
Yelkenli	77	K3
Yell	56	A1
Yellandu	92	F5
Yellel	67	G5
Yellowhead Pass	119	M5
Yellowknife *Canada*	119	N3
Yellowknife *Canada*	119	N3
Yellow River	87	M4
Yellow Sea	87	N4
Yellowstone	123	M4
Yellowstone Lake	123	J5
Yell Sound	56	A1
Yelnya	78	E5
Yemen Arab Republic	96	G8
Yemen, People's Democratic Republic of	97	J8
Yemetsk	78	G3
Yemtsa	78	G3
Yen Bai	93	K4
Yendi	104	E4
Yengisar *China*	86	D4
Yengisar *China*	86	E3
Yengue	105	G5
Yenice *Turkey*	76	B3
Yenice *Turkey*	77	F3
Yenice *Turkey*	76	F4
Yeniceoba	76	E3
Yenikem	76	E3
Yenikoy *Turkey*	77	G4
Yenikoy *Turkey*	77	K2
Yenipazar	76	C4
Yenisarbademli	76	D4
Yenisehir	76	C2
Yenisey	84	D3
Yeniseysk	84	E5
Yeniseyskiy Zaliv	84	C2
Yenotayevka	79	H6
Yeoryios	75	G4
Yeovil	52	E4
Yeraliyev	79	J7
Yerbent	95	P2
Yerbogachen	84	H4
Yerema	84	H4
Yerevan	77	L2
Yergeni	79	G6
Yerkoy	76	F3
Yermak	84	B6
Yermaki	84	H5
Yermakovo	84	D3
Yermitsa	78	J2
Yermolayevo	79	K5
Yerofey-Pavlovich	85	L6
Yerolimin	75	G4
Yershov	79	H5
Yerupaja, Cerro	136	B6
Yerushalayim	94	B6
Yesil	77	G2
Yesilcay	76	C2
Yesilgolcuk	76	F3
Yesilhisar	76	F3
Yesilkent	77	G4
Yesilova	76	C4
Yesilova	76	E3
Yesilyurt	77	G3
Yessey	84	G3
Yeste	66	E3
Yeu, Ile d'	65	B5
Yevlakh	79	H7
Yevpatoriya	79	E6
Yevreyskaya Ao	88	D1
Ye Xian	87	M4
Yeysk	79	F6
Y-Fenni	52	D3
Yhu	138	E5
Yian	87	P2
Yiannitsa	75	G2
Yibin	93	K3
Yichang	93	M2
Yicheng	93	M2
Yichun	87	P2
Yidu	93	M2
Yidun	93	J2
Yigilca	76	D2
Yilan	88	B2
Yildizeli	77	G3
Yimianpo	88	A3
Yimuhe	87	N1
Yinchuan	87	K4
Yindarlgooda, Lake	112	E5
Yingde	93	M4
Ying He	93	M2
Yingkou	87	N3
Yining	86	E3
Yin Shan	87	K3
Yinxian	87	N6
Yioura *Greece*	75	H4
Yioura *Greece*	75	H3
Yirga Alem	103	G6
Yirol	102	F6
Yishui	87	M4
Yithion	75	G4
Yitong	87	P3
Yi Xian	87	N3
Yixing	87	M5
Yiyang	93	M3
Yliharma	62	N4
Yli-kitka	62	N3
Yli-li	62	L4
Ylitornio	62	K3
Ylivieska	62	L4
Y Llethr	52	C2
Yntaly	86	C2
Yoakum	128	D6
Yogope Yaveo	131	M9
Yogyakarta	90	E7
Yojoa, Laguna de	132	D7
Yokadouma	105	J5
Yokkaichi	89	F8
Yokohama *Japan*	89	G8
Yokohama *Japan*	88	H5
Yokosuka	89	G8
Yokote	88	H6
Yola	105	H4
Yolaina, Cordillera de	132	E9
Yom, Mae Nam	93	J5
Yonabaru	89	H10
Yonago	89	D8
Yonam-dong	88	B5
Yon dok	89	B7
Yonezawa	89	H7
Yong-an	88	B5
Yongan	87	M6
Yongchang	86	J4
Yongchuan	93	L3
Yongdeng	93	K1
Yongfeng	87	M6
Yongfu	93	L4
Yonghe	87	L4
Yonghung	87	P4
Yongju	89	B7
Yongkang	87	N6
Yongren	93	K3
Yongsanpo	87	P4
Yongsheng	93	K3
Yonkers	125	P6
Yonne	65	E5
York *U.K.*	55	H3
York *Nebraska, U.S.A.*	123	R7
York *Pennsylvania, U.S.A.*	125	M7
York, Cape *Australia*	113	J1
York, Cape *Papua New Guinea*	114	C4
Yorke Peninsula	113	H6
Yorketown	113	H6
York Factory	119	S4
York, Kap	120	N2
Yorkshire Moors	55	J2
Yorkshire Wolds	55	J3
Yorkton	123	N2
York, Vale of	55	H2
Yoro	132	D7
Yosemite Valley	126	C2
Yosemite Village	126	C2
Yoshioka	88	H6
Yoshkar-Ola	78	H4
Yosu	87	P5
Yotsukura	89	H7
Youghal	59	G9
Youghal Bay	59	G9
Youhao	88	B2
You Jiang	93	L4
Youkounkoun	104	C3
Young	113	K5
Young, Cape	115	F6
Youngstown	125	K6
Youssoufia	100	D2
You Xian	93	M3
Youyang	93	L3
Yozgat	76	F3
Ypres	64	E3
Yreka	122	C7
Ysabel Channel	114	E2
Ysbyty Ifan	54	F3
Ysgubor-y-coed	52	D2
Yssingeaux	65	F6
Ystad	63	E9
Ythan	56	F3
Ytterbyn	62	K4
Ytterhogdal	63	F5
Yuanjiang	93	K4
Yuan Jiang	93	M3
Yuanling	93	M3
Yuanmou	93	K3
Yuanping	87	L4
Yuba City	126	B1
Yubari	88	H4
Yucatan Channel	132	E4
Yucebag	77	J3
Yuci	87	L4
Yudaokou	87	M3
Yudoma	85	P5
Yudu	87	M6
Yuendumu	112	G3
Yueqing	87	N6
Yuexi	93	N2
Yuexi He	93	K3
Yueyang	93	M3
Yug	78	H3
Yugorskiy Poluostrov	84	Ad3
Yugoslavia	72	D3
Yuhebu	87	K4
Yuhuan	87	N6
Yuilsk	84	Ae4
Yu Jiang	93	L4
Yukon	118	D3
Yukon Delta	118	C3
Yuksekova	77	L4
Yukta	84	H4
Yukutat Bay	118	H4
Yula	78	G3
Yuli	86	F3
Yulin *Guangxi, China*	93	M4
Yulin *Shaanxi, China*	87	K4
Yuma	126	E4
Yumen	86	H4
Yumenzhen	86	H3
Yumurtalik	77	F4
Yuna	133	N5
Yunak	76	D3
Yunaska Island	118	Ad9
Yuncheng	93	M2
Yungay	136	B5
Yunnan	93	K4
Yunotsu	89	D8
Yunta	113	H5
Yunxiao	87	M7
Yurga	84	C5
Yurgamysh	84	Ad5
Yuribey *U.S.S.R.*	84	A3
Yuribey *U.S.S.R.*	84	B2
Yurimaguas	136	B5
Yurla	78	J4
Yurya	78	H4
Yuryevets	78	G4
Yuryev Polskiy	78	F4
Yusef, Bahr	102	F2
Yushan	87	M6
Yushino	78	J2
Yushkozero	62	Q4
Yushu *Jilin, China*	87	P3
Yushu *Qinghai, China*	93	J2
Yushugou	86	F3
Yusta	79	H6
Yusufeli	77	J2
Yutian	92	F1
Yuty	138	E5
Yuxi	93	K4
Yu Xian	87	L4
Yuzha	78	G4
Yuzhno Kamyshovyy Khrebet	88	J2
Yuzhno-Sakhalinsk	88	J2
Yuzhnoye	88	J2
Yuzhnyy Bug	79	E6
Yverdon	68	A2
Yvetot	64	D4

Z

Place	Page	Ref
Zaandam	64	F2
Zabal Saghir, Nahr al	77	K5
Zabaykalsk	85	K7
Zab-e Kuchek	94	G3
Zabid	96	F9
Zabok	72	C2
Zabol	95	Q6
Zaboli	95	Q8
Zabren	71	G4
Zabrze	71	H3
Zaburunye	79	J6
Zacapa	132	C7
Zacapu	130	J8
Zacatecas	130	H6
Zacatecoluca	132	C8
Zacoalco	130	H7
Zadar	72	C3
Zadetkyi Kyun	93	J7
Zafora	75	J4
Zafra	66	C3
Zagan	70	F3
Zagazig	102	F1
Zagorsk	78	F4
Zagreb	72	C3
Zagros, Kuhha-ye	95	K6
Zagubica	73	F3
Zagyva	72	F2
Zahedan	95	Q7
Zahle	77	F6
Zahran	96	F8
Zahrat al Batin	94	F6
Zaindeh	95	L5
Zaire	106	C3
Zaire	106	D3
Zajecar	73	G4
Zakamensk	84	G6
Zakatly	79	H7
Zakharovka	86	C2
Zakhmet	95	R3
Zakho	94	F3
Zakho	77	K4
Zakinthos *Greece*	75	F4
Zakinthos *Greece*	75	F4
Zakros	75	J5
Zala	72	D2
Zalaegerszeg	72	D2
Zalalovo	72	D2
Zalau	73	G2
Zaleshchiki	73	H1
Zalim	96	F5
Zalingei	102	D5
Zamakh	97	H8
Zambales Mountains	91	G2
Zambeze	109	F3
Zambezi	106	D5
Zambia	107	E5
Zamboanga	91	G4
Zambrow	71	K2
Zamora *Ecuador*	136	B4
Zamora *Spain*	66	D2
Zamora de Hidalgo	130	H7
Zamosc	71	K3
Zancara	66	E3
Zanesville	124	K8
Zangezurskiy Khrebet	94	G2
Zanjan	94	J3
Zanjon	138	C6
Zante	75	F4
Zanthus	112	E5
Zanule	78	H3
Zanzibar	107	G4
Zanzibar Island	107	G4
Zaoyang	93	M2
Zaozernyy	84	E5
Zaozhuang	87	M5
Zapadna Morava	72	F3
Zapadnaya Dvina	78	E4
Zapadno Sibirskaya Ravnina	84	Ae4
Zapadnyy Chink Ustyurta	79	J7
Zapadnyy Sayan	84	E6
Zapata	128	C7
Zapata, Peninsula de	132	G3
Zapatosa	136	C2
Zapatoza, Cienaga de	133	L10
Zapiga	138	C3
Zapolyarnyy	62	P2
Zaporozhye	79	F6
Zapotlanejo	130	H7
Zap Suyu	77	K4
Zara *Turkey*	77	G3
Zara *Yugoslavia*	72	C3
Zaragoza *Colombia*	136	C2
Zaragoza *Spain*	67	F2
Zarand *Iran*	95	K4
Zarand *Iran*	95	N6
Zarandului, Muntii	73	G2
Zaranj	95	Q6
Zarasai	63	M9
Zarate	139	E6
Zaraysk	78	F5
Zaraza	136	D2
Zardak	95	P4
Zard Kuh	95	K5
Zaria	105	G3
Zarnesti	73	H3
Zarqa	94	C5
Zarqan	95	L7
Zary	70	F3
Zarzaitine	101	G3
Zarzis	101	H2
Zaschhita	84	C6
Zaskar Mountains	92	E2
Zaslavl	71	M1
Zastron	108	E6
Zatec	70	E3
Zatishye	73	K2
Zator	71	H4
Zavitinsk	85	M6
Zavodskoy	84	C6
Zawiercie	71	H3
Zawr, Ra's az	97	J3
Zaysan	86	E2
Zaysan, Ozero	86	E2
Zbarazh	71	L4
Zbaszyn	70	F2
Zborov	71	L4
Zbruch	71	M4
Zdolbunov	71	M3
Zdunska Wola	71	H3
Zebak	92	D1
Zebirget	96	C5
Zeebrugge	64	E3
Zeerust	108	E5
Zefat	94	B5
Zehdernick	70	E2
Zei Badinan	94	F3
Zei Koya	94	F4
Zeitz	70	E3
Zelenoborskiy	62	Q3
Zelenodolsk	78	H4
Zelenogorsk	63	N6
Zelenogradsk	71	J1
Zelenokumsk	79	G7
Zelina	72	D3
Zella Mehlis	70	D3
Zell am See	68	D2
Zelva	71	L2
Zemaitija	63	K9
Zemetchino	79	G5
Zemgale	63	L8
Zemio	102	E6
Zemlya Bunge	85	Q1
Zemmora	67	G5
Zempoala	131	K8
Zempoaltepec	131	M9
Zemun	72	F3
Zenica	72	D3
Zepce	72	E3
Zerbst	70	E3
Zerkow	71	G2
Zermatt	68	A2
Zernograd	79	G6
Zerqan	75	F2
Zestafoni	77	K1
Zetouji	87	N4
Zeya *U.S.S.R.*	85	M6
Zeya *U.S.S.R.*	85	M6
Zeysk	85	M6
Zeytinbagi	76	C2
Zeytinlik	77	J2
Zezere	66	C2
Zgierz	71	H3

Zgorzelec	70	F3
Zhabe	71	L4
Zhalanash	84	Ae6
Zhamansor	79	J6
Zhamshi	86	C2
Zhanabas	86	B2
Zhanatas	86	B3
Zhangbei	87	L3
Zhangdian	87	M4
Zhangguangcai Ling	88	B3
Zhangiz-Tobe	86	E2
Zhangjiakou	87	L3
Zhangping	87	M6
Zhangpu	87	M7
Zhangzhou	87	M7
Zhanjiang	93	M4
Zhaoan	87	M7
Zhaoguang	88	A1
Zhaoqing	93	M4
Zhaotong	93	K3
Zhaoxing	88	C2
Zhaoyuan	87	P2
Zharbulak	86	F2
Zharma	86	E2
Zharyk	86	C2
Zhashkov	79	E6
Zhatay	85	M4
Zhaxigang	92	E2
Zhdanov	79	F6
Zhejiang	87	M6
Zhelaniya, Mys	80	H2
Zheldyadyr	84	Ae7
Zheleznodorozhnyy *U.S.S.R.*	84	G5
Zheleznodorozhnyy *U.S.S.R.*	71	J1
Zheleznodorozhnyy *U.S.S.R.*	78	J3
Zheleznogorsk	79	F5
Zhenan	93	L2
Zhengan	93	L3
Zhenglan Qi	87	M3
Zhengzhou	93	M2
Zhenjiang	87	M5
Zhenyuan	93	L3
Zherdevka	79	G5
Zhigalovo	84	H6
Zhigansk	85	L3
Zhijiang	93	L3
Zhilaya Kosa	79	J6
Zhiloy, Ostrov	79	J7
Zhitkovichi	79	D5
Zhitomir	79	D5
Zhlobin	79	E5
Zhmerinka	79	D6
Zhob *Pakistan*	92	C2
Zhob *Pakistan*	92	C2
Zhodino	78	D5
Zhokhova, Ostrov	85	S1
Zholymbet	84	A6
Zhongba	92	F3
Zhongdian	93	J3
Zhongwei	93	L1
Zhong Xian	93	L2
Zhongyaozhan	87	P1
Zhoushan Dao	87	M6
Zhovten	73	L2
Zhucheng	87	M4
Zhukovka	79	E5
Zhulong	87	M4
Zhuozi	87	L3
Zhuxi	93	L2
Zhuzhou	93	M3
Ziama-Mansouria	67	J4
Zibo	87	M4
Zicavo	69	B5
Zidani Most	72	C2
Zidarovo	73	J4
Ziel, Mount	112	G3
Zielona Gora	70	F3
Ziesar	70	E2
Zigazinskiy	78	K5
Zigong	93	K3
Ziguinchor	104	B3
Zihuatanejo	131	J9
Zilair	79	K5
Zile	77	F2
Zilina	71	H4
Zima	84	G6
Zimapan	131	K7
Zimbabwe	108	E3
Zimkan	94	H4
Zimnicea	73	H4
Zimniy Bereg	78	G2
Zimovniki	79	G6
Zinapecuaro	131	J8
Zindajan	95	Q4
Zinder	101	G6
Zinjibar	96	G10
Zipaquira	136	C2
Zirje	72	C4
Zi Shui	93	M3
Zitacuaro	131	J8
Ziyun	93	L3
Zizhong	93	K3
Zlatibor	72	E4
Zlitan	101	H2
Zloczew	71	H3
Zlutice	70	E3
Zmigrod	71	G3
Zmiyevka	79	F5
Znamenka *Rossiyskaya S.F.S.R., U.S.S.R.*	84	B6
Znamenka *Ukraine S.S.R., U.S.S.R.*	79	E6
Znamenskoye	84	A5
Znin	71	G2
Znojmo	70	G4
Zohreh	95	K6
Zoige	93	K2
Zolochev *U.S.S.R.*	79	F5
Zolochev *U.S.S.R.*	71	L4
Zolotinka	85	L5
Zolotonosha	79	E6
Zolotoy, Mys	88	G2
Zomba	107	G6
Zongo	106	C2
Zonguldak	76	D2
Zongyang	87	M5
Zonza	69	B5
Zorleni	73	J2
Zouar	102	C3
Zouerate	100	C4
Zrenjanin	72	F3
Zubayr, Jazair az	96	F9
Zuenoula	104	D4
Zufaf	96	E8
Zufar	97	M8
Zug	68	B2
Zugdidi	77	J1
Zugspitze	70	D5
Zujar	66	D3
Zula	96	D9
Zulia	133	L10
Zumbo	108	F3
Zumpango	131	K8
Zungeru	105	G4
Zuni	127	H3
Zuni Mountains	127	H3
Zunyi	93	L3
Zuo Jiang	93	L4
Zupanja	72	E3
Zuqaq	96	E7
Zurich	68	B2
Zurichsee	68	B2
Zuru	105	G3
Zut	72	C4
Zutphen	64	G2
Zuwarah	101	H2
Zuyevka	78	J4
Zvishavane	108	F4
Zvornik	72	E3
Zwedru	104	D4
Zweibrucken	70	B4
Zwettl	68	E1
Zwickau	70	E3
Zwiesel	70	E4
Zwolen	71	J3
Zwolle	64	G2
Zyrardow	71	J2
Zyryanka *U.S.S.R.*	84	C2
Zyryanka *U.S.S.R.*	85	S3
Zyryanovsk	86	E2

Produced by Engineering Surveys
Reproduction Ltd.

Cartographic Design and Production Manager
Keith Brook

Senior Cartographic Editor
Zoë Goodwin

Cartographic Editor
Lindsay Evans

Cartographers
Nicky Chapman
Mike Larby
Gill Dalton
David Handley-Clarke
Chris Major

Cartographic Illustrator
Janos Marffy

Text by
Simon Palfrey

Pictorial Section Design
Sue Cook

Commissioning Editor
Andrew Preston

The publishers wish to thanks all those involved in the production of
this atlas, and in particular the photo technicians at ESR Ltd, Richard
Ross, John Gill, Michael Hodson Designs, Apollo Colour Repro Ltd,
E.S. Computing Ltd, Typogram Ltd, Link-Line Ltd.

Photographic Acknowledgements
Gamma, Paris; James Davis Travel Photography; Compix;
Daily Telegraph Colour Library; J. Allan Cash;
Colour Library Books Ltd; Philippine Embassy, London;
Pakistan Embassy, London; Qatar Embassy, London;
Contact Press Images; Cyprus Tourism Organisation,
Planet Earth Pictures Ltd.